Enhancing Higher Education and Research With OpenAI Models

Şirvan Şen Demir
Süleyman Demirel University, Turkey

Mahmut Demir
Isparta University of Applied Sciences, Turkey

A volume in the Advances in Higher Education and Professional Development (AHEPD) Book Series

IGI Global
PUBLISHER of TIMELY KNOWLEDGE

Published in the United States of America by
IGI Global
Information Science Reference (an imprint of IGI Global)
701 E. Chocolate Avenue
Hershey PA, USA 17033
Tel: 717-533-8845
Fax: 717-533-8661
E-mail: cust@igi-global.com
Web site: http://www.igi-global.com

Library of Congress Cataloging-in-Publication Data

CIP DATA PROCESSING

2024 Information Science Reference
ISBN(hc) 9798369316665 | ISBN(sc) 9798369346099 | eISBN 9798369316672

This book is published in the IGI Global book series Advances in Higher Education and Professional Development (AHEPD) (ISSN: 2327-6983; eISSN: 2327-6991)

British Cataloguing in Publication Data
A Cataloguing in Publication record for this book is available from the British Library.

Advances in Higher Education and Professional Development (AHEPD) Book Series

ISSN:2327-6983
EISSN:2327-6991

MISSION

As world economies continue to shift and change in response to global financial situations, job markets have begun to demand a more highly-skilled workforce. In many industries a college degree is the minimum requirement and further educational development is expected to advance. With these current trends in mind, the **Advances in Higher Education & Professional Development (AHEPD) Book Series** provides an outlet for researchers and academics to publish their research in these areas and to distribute these works to practitioners and other researchers.

AHEPD encompasses all research dealing with higher education pedagogy, development, and curriculum design, as well as all areas of professional development, regardless of focus.

COVERAGE

- Adult Education
- Assessment in Higher Education
- Career Training
- Coaching and Mentoring
- Continuing Professional Development
- Governance in Higher Education
- Higher Education Policy
- Pedagogy of Teaching Higher Education
- Vocational Education

IGI Global is currently accepting manuscripts for publication within this series. To submit a proposal for a volume in this series, please contact our Acquisition Editors at Acquisitions@igi-global.com or visit: http://www.igi-global.com/publish/.

The Advances in Higher Education and Professional Development (AHEPD) Book Series (ISSN 2327-6983) is published by IGI Global, 701 E. Chocolate Avenue, Hershey, PA 17033-1240, USA, www.igi-global.com. This series is composed of titles available for purchase individually; each title is edited to be contextually exclusive from any other title within the series. For pricing and ordering information please visit http://www.igi-global.com/book-series/advances-higher-education-professional-development/73681. Postmaster: Send all address changes to above address.

Titles in this Series

For a list of additional titles in this series, please visit:
http://www.igi-global.com/book-series/advances-higher-education-professional-development/73681

Global Perspectives on Decolonizing Postgraduate Education
Mishack Thiza Gumbo (University of South Africa, South Africa) Michael Gaotlhobogwe (University of Botswana, Botswana) Constantino Pedzisai (Chinhoyi University of Technology, Zimbabwe) Zingiswa Mybert Monica Jojo (Rhodes University, South Africa) and Christopher B. Knaus (University of Washington, Tacoma, USA & University of South Africa, South Africa)
Information Science Reference • copyright 2024 • 339pp • H/C (ISBN: 9798369312896) • US $230.00 (our price)

Emerging Research in Agricultural Teacher Education
R. Kirby Barrick (University of Florida, USA (Retired)) and Andrew C. Thoron (Abraham Baldwin Agricultural College, USA)
Information Science Reference • copyright 2024 • 426pp • H/C (ISBN: 9798369327661) • US $245.00 (our price)

Engaging Higher Education Teachers and Students With Transnational Leadership
Gareth Richard Morris (University of Nottingham, Ningbo, China) and Shayna Kozuch (University of Nottingham, Ningbo, China)
Information Science Reference • copyright 2024 • 306pp • H/C (ISBN: 9798369361009) • US $245.00 (our price)

Preparing Students From the Academic World to Career Paths A Comprehensive Guide
Cassandra Sligh Conway (South Carolina State University, USA) and Andy Jiahao Liu (University of Arizona, USA)
Information Science Reference • copyright 2024 • 334pp • H/C (ISBN: 9781799879992) • US $215.00 (our price)

For an entire list of titles in this series, please visit:
http://www.igi-global.com/book-series/advances-higher-education-professional-development/73681

IGI Global
PUBLISHER of TIMELY KNOWLEDGE

701 East Chocolate Avenue, Hershey, PA 17033, USA
Tel: 717-533-8845 x100 • Fax: 717-533-8661
E-Mail: cust@igi-global.com • www.igi-global.com

Table of Contents

Detailed Table of Contents

Chatbots have emerged as innovative tools with the potential to significantly impact academic literacy skills across various domains. This study investigates the impact of chatbots on academic literacy skills across four domains: source evaluation, writing, critical thinking, and accessibility. Comparative analysis of Google Bard, Microsoft Bing Chat, and QuillBot reveals distinct features. Bard excels in source evaluation, offering robust fact-checking and citation assistance. It also provides comprehensive writing support and tools for critical thinking. Moreover, Bard offers personalized, accessible support, including 24/7 availability and language learning assistance. Bing Chat and QuillBot offer limited features compared to Bard. Overall, chatbots show promise in enhancing academic literacy, particularly in source evaluation, writing, and critical thinking skills.

Chapter 3
Building Democratisation and Agency: The Adoption of Ethical AI Practice in Pedagogy 60
Catherine Hayes, University of Sunderland, UK

The aims of this chapter are threefold, namely to consider global ethics and the impact that AI could potentially have in terms of increasing societal inequalities in terms of existing infrastructure, to provide an insight into the developmental and progressive use of AI across organizational infrastructures in pedagogic practice and finally, and to embed the concept of ethical AI and the potential for its praxis across all aspects of its integration in the building of global democracy and agency. Debates and sensationalized presentations of artificial intelligence (AI) across the media and in scientific and industrial contexts have shaped public perception of its potential benefits and the profound way the potential for harm ought to be acknowledged. This chapter provides a theoretical insight into how AI can be objectively debated amidst the controversy surrounding its implementation and the potential for the inaccessible to be made accessible over forthcoming months and years.

Chapter 4
Democratizing Education AI and OpenAI Models for Global Access to Knowledge 79
Sevinj Isayeva, Süleyman Demirel University, Turkey

This chapter delves into an examination of the role of artificial intelligence models in the democratization of education. The central focus of the study revolves around the utilization of AI-supported technologies in education, with particular emphasis on enhancing the learning experience and ensuring accessibility to education and knowledge. Moreover, the chapter comprehensively addresses the advantages of employing AI technologies in the process of transitioning towards democratizing education, along with potential challenges encountered during the adaptation phase, aiming to comprehend their overall impact. Additionally, the chapter provides nuanced

insights into various applications and usage fields for diverse AI technologies. In conclusion, it underscores that the effective and efficient deployment of these technologies is contingent upon a holistic consideration of ethical, regulatory, and social issues.

This chapter explains the transformative impact of artificial intelligence (AI) on tourist guidance education, exploring the paradigm shift in teaching methodologies and industry practices. As AI technologies continue to advance, their integration into tourism education has revolutionized the way students acquire knowledge and skills essential for guiding travelers effectively. The chapter reviews incorporating AI-driven tools such as virtual reality simulations, chatbots, and machine learning algorithms into educational frameworks, fostering immersive and dynamic learning experiences. This chapter also underscores the economic implications, as AI-equipped guides contribute to the sustainability and competitiveness of tourist destinations.

Artificial intelligence has had a significant impact on education, particularly owing to its ability to personalize students' learning experiences. AI-driven adaptive systems ensure that education aligns with each student's unique learning styles and abilities by analyzing their strengths and weaknesses, adapting content to their pace and specific needs. This encompasses a range of applications, from intelligent tutoring systems that provide real-time guidance to personalized content recommendations. In addition to fostering engagement and motivation, this approach enhances students'

have influenced materials science, data analytics, public health, urban design, and entertainment experiences. The study examines equity, access, and ethical dimensions of NBA-driven engineering innovations, focusing on data privacy, algorithmic bias, and commodification of athlete performance. The goal is to foster inclusivity, equity, and sustainable development, fostering collaboration between the sports industry and engineering disciplines. This approach emphasizes the transformative power of sports-driven innovation in engineering for societal betterment.

Preface

OVERVIEW

In the ever-evolving education environment, integrating artificial intelligence (AI) is a monumental paradigm shift, reshaping traditional pedagogical approaches and opening new frontiers of learning and research. Integrating artificial intelligence (AI) into the education system represents a watershed moment in the history of learning and pedagogy. As we navigate the complexities of the 21st century, characterized by rapid technological advancement and unprecedented access to information, the role of AI in shaping the future of education becomes increasingly paramount. As we embark on this transformative journey, the concept of AI in education emerges as a catalyst for unlocking the full potential of learners, educators, and institutions alike.

At its core, the concept of AI in education embodies the fusion of cutting-edge technology with pedagogical principles, aiming to enhance the learning experience and optimize educational outcomes. From personalized learning pathways to adaptive assessment strategies, AI promises to revolutionize traditional educational practices, transcending time, space, and resource limitations. By harnessing the power of machine learning algorithms, natural language processing, and data analytics, educators have opportunities to tailor instruction to individual learners' unique needs and preferences, fostering a more engaging, immersive, and effective learning environment.

The implications of integrating AI into the education system extend far beyond the confines of the classroom. AI has the potential to democratize access to education on a global scale, breaking down geographical and socioeconomic barriers and empowering learners from all walks of life to pursue their academic aspirations. Through online learning platforms, virtual classrooms, and interactive learning resources, students around the globe can engage in collaborative knowledge construction, transcending traditional constraints of time and space. Moreover, AI-driven insights and analytics offer unprecedented opportunities for educational research, enabling educators and policymakers to gain deeper insights into learning processes, pedagogical effectiveness, and student outcomes.

However, integrating AI into the education system is not without its challenges. Ethical considerations loom large as questions of data privacy, algorithmic bias, and digital equity come to the forefront. As educators navigate the complexities of AI adoption, they must grapple with transparency, accountability, and inclusivity issues, ensuring that AI technologies are deployed responsibly and ethically. The rapid pace of technological advancement demands a paradigm shift in teacher training and professional development, ensuring that educators are equipped with the necessary skills and competencies to harness the full potential of AI in the classroom. Additionally, concerns about job displacement and the role of AI in reshaping the future of work underscore the need for thoughtful and strategic approaches to AI integration in education. Moreover, the rapid pace of technological innovation necessitates ongoing professional development and training for educators, empowering them to leverage AI tools effectively and ethically in the classroom.

Against this backdrop, the chapters of *Enhancing Higher Education and Research With OpenAI Models* offer a nuanced exploration of the multifaceted dimensions of AI in education. From the evolution of traditional classrooms to AI-driven learning environments to the democratization of education through global access to knowledge, each chapter delves into the transformative potential of AI in reshaping the educational environment. By examining case studies, innovative approaches, and ethical considerations, this book provides a comprehensive framework for understanding and harnessing the power of AI to enhance learning, teaching, and research in the 21st century and beyond. By embracing innovation, fostering collaboration, and upholding ethical principles, this book also serves as a roadmap for navigating the complexities and opportunities of the AI-enabled educational environment to create a more inclusive, equitable, and empowering educational ecosystem for future generations.

ORGANIZATION OF THE BOOK

The book is organized into 10 chapters with brief descriptions as follows:

Chapter 1: Evolution of Higher Education in the Social Science From Traditional Classrooms to AI-Driven Learning Environments

Chapter 1 scrutinizes the changing landscape of higher education, focusing on the transition from conventional classrooms to AI-enhanced learning settings. It contrasts traditional and online education, weighing their pros and cons. Additionally, it explores the benefits of AI in personalizing learning, enhancing student outcomes, and simplifying administrative tasks. Despite its promise, the chapter acknowledges challenges like global inequality and ethical dilemmas, offering a nuanced perspective on AI's impact on higher education in the social sciences.

Chapter 2: Chatbots in Academic Literacy Exploring AI in Education

Chapter 2 investigates how chatbots impact academic literacy across four domains: source evaluation, writing, critical thinking, and accessibility. A comparative analysis of Google Bard, Microsoft Bing Chat, and QuillBot reveals distinct features. Bard excels in source evaluation, writing, and critical thinking, offering personalized and accessible support, while Bing Chat and QuillBot offer limited features. Overall, chatbots show promise in enhancing academic literacy skills.

Chapter 3: Building Democratisation and Agency: The Adoption of Ethical AI Practice in Pedagogy

Chapter 3 addresses three main objectives: examining global ethics and the potential impact of AI on societal inequalities, exploring the progressive use of AI in educational settings, and advocating for the integration of ethical AI principles in building global democracy and agency. It provides a theoretical framework for objective debate on AI implementation, emphasizing accessibility and ethical considerations amidst its potential benefits and harms.

Chapter 4: Democratizing Education AI and OpenAI Models for Global Access to Knowledge

Chapter 4 explores the role of artificial intelligence in making education more accessible worldwide. It emphasizes utilizing AI to enhance learning experiences and ensure educational accessibility. The chapter discusses the benefits of AI in democratizing education while addressing challenges in its implementation. It provides insights into various AI applications and highlights the importance of considering ethical, regulatory, and social factors for effective deployment.

Chapter 5: How Artificial Intelligence in Tourist Guidance Education Is Changing the Game

Chapter 5 elucidates the revolutionary effect of AI on tourist guidance education, reshaping teaching approaches and industry standards. It explores the integration of AI technologies like virtual reality simulations, chatbots, and machine learning algorithms into educational curricula, offering immersive learning experiences. Additionally, it discusses the economic benefits, highlighting how AI-equipped guides enhance destination sustainability and competitiveness.

Chapter 6: Transforming Education with the Power of Artificial Intelligence: Case Studies

Chapter 6 delves into AI's profound impact on education, particularly its role in personalizing learning experiences. Through adaptive systems, AI tailors education to individual learning styles, pacing, and needs, enhancing engagement and comprehension. It explores various applications, from intelligent tutoring systems to personalized content recommendations, addressing challenges in higher education and offering insights into enhancing audiovisual materials, mentoring, and information dissemination for students and staff.

Chapter 7: The Technological Transformation of Social Science Education: An Overview

Chapter 7 traces the evolution of social science education from traditional classrooms to AI-driven learning environments. It discusses the historical reliance on traditional methods and the gradual integration of technology, particularly AI, which revolutionized education through personalized learning experiences. The chapter examines the contemporary landscape of AI-driven education in social sciences, acknowledging its exciting possibilities alongside challenges and ethical considerations.

Chapter 8: AI and OpenAI in Education: Unveiling the Future of Learning and Teaching

Chapter 8 delves into the transformative possibilities of artificial intelligence (AI) and OpenAI models in education. It explores the core principles of AI, including machine learning and deep learning, and reveals their applications in personalized learning and administrative efficiency. By demystifying these technologies, the chapter equips educators and policymakers with essential knowledge to harness AI's potential for improving learning outcomes.

Chapter 9: Can the Potential Contributions of ChatGPT in Tourism Education Be Realized?

Chapter 9 delves into the impacts of ChatGPT on tourism students as perceived by academics. It presents a nuanced evaluation of both positive and negative effects. While ChatGPT enhances learning performance and digital literacy, some academics express concerns about students' ability to internalize information and develop critical skills. Positive effects include fostering innovation awareness and time management, while negative effects involve potential laziness and decreased student motivation.

Chapter 10: The Impact of NBA Implementation Across Engineering Disciplines: Innovative Approaches

Chapter 10 explores how NBA principles have revolutionized various engineering fields, from materials science to urban design. It delves into the equity, access, and ethical implications of NBA-driven innovations, addressing data privacy and algorithmic bias concerns. The chapter emphasizes the transformative potential of sports-driven innovation for societal advancement by fostering collaboration between sports and engineering.

Sirvan Sen Demir
Süleyman Demirel University, Turkey

Mahmut Demir
Isparta University of Applied Sciences, Turkey

Chapter 1
Evolution of Higher Education in the Social Sciences From Traditional Classrooms to AI-Driven Learning Environments

Onur Aktürk
Süleyman Demirel University, Turkey

ABSTRACT

This chapter examines the evolving landscape of higher education in the social sciences, specifically the shift from traditional classroom settings to AI-powered learning environments. It contrasts the features of traditional and online education, highlighting the advantages and disadvantages of each approach. The chapter then delves into the positive impacts of artificial intelligence (AI) on higher education, showcasing how AI can personalize learning experiences, improve student outcomes, and streamline administrative tasks. However, the chapter also acknowledges the challenges associated with integrating AI into higher education, including issues of global inequality, uneven distribution of AI resources, and ethical concerns. By addressing both the opportunities and challenges, this chapter provides a comprehensive overview of the transformative potential of AI in higher education and its implications for the social sciences.

INTRODUCTION

Education is one of the most crucial instruments for societies' economic, social, and cultural development, unveiling the potential of individuals and forming the

DOI: 10.4018/979-8-3693-1666-5.ch001

foundational stones of societal progress. Another significant driving force behind societal development is the groundbreaking advancements in technology. Thus, the synergy between these two pivotal actors, education and technology, transforms teaching and learning practices by integrating technological developments into the education sector. In particular, advances in cloud computing, learning analytics, big data, and artificial intelligence present significant opportunities for enhancing students' learning skills (Cheung et al., 2021).

The traditional education system, dominated by a one-size-fits-all approach, is often criticized for overlooking individual differences, thus lacking the capacity to meet the diverse needs of learners. At this juncture, education systems worldwide are increasingly adopting a personalized approach that does not ignore individual differences, focusing on student-centered and needs-based education (Bhutoria, 2022). It is crucial to embrace methods and techniques to produce high-quality educational outcomes to adapt to current and future developments and solve problems effectively (Toniş et al., 2022). The challenges faced globally during the pandemic have necessitated a transformation in the education system (Van et al., 2020). During this period, institutions and educators were forced to rapidly transition from face-to-face to remote learning, making the creation of new learning environments inevitable (Carrillo & Flores, 2020). This situation reiterated that the education sector, a key factor in societal progress, must quickly adapt to unforeseen life conditions and changes in the economy and technology while meeting student demands (Alotaibi & Alshehri, 2023).

The advancements in information technology, coupled with the widespread adoption of artificial intelligence across nearly all aspects of societal life, have inevitably led to its integration into the education sector, embracing these new technologies for educational applications (Ouyang & Jiao, 2021). Compared to traditional educational models, which come with numerous challenges, artificial intelligence is considered a potent tool in the design of effective teaching and offers new and more efficient methods for educational research, positioning AI as a powerful and effective instrument in educational applications (Holmes et al., 2019; Hwang et al., 2020).

This study focuses on the evolution from traditional classroom environments to AI-driven learning spaces at the intersection of education and technology. It investigates how technological advancements in cloud computing, learning analytics, big data, and artificial intelligence have spurred a transformation within the education sector and examines the impact of this transformation on students' learning abilities. Furthermore, it will explore how the pandemic has accelerated the need for an urgent transformation in educational systems and detail the role of artificial intelligence in this process. The research aims not only to evaluate the current state of this transformation in higher education but also to shed light on future educational models.

The structure of the research will begin with an introduction, addressing the impact of technology on education, followed by an examination of the rise and characteristics of AI-driven learning environments. Subsequently, it will focus on the effects of these new learning environments on student skills and educational outcomes. Additionally, the rapid transformation in education during the pandemic and the role of artificial intelligence in this period will be assessed. Finally, the research will conclude by discussing the future trends and potential impacts of this transformation in higher education.

BACKGROUND

Evolution of Higher Education

Education is not only a human right but also an important factor in social development. It contributes to poverty reduction, improved health conditions, gender equality, and social stability. It is also an effective way to increase employment and earnings for individuals (World Bank, 2023). The education sector, which has such an important place in terms of social development, has constantly evolved due to its dynamic structure (Gowda & Suma, 2017). Especially the increasing transparency of physical borders between countries brought about by globalization, the increasing use of information technology, and the emergence of work organization structures based on networks and teams have significantly altered the external environment individuals interact with. Furthermore, transformations in the business world have also impacted employer expectations of employees. In highly competitive environments, the ability to critically select and use information, as well as communication and cooperation skills, are standout characteristics. Education systems are expected to rapidly adapt to this transformation to train experts with the necessary skills for future employment (Tynjälä, 1999).

For the rapid adaptation process to be successful, the education subjects must have the necessary equipment. At this point, students, the most important subjects of education, must acquire and develop the necessary skills to adapt to the rapidly changing social structure. Learning to learn and the ability to manage one's learning processes are issues that are gaining importance day by day. Therefore, the educational environment plays an important role in helping students develop their ability to manage their learning processes and shape their learning attitudes (Park & Choi, 2014; Schuitema, Peetsma & Veen, 2012). When the literature is examined, it is clear that designing an educational environment that encourages student autonomy and freedom to choose their learning processes, clearly expressing the importance of the information being taught and linking it to prior knowledge, as well as encouraging collaboration, will promote greater sharing and discussion of ideas. As a result, the design of the educational environment plays a crucial role in developing students' learning processes (Dalgıç et al., 2024; Schuitema et al., 2012). At this point, it is clear that the creation of traditional and technology-integrated educational environments will have different results in terms of students' development processes. At this point, higher education institutions play a crucial role in social progress, not only by preparing students for social and professional life, but also by making significant contributions to various aspects of society.

Due to the significance attributed to higher education by policymakers and the corresponding investments, both students and society reap the rewards. Individuals with a university degree earn more and enjoy better living conditions commensurate with their qualifications than those without such a degree. Higher earnings translate to increased tax contributions and greater civic engagement. A better future for their children also raises the living standards of future generations. Beyond its benefits, higher education leads to an increase in the labor force participation rate, employment, and earnings, as well as an increase in the material welfare of society (Baum, Ma & Payea, 2010). Due to the significant role that higher education institutions play in society, it is crucial to implement effective strategies and policies. To achieve this, it is necessary to analyze the historical evolution of these institutions from the past to the present objectively and comprehensively. Higher education institutions play a crucial role in the context of knowledge economies, as they are increasingly becoming research subjects. The effects of expanding higher education and research systems are not only regional but also national and even global. With this multifaceted impact, higher education research began to attract more attention from the scientific community as a field of knowledge in its own right in European countries in the 1970s (Brennan & Teichler, 2008).

It is helpful to review its history to predict the future of higher education, which is a crucial tool for development, and to plan and strategize accordingly. Higher education is an institution that has been essential for the development of civilizations. It is characterized by the concepts of institutional autonomy and academic freedom. While administrators, military personnel, priests, and other service elites are trained through higher education, the existence of universities can be traced back to medieval Europe. Since the twelfth century, an autonomous higher education institution has only emerged in Europe and continues to exist. The history of higher education is primarily the history of the European university and its evolution into an adaptable institutional structure that caters to the requirements of diverse societies across the globe. In this context, the mentioned historical process can be handled in five stages (Perkin, 2007):

- From the twelfth century to the 1530s, cosmopolitan European universities rose and played a significant role in the collapse of the medieval order with the Reformation;
- The integration of universities into their national structures by the rising "nationalization" during the Wars of Religion and the subsequent decline in the influence of universities during the Enlightenment of the eighteenth century (1530-1789);
- The revival of the university after the French Revolution and its growing role in industrial society (1789-1939);
- The expansion of universities to the non-European world and their adaptation to the needs of developing societies and anti-colonial reactions (1538-1960s);
- The transition from elite to mass education and the roles of the university and its diversified institutions in post-industrial society (1945-present).

TRADITIONAL EDUCATION

In Europe, university education is less standardized and formalized than in other regions. Instead of classroom instruction, it is structured around exams that span a year or more. In England, where university education has been deeply established, the traditional form of education is the tutorial system, characterized by one-on-one interactions between professor and student (Rhoades, 1991). Some third world societies still prefer traditional education (Oda Abunamus et al., 2022). In general, the evaluation of the traditional education system reveals that many universities employ an instructor-centered teaching style. This approach gives the instructor sole responsibility for deciding what and how to teach, which can make it difficult for students to retain even the most basic concepts. Therefore, it is suggested that these traditional methods may not be the most effective way to encourage student learning (Alters & Nelson, 2002). Zhao (2011) argues that traditional education follows a passive model, where students are expected to simply listen, take notes, and be monitored. This creates a one-way teaching channel, with information flowing solely from teacher to student, leaving the student as a mere consumer of information. It is also emphasized that traditional education is based on transfer learning. One of the important components of the educational environment is the classroom, where educational activities take place.

The design of classrooms in traditional universities can be traced back to the teaching spaces that emerged in medieval universities and has remained largely unchanged, except for dimensions. Throughout history, educational environments and methods have evolved in line with social and technological changes. When we look at the Ancient Greek period, when education gained a formal structure, teaching was generally based on rhetoric and students used to learn through dialogues, gathering around their teachers. On the other hand, the medieval period stands out as the first period to offer more organized educational spaces. In this period, the need for large and purpose-designed spaces became apparent, and universities became the pioneers of this structural transformation. Since the Industrial Revolution until today, the educational model has generally taken on a lecture-based structure with an instructor standing in front and students sitting in rows (Park & Choi, 2014). Given the increasing population and demand for high-quality education, traditional classrooms may not provide an efficient learning environment, prompt assessment, and active participation (Demir & Demir, 2023a; 2023b; Haleem et al., 2022).

Looking at the concept of the classroom from a broader perspective within the traditional education system, there are two types of traditional classrooms: teacher-centered and student-centered. Teacher-centered traditional classrooms in universities have a structure in which the teacher takes the main role and students usually focus on what the teacher says. In such classrooms, students exhibit passive behavior rather than actively processing the information the teacher provides. However, as changes in teaching approach occur, traditional classrooms are transforming into student-centered classrooms. In traditional student-centered classrooms, in addition to listening, writing and thinking skills, students are expected to participate in the lessons actively. Students can answer questions, collaborate, and make presentations in such classrooms. In this way, learning behaviors are activated, and students are proven more effective in learning outcomes (Li et al., 2014).

The general characteristics of traditional education can be summarized as follows: it relies heavily on printed materials, and students are constrained by time and space during the learning process, as they are required to attend classes at specific times and locations determined by the institution and teacher (Gowda & Suma, 2017), Learning outcomes and assessment methods are implemented according to predetermined plans and programs (Babić, 2011), in addition, traditional assessment and evaluation refer to tools that primarily measure cognitive abilities, such as open-ended, short-answer, true-false, multiple-choice, and matching tests (Çalışkan & Kaşıkçı, 2010), enables spontaneous discussions, instant feedback and personal, face-to-face communication (Clayton, Blumberg & Anthony, 2018), passive teaching is the dominant approach, which requires no action beyond listening, watching, and note-taking by students during the teaching process (Zhao, 2011).

IMPACT OF TECHNOLOGY ON HIGHER EDUCATION

Education, research, innovation, and leadership are essential in addressing sustainable development challenges. Universities have a critical role to play in the achievement of sustainable development goals. As they hold a unique position within society and have an educational mandate, universities must prioritize this role (Ahel & Lingenau, 2020). The only way to achieve Sustainable Development goals is through the rapid adoption of innovative digital technologies in digital transformation (Alojail & Khan, 2023). However, some countries have not been able to keep up with technological change due to a lack of digital skills and awareness. In today's competitive and rapidly advancing digital world, this is a significant disadvantage (Nordhaus, 2019). At this point that higher education institutions play a crucial role in addressing the gap in the development of digital skills and the acquisition of digital capabilities (Strielwowski, Korneeva & Gorina, 2022).

The penetration of digital technologies into our daily lives and their becoming an indispensable part of life inevitably have a profound impact on all strata of society. Such an impact leads to radical changes from the way we work to the way we communicate, from social activities to our understanding of entertainment (OECD, 2016). In today's fierce competition conditions, gaining digital skills, especially in business life, and being able to evaluate the advantages brought by digitalization effectively will inevitably make significant contributions to both individuals, businesses and societies on a wider scale. Therefore, it has become a necessity to keep up with the digital transformation rapidly (Alenezi & Akour, 2023). There is a strong correlation between education and skills in digital transformation and adaptation to digital technologies (OECD, 2016). In this sense, higher education has a key role in providing individuals with vital skill sets, including information literacy, and the development of professional skills (Alenezi & Akour, 2023; Kurbanov et al., 2020). The fact that technology has made its presence felt in almost every aspect of life has naturally made it inevitable for educational institutions to be affected by this transformation process. On the one hand, the need to utilize the use of technology in schools, colleges and universities is radically changing the way of teaching and learning, while on the other hand, it is necessary to equip the generations that have come into contact with these technologies and will continue to do so in the future with the necessary knowledge, tools and capabilities (Díaz-García et al., 2022).

FROM EDUCATION 1.0 TO EDUCATION 5.0

Education became widespread after the first industrial revolution at the end of the 18th century, ushering in the era of Education 1.0 (Miranda et al., 2021). In general, Education 1.0 is an education model based on the method of receiving, responding and repeating, where certain life skills are transferred to a limited number of students, where information is transferred directly from the teacher to the student in a one-way way. In this model, the student receives information from the teacher, responds to what he/she has learnt in line with learning methods and finally presents what he/she has learnt again as an output (Kalaichelvan & Subramanian, 2023).

Education 2.0 coincides with the second industrial revolution period. The primary source of information of this period was open-source materials accessible through libraries. In the Education 2.0 period, thanks to advances in technology, electronic devices such as printers, calculators and computers started to be used in the field of education (Miranda et al., 2021). In Education 2.0, blogs, podcasts and participatory technologies are used, but the conditions are largely the same as in Education 1.0 (Gerstein, 2014).

Education 3.0, which emerged at the end of the 20th century during the third industrial revolution, marked a significant shift towards computerization, automation, and control in the educational landscape. This era introduced a new paradigm where synchronous sessions between students and teachers were no longer a prerequisite for learning. Instead, the teaching-learning processes were enhanced by an array of resources such as multimedia, online tools, and virtual laboratories, supporting a more heutagogical and connectivist approach. Teachers transitioned into roles as orchestrators, curators, and collaborators, empowering students to actively construct their knowledge. Mirroring the personalized nature of Web 3.0, Education 3.0 emphasized interest-based learning, allowing for a student-centered approach that tailors the educational experience to each learner's unique internet profile and browsing history (Miranda et al., 2021; Songkram et al., 2021).

Education 4.0 corresponds with the fourth industrial revolution, focusing on revolutionizing the educational landscape through cutting-edge technologies and innovative pedagogical practices. Placing the student at the forefront of their learning journey, Education 4.0 integrates advanced technologies from Industry 4.0 to enrich the learning experience. This approach aims to future-proof education by leveraging technologies such as virtual reality, robotics, big data, artificial intelligence, and smart technologies. The goal is to create an educational environment where students are the protagonists of their learning, supported by the transformative potential of these technological advancements (Kalaichelvan & Subramanian, 2023; Miranda et al., 2021; Moraes et al, 2023).

Education 5.0 conceptually represents a new paradigm in the field of education. At the center of this paradigm is an understanding that puts the student at the center using the latest technologies and teaching methods. The main objective of Education 5.0, which integrates artificial intelligence into the field of education, is to optimize the learning process and improve learning outcomes by adapting the content, pace and assessments in the context of each student's abilities and learning style (Ahmad et al., 2023; Rane et al., 2023).

The transformation of higher education through digital means presents a contrast to digitalization efforts in the business sector, which typically focus on new business models and the evolution of organizational identities. In the realm of higher education, the emphasis shifts towards enhancing the development of knowledge through the establishment of digital learning spaces. Unlike the digital transformation in businesses, higher education's digital shift does not adhere to the same criteria. The emergence of digital learning environments is underpinned by three pivotal elements. Firstly, the integration of digital education with digital subjects lays a crucial technical foundation. Secondly, this digital space is characterized by a dynamic redefinition of roles between students and teachers, fostering deeper and innovative forms of learning. Lastly, it empowers universities to extend beyond traditional physical and institutional limits, facilitating broader societal engagement. Thus, while still in its early stages, this shift towards a digital learning environment indeed marks a significant transformation in the realm of higher education (Bygstad et al., 2022). The phases of effectively realizing digital transformation within the scope of higher education can be expressed as follows (Alenezi & Akour, 2023; Benavides et al., 2020; Rashid et al; 2021; Abad-Segura et al., 2020):

- To convey the importance of being a university that has completed the digital transformation process to all parties that will be affected and benefit from the digital transformation process, in other words, to disseminate the digital transformation culture,
- To provide financial and moral support from the leadership and employees of the university,
- Determining the requirements ranging from the infrastructure needed, equipped employees and legal aspects,
- Reviewing and benchmarking the results of successful models that have experienced the digital transformation process both locally and internationally,
- Updating the current vision, mission, goals and objectives of the university in line with the digital transformation strategy,
- Identifying the parties that will benefit from the digital transformation process, such as students, alumni, board members, faculty members and administrators, and how they will participate in this process,
- Developing an operational plan with objectives, targets, activities, processes, financing needed, technical resources and timetable,
- Setting criteria and indicators to facilitate the monitoring of progress at each step and providing feedback until the final step is reached.

Acknowledgment of digital transformation's significance is widespread, yet information on its maturity levels and associated challenges remains limited, particularly in the context of developing countries and within the sphere of higher education. It is the view of researchers that the maturity criteria outlined in Deloitte's maturity assessment framework are thorough, concrete, accessible, and accurately mirror the state of digital transformation. To help guide higher education institutions in this context, Deloitte provides a Digital Maturity Assessment Framework using five key criteria (Marks et al, 2021):

- Does the organization have the right vision and strategy for digital, and the leadership, communications, and focus required to support this vision?
- Does the organization have the right talent, skills, and knowledge to support its vision, products, and services?
- Does the organization have the right processes, controls, and digital technologies to support the operations of the organization?
- Does the organization have the right technologies and infrastructure as well as the ability to develop, manage and deliver?
- Does the organization have the right approach to understanding and communicating with its customers to succeed in a digital environment? (Deloitte, 2019).

In addition to Deloitte's Maturity Assessment Framework, to assess capability in higher education, in 2018, HolonIQ introduced a comprehensive 16-point framework aimed at enhancing digital higher education. This framework delineates critical capabilities and pinpoints strategic areas for focus and development, offering institutions a concrete means of assessing their progress in digital transformation. Comprising four main dimensions-Demand and Discovery (DD), Learning Design (LD), Learner Experience (LX), and Work and Lifelong Learning (WL)-the model encapsulates key competencies across various facets of education, including recruitment, curriculum design, assessment, and career planning (Figure 1). Furthermore, it provides a structured approach to the developmental aspects necessary to implement digital learning successfully (HolonIQ, 2023).

Adopting digital technology in education has led to various changes in learning processes; however, whether this technology has fundamentally transformed education is controversial. The integration of technology into education varies depending on societal conditions, and this depends on factors such as socio-economic level, teachers' interest in and readiness for technology, their level of education, and the country's economic situation. Computers and other technological devices are generally not widely used in classrooms except in technologically advanced countries. Moreover, evidence on the effects of digital technology on education is contradictory, and the short and long-term costs of technology use often seem to be underestimated. The most disadvantaged groups are often left behind in utilizing technological advances (UNESCO, 2023).

Figure 1. Higher Education Digital Capability Framework
Sources: HolonIQ (2023). "Higher Education Digital Transformation Survey". https://www.holoniq.com/notes/2023-higher-education-digital-transformation-survey

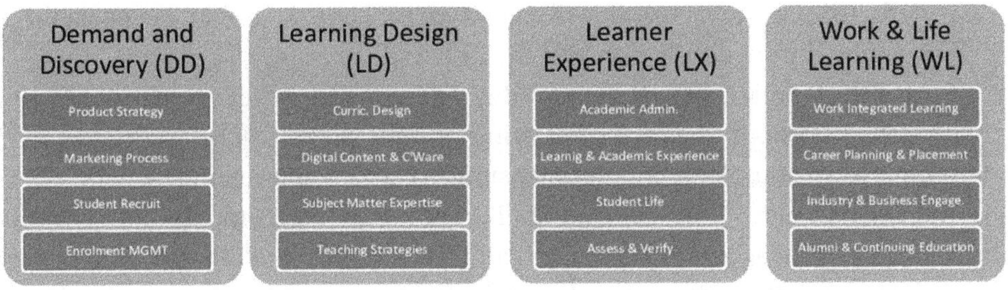

While the digital transformation process continues progressing in line with certain plans and strategies, a disruptive event such as Covid 19 has had a significant impact worldwide. This situation, which radically changed the socio-economic functioning on a global scale, forced individuals and institutions to adapt to new lifestyles. The biggest impact of the pandemic was to accelerate the digital transformation process. The higher education sector suspended the face-to-face education and training process and closed its campuses, necessitating the fastest paradigm shift ever seen. Firstly, a sudden shift towards online learning based on digital technologies (Mhlanga et al., 2022). Due to the comparison between traditional education and online education, particularly during the pandemic and subsequent transition to remote learning, it is now possible to more clearly analyze the advantages and disadvantages of these two distinct educational environments.

In recent years, the diversity of the student population, the increase in class sizes, and changes in student expectations have led to the increasing adoption of more flexible approaches that include the use of ICT (Saunders, 2000; Saunders & Klemming, 2003). The flexibility that has emerged with the widespread use of Internet-based technologies has created many advantages for the education sector. One of the most important of these advantages is that individuals can receive education at any time and place they want, without being bound to a specific place and/or time during their education process, and they can organize their own education programs to suit their lifestyles (Campbell et al., 2008).

OECD (2016) explains the necessity of embedding information and communication technologies (ICT) in schools and teachers' practices with the following statements:

- Firstly, while the use of ICT devices and the internet will enhance the traditional learning experience, the use of these technologies will also act as a catalyst for the larger-scale change that will be needed in the future,

- In the processes of education and learning, Information and Communication Technologies (ICT), even if they occur outside of school, can play a crucial role in enabling initial education to make the use of these technologies and benefit from them accessible for everyone. Thus, it might be possible to bridge the digital divide between the rich and the poor,
- School ICT policies may be grounded in the desire to reduce administrative and other costs. In the face of existing or anticipated teacher shortages, ICT policies can complement other measures to attract and retain teachers.
- Information and Communication Technologies can support and enhance learning. With access to computers and the Internet, students are able to seek and acquire knowledge beyond what is offered by teachers and textbooks.
- ICT provides students new ways to practice their skills - such as maintaining a personal webpage or online publication, programming, conversing with native speakers while learning a second language, and/or preparing multimedia presentations. These activities can be undertaken either individually or as part of a remotely connected team.
- ICT devices integrate traditionally separate educational media (books, writing, audio recordings, video recordings, databases, etc.).

Evaluated the features of traditional education and virtual and web-based education in their study and came to the following conclusion (Pakdaman et al., 2019):

- Traditional education: Many schools and universities worldwide widely use traditional lecturing methods. The course typically involves memorization, repetition, and straight lectures, with the lecturer providing verbal information and the students taking notes. This method places the lecturer in an active role and the students in a passive position (Lehmann et al., 2013; Woltering et al., 2009)
- E-Learning: E-learning is a combination of software and information technology-based teaching methods (computer, network, internet, and virtual university) that offer lifelong opportunities for education and learning without any limitations regardless of time and place, where courses can be repeated, access to information can be accessed without time and space restrictions (Ellaway, 2011; Kremer & Holla, 2009).

The emergence of new educational technologies and e-learning undoubtedly offers opportunities, but these technologies alone do not lead to deep and effective learning. For all its advantages, virtual education has disadvantages, such as high initial costs, limited access, restricted access to computers and accessories, limited management and monitoring of computer resources and educational services, and lack of ethical

Table 1. Traditional Learning vs. E-Learning

Differences	Traditional Education	E-Learning
Organization	One type of organization: teacher and student come together	Can be tailored to different situations, such as communication rules, access to materials, etc.
Time and Venue	Be present at the predetermined time and place	There are no restrictions on the time and place of learning
Communication	Natural	The communication method must be selected depending on the course type and purpose
Teacher	Identifying the learning outcomes, creating educational activities, exercises and educational process, evaluating students' knowledge	Depending on the model of the Internet Course (Person/Virtual Teacher/the system that controls the education process)
Learner	Teacher-centered: Passive learning	More active learning, communicating with the teacher and other students regardless of time and place
	Learner-centered: Active learning	
Content	Textual, audio-video, teacher chooses the content	Multimedia format, unlimited access, adapted to different learning styles

and educational relationships with teachers. On the other hand, traditional education offers some advantages, such as assisting lecturers in teaching content, stimulating students' desire to learn, contextualizing students' past and present experiences, accelerating and facilitating knowledge acquisition, and enabling feedback, which cannot be completely ignored (Pakdaman et al., 2019).

The differences between traditional learning and e-learning can generally be expressed in Table 1 (Babić, 2011; Li et al., 2014; Rudak, 2013).

ARTIFICIAL INTELLIGENCE IMPACT ON HIGHER EDUCATION

The digital revolution has had a huge societal impact, from our work to the functioning of companies, from our consumption habits to our employment patterns. With the integration of artificial intelligence into social life, the coefficient of this impact continues to increase. It brings to mind negative scenarios as well as positive aspects. While it is seen as a groundbreaking revolution in a positive sense by various circles, it is defined as the beginning of the end by a group (Makridakis, 2017). These changes, which will trigger global growth along with productivity, may also lead to the disappearance of many jobs, further deepening the already existing inequality. In the analysis carried out by the IMF, it is stated that approximately 40 percent of global employment interacts with artificial intelligence, and approximately 60 percent of employment in developed economies will be affected by artificial intelligence (Georgieva, 2024). Artificial intelligence (AI) is revolutionizing the development of public services with innovative technologies such as autonomous vehicles and automated customer service. In China, Alibaba's AI algorithms turn traffic lights in Shanghai green as ambulances approach. At the same time, in the US, BrainScope's portable electrode headset detects traumatic brain injuries at accident scenes with 98% accuracy. These examples offer a glimpse of how AI can change our lives. Moreover, the incorporation of AI into public education promises to overcome previous failed attempts at technology in this field.

Before addressing the multifaceted impact of artificial intelligence in the field of education, starting with the question "What is artificial intelligence?" will be a healthy first step to predict the point that this technology integrated into the education sector will reach in the future. However, it would be a more accurate approach to start with the question, "What is intelligence?" The ability to achieve set goals through computation is present in varying degrees in humans, many animals, and some machines. Intelligence can be defined as the computational aspect of the ability to achieve set goals. This ability is found to varying degrees in humans, many animals, and some machines. Artificial intelligence is the science and engineering of making intelligent machines, especially intelligent computer programs (McCarthy, 2004).

According to the results of McKinsey's annual research survey, the proportion of companies integrating and adopting artificial intelligence into their businesses in 2022 has doubled compared to 2017. Still, this rate has hovered between 50% and 60% in recent years. The contribution of artificial intelligence is also significant in terms of fulfilling tasks more efficiently and effectively. In the survey conducted on the use of GitHub's artificial intelligence system Copilot, it was revealed that 88% of the respondents felt more productive when using the system, 74% were able to produce more satisfying jobs, and 88% were able to complete tasks much faster (Chui et al., 2022; Kalliamvakaou, 2022).

Artificial Intelligence, which has a striking impact in the economic field, has also had a high impact on higher education institutions, which have an important mission in terms of bringing well-equipped individuals to society. According to the Artificial Intelligence Index Report (2023), interest in AI majors, which are usually part of computer science curricula, has been increasing yearly. According to North American-based data, the number of computer science bachelor's degree graduates on the road to 2021 has increased nearly four times compared to 2021 (33,059). Regarding international students, the situation is not much different: the proportion of computer science undergraduates with international student status is 16.5%, corresponding to an increase of about 9.5 percentage points compared to 2012 (Maslej et al., 2023). According to the "2023 Educade Horizon Report," the most influential trends shaping higher education teaching and learning across

Figure 2. AI in University Programs by Level of Studies (%)
Source: European Commission, JRC Technical Report (2022)

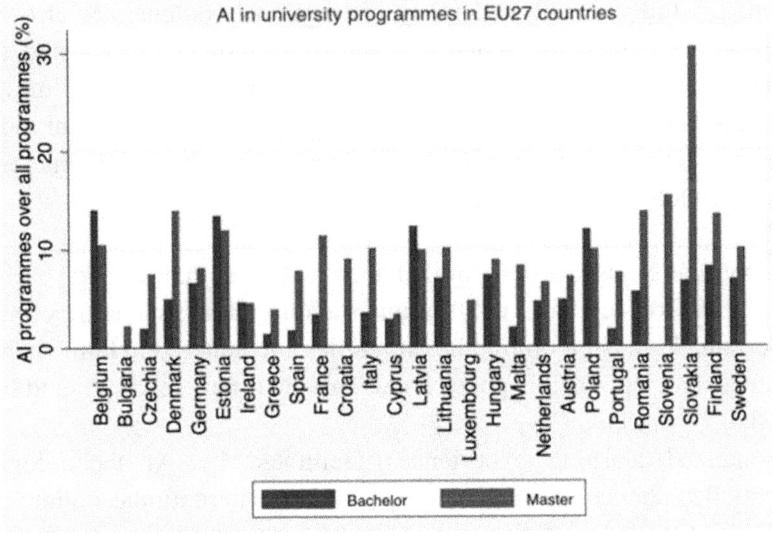

five categories: social, technological, economic, environmental, and political. Within technological trends, it is stated that artificial intelligence has now become mainstream and technologies that simplify complex processes without the need for code enable many more people to create digital content (Pelletier et al., 2023). In addition, in the "AI Watch Index 2021" report, the indicators that consider the ratio of programs with Artificial Intelligence content in the total number of programs in the 2020-2021 academic year are given in Figure 2.

Figure 2 shows that in most member states, AI content in master's degree programs is higher than in bachelor's degree programs. At this point, Belgium, Estonia, Latvia, and Poland are the four exceptions that have more AI content in their undergraduate programs. The second country with the highest concentration of AI content in master's curricula is Slovenia (15.3%). Another striking feature in the graph belongs to Slovenia. It is the leading country in the EU regarding AI content (30.4%) (Righi et al., 2022). Apart from introducing artificial intelligence into the course content of higher education programs, with its penetration into almost all areas of higher education, its effects on all parties of higher education are inevitable. Therefore, how AI is utilized will also differ for the parties involved in higher education. For example, AI can provide 24/7 support to students during the registration process, help instructors grade students and provide them with the resources they need, provide counseling services to help students overcome deficiencies by analyzing their past performance, or bring together information from multiple campus systems to guide administrative decisions or to create curricula (Klutka et al., 2018).

In terms of students studying, many international students are also involved in student mobility in higher education and this number is expected to reach approximately eight million by 2025. One of the important ways to mitigate the disadvantages as well as the advantages of such a high level of student mobility is through artificial intelligence applications. The benefits of these applications can be expressed as follows (Wang et al., 2023):

- Chatbots can be used as a helpful element to overcome language barriers and cultural differences, especially for international students, and they are also an important aid in overcoming the difficulties encountered in homework due to language barriers. At this point, it can provide timely feedback and language translation services,
- Personalized learning experiences facilitated by AI technologies can potentially enhance the educational journey of international students,
- Search and recommendation systems of AI-powered applications can enhance the user experience and increase the functionality of libraries (Cox et al., 2019),
- Predictive practices in education can provide insight into the overall trajectory of students in general, including international students. Data such as attendance, grades, completion rates, etc. can help to see the current status of a student and identify students who are falling behind or dropping out, making it easier to take timely action.

Chen et al. (2020) grouped the functions of AI under areas such as instructions, learning, and management in their study, and in management, to perform administrative tasks such as grading exams and providing feedback quickly, to support instructors in decision support and data-based studies. In the instruction area, instructors can develop personalized learning plans and specific teaching methods for each student, as well as analyze syllabi and materials to create customized content. In the field of learning, they stated that it can be used in areas such as identifying student learning deficiencies and determining an appropriate career path. In addition, in their study, Crompton and Burke (2023) identified five categories of how artificial intelligence will be used in higher education;

1. Assessment-Evaluation: Phase of assessment/evaluation instructors in generating questions and creating multiple question tests. AI technologies can generate highly realistic short-answer questions. However, it would be

important for instructors always to confirm questions provided by the AI to ensure they are correct and that they match the learning objectives for the class

2. Predicting: Phase of predicting AI can be used to predict different topics such as career decision, development track, academic performance.
3. AI Assistant: AI assistant can support depending on student needs such as answering questions, performance, and out-of-class sports.
4. Intelligent Tutoring System: Intelligent tutoring systems are instructional systems that use artificial intelligence techniques and training methods. ITS systems customize educational activities and strategies per the student's wishes and needs (Mousavinasab et al., 2021).
5. Managing Student Learning: Measurement, collection, analysis and reporting of relevant data to optimize learning and the environments in which learning takes place, as well as to perform tasks such as curriculum sequencing.

Undoubtedly, one of the most striking developments in the field of AI took place on 30 November 2022 with the launch of the AI-based chatbot ChatGPT (Chat Generative Pre-trained Transformer) by OpenAI (Wikipedia, 2024). ChatGPT is the sister model of InstructGPT, which is trained to understand a command and provide a detailed response (OpenAI, 2022). In particular, it has influenced the education sector due to its ability to generate human-like text and some features that make automated conversations much easier (Grassini, 2023). ChatGPT could serve various roles in education settings, such as providing information, facilitating debates and discussions, supporting self-directed learning, and creating course materials (Smith et al., 2023). In academic studies analyzing the impact of ChatGPT on education, it is stated that it can significantly help both students and instructors (Lo, 2023). ChatGPT is a useful tool for instructors to organize and draft article components, as well as assess students' assessment and evaluation skills (Zhai, 2022). For students, ChatGPT facilitates language acquisition by empowering learners to manipulate sentence structures, refine pronunciation and terminology usage, comprehend grammatical nuances, and receive instantaneous feedback on their interpretations (Gill et al., 2024). In the report prepared by Unesco (2023) (ChatGPT and Artificial Intelligence in Higher Education), the main applications of ChatGPT in higher education are shown in Table 2 (Sabzalieva & Valentini, 2023).

Table 2 shows that ChatGPT is used in three main areas of higher education institutions. From the students' perspective, ChatGPT offers support in completing homework and assigned tasks, as well as providing feedback on areas for improvement, similar to a private instructor. The full support of ChatGPT in all stages of the research process is invaluable to instructors. ChatGPT is a helpful tool for research design and data analysis. It also has the potential to reduce administrative work time significantly.

Table 2. Applications of ChatGPT in Higher Education

Students	Students doing group work can complete the tasks and assignments given to them by using ChatGPT by using time effectively.
	Artificial intelligence can function as a personal tutor, providing learners with specific information on specific topics of interest and providing feedback
	They may request alternative learning materials or methods to better understand a topic.
Researchers	ChatGPT can help researchers to shape the research process
	Research design /Generate ideas for research question, suggest data sources
	Assists in the data collection phase, querying archives and datasets and translating sources into different languages
	Improve the quality of writing in the writing phase, and be able to reorganise citations and references
	Provides necessary support during the data analysis phase Provides necessary support during the data analysis phase
Administration	Responding to queries from applicants (potential students)
	Send reminders or notifications
	Helping students to complete courses and fulfil the required requirements, checking administrative information (e.g. location of classes, exam timetable)

One of the key stakeholders affected by the rapid developments in the field of artificial intelligence is undoubtedly educators. This rapid development inevitably raises questions such as whether artificial intelligence technology will completely take over the role of educators in the future. This rapid development inevitably raises questions such as whether artificial intelligence technology will completely assume the role of educators in the future. At this point, one of the two extreme views that differ from each other is that artificial intelligence aims to reduce costs and, therefore, will lead to a decrease in the number of educators, which is one of the main cost items. In contrast, the other view suggests that machines can never replace humans, but can be seen as an auxiliary element that will increase the productivity of educators (Bates et al., 2020). One of the most well-known benefits of artificial intelligence applications is the use of humanoid and web-based robots designed to fulfil the tasks and functions of instructors, enabling instructors to perform different administrative tasks such as reviewing students' homework and grading much more effectively and efficiently, thereby improving the quality of teaching activities. Machine learning systems contribute to improving the quality of learning by customizing the curriculum and course content in line with student needs (Chen et al., 2020). The shortcomings of traditional education systems have also contributed to the professional development of educators who have to keep up with the requirements of the digital age. Especially the inadequacy of the training programs of traditional education systems to encourage professional development, as well as the intervals between training programs up to a few years and the lack of strategic planning make such a change process compulsory for educators (Al-Zyoud, 2020).

EXAMPLES OF ARTIFICIAL INTELLIGENCE APPLICATIONS IN HIGHER EDUCATION

The integration of artificial intelligence (AI) in the field of education has led to the increased utilization of AI applications in the world of education. This has significantly altered how teaching, learning and administrative processes are conducted. A noteworthy example in this field is Georgia State University. The "Pounce" artificial intelligence system developed by AdmitHub provides an important support service and offers a kind of guidance service to students. For example, with "Pounce", students can learn about the importance of applying for financial aid, as well as receive step-by-step guidance throughout the process. They can also get quick answers to their questions such as orientation dates, driving on campus and study opportunities. In comparison to students who received GSU's standard support before and during the registration process, "Pounce" was found to have significantly contributed to students completing the registration process without any errors (Page & Gehlbach, 2018). Another example of the use of AI in higher education is the University of Technology Sydney (Australia). Especially during the pandemic period, with the breakdown of physical communication between students and lecturers, it has become increasingly difficult to track students' interactions with the course, and to overcome this difficulty, a program was created that tracks students' facial and eye movements as well as keyboard activity and mouse movements during online courses to determine students' instant reactions to the course content or their level of participation in the lessons (Bamford, 2020). In this way, students' level of interest in course content can be determined, future arrangements can be made more appropriately, and more interesting course content can be prepared (Liu et al., 2023). Another example of the utilization of Chatbots to facilitate the teaching process is the Georgia Institute of Technology (USA). As of 2016, the artificial intelligence Chatbot named "Jill Watson" has been enhanced with additional functions, including the ability to respond to students' online queries and provide motivational support to reduce dropout rates in online courses (Georgia Tech, 2016).

A team of researchers studying student online behavior using anonymized and aggregated metadata from student learning management systems started with hand-crafted algorithms. Over time, they added more data, switched to machine learning, and made important findings; for example, as students' online interactions increased, their course grades improved. Within two weeks of the beginning of the semester, these algorithms could predict students' grades with 60-70% accuracy. In a pilot launched in the fall of 2016, 16,000 students were identified and contacted as being at risk of failing early on. The barriers encountered were mostly non-academic and easily resolved by the institution's intervention. By the end of the semester, these interventions resulted in 3,000 students achieving a C grade or better, the biggest drop at the college in fifty years. To date, the project has helped 34,712 students (Hinton, n.d.). Another illustrative example is M-Write, a software developed by the University of Michigan. The algorithmic approach employed by M-Write enables the identification of areas where students may encounter difficulties and make mistakes during the writing process. Additionally, the algorithm facilitates the identification of the underlying issues that may contribute to suboptimal writing, and it supports students during the writing process (O'Brien, 2023). The examples of similar artificial intelligence applications offer a small insight into the current examples of artificial intelligence applications but also offer a strong perspective in terms of predicting the point it can reach in the field of education in the future.

KEY CHALLENGES AND CONCERNS IN THE INTEGRATION OF ARTIFICIAL INTELLIGENCE IN HIGHER EDUCATION

While the advantages of AI for educators, students, and administrators in educational institutions are evident, the rapid integration of artificial intelligence applications into the field of education also poses several challenges and concerns. UNESCO's 2023 report reveals that the current global inequality is inevitable to bring many difficulties and inequalities related to the use of artificial intelligence. The second major concern is that AI is not evenly distributed across countries in terms of education, training and research. There is a striking disparity in the adoption and development of AI between the US and China, and between sub-Saharan Africa, parts of Central and South Asia and parts of Latin America (Liu et al., 2023; Yu et al., 2023). In addition to the aforementioned challenges, colleges and universities are still facing enrolment and funding issues in some parts of the world due to the negative impact of the pandemic (Kuleto et al., 2021). Another notable difficulty is experienced in the planning and implementation phase. In order for technological innovations to be implemented effectively in vocational schools or universities, the arrangements should be designed in accordance with the aims and objectives of each institution (Cabaleiro-Cerviño & Vera, 2020).

Ethics is one of the most important concerns raised by the use of artificial intelligence technologies in higher education. One of the major concerns is that with the rise of educational technologies, whether or not they include artificial intelligence technology, a significant amount of student data will be collected during enrolment, and issues such as who will access this data and how long it will be stored (Boulay, 2022). Furthermore, transparency becomes a critical issue when chatbots employing artificial intelligence technology are used in contexts that may influence a student's academic career, such as career advice or counseling services. Additionally, concerns about justice, fairness, equity, privacy, and security are paramount. If the records of a student's interactions with chatbots are accessible to others, this could raise serious concerns regarding privacy and security principles (Chen et al., 2022). In research conducted specifically on ChatGPT, the barriers to fully utilizing the benefits of ChatGPT are listed as follows; lack of awareness, technological barriers, resistance to change, concerns about ethical issues, investment costs and financial constraints, insufficiency of multidisciplinary studies, legal regulations (such as copyrights and privacy regulations) (Michel-Villarreal et al., 2023). Another significant challenge is the potential for algorithmic bias in data analysis. Preventing biases resulting from using artificial intelligence in pattern identification is a crucial issue that requires greater emphasis (Yousuf & Wahid, 2024).

The performance of modern artificial intelligence applications is directly related to the quality of the data they utilize. The qualitative and quantitative characteristics inherent in the data directly affect the algorithm. For example, if the data has an unbalanced distribution and reflects the general trend of students to the extent that minority students are ignored, algorithms may systematically produce erroneous data in terms of minority students. Given the value placed on each student, it is essential to adopt a meticulous approach to data collection, ensuring that minority students are not disadvantaged by being overlooked (Luan et al., 2020).

POTENTIAL IMPACTS OF INTEGRATING ARTIFICIAL INTELLIGENCE INTO HIGHER EDUCATION IN THE FUTURE

Higher education is undergoing a radical and important transformation process with the integration of artificial intelligence technologies in this era of non-stop advancement of knowledge and technology. The integration of AI into higher education offers a wide range of innovations from learning methods to teaching strategies, from academic research to campus management, and brings unique opportunities in areas such as deep learning, natural language processing and machine learning (Li et al., 2024; Lund et al., 2023; Popenici & Kerr, 2017).

The spread of artificial intelligence (AI) will inevitably profoundly impact almost all aspects of social life. This will inevitably lead to a widening of the digital divide between those who can utilize AI effectively and those who are not. Higher education is undoubtedly one of the areas where these differences will be experienced. Therefore, on the one hand, students' acquisition of relevant competencies in AI literacy and then interdisciplinary studies should be encouraged much more by institutions (Chiu, 2024). In addition, higher education institutions should incorporate AI-related course content to ensure equitable educational opportunities and to enhance the effective utilization of these tools. Neglecting advancements in artificial intelligence could result in a disinterest among students in this critical field, potentially stifling the progress of higher education institutions (Neumann, Rauschenberger & Schön, 2023).

In general terms, it can be stated that the impact of artificial intelligence on higher education will be as follows;

1. AI will be a significant tool for enhancing productivity and efficiency for both educators and students. Faculty will increasingly utilize AI tools for grading, assessment, and other time-consuming tasks (Shaw et al., 2023).
2. The findings of a survey conducted with over 1,000 faculty members, shared in the Spring 2023 Time for Class report, indicate that both students and faculty believe that Generative AI (GenAI) tools will be necessary to succeed in the highly competitive work environment. A substantial percentage of faculties using GenAI (75%) emphasize that graduates need to know how to effectively utilize these tools for success in the workplace (Shaw et al., 2023).
3. Future higher education institutions must update themselves in line with the characteristics and needs of the future workforce. Skills working with GenAI should be acquired, emphasis should be placed on AI literacy, and an interdisciplinary learning mindset should be adopted (Chiu, 2024).
4. Since Metaverse environments offer participants the opportunity to create their own maker spaces, Maker learning should be incorporated into many courses (Burke, 2015; Chiu, 2024).
5. AI systems will play a significant role in alleviating students' fears towards learning by providing an independent learning environment free from the limitations they offer. This shift will also transform the role of teachers (Aldosari, 2020).

CONCLUSION

The radical changes brought about by artificial intelligence in the education sector have resulted in all stakeholders of the education sector being influenced by this change and entering into a process of change and transformation. Consequently, the potential of artificial intelligence technologies to shape teaching and learning in higher education has led to a critical discussion on their integration (Popenici & Kerr, 2017). This innovative destruction environment brought about by artificial intelligence brings along a number of challenges as well as opportunities, and solutions must be produced rapidly to overcome these problems.

Luan et al. (2020) addressed the problems that the integration of big data and artificial intelligence into the field of education will create in three main areas: research, policy-making and industry. The unequal distribution of learning opportunities and the contrasts arising from differences in development as a result of rapidly developing technology in the field of research create significant obstacles in terms of utilizing digital technologies. In the field of policy-making, the need for much stricter measures to protect private and personal data, as well as the fact that many pre-service educators have not yet fully adapted to new technologies, appear to be a serious problem. In the field of industry, the necessity of academia-industry collaboration is emphasized due to the challenges inherent in the integration of big data and artificial intelligence into the education sector. These challenges include the timely publication of advances in educational research on commercial platforms. In a separate study, the difficulties associated with integrating AI technologies into the field of education were broadly categorized as follows: strategy (an implementation plan to achieve the goals in line with a programme agreed upon after the common opinion of the stakeholders); institutional maturity (readiness and capability in terms of employees, processes and technology); data management and infrastructure (Owoc, Sawicka & Weichbroth, 2021).

In order to make optimal use of the advantages brought by Artificial Intelligence technologies, which are likely to bring much more in the future, it will positively affect the efficiency of the education sector, which has a key role in social development, to produce strategies for the problems that arise and are likely to arise. First of all, when proposing solutions to problems, the implementation process should take into account compliance with higher education laws, as well as the capacity of the university. Educational training should be designed to enable the more effective use of new technologies. New teaching and evaluation methods should be developed in formal education systems. In addition, the government should take measures to ensure data security during the policy-making and implementation phase. Much more research is needed on the use of artificial intelligence for individual differences in student learning. Finally, academic and industrial co-operation should be strengthened and more co-ordinated research projects should be supported (Luan et al., 2020; Owoc et al., 2021). In conclusion, as we navigate through the transformative waves that artificial intelligence brings to higher education, it is imperative that educators, policymakers, and institutions collaboratively refine strategies that harness AI's potential while mitigating its risks, ensuring that the evolution of educational practices aligns with both technological advancements and the fundamental values of equitable and inclusive learning.

REFERENCES

Abad-Segura, E., González-Zamar, M. D., Infante-Moro, J. C., & Ruipérez García, G. (2020). Sustainable management of digital transformation in higher education: Global research trends. *Sustainability (Basel)*, *12*(5), 21–27. doi:10.3390/su12052107

Ahel, O., & Lingenau, K. (2020). Opportunities and Challenges of Digitalization to Improve Access to Education for Sustainable Development in Higher Education. In *Universities as Living Labs for Sustainable Development. World Sustainability Series*. Springer. doi:10.1007/978-3-030-15604-6_21

Ahmad, S., Umirzakova, S., Mujtaba, G., Amin, M. S., & Whangbo, T. (2023). Education 5.0: requirements, enabling technologies, and future directions. *arXiv preprint arXiv:2307.15846*.

Al-Zyoud, H. M. M. (2020). The role of artificial intelligence in teacher professional development. *Universal Journal of Educational Research*, *8*(11B), 6263–6272. doi:10.13189/ujer.2020.082265

Aldosari, S. A. M. (2020). The future of higher education in the light of artificial intelligence transformations. *International Journal of Higher Education*, *9*(3), 145–151. doi:10.5430/ijhe.v9n3p145

Alenezi, M., & Akour, M. (2023). Digital Transformation blueprint in Higher Education: A case study of PSU. *Sustainability (Basel)*, *15*(10), 8204. Advance online publication. doi:10.3390/su15108204

Alojail, M., & Khan, S. B. (2023). Impact of digital transformation toward sustainable development. *Sustainability (Basel)*, *15*(20), 14697. Advance online publication. doi:10.3390/su152014697

Alotaibi, N. S., & Alshehri, A. H. (2023). Prospers and obstacles in using artificial intelligence in Saudi Arabia higher education institutions—The potential of AI-based learning outcomes. *Sustainability (Basel)*, *15*(13), 10723. doi:10.3390/su151310723

Alters, B. J., & Nelson, C. E. (2002). Perspective: Teaching evolution in higher education. *Evolution; International Journal of Organic Evolution*, *56*(10), 1891–1901. doi:10.1111/j.0014-3820.2002.tb00115.x PMID:12449476

Babić, S. (2011, May). E-learning environment compared to traditional classroom. In *2011 Proceedings of the 34th International Convention MIPRO* (pp. 1299-1304). IEEE.

Bamford, M. (2020) *Tracking technology aims to improve online learning for students during COVID-19, ABC News*. https://www.abc.net.au/news/2020-05-08/tracking-technology-aims-to-improve-online-learning/12211996

Baum, S., Ma, J., & Payea, K. (2010). *Education Pays, 2010: The Benefits of Higher Education for Individuals and Society. Trends in Higher Education Series*. College Board Advocacy & Policy Center.

Benavides, L. M. C., Tamayo Arias, J. A., Arango Serna, M. D., Branch Bedoya, J. W., & Burgos, D. (2020). Digital transformation in higher education institutions: A systematic literature review. *Sensors (Basel)*, *20*(11), 3291. Advance online publication. doi:10.3390/s20113291 PMID:32526998

Bhutoria, A. (2022). Personalized education and artificial intelligence in the United States, China, and India: A systematic review using a human-in-the-loop model. *Computers and Education: Artificial Intelligence*, *3*, 100068. Advance online publication. doi:10.1016/j.caeai.2022.100068

Brennan, J., & Teichler, U. (2008). The future of higher education and of higher education research: Higher education looking forward: An introduction. *Higher Education*, *56*(3), 259–264. doi:10.1007/s10734-008-9124-6

Bucea-Manea-Ţoniş, R., Kuleto, V., Gudei, S. C. D., Lianu, C., Lianu, C., Ilić, M. P., & Păun, D. (2022). Artificial intelligence potential in higher education institutions enhanced learning environment in Romania and Serbia. *Sustainability (Basel)*, *14*(10), 5842. doi:10.3390/su14105842

Bygstad, B., Øvrelid, E., Ludvigsen, S., & Dæhlen, M. (2022). From dual digitalization to digital learning space: Exploring the digital transformation of higher education. *Computers & Education*, *182*, 104463. Advance online publication. doi:10.1016/j.compedu.2022.104463

Cabaleiro-Cerviño, G., & Vera, C. (2020). The Impact of Educational Technologies in Higher Education. *GIST Education and Learning Research Journal*, *20*, 155–169. doi:10.26817/16925777.711

Çalışkan, H., & Kaşıkçı, Y. (2010). The application of traditional and alternative assessment and evaluation tools by teachers in social studies. *Procedia: Social and Behavioral Sciences*, *2*(2), 4152–4156. doi:10.1016/j.sbspro.2010.03.656

Campbell, M., Gibson, W., Hall, A., Richards, D., & Callery, P. (2008). Online vs. face-to-face discussion in a web-based research methods course for postgraduate nursing students: A quasi-experimental study. *International Journal of Nursing Studies*, *45*(5), 750–759. doi:10.1016/j.ijnurstu.2006.12.011 PMID:17306272

Carrillo, C., & Flores, M. A. (2020). COVID-19 and teacher education: A literature review of online teaching and learning practices. *European Journal of Teacher Education*, *43*(4), 466–487. doi:10.1080/02619768.2020.1821184

Chen, L., Chen, P., & Lin, Z. (2020). Artificial intelligence in education: A review. *IEEE Access : Practical Innovations, Open Solutions*, *8*, 75264–75278. doi:10.1109/ACCESS.2020.2988510

Chen, Y., Jensen, S., Albert, L. J., Gupta, S., & Lee, T. (2023). Artificial intelligence (AI) student assistants in the classroom: Designing chatbots to support student success. *Information Systems Frontiers*, *25*(1), 161–182. doi:10.1007/s10796-022-10291-4

Cheung, S. K., Kwok, L. F., Phusavat, K., & Yang, H. H. (2021). Shaping the future learning environments with smart elements: Challenges and opportunities. *International Journal of Educational Technology in Higher Education*, *18*(1), 1–9. doi:10.1186/s41239-021-00254-1 PMID:34778521

Chiu, T. K. (2024). Future research recommendations for transforming higher education with generative AI. *Computers and Education: Artificial Intelligence*, *6*, 100197. Advance online publication. doi:10.1016/j.caeai.2023.100197

Chui. (2022). The State of AI in 2022-and a half decade in review. McKinsey. https://www.mckinsey.com/capabilities/quantumblack/our-insights/the-state-of-ai-in-2022-and-a-half-decade-in-review#review

Clayton, K. E., Blumberg, F. C., & Anthony, J. A. (2018). Linkages between course status, perceived course value, and students' preference for traditional versus non-traditional learning environments. *Computers & Education*, *125*, 175–181. doi:10.1016/j.compedu.2018.06.002

Cox, A. M., Pinfield, S., & Rutter, S. (2019). The intelligent library: Thought leaders' views on the likely impact of artificial intelligence on academic libraries. *Library Hi Tech*, *37*(3), 418–435. doi:10.1108/LHT-08-2018-0105

Crompton, H., & Burke, D. (2023). Artificial intelligence in higher education: The state of the field. *International Journal of Educational Technology in Higher Education*, *20*(1), 22. doi:10.1186/s41239-023-00392-8

Dalgıç, A., Yaşar, E., & Demir, M. (2024). ChatGPT and learning outcomes in tourism education: The role of digital literacy and individualized learning. *Journal of Hospitality, Leisure, Sport and Tourism Education, 34*, 100481. doi:10.1016/j.jhlste.2024.100481

Deloitte. (2019). National Transformation in the Middle East a Digital Journey. *Deloitte* https://www2.deloitte.com/content/dam/Deloitte/xe/Documents/technology-media-telecommunication

Demir, M., & Demir, Ş. Ş. (2023). Is ChatGPT the right technology for service individualization and value co-creation? Evidence from the travel industry. *Journal of Travel & Tourism Marketing, 40*(5), 383–398. doi:10.1080/10548408.2023.2255884

Demir, Ş. Ş., & Demir, M. (2023). Professionals' perspectives on ChatGPT in the tourism industry: Does it inspire awe or concern? *Journal of Tourism Theory and Research, 9*(2), 61–77. doi:10.24288/jttr.1313481

Díaz-García, V., Montero-Navarro, A., Rodríguez-Sánchez, J. L., & Gallego-Losada, R. (2022). Digitalization and digital transformation in higher education: A bibliometric analysis. *Frontiers in Psychology, 13*, 1081595. Advance online publication. doi:10.3389/fpsyg.2022.1081595 PMID:36533011

du Boulay, B. (2022). Artificial intelligence in education and ethics. In *Handbook of open, distance and digital education* (pp. 1–16). Springer Nature Singapore. doi:10.1007/978-981-19-0351-9_6-2

Ellaway, R. (2011). E-learning: Is the revolution over? *Medical Teacher, 33*(4), 297–302. doi:10.3109/0142159X.2011.550968 PMID:21456987

Georgia Tech. (2016). Artificial Intelligence Course Creates AI Teaching Assistant. Available at: https://news.gatech.edu/news/2016/05/09/artificial-intelligence-course-createsai-teaching-assistant

Georgieva, K. (2024, January 14). AI will transform the global economy; let's make sure it benefits humanity. International Monetary Fund. https://www.imf.org/en/Blogs/Articles/2024/01/14/ai-will-transform-the-global-economy-lets-make-sure-it-benefits-humanity

Gerstein, J. (2014). Moving from education 1.0 through education 2.0 towards education 3.0. In L. M. Blaschke, C. Kenyon, & S. Hase (Eds.), Experiences in self-determined learning (pp. 83-97). Amazon.com.

Gill, S. S., Xu, M., Patros, P., Wu, H., Kaur, R., Kaur, K., & Buyya, R. (2024). Transformative effects of ChatGPT on modern education: Emerging Era of AI Chatbots. *Internet of Things and Cyber-Physical Systems*, *4*, 19–23. doi:10.1016/j.iotcps.2023.06.002

Gowda, R. S., & Suma, V. (2017, February). A comparative analysis of traditional education system vs. e-Learning. In *2017 International conference on innovative mechanisms for industry applications (ICIMIA)* (pp. 567-571). IEEE. 10.1109/ICIMIA.2017.7975524

Grassini, S. (2023). Shaping the future of education: Exploring the potential and consequences of AI and ChatGPT in educational settings. *Education Sciences*, *13*(7), 692. doi:10.3390/educsci13070692

Haleem, A., Javaid, M., Qadri, M. A., & Suman, R. (2022). Understanding the role of digital technologies in education: A review. *Sustainable Operations and Computers*, *3*, 275–285. doi:10.1016/j.susoc.2022.05.004

Hinton, P. J. (n.d.). *Ivy Tech develops machine learning algorithm to identify at-risk students and provide early intervention.* Google for Education. https://edu.google.com/why-google/customer-stories/ivytech-gcp/

Holmes, W., Bialik, M., & Fadel, C. (2019). *Artificial intelligence in education: Promises and implications for teaching and learning*. Center for Curriculum Redesign.

HolonIQ. (2023). *2023 Higher Education Digital Transformation Survey*. https://www.holoniq.com/notes/2023-higher-education-digital-transformation-survey

Hwang, G. J., Xie, H., Wah, B. W., & Gašević, D. (2020). Vision, challenges, roles and research issues of Artificial Intelligence in Education. *Computers and Education: Artificial Intelligence*, *1*, 100001. Advance online publication. doi:10.1016/j.caeai.2020.100001

Kalaichelvan, R., & Subramanian, P. (2023). Historical perspective of education 1.0 to education 5.0. In S. Prakash, M. A. Muniammal, M. Maruthavanan, S. Raja Kumar, K. Thangavel, & N. Sundar (Eds.), *Education 5.0: Revolutionizing learning for the future* (pp. 53–56). Thiagarajar College of Preceptors.

Kalliamvakaou. (2022). Quantifying GitHub Copilot's Impact on Developer Productivity and Happiness. https://github.blog/2022-09-07-research-quantifying-github-copilots-impact-on-developer-productivity-and-happiness

Klutka, J., Ackerly, N., & Magda, A. J. (2018). *Artificial intelligence in higher education: Current uses and future applications*. Learning House.

Kremer, M., & Holla, A. (2009). Improving education in the developing world: What have we learned from randomized evaluations? *Annual Review of Economics*, *1*(1), 513–542. doi:10.1146/annurev.economics.050708.143323 PMID:23946865

Kuleto, V., Ilić, M., Dumangiu, M., Ranković, M., Martins, O. M., Păun, D., & Mihoreanu, L. (2021). Exploring opportunities and challenges of artificial intelligence and machine learning in higher education institutions. *Sustainability (Basel)*, *13*(18), 10424. doi:10.3390/su131810424

Kurbanov, R. A., Belyalova, A. M., Yarygina, N. A., Schetinina, S. Y., Feshina, S. S., Buslaev, S. I., & Dugarskaya, T. A. (2020). Student attitude to future profession in field of information technology at university training stage. *International Journal of Psychosocial Rehabilitation*, *24*(4), 5019–5026. doi:10.37200/IJPR/V24I4/PR201601

Lehmann, R., Bosse, H. M., Simon, A., Nikendei, C., & Huwendiek, S. (2013). An innovative blended learning approach using virtual patients as preparation for skills laboratory training: Perceptions of students and tutors. *BMC Medical Education*, *13*(1), 1–9. doi:10.1186/1472-6920-13-23 PMID:23402663

Li, C. H., Yuen, H. Y., Lee, T. T., Tang, W. F., Lee, C. C., Ng, C., & Mak, S. L. (2023). How to Embed AI Applications of Building Management System in Campus Management. In *International conference on WorldS4* (pp. 403-411). Singapore: Springer Nature Singapore.

Li, F., Qi, J., Wang, G., & Wang, X. (2014). Traditional classroom vs e-learning in higher education: Difference between students' behavioral engagement. *International Journal of Emerging Technologies in Learning*, *9*(2), 48. doi:10.3991/ijet.v9i2.3268

Liu, B. L., Morales, D., Roser-Chinchilla, J., Sabzalieva, E., Valentini, A., Vieira do Nascimento, D., & Yerovi, C. (2023). Harnessing the era of artificial intelligence in higher education: a primer for higher education stakeholders. https://policycommons.net/artifacts/6942527/harnessing-the-era-of-artificial-intelligence-in-higher-education/7852431/

Luan, H., Geczy, P., Lai, H., Gobert, J., Yang, S. J., Ogata, H., Baltes, J., Guerra, R., Li, P., & Tsai, C. C. (2020). Challenges and future directions of big data and artificial intelligence in education. *Frontiers in Psychology*, *11*, 580820. Advance online publication. doi:10.3389/fpsyg.2020.580820 PMID:33192896

Lund, B. D., Wang, T., Mannuru, N. R., Nie, B., Shimray, S., & Wang, Z. (2023). ChatGPT and a new academic reality: Artificial Intelligence-written research papers and the ethics of the large language models in scholarly publishing. *Journal of the Association for Information Science and Technology*, *74*(5), 570–581. doi:10.1002/asi.24750

Makridakis, S. (2017). The forthcoming Artificial Intelligence (AI) revolution: Its impact on society and firms. *Futures*, *90*, 46–60. doi:10.1016/j.futures.2017.03.006

Marks, A., Al-Ali, M., Atassi, R., Elkishk, A. A., & Rezgui, Y. (2021). Digital transformation in higher education: maturity and challenges post COVID-19. In Information Technology and Systems: ICITS 2021, Volume 1 (pp. 53-70). Springer International Publishing. doi:10.1007/978-3-030-68285-9_6

Maslej, N., Fattorini, L., Brynjolfsson, E., Etchemendy, J., Ligett, K., Lyons, T., Manyika, J., Ngo, H., Niebles, J. C., Parli, V., Shoham, Y., Wald, R., Clark, J., & Perrault, R. (2023). The AI Index 2023 Annual Report. AI Index Steering Committee, Institute for Human-Centered AI, Stanford University.

McCarthy, J. (n.d.). What is artificial intelligence? http://jmc.stanford.edu/artificial-intelligence/what-is-ai/

Mhlanga, D., Denhere, V., & Moloi, T. (2022). COVID-19 and the key digital transformation lessons for higher education institutions in South Africa. *Education Sciences*, *12*(7), 464. Advance online publication. doi:10.3390/educsci12070464

Michel-Villarreal, R., Vilalta-Perdomo, E., Salinas-Navarro, D. E., Thierry-Aguilera, R., & Gerardou, F. S. (2023). Challenges and opportunities of generative AI for higher education as explained by ChatGPT. *Education Sciences*, *13*(9), 856. doi:10.3390/educsci13090856

Miranda, J., Navarrete, C., Noguez, J., Molina-Espinosa, J. M., Ramírez-Montoya, M. S., Navarro-Tuch, S. A., Bustamante-Bello, M.-R., Rosas-Fernández, J.-B., & Molina, A. (2021). The core components of education 4.0 in higher education: Three case studies in engineering education. *Computers & Electrical Engineering*, *93*, 107278. Advance online publication. doi:10.1016/j.compeleceng.2021.107278

Moraes, E. B., Kipper, L. M., Hackenhaar Kellermann, A. C., Austria, L., Leivas, P., Moraes, J. A. R., & Witczak, M. (2023). Integration of Industry 4.0 technologies with Education 4.0: Advantages for improvements in learning. *Interactive Technology and Smart Education*, *20*(2), 271–287. doi:10.1108/ITSE-11-2021-0201

Mousavinasab, E., Zarifsanaiey, N., & Niakan Kalhori, S., Rakhshan, M., Keikha, L., & Ghazi Saeedi, M. (2021). Intelligent tutoring systems: A systematic review of characteristics, applications, and evaluation methods. *Interactive Learning Environments*, *29*(1), 142–163. doi:10.1080/10494820.2018.1558257

Neumann, M., Rauschenberger, M., & Schön, E. M. (2023). "We Need To Talk About ChatGPT": The Future of AI and Higher Education. In *2023 IEEE/ACM 5th International Workshop on Software Engineering Education for the Next Generation (SEENG)* (pp. 29-32). IEEE.

Nordhaus, W. (2019). Climate change: The ultimate challenge for economics. *The American Economic Review*, *109*(6), 1991–2014. doi:10.1257/aer.109.6.1991

O'Brien, C. (2023). 8 Universities Leveraging AI to Drive Student Success. Digital Marketing Institute. https://digitalmarketinginstitute.com/blog/8-universities-leveraging-ai-to-drive-student-success

Oda Abunamous, M., Boudouaia, A., Jebril, M., Diafi, S., & Zreik, M. (2022). The decay of traditional education: A case study under covid-19. *Cogent Education*, *9*(1), 2082116. Advance online publication. doi:10.1080/2331186X.2022.2082116

OECD. (2016). *Innovating Education and Educating for Innovation: The Power of Digital Technologies and Skills*. OECD Publishing. doi:10.1787/9789264265097-

Open, A. I. (2022, November 30). Introducing ChatGPT. https://openai.com/blog/chatgpt

Ouyang, F., & Jiao, P. (2021). Artificial intelligence in education: The three paradigms. *Computers and Education: Artificial Intelligence*, *2*, 100020. Advance online publication. doi:10.1016/j.caeai.2021.100020

Owoc, M. L., Sawicka, A., & Weichbroth, P. (2021). Artificial Intelligence Technologies in Education: Benefits, Challenges and Strategies of Implementation. In M. L. Owoc & M. Pondel (Eds.), *Artificial Intelligence for Knowledge Management*. Springer. doi:10.1007/978-3-030-85001-2_4

Page, L., & Gehlbach, H. (2018, January 16). How Georgia State University Used an Algorithm to Help Students Navigate the Road to College. *Harward Business Review*. https://hbr.org/2018/01/how-georgia-state-university-used-an-algorithm-to-help-students-navigate-the-road-to-college

Pakdaman, M., Moghadam, M. N., Dehghan, H. R., Dehghani, A., & Namayandeh, M. (2019). Evaluation of the cost-effectiveness of virtual and traditional education models in higher education: A systematic review. *Health Technology Assessment in Action*, 1-14.

Park, E. L., & Choi, B. K. (2014). Transformation of classroom spaces: Traditional versus active learning classroom in colleges. *Higher Education*, *68*(5), 749–771. doi:10.1007/s10734-014-9742-0

Pelletier, K., Robert, J., Muscanell, N., McCormack, M., Reeves, J., Arbino, N., . . . Zimmern, J. (2023). 2023 EDUCAUSE Horizon Report, Teaching and Learning Edition. EDUCAUSE. Erişim adresi: https://library.educause.edu/-/media/files/library/2023/4/20 23hrteachinglearning.pdf?#page=18

Perkin, H. (2007). History of Universities. In J. J. F. Forest & P. G. Altbach (Eds.), *International Handbook of Higher Education. Springer International Handbooks of Education* (Vol. 18). Springer. doi:10.1007/978-1-4020-4012-2_10

Popenici, S. A., & Kerr, S. (2017). Exploring the impact of artificial intelligence on teaching and learning in higher education. *Research and Practice in Technology Enhanced Learning*, *12*(1), 22. doi:10.1186/s41039-017-0062-8 PMID:30595727

RaneN.ChoudharyS.RaneJ. (2023). Education 4.0 and 5.0: Integrating Artificial Intelligence (AI) for personalized and adaptive learning. *Available at* SSRN 4638365. doi:10.2139/ssrn.4638365

Rashid, S., Fayez, O., Ismail, H., & Khan, R. F. (2021). Digital social support for undergraduate students during COVID-19: Pivotal support for the digital transformation. *Journal of Public Health Research*, *10*(4), jphr.2021.2148. Advance online publication. doi:10.4081/jphr.2021.2148 PMID:34278768

Rhoades, G. (1991). Graduate Education. In International Higher Education Volume 1: An Encyclopedia (1st ed.). Routledge. doi:10.4324/9780203802748

Rudak, L. (2013). Spot-The-Difference–Traditional Education Vs. E-Education. Use of E-learning in the Training of Professionals in the Knowledge Society. STUDIO NOA, Cieszyn–Katowice.

Sabzalieva, E., & Valentini, A. (2023). ChatGPT and artificial intelligence in higher education: quick start guide. https://www.ucd.ie/artshumanities/t4media/ChatGPT-and-Artifi cial-Intelligence-in-higher-education-Quick-Start-guide_EN_F INAL.pdf

Saunders, G. (2000). *Getting Started with On-line Learning*. Winchcombe: Learning Partners.

Saunders, G., & Klemming, F. (2003). Integrating technology into a traditional learning environment: Reasons for and risks of success. *Active Learning in Higher Education*, *4*(1), 74–86. doi:10.1177/1469787403004001006

Schuitema, J., Peetsma, T., & van der Veen, I. (2012). Self-regulated learning and students' perceptions of innovative and traditional learning environments: A longitudinal study in secondary education. *Educational Studies*, *38*(4), 397–413. doi:10.1080/03055698.2011.643105

Shaw, C., Yuan, L., Brennan, D., Martin, S., Janson, N., Fox, K., & Bryant, G. (2023). *Generative AI in Higher Education: Fall 2023 Update of Time for Class Study*. Tyton Partners. https://tytonpartners.com/time-for-class-2023/GenAI-Update

Smith, A., Hachen, S., Schleifer, R., Bhugra, D., Buadze, A., & Liebrenz, M. (2023). Old dog, new tricks? Exploring the potential functionalities of ChatGPT in supporting educational methods in social psychiatry. *The International Journal of Social Psychiatry*, *69*(8), 1882–1889. doi:10.1177/00207640231178451 PMID:37392000

Songkram, N., Chootongchai, S., Khlaisang, J., & Koraneekij, P. (2021). Education 3.0 system to enhance twenty-first century skills for higher education learners in Thailand. *Interactive Learning Environments*, *29*(4), 566–582. doi:10.1080/10494820.2019.1592197

Strielkowski, W., Korneeva, E., & Gorina, L. (2022). Sustainable development and the digital transformation of educational systems. *Intelektinė ekonomika, 16*(1), 134-150. doi:10.1016/S0883-0355(99)00012-9

UNESCO. (2023). *Global Education Monitoring Report 2023: Technology in education – A tool on whose terms?* UNESCO. doi:10.54676/UZQV8501

Van, N. T., Irum, S., Abbas, A. F., Sikandar, H., & Khan, N. (2022). Online Learning—Two Side Arguments Related to Mental Health. *International Journal of Online & Biomedical Engineering*, *18*(9), 131–143. Advance online publication. doi:10.3991/ijoe.v18i09.32317

Wang, T., Lund, B. D., Marengo, A., Pagano, A., Mannuru, N. R., Teel, Z. A., & Pange, J. (2023). Exploring the potential impact of artificial intelligence (AI) on international students in higher education: Generative AI, chatbots, analytics, and international student success. *Applied Sciences (Basel, Switzerland)*, *13*(11), 6716. Advance online publication. doi:10.3390/app13116716

Wikipedia. (2024). ChatGPT. Available at: https://en.wikipedia.org/wiki/ChatGPT

Woltering, V., Herrler, A., Spitzer, K., & Spreckelsen, C. (2009). Blended learning positively affects students' satisfaction and the role of the tutor in the problem-based learning process: Results of a mixed-method evaluation. *Advances in Health Sciences Education : Theory and Practice*, *14*(5), 725–738. doi:10.1007/s10459-009-9154-6 PMID:19184497

World Bank. (2023, October 11). Education overview. https://www.worldbank.org/en/topic/education/overview

Yousuf, M., & Wahid, A. (2021, November). The role of artificial intelligence in education: Current trends and future prospects. In *2021 International conference on information science and communications technologies (ICISCT)* (pp. 1-7). IEEE. 10.1109/ICISCT52966.2021.9670009

Yu, D., Rosenfeld, H., & Gupta, A. (2023) 'The "AI divide" between the Global North and the Global South', *World Economic Forum*. Available at: https://www.weforum.org/agenda/2023/01/davos23-ai-divideglobal-north-global-south/

ZhaiX. (2022). ChatGPT user experience: Implications for education. *Available at* SSRN 4312418.

Zhao, H. (2011). Introducing ICT in a Traditional Higher Education Environment. In S. Lin & X. Huang (Eds.), *Advances in Computer Science, Environment, Ecoinformatics, and Education. CSEE 2011. Communications in Computer and Information Science* (Vol. 216). Springer. doi:10.1007/978-3-642-23345-6_25

ADDITIONAL READING

Baker, B., Mills, K. A., McDonald, P., & Wang, L. (2023). AI, Concepts of Intelligence, and Chatbots: The "Figure of Man," the Rise of Emotion, and Future Visions of Education. *Teachers College Record*, *125*(6), 60–84. doi:10.1177/01614681231191291

Hinojo-Lucena, F. J., Aznar-Díaz, I., Cáceres-Reche, M. P., & Romero-Rodríguez, J. M. (2019). Artificial intelligence in higher education: A bibliometric study on its impact in the scientific literature. *Education Sciences*, *9*(1), 51–61. doi:10.3390/educsci9010051

Roumate, F. (Ed.). (2023). *Artificial Intelligence in Higher Education and Scientific Research: Future Development*. Springer Nature. doi:10.1007/978-981-19-8641-3

Tan, S. (2023). Harnessing Artificial Intelligence for Innovation in Education. In *Learning Intelligence: Innovative and Digital Transformative Learning Strategies*. Springer. doi:10.1007/978-981-19-9201-8_8

KEY TERMS AND DEFINITIONS

AI Assistant: Software designed to perform tasks or services for an individual or a group in an educational context. In higher education, AI assistants can support learning by answering questions, providing material suggestions, or assisting with administrative tasks.

Artificial Intelligence (AI): The science and engineering of making intelligent machines, particularly intelligent computer programs, which involves the automation of intelligent behavior and machine learning.

Chatbot: An AI-driven program designed to simulate human-like conversation based on user inputs. In educational settings, chatbots can function as virtual assistants to provide information, facilitate learning, support administrative tasks, and enhance student engagement by offering instant responses to queries.

Digital Learning Environments (DLEs): Platforms and applications that facilitate digital learning, characterized by integrating technology with educational processes to provide dynamic, personalized, and flexible learning experiences.

Digital Maturity Assessment: A framework used by organizations, including educational institutions, to evaluate their level of technological advancement and integration. It measures the organization's readiness and capability to adopt and utilize digital technologies effectively.

Digital Transformation: The process of using digital technologies to radically change how an organization operates and delivers value to its customers. In the context of higher education, it involves incorporating digital tools and platforms to enhance learning and administrative processes.

Digital Transformation Strategy: A plan developed by educational institutions to integrate digital technologies into their operations, which includes updating the institution's vision, mission, and objectives to align with digital goals.

Higher Education Digital Capability Framework: A model that delineates critical capabilities and pinpoints strategic areas for focus and development in higher education to enhance digital transformation. It covers recruitment, curriculum design, assessment, and career planning.

Intelligent Tutoring System (ITS): Advanced computer systems that provide immediate and personalized instruction or feedback to learners, typically without requiring intervention from a human teacher. ITS systems adapt to the needs of individual students, often using AI to tailor the learning experience.

Traditional Learning: A conventional education system where teaching predominantly occurs in classroom settings. This method typically involves direct instruction from a teacher to students who passively receive information through lectures and note-taking, often focused on memorization and repetition.

Chapter 2
Chatbots in Academic Literacy Exploring AI in Education

Mariam Hadi Ali
Niagara College KSA, Pakistan

Maria Kainat
University of Agriculture, Faisalabad, Pakistan

Maida Maqsood
Government College Women University, Sialkot, Pakistan

Sanny F. Fernandez
https://orcid.org/0000-0003-0024-4542
Iloilo State University of Fisheries Science and Technology, Philippines

Sijjad Ali
https://orcid.org/0000-0002-9141-8837
Shenzhen University, China

Munir Ahmad
https://orcid.org/0000-0003-4836-6151
Survey of Pakistan, Pakistan

ABSTRACT

Chatbots have emerged as innovative tools with the potential to significantly impact academic literacy skills across various domains. This study investigates the impact of chatbots on academic literacy skills across four domains: source evaluation, writing, critical thinking, and accessibility. Comparative analysis of Google Bard, Microsoft Bing Chat, and QuillBot reveals distinct features. Bard excels in source evaluation, offering robust fact-checking and citation assistance. It also provides comprehensive writing support and tools for critical thinking. Moreover, Bard offers personalized, accessible support, including 24/7 availability and language learning assistance. Bing Chat and QuillBot offer limited features compared to Bard. Overall, chatbots show promise in enhancing academic literacy, particularly in source evaluation, writing, and critical thinking skills.

DOI: 10.4018/979-8-3693-1666-5.ch002

INTRODUCTION

Artificial Intelligence (AI) has become a ubiquitous force in shaping the future of education. The use of AI in education has progressed in many parts of the world, especially in developed countries. It has the potential to enhance science, technology, engineering, and mathematics (STEM) education as noted by Xu & Ouyang (2022). AI applications can support quality education by addressing significant challenges in the field of education, such as identifying students who are at risk of dropping out (Salas-Pilco & Yang, 2022).

AI-based chatbots have rapidly evolved and found applications in various fields, including Marketing, Supporting Systems, Education, Health Care, Cultural Heritage, and Entertainment (Adamopoulou & Moussiades, 2020). AI Chatbots can improve human interaction with machines by using Natural Language Processing and Machine Learning techniques to simulate chats in various domains like science, education, and healthcare (Singh & Thakur, 2020). Chatbots in education can enhance student learning and improve services, with various currently used types and the potential for similar effects to human tutors (Pérez et al., 2020). It can revolutionize foreign language learning (Dokukina & Gumanova, 2020), enhance smart LMS by supporting 24-hour interactive learning processes (Murad et al., 2019), increase learning accomplishment by providing course alerts, grade books, attendance statistics, and assignment feedback (Chaiprasurt et al., 2022). Chatbots can improve the quality of education by aiding in achieving every student's potential and combining traditional and automated educational approaches in the digital age (Ouatu & Gifu, 2021).

These conversational agents can help students engage with academic content and develop literacy skills such as critical thinking and analysis, research skills, information literacy, writing and communication skills, and source evaluation. They can improve the academic research experience for university students by adapting emerging technologies and designing a positive user experience (Mckie & Narayan, 2019). In the context of academic literacy, they can support identifying students' misunderstandings and directing them to the parts of the course dealing with concepts they have not yet mastered (Gaglo et al., 2022). Thus, they can positively impact students' communication skills by expanding interactions, increasing motivation, and enhancing interest in learning English (N.-Y. Kim et al., 2019).

Many chatbots have been developed for various educational purposes. For example, chatbots like StudyBuddy can promote behavioral change in college students by providing study tips and assessments, breaking down assignments, and recommending academic resources (Tian et al., 2021). Similarly, "Ellie" is a well-designed AI chatbot that can encourage students to engage in conversation in EFL classes (Yang et al., 2022). Moreover, using concept mapping and probability distribution analysis, the AI-IESLS chatbot improves students' learning experience and enhances their thinking ability and expectations in higher education platforms (Liu et al., 2022). The FIT-EBot chatbot can improve higher education services, reduce labor costs, and create new innovative services by automatically answering students' questions on behalf of academics (Hien et al., 2018). Tashi-Bot, for example, can help applicants and university students acquire information on academic and administrative processes without human interaction (Carlos et al., 2021). Similarly, chatbots, based on Google DialogFlow, can enhance teaching assistant training courses by enhancing online and face-to-face content, addressing challenges faced in teaching (Gonda & Chu, 2019).

Artificial Intelligence in Education represents a burgeoning field, still in its nascent stages of development for both researchers and practitioners (Chiu et al., 2023; Dalgıç et al., 2024). Given this evolving landscape, a crucial area of investigation lies in understanding the dynamics of AI-enabled chatbots within the realm of academic literacy. The diverse applications of chatbots in education underscore the necessity to delve into their role across various dimensions of academic literacy, including critical thinking, writing skills, communication skills, research abilities, and more. Furthermore, the proliferation of different types of chatbots emphasizes the importance of characterizing these technologies within the academic literacy paradigm. Therefore, the primary objectives of this chapter are outlined as follows:

Objective 1: Synthesize existing research on the impact of chatbots and AI in education on academic literacy skills.

Objective 2: Conduct a comparative analysis of chatbots designed for academic literacy support (e.g., Bard, Bing Chat, QuillBot).

A mixed-methods approach combining a literature review and a case study comprehensively addresses the research objectives. This chapter is structured as follows: The second section describes the impact of chatbots on academic literacy skills. The examination of various aspects concerning three chatbot cases such as Bard, Bing Chat, QuillBot are discussed in the next section. Finally, conclusions are drawn, and recommendations for future research directions are presented.

IMPACT OF CHATBOTS ON ACADEMIC LITERACY SKILLS

Chatbots can affect student learning and improve services in various areas, providing a framework for research and development in the educational field as noted by Pérez et al. (2020). They can significantly improve explicit reasoning, learning achievement, knowledge retention, and learning interest (Deng & Yu, 2023). They can also improve the academic research experience for university students by adapting emerging technologies and designing a positive user experience (Mckie & Narayan, 2019). To address the first objective of the chapter, an exhaustive analysis is performed via a comprehensive literature review using the Google Scholar engine. Through this process, the impact of chatbots on academic literacy has been categorized into four distinct aspects: Source Evaluation and Research, Writing and Communication, Critical Thinking and Analysis, and Accessibility and Personalized Support.

Source Evaluation and Research

It includes determining whether a source is scholarly, peer-reviewed, and trustworthy in academic contexts. It implies examining a particular subject matter in the quest to expand current knowledge, evaluate existing concepts and suggestions, or resolve particular problems. Its scope of engagement can involve undertaking actions like gathering data, analysis, interpretation, and data synthesis. Detailed results of this aspect are as follows.

Fact-Checking and Information Verification

Verifying the truthfulness and reliability of facts is called the facts check and information verification. This is the process of confirming the accuracy, dependability, and truthfulness of the facts, statements, or data. The verification process normally consists of researching many reputable sources, observing a particular information background or context, and examining the reliability and authority of these sources. Chatbots can be trained to identify potentially biased or unreliable sources, prompting users to consider the origin and credibility of information. For example, TruthBot, a multilingual chatbot, can provide trustworthy information, fact-checking, and news alerts on specific topics, endorsed by Gupta et al. (2021). Similarly, ChatGPT can be used for auxiliary gathering information and detecting falsehoods (Cuartielles et al., 2023).

Keyword and Topic Exploration

The keyword and topic research involves the steps of listing, comparing, and choosing important terms, subjects, questions, or other issues in the field of study or area of interest. This process involves searching for the information, studying the search results, and discerning varied information sources to shed more light on the research area of concern. While a keyword search enables the researcher to achieve significant results on the focused queries, which leads to finding relevant sources, a topic review brings up more facets of the themes and mainly the debates within an area of study. Chatbots can help users refine their research queries by suggesting relevant keywords, suggesting alternative search terms, and guiding them toward scholarly databases. Chatbots can identify keywords from sentences and answer queries using natural language processing, with the potential for further processing by expert systems (Athota et al., 2020).

Citation Assistance

Bibliographic services offer help, direction, and resources to ensure writers cite and reference their source information in an acceptable format. It comprises getting a grip on citation styles like APA, MLA, Chicago, or Harvard, arranging other sources accordingly, understanding academic integrity, and making the right use of citations. Chatbots can automatically generate citations in various academic styles based on source information, reducing formatting errors and promoting proper citation practices.

Writing and Communication

Writing is somehow connected with developing a person's ability to build sentences that contain word meanings and intentions in corresponding written language. Writing in an academic environment enjoins not only two or three essay styles but also various longer texts such as research papers, reports, and dissertations. Communicating properly implies putting neat and comprehensible ideas from the writer to the reader into the writing. It concerns language precision, laying it out, cohesion, and following academic traditions.

Grammar and Mechanics Checks

The grammar and mechanics audit consist of inspecting the written works for issues related to parts of grammar as well as punctuation, spelling, syntax, and word and sentence order. Using proper spelling, capitalization, punctuation, and grammar throughout writing makes the communication help to align with the established rules and conventions of the language and make the writing appear more clear, readable, and coherent. The grammar and mechanics checks allow writers to assemble professional and perfect texts delivered to the audience without any mistakes and errors. Chatbots can identify and correct common grammatical errors, offering instant feedback and helping users improve their writing mechanics. For example, they can improve punctuation correctness in Spanish, mainly by using commas, colons, and periods in different syntactic patterns (Vázquez-Cano et al., 2021). Similarly, they can improve students' Chinese vocabulary learning achievement, with perceived usefulness being a key predictor of behavioral intention, as noted by Chen et al. (2020).

Paraphrasing and Summarizing

Paraphrasing is a word-by-word restatement of the source in the author's way with different words or sentence structure, whereas summarizing represents just the main thoughts or intentions of a longer text in a clear sentence or two. Chatbots can assist with paraphrasing complex texts to avoid plagiarism and aid in summarizing key points, helping users understand and retain information effectively.

Feedback and Self-Revision

Feedback and self-revision are complex notions implying the evaluation and subsequent changing of the writing into better form. Feedback can be considered as the exchange of ideas and information executed by receiving constructive criticism, suggestions, and comments from others, such as teachers, peers, and editors, regarding authors' work and possible improvement. Self-revision hinges on critically examining, amending, and enhancing one's written piece according to the review received. Chatbots can provide personalized feedback on drafts, suggesting improved word choice, sentence structure, and clarity, promoting self-reflection and revision skills.

Critical Thinking and Analysis

Critical thinking involves taking apart facts, arguments, and data for evaluation on a one-dimensional plane of logic and systematic reasoning. It is about challenging assumptions and the process of considering biases and different perspectives and making reasonable decisions.

Argument Analysis and Identification of Fallacies

Argument analysis makes the reader look at the structure, logic, and soundness of the arguments used in both written and verbal communication. It also involves evaluating the strength of the argument and critically analyzing whether the argument is logically perfect or is supported with relevant and reliable data. Bringing out fallacies requires revealing the common mistakes in reasoning or the gaps in logical range that might make the argument shaky or unconvincing. Chatbots can highlight logical fallacies and inconsistencies in arguments, prompting users to evaluate presented information and develop stronger critical thinking skills critically.

Exploring Multiple Perspectives

Investigating multiple perspectives means considering different points of view, as well as evaluating the opinions and interpretations of numerous people regarding any particular problem, issue, or notion. It embraces that not all people may share the same experiences but may rather find their life in the spectrum of their perceptions, beliefs, and values. By mirroring various standpoints, people can identify more important aspects of the problems, comprehend the outlook of people with different beliefs, and post-up virtues of empathy and tolerance. Chatbots can access and present diverse viewpoints on specific topics, encouraging users to consider different interpretations and form well-rounded conclusions.

Practicing Socratic Dialogue

Socratic dialogue is a philosophical technique of inquiry and discussion in which questions are put forward and answers are offered to advance critical thinking and daub their concepts. Socrates, the famous Greek philosopher, was the inspiration for the approach. He encouraged his listeners to question and go into dialogue to explore fundamental concepts as well as to challenge take-it-for-grantedness and get deeper insights. The Socratic dialogue combines deliberation, in which one asks clarifying and probing open-ended questions, distinguishing various viewpoints. It adds reasoned arguments to understand the emerging picture at the end of the discussion. Chatbots can engage in simulated discussions on various topics, allowing users to test their understanding, ask clarifying questions, and refine their ability to analyze and synthesize information. For example, IntelliBot is a domain-specific chatbot that uses multiple strategies to generate a response and is superior in engaging with users and providing complete answers in the insurance domain (Nuruzzaman & Hussain, 2020).

Accessibility and Personalized Support

Accessibility is measured by the ability to reach the facilities, the materials, and the assistants for the disabled and people having varied needs, in particular. In terms of academic literacy, the accessibility covers offering direct writing help, a feedback system as well as assistance sources. Individual orientation is more specific and includes tailored guidance, feedback, and help regarding individually attributed factors like personal needs, preferences, and learning style.

24/7 Availability and On-Demand Assistance

24/7 availability and live assistance features empower students to access assistance or help anytime, either early in the morning or late at night. There is no limitation to things like time zones and working hours. An immediately available/as-needed service means individuals can request help/ support at their convenience in a way that does not require pre-scheduled appointments or wait specific hours of operations. Chatbots offer constant access to academic literacy support, overcoming time zone limitations and providing personalized feedback at the user's pace. For example, the chatbot can efficiently and accurately answer university-related FAQs using AIML and LSA, reducing customer service costs and improving user satisfaction (Ranoliya et al., 2017).

Catering to Diverse Learning Styles

Addressing diverse learning styles entails designing teaching materials, activities, and events oriented toward various styles in which students receive, comprehend, and uniquely apply information. An example of a learning style may be visual, auditory, kinesthetic, or tactile, in the picture, combined with other factors such as cognitive abilities, interests, and background. Educators and instructional designers can achieve inclusive and highly effective learning environments by recognizing how students learn differently and providing individualized attention and relevant information. This growing engulfment of students can lead to a better learning experience that enables learners to grasp the subject matter and improve their retention of information. Chatbots can adapt their interactions based on individual learning needs and preferences, offering tailored guidance and promoting inclusive learning environments.

Language Learning and Support

Language learning and support render getting, developing, and strengthening some proficiencies in one or more languages. It includes everything to do with the language learning process, including vocabulary, grammar, pronunciation, fluency, and comprehension. Language support mechanisms may include tools, resources, and services like language courses, language tutoring, language exchange programs, language learning apps, dictionaries, and language immersion experiences to help learners master their language and learn new languages.

Chatbots in language learning have positive perceptions, particularly in terms of perceived ease of use and attitudes, but behavioral intention is more moderate (Belda-Medina & Calvo-Ferrer, 2022). For example, chatbot usage can significantly improve English listening and reading skills in both experimental and control groups, with the experimental group showing more improvements in listening proficiency (N. Kim, 2018). Chatbots can facilitate language learning by providing feedback on grammar and vocabulary used in written communication, particularly helpful for students with English as a second language.

CASE STUDY OF CHATBOTS

The swift advancements of chatbots are significantly influencing higher education, as millions of students and academics are now embracing bots such as ChatGPT, Bing Chat, Bard, QuillBot, Ernie, and similar technologies for a diverse array of tasks and functions (Rudolph et al., 2023). To address the second objective of the chapter, this case study makes use of three chatbots, i.e., Google Bard, Microsoft Bing Chat, and Quillbot, to assess the four distinct aspects of academic literacy Source Evaluation and Research, Writing and Communication, Critical Thinking and Analysis, and Accessibility and Personalized Support.

Bard

Google releases its AI chatbot, Bard, on March 21, 2023, to compete with Microsoft and OpenAI. Bard is based on LaMDA, a large language model showcased by Google in May 2021. Bard can answer questions, write text, and engage in informative conversations on various subjects (De Vynck & Tiku, 2023; Fowler, 2023). Bard simulates and processes human conversation in written or spoken form (Egli, 2023), having potential applications in education, particularly in assessment and teaching (Khademi, 2023). Google Bard can engage users in dynamic conversational interactions and provide contextually relevant responses and personalized guidance (Adetayo & Oyeniyi, 2023).

Bing Chat

Bing Chat, serves as an AI-driven search assistant, offering comprehensive results and generating text in various tones and formats. It delivers detailed responses to complex queries, including text-based answers, images, and relevant links, enhancing browsing experiences. It is an advanced conversational AI that helps learners develop reflective and critical thinking, creativity, problem-solving skills, and concept comprehension (Vasconcelos & dos Santos, 2023), showing superior performance in English compared to ChatGPT and Bard (DAO, 2023).

Table 1. Analysis of Source Evaluation and Research Aspect

Features	Bard	Bing Chat	QuillBot
Fact-Checking and Information Verification	Guides information on scholarly sources but cannot directly evaluate source credibility.	Offers basic fact-checking but may not be as comprehensive.	Focuses more on paraphrasing and generating content rather than fact-checking.
Keyword and Topic Exploration	May offers an in-depth exploration of keywords and topics.	Limited keyword and topic exploration capabilities.	Provides keyword-based suggestions for paraphrasing and expanding on topics.
Citation Assistance	Supports citation formats and provides guidance on citing sources.	Doesn't offer citation assistance directly.	Doesn't directly assist with citation, but can help generate paraphrased content that can be cited properly.

QuillBot

QuillBot is an online application that paraphrases writing, avoids plagiarism, summarizes long sentences, and improves grammar to be more precise and look professional (Fitria, 2021; Nurmayanti & Suryadi, 2023), assisting post-graduate students in improving the quality of their writing and enhancing their positive attitudes toward writing (Kurniati & Fithriani, 2022). Students can use QuillBot as a tool to rewrite texts or as an alternative when manual paraphrasing is challenging (Fitria, 2022), serving as a valuable tool for nurturing students' interest in literacy and enhancing their writing skills through its innovative features and intuitive interface (Nur Azizah & Tira Erlangga, 2023). QuillBot is a multifaceted writing and paraphrasing tool that enhances students' writing skills and fosters curiosity in language exploration (Chui Chui, 2022).

The comparative analysis of three chatbots i.e. Google Bard, Microsoft Bing Chat, and Quillbot regarding four aspects of academic literacy is presented below.

Source Evaluation and Research

Table 1 showcases the comparison of this aspect with respect to three features i.e. fact-checking and information verification, keyword and topic exploration, and citation assistance.

Fact-Checking and Information Verification

Bard seems to excel in this aspect, prioritizing sources and information. Bing Chat offers basic fact-checking but may not provide as comprehensive results as Bard.

QuillBot, however, focuses more on content generation and paraphrasing, which may not prioritize fact-checking as strongly.

Keyword and Topic Exploration

Bard offers an exploration of keywords and topics, providing in-depth information. Bing Chat's capabilities in this area are limited compared to Bard. QuillBot provides suggestions based on keywords for generating content but might not delve deeply into exploration as Bard does.

Citation Assistance

Bard supports citation formats and assists users in citing sources. Bing Chat doesn't directly offer citation assistance. QuillBot doesn't provide direct citation assistance either, but it can assist in generating paraphrased content that can be cited properly, albeit indirectly. While Bard appears to be the most robust option for academic literacy aspects such as source evaluation and research, QuillBot focuses more on content generation and paraphrasing than direct fact-checking and citation assistance. Bing Chat falls somewhere in between, offering some basic features but not as comprehensive as Bard. The choice depends on the user's specific needs and the depth of assistance required for academic tasks.

Writing and Communication

The comparison of this aspect is presented in Table 2 with respect to three features, i.e., grammar and mechanics checks, paraphrasing and summarizing, and feedback and self-revision.

Grammar and Mechanics Checks

Bard excels in this aspect, offering detailed grammar and mechanics checks. Bing Chat provides basic checks but might not offer as much depth or detail as Bard. QuillBot, while offering checks, may prioritize other features like paraphrasing, potentially leading to less comprehensive grammar and mechanics assistance.

Paraphrasing and Summarizing

Bard offers paraphrasing and summarizing capabilities, aiding in rewriting and condensing content effectively. Bing Chat provides some paraphrasing and summarizing features but may not be as versatile as Bard. QuillBot heavily emphasizes

Table 2. Analysis of Writing and Communication Aspect

Features	Bard	Bing Chat	QuillBot
Grammar and Mechanics Checks	Offers basic grammar and mechanics checks.	Provides basic grammar and mechanics checks but may lack depth.	Offers grammar and mechanics checks but may prioritize other features like paraphrasing.
Paraphrasing and summarizing	Offers paraphrasing and summarizing functionalities with various options for style and length.	Provides some paraphrasing and summarizing features.	Focuses heavily on paraphrasing and summarizing, offering various options and suggestions.
Feedback and Self-Revision	Provides detailed feedback and suggestions for self-revision.	Offers some feedback but may not be as comprehensive as Bard.	Provides feedback primarily through paraphrasing and suggesting alternatives.

paraphrasing and summarizing, providing various options and suggestions for rewriting content.

Feedback and Self-Revision

Bard provides detailed feedback and suggestions for self-revision, aiding users in improving their writing effectively. Bing Chat offers some feedback but may not be as comprehensive as Bard. QuillBot primarily provides feedback through paraphrasing and suggesting alternatives, which may not cover all aspects of self-revision as extensively as Bard. Bard appears to be the most comprehensive option for academic literacy aspects of writing and communication, offering robust grammar checks, paraphrasing and summarizing capabilities, and detailed feedback for self-revision. QuillBot focuses heavily on paraphrasing and summarizing, while Bing Chat falls somewhere in between, offering basic features in each aspect but not as comprehensively as Bard. Again, the choice depends on the specific needs and preferences of the user for writing and communication tasks.

Critical Thinking and Analysis

Table 3 demonstrates the comparison of this aspect with respect to three features, i.e., argument analysis and identification of fallacies, exploring multiple perspectives, and practicing Socratic dialogue.

Table 3. Analysis of Critical Thinking and Analysis Aspect

Features	Bard	Bing Chat	QuillBot
Argument Analysis and Fallacy Identification	Offers tools for analyzing arguments and identifying fallacies.	Provides some tools for basic argument analysis but may need more depth.	Offers limited support for argument analysis and fallacy identification.
Exploring Multiple Perspectives	Provides resources for exploring multiple perspectives on a topic or issue.	Offers limited resources for exploring multiple perspectives.	Provides suggestions for paraphrasing and presenting different viewpoints.
Practicing Socratic Dialogue	Offers guidance and prompts for practicing Socratic dialogue.	Does not specifically support Socratic dialogue practice.	Does not specifically support Socratic dialogue practice.

Argument Analysis and Fallacy Identification

Bard excels in this aspect, offering tools and support for analyzing arguments and identifying fallacies effectively. Bing Chat provides some basic tools for argument analysis but may not offer as much depth or comprehensive support as Bard. QuillBot offers limited support in this area, potentially focusing more on paraphrasing and content generation rather than critical analysis.

Exploring Multiple Perspectives

Bard provides resources and guidance for exploring multiple perspectives on a topic or issue, aiding in critical thinking and analysis. Bing Chat offers limited resources for exploring multiple perspectives, potentially limiting its effectiveness in fostering critical thinking. QuillBot provides suggestions for paraphrasing and presenting different viewpoints, but it may not offer as comprehensive support for exploring multiple perspectives as Bard.

Practicing Socratic Dialogue

Bard offers guidance and prompts for practicing Socratic dialogue, facilitating the development of critical thinking skills through interactive questioning and discussion. Bing Chat and QuillBot do not specifically support Socratic dialogue practice, potentially limiting their effectiveness in promoting critical thinking through this method. Bard emerges as the most suitable option for academic literacy aspects related to critical thinking and analysis, offering robust tools for argument analysis and fallacy identification, resources for exploring multiple perspectives, and support for practicing Socratic dialogue. Bing Chat and QuillBot offer some support in

Table 4. Analysis of Accessibility and Personalized Support Aspect

Features	Bard	Bing Chat	QuillBot
24/7 Availability and On-Demand Assistance	Available for assistance around the clock, offering on-demand support.	May be available 24/7 and might not offer on-demand assistance.	Availability might vary, potentially offering on-demand assistance.
Catering to Diverse Learning Styles	Offers personalized support tailored to various learning styles and preferences.	May provide some level of customization but might not cater extensively to diverse learning styles.	Offers suggestions and tools for adapting content but may not cater extensively to diverse learning styles.
Language Learning and Support	Provides language learning support and assistance in various languages.	Might offer basic language support but may not be as comprehensive as Bard.	Offers some language support features but may prioritize other functionalities over language learning.

these areas but may not be as comprehensive or specialized as Bard, particularly in fostering critical thinking skills through methods like Socratic dialogue.

Accessibility and Personalized Support

The comparison of this aspect is described in Table 4 concerning three features, i.e., 24/7 availability and on-demand assistance, catering to diverse learning styles, and language learning and support.

24/7 Availability and On-Demand Assistance

Bard excels in this aspect, providing assistance 24/7 and offering on-demand support whenever needed. Bing Chat may provide 24/7 availability and might not offer on-demand assistance. QuillBot's availability may vary, and it might offer on-demand assistance and 24/7 availability.

Catering to Diverse Learning Styles

Bard offers personalized support tailored to various learning styles and preferences, catering extensively to individual needs. Bing Chat may provide some level of customization but might not cater as extensively to diverse learning styles as Bard. QuillBot offers suggestions and tools for adapting content but may not cater as extensively to diverse learning styles as Bard.

Language Learning and Support

Bard provides robust language learning support and assistance in various languages, making it versatile for users with different language needs. Bing Chat might offer basic language support but may not be as comprehensive as Bard. QuillBot offers some language support features, but its primary focus may not be on language learning, potentially prioritizing other functionalities. Bard emerges as the most suitable option for academic literacy related to accessibility and personalized support, offering 24/7 availability, personalized assistance catering to diverse learning styles, and robust language learning support. While Bing Chat and QuillBot offer some features in these areas, they may not be as comprehensive or specialized as Bard, particularly in providing round-the-clock assistance and catering extensively to diverse learning needs and language support.

CHALLENGES AND CONCERNS IN CHATBOT IMPLEMENTATION

Addressing the integration of chatbots in academic literacy poses various challenges and concerns that need careful consideration. Natural Language Understanding (NLU) emerges as a pivotal obstacle. Chatbots must grapple with the complexities of human language, including nuances, slang, and informal expressions, to ensure accurate and meaningful interactions. Multilingual capabilities and swift adaptation to diverse linguistic environments further compound the intricacies of deployment, as highlighted by Shawar & Atwell (2005). Mastery of NLU is imperative for chatbots to furnish precise and contextually relevant responses, thus enhancing user experiences and communication efficacy.

Another critical challenge is contextual understanding, as underscored by Ait-Mlouk and Jiang (2020). Chatbots must be able to discern and retain conversational context to furnish pertinent and coherent responses. Skillful navigation of shifting discussion topics, user intents, and subtle cues is essential to prevent misunderstanding and foster engaging interactions. Personalization and user experience present further hurdles, as noted by Athreya, Ngonga Ngomo, and Usbeck (2018). Achieving tailored experiences demands efficient collection and analysis of user data while adhering to stringent privacy protocols. Chatbots leverage user preferences, behavioral patterns, and interaction histories to deliver individualized recommendations and responses, necessitating adept data utilization and analysis.

Moreover, training and maintenance are indispensable for ensuring chatbot efficacy and longevity, according to Daniel et al. (2020). Continuous training enables chatbots to adapt to evolving user needs, handle new challenges, and sustain performance standards. Leveraging diverse datasets, user feedback, and machine learning algorithms is crucial to enhancing language comprehension, response generation, and conversational prowess. Ethical considerations and biases represent significant concerns in chatbot development and implementation, as highlighted by Murtarelli, Gregory, and Romenti (2021). Biased training data or algorithms can inadvertently perpetuate unfair or discriminatory outcomes, underscoring the importance of justice, accountability, and transparency in chatbot design. Detecting and mitigating biases through rigorous evaluation of training data and algorithms and implementing bias detection mechanisms are imperative steps to ensure fairness and equity in chatbot interactions.

CONCLUSION

Chatbots in education and research face ethical challenges, potential misuse, and potential exploitation, but can be considered an opportunity for development rather than a threat (Kooli, 2023). The analysis presented above evidences that chatbots contribute to academic literacy skills such as research and writing, source evaluation and communication, critical thinking, accessibility and personalized support. Conducting a comparison of the three leading chatbots: Google Bard, Microsoft Bing Chat, and QuillBot. It becomes manifest how the platforms are distinguished for their features and capabilities meant to assist in academic literacy.

Regarding source assessment and research, Bard comes out as an advancer in this case, through fact-checking and information verification, keyword and topic exploration, and citation assistance. Nevertheless, QuillBot concentrates on written text generation using paraphrasing, while Bing Chat is somewhere in between, addressing the area of basic fact-checking without going deep. Bard proceeds to dictate excellent grammar and mechanics revising along with paraphrasing, and summarizing capabilities. Quillbot relies mostly on rephrasing and summary, while Bong Chat lacks comprehensive services like Bard.

Critical thinking and analytical skills are helped to strengthen through the tools of coping with the argument analysis, fallacies of reasoning, various points of view, and dialogue of Socrates. While Bing Chat and QuillBot indeed come up with some suggestions, they still might not be enough and might not be as specific in these issues as Bard is. As regards accessibility and personal support, Bard does not fall short with 24/7 availability and on-demand help, which is designed for numerous learning styles and powerful language support. Though Bing Chat and QuillBot have some aspects of research and writing, they may not present Bard's degree of greatness and diversity.

Despite the advancements in chatbot technology for enhancing academic literacy skills, there are several avenues for future research and development. The future bots should look into an advanced distinguishing factor between themselves and the teachers, namely the ability to give more personal feedback and assistance, including applying complex academic tasks. In addition, progress in the domain of natural language processing can help chatbots in their ability to comprehend and respond to commands more conveniently, thus increasing their efficiency in supporting users' needs.

REFERENCES

Adamopoulou, E., & Moussiades, L. (2020). An Overview of Chatbot Technology. *IFIP Advances in Information and Communication Technology, 584 IFIP*. doi:10.1007/978-3-030-49186-4_31

Adetayo, A. J., & Oyeniyi, W. O. (2023). Revitalizing reference services and fostering information literacy: Google Bard's dynamic role in contemporary libraries. *Library Hi Tech News*. Advance online publication. doi:10.1108/LHTN-08-2023-0137

Ait-Mlouk, A., & Jiang, L. (2020). KBot: A Knowledge Graph Based ChatBot for Natural Language Understanding over Linked Data. *IEEE Access : Practical Innovations, Open Solutions*, *8*, 149220–149230. Advance online publication. doi:10.1109/ACCESS.2020.3016142

Athota, L., Shukla, V. K., Pandey, N., & Rana, A. (2020). Chatbot for Healthcare System Using Artificial Intelligence. *ICRITO 2020 - IEEE 8th International Conference on Reliability, Infocom Technologies and Optimization (Trends and Future Directions)*. 10.1109/ICRITO48877.2020.9197833

Athreya, R. G., Ngonga Ngomo, A. C., & Usbeck, R. (2018). Enhancing Community Interactions with Data-Driven Chatbots - The DBpedia Chatbot. *The Web Conference 2018 - Companion of the World Wide Web Conference, WWW 2018*. 10.1145/3184558.3186964

Belda-Medina, J., & Calvo-Ferrer, J. R. (2022). Using Chatbots as AI Conversational Partners in Language Learning. *Applied Sciences (Basel, Switzerland)*, *12*(17), 8427. Advance online publication. doi:10.3390/app12178427

Carlos, H., Germán, S.-T., & Dixon, S. (2021). Tashi-bot: A intelligent personal assistant for users in an educational institution. In Journal of Management Information and Decision Sciences (Vol. 24, Issue 6).

Chaiprasurt, C., Amornchewin, R., & Kunpitak, P. (2022). Using motivation to improve learning achievement with a chatbot in blended learning. *World Journal on Educational Technology: Current Issues, 14*(4), 1133–1151. Advance online publication. doi:10.18844/wjet.v14i4.6592

Chen, H. L., Vicki Widarso, G., & Sutrisno, H. (2020). A ChatBot for Learning Chinese: Learning Achievement and Technology Acceptance. *Journal of Educational Computing Research, 58*(6), 1161–1189. Advance online publication. doi:10.1177/0735633120929622

Chiu, T. K. F., Xia, Q., Zhou, X., Chai, C. S., & Cheng, M. (2023). Systematic literature review on opportunities, challenges, and future research recommendations of artificial intelligence in education. In *Computers and Education* (Vol. 4). Artificial Intelligence., doi:10.1016/j.caeai.2022.100118

Chui Chui, H. (2022). The QuillBot grammar checker: Friend or foe of ESL student writers. *Journal of Creative Practices in Language Learning and Teaching, 10*(1).

Cuartielles, R., Ramon-Vegas, X., & Pont-Sorribes, C. (2023). Retraining fact-checkers: The emergence of ChatGPT in information verification. *Profesional de La Informacíón/Information Professional, 32*(5), 1-12.

Dalgıç, A., Yaşar, E., & Demir, M. (2024). ChatGPT and learning outcomes in tourism education: The role of digital literacy and individualized learning. *Journal of Hospitality, Leisure, Sport and Tourism Education, 34*, 100481. doi:10.1016/j.jhlste.2024.100481

Daniel, G., Cabot, J., Deruelle, L., & Derras, M. (2020). Xatkit: A Multimodal Low-Code Chatbot Development Framework. *IEEE Access : Practical Innovations, Open Solutions, 8*, 15332–15346. Advance online publication. doi:10.1109/ACCESS.2020.2966919

Dao, X.-Q. (2023). Which Large Language Model should You Use in Vietnamese Education: ChatGPT, Bing Chat, or Bard? SSRN *Electronic Journal*. doi:10.2139/ssrn.4527476

De Vynck, G., & Tiku, N. (2023). *Google's catch-up game on AI continues with Bard launch*. The Washington Post. https://www.washingtonpost.com/technology/2023/03/21/bard-go
ogle-ai/

Deng, X., & Yu, Z. (2023). A Meta-Analysis and Systematic Review of the Effect of Chatbot Technology Use in Sustainable Education. In Sustainability (Switzerland) (Vol. 15, Issue 4). doi:10.3390/su15042940

Dokukina, I., & Gumanova, J. (2020). The rise of chatbots-new personal assistants in foreign language learning. *Procedia Computer Science, 169*, 542–546. Advance online publication. doi:10.1016/j.procs.2020.02.212

Egli, A. (2023). ChatGPT, GPT-4, and Other Large Language Models: The Next Revolution for Clinical Microbiology? In Clinical Infectious Diseases (Vol. 77, Issue 9). doi:10.1093/cid/ciad407

Fitria, T. N. (2021). QuillBot as an online tool: Students' alternative in paraphrasing and rewriting of English writing. *Englisia: Journal of Language, Education, and Humanities, 9*(1), 183. Advance online publication. doi:10.22373/ej.v9i1.10233

Fitria, T. N. (2022). Avoiding Plagiarism of Students' Scientific Writing by Using the QuillBot Paraphraser. *Elsya : Journal of English Language Studies, 4*(3). Advance online publication. doi:10.31849/elsya.v4i3.9917

Fowler, G. A. (2023). *Say what, Bard? What Google's new AI gets right, wrong and weird.* The Washington Post. https://www.washingtonpost.com/technology/2023/03/21/google-bard/

Gaglo, K., Degboe, B. M., Kossingou, G. M., & Ouya, S. (2022). Proposal of conversational chatbots for educational remediation in the context of covid-19. *International Conference on Advanced Communication Technology, ICACT, 2022-February*. 10.23919/ICACT53585.2022.9728860

Gonda, D. E., & Chu, B. (2019). Chatbot as a learning resource? Creating conversational bots as a supplement for teaching assistant training course. *TALE 2019 - 2019 IEEE International Conference on Engineering, Technology and Education*. 10.1109/TALE48000.2019.9225974

Gupta, A., Varun, Y., Das, P., Muttineni, N., Srivastava, P., Zafar, H., Chakraborty, T., & Nath, S. (2021). TruthBot: An Automated Conversational Tool for Intent Learning, Curated Information Presenting, and Fake News Alerting. *ArXiv Preprint ArXiv:2102.00509*.

Hien, H. T., Cuong, P. N., Nam, L. N. H., Nhung, H. L. T. K., & Thang, L. D. (2018). Intelligent assistants in higher-education environments: The FIT-EBOt, a chatbot for administrative and learning support. *ACM International Conference Proceeding Series*. 10.1145/3287921.3287937

Khademi, A. (2023). Can ChatGPT and Bard generate aligned assessment items? A reliability analysis against human performance. *Journal of Applied Learning and Teaching, 6*(1). Advance online publication. doi:10.37074/jalt.2023.6.1.28

Kim, N. (2018). A Study on Chatbots for Developing Korean College Students' English Listening and Reading Skills. *Journal of Digital Convergence, 16*(8).

Kim, N.-Y., Cha, Y., & Kim, H.-S. (2019). Future English Learning: Chatbots and Artificial Intelligence. *Multimedia-Assisted Language Learning, 22*(3).

Kooli, C. (2023). Chatbots in Education and Research: A Critical Examination of Ethical Implications and Solutions. *Sustainability (Basel), 15*(7), 5614. Advance online publication. doi:10.3390/su15075614

Kurniati, E. Y., & Fithriani, R. (2022). Post-Graduate Students' Perceptions of Quillbot Utilization in English Academic Writing Class. *Journal of English Language Teaching and Linguistics, 7*(3), 437. Advance online publication. doi:10.21462/jeltl.v7i3.852

Liu, L., Subbareddy, R., & Raghavendra, C. G. (2022). AI Intelligence Chatbot to Improve Students Learning in the Higher Education Platform. *Journal of Interconnection Networks, 22*(Supp02), 2143032. Advance online publication. doi:10.1142/S0219265921430325

Mckie, I. A. S., & Narayan, B. (2019). Enhancing the Academic Library Experience with Chatbots: An Exploration of Research and Implications for Practice. *Journal of the Australian Library and Information Association, 68*(3), 268–277. Advance online publication. doi:10.1080/24750158.2019.1611694

Murad, D. F., Iskandar, A. G., Fernando, E., Octavia, T. S., & Maured, D. E. (2019). Towards smart LMS to improve learning outcomes students using LenoBot with natural language processing. *2019 6th International Conference on Information Technology, Computer and Electrical Engineering, ICITACEE 2019*. 10.1109/ICITACEE.2019.8904311

Murtarelli, G., Gregory, A., & Romenti, S. (2021). A conversation-based perspective for shaping ethical human–machine interactions: The particular challenge of chatbots. *Journal of Business Research, 129*, 927–935. Advance online publication. doi:10.1016/j.jbusres.2020.09.018

Nur Azizah, N., & Tira Erlangga, D. (2023). The effectiveness of quillbot in developing students' literation. *Pustakailmu.Id, 3*(1).

Nurmayanti, N., & Suryadi, S. (2023). The Effectiveness Of Using Quillbot In Improving Writing For Students Of English Education Study Program. *Jurnal Teknologi Pendidikan : Jurnal Penelitian Dan Pengembangan Pembelajaran, 8*(1), 32. Advance online publication. doi:10.33394/jtp.v8i1.6392

Nuruzzaman, M., & Hussain, O. K. (2020). IntelliBot: A Dialogue-based chatbot for the insurance industry. *Knowledge-Based Systems, 196*, 105810. Advance online publication. doi:10.1016/j.knosys.2020.105810

Ouatu, B. I., & Gifu, D. (2021). Chatbot, the future of learning? *Smart Innovation. Systems and Technologies, 197*, 263–268. Advance online publication. doi:10.1007/978-981-15-7383-5_23

Pérez, J. Q., Daradoumis, T., & Puig, J. M. M. (2020). Rediscovering the use of chatbots in education: A systematic literature review. In Computer Applications in Engineering Education (Vol. 28, Issue 6). doi:10.1002/cae.22326

Ranoliya, B. R., Raghuwanshi, N., & Singh, S. (2017). Chatbot for university related FAQs. *2017 International Conference on Advances in Computing, Communications and Informatics, ICACCI 2017, 2017-January*. 10.1109/ICACCI.2017.8126057

Rudolph, J., Tan, S., & Tan, S. (2023). War of the chatbots: Bard, Bing Chat, ChatGPT, Ernie and beyond. The new AI gold rush and its impact on higher education. *Journal of Applied Learning and Teaching, 6*(1). Advance online publication. doi:10.37074/jalt.2023.6.1.23

Salas-Pilco, S. Z., & Yang, Y. (2022). Artificial intelligence applications in Latin American higher education: a systematic review. In International Journal of Educational Technology in Higher Education (Vol. 19, Issue 1). doi:10.1186/s41239-022-00326-w

Shawar, B. A., & Atwell, E. S. (2005). Using corpora in machine-learning chatbot systems. *International Journal of Corpus Linguistics, 10*(4), 489–516. Advance online publication. doi:10.1075/ijcl.10.4.06sha

Singh, S., & Thakur, H. K. (2020). Survey of Various AI Chatbots Based on Technology Used. *ICRITO 2020 - IEEE 8th International Conference on Reliability, Infocom Technologies and Optimization (Trends and Future Directions)*. 10.1109/ICRITO48877.2020.9197943

Tian, X., Risha, Z., Ahmed, I., Lekshmi Narayanan, A. B., & Biehl, J. (2021). Let's Talk It Out. *Proceedings of the ACM on Human-Computer Interaction, 5*(CSCW1). 10.1145/3449171

Vasconcelos, M. A. R., & dos Santos, R. P. (2023). Enhancing STEM learning with ChatGPT and Bing Chat as objects to think with: A case study. *Eurasia Journal of Mathematics, Science and Technology Education, 19*(7), em2296. Advance online publication. doi:10.29333/ejmste/13313

Vázquez-Cano, E., Mengual-Andrés, S., & López-Meneses, E. (2021). Chatbot to improve learning punctuation in Spanish and to enhance open and flexible learning environments. *International Journal of Educational Technology in Higher Education*, *18*(1), 33. Advance online publication. doi:10.1186/s41239-021-00269-8

Xu, W., & Ouyang, F. (2022). The application of AI technologies in STEM education: a systematic review from 2011 to 2021. In International Journal of STEM Education (Vol. 9, Issue 1). doi:10.1186/s40594-022-00377-5

Yang, H., Kim, H., Lee, J. H., & Shin, D. (2022). Implementation of an AI chatbot as an English conversation partner in EFL speaking classes. *ReCALL*, *34*(3), 327–343. Advance online publication. doi:10.1017/S0958344022000039

ADDITIONAL READING

Černý, M. (2023). Educational Psychology Aspects of Learning with Chatbots without Artificial Intelligence: Suggestions for Designers. *European Journal of Investigation in Health, Psychology and Education*, *13*(2), 284–305. Advance online publication. doi:10.3390/ejihpe13020022 PMID:36826206

Chamorro-Atalaya, O., Olivares-Zegarra, S., Sobrino-Chunga, L., Guerrero-Carranza, R., Vargas-Diaz, A., Huarcaya-Godoy, M., Rasilla-Rovegno, J., Suarez-Bazalar, R., Poma-Garcia, J., & Cruz-Telada, Y. (2023). Application of the Chatbot in University Education: A Bibliometric Analysis of Indexed Scientific Production in SCOPUS, 2013-2023. *International Journal of Learning. Teaching and Educational Research*, *22*(7), 281–304. Advance online publication. doi:10.26803/ijlter.22.7.15

Hwang, G. J., & Chang, C. Y. (2023). A review of opportunities and challenges of chatbots in education. In Interactive Learning Environments (Vol. 31, Issue 7). do i:10.1080/10494820.2021.1952615

Nee, C. K., Rahman, M. H. A., Yahaya, N., Ibrahim, N. H., Razak, R. A., & Sugino, C. (2023). Exploring the Trend and Potential Distribution of Chatbot in Education: A Systematic Review. *International Journal of Information and Education Technology (IJIET)*, *13*(3), 516–525. Advance online publication. doi:10.18178/ijiet.2023.13.3.1834

Wan Hamzah, W. M. A. F., Ismail, I., Yusof, M. K., Saany, S. I. M., & Yacob, A. (2021). Using Learning Analytics to Explore Responses from Student Conversations with Chatbot for Education. *International Journal of Engineering Pedagogy*, *11*(6), 70–84. Advance online publication. doi:10.3991/ijep.v11i6.23475

Zhang, R., Zou, D., & Cheng, G. (2023). A review of chatbot-assisted learning: pedagogical approaches, implementations, factors leading to effectiveness, theories, and future directions. In Interactive Learning Environments. doi:10.1080/10494820.2023.2202704

KEY TERMS AND DEFINITIONS

Academic Literacy: Academic literacy refers to the ability to read, write, and critically engage with texts, ideas, and information within an academic context. It involves understanding disciplinary conventions, analyzing complex texts, synthesizing information, and effectively communicating ideas through writing and speaking.

Artificial Intelligence (AI): AI is a branch of computer science that focuses on creating systems or machines capable of performing tasks that typically require human intelligence. These tasks include reasoning, problem-solving, learning, perception, understanding natural language, and decision-making.

Chatbot: A chatbot is a computer program or an AI application designed to simulate conversation with human users, typically through text or speech interfaces. Chatbots can be programmed to respond to user queries, provide information, complete tasks, or engage in casual conversation.

Conversational Agents: Conversational agents, also known as dialogue systems or virtual assistants, are AI-based systems designed to engage in natural language conversations with users. These agents can understand and generate human-like responses, allowing users to interact with them conversationally to obtain information, perform tasks, or receive assistance.

Machine Learning: Machine learning is a subset of artificial intelligence that focuses on developing algorithms and statistical models that enable computers to learn from and make predictions or decisions based on data without being explicitly programmed.

Chapter 3
Building Democratisation and Agency:
The Adoption of Ethical AI Practice in Pedagogy

Catherine Hayes
University of Sunderland, UK

ABSTRACT

The aims of this chapter are threefold, namely to consider global ethics and the impact that AI could potentially have in terms of increasing societal inequalities in terms of existing infrastructure, to provide an insight into the developmental and progressive use of AI across organizational infrastructures in pedagogic practice and finally, and to embed the concept of ethical AI and the potential for its praxis across all aspects of its integration in the building of global democracy and agency. Debates and sensationalized presentations of artificial intelligence (AI) across the media and in scientific and industrial contexts have shaped public perception of its potential benefits and the profound way the potential for harm ought to be acknowledged. This chapter provides a theoretical insight into how AI can be objectively debated amidst the controversy surrounding its implementation and the potential for the inaccessible to be made accessible over forthcoming months and years.

INTRODUCTION

"I believe that at the end of the century the use of words and general educated opinion will have altered so much that one will be able to speak of machines thinking

DOI: 10.4018/979-8-3693-1666-5.ch003

without expecting to be contradicted."

– Alan Turing (1912-1954)

This chapter will consider applied ethics in the context of pedagogical practice in relation to the potential impact of Artificial Intelligence (AI) in pedagogic practice. The extent to which AI has been progressively integrated into society over the last three years, has exponentially increased media and scientific debates of what is and what might be, if all we are to believe about AI is realised (Bareis & Jatzenbach, 2022). As with any landmark paradigmatic shift in society's use of and access to technological advance, the widespread introduction of AI has both positive and negative aspects which can be harnessed for both human progression and decimation (Mikalef et al, 2022). Initial debates surrounding AI focused predominantly on their functionalist capacities to reduce the complexity and challenge of largely physical tasks, where algorithmic decision-making could be used as an adjunct support to mundane and burdensome human work (Mirbabaie et al 2022). This has now progressed to the widespread cognitive debates as to how AI can address tasks which before, seemed impossible and largely inaccessible, in terms of the decision-making processes necessary to undertake them (Madhav & Tyagi, 2022). One of the key aspects of these debates is how humanity has often designed AI in human form, to the extent technological artefacts are often perceived as robots with a high degree of sentient ambition (Owe and Baum, 2021). It is often thought AI can compete for cognitive advantage rather than simply being a design artefact used to extend the reach of humanity's applied intellect (Mele, & Russo-Spena, 2023; Yamin, et al, 2021). This has led to widespread hyperbole that AI somehow has the capacity to override human cognition and that its capacity for extended algorithmic thinking may eventually pose a huge threat to mankind, alongside offering some of the greatest technological developments of our age (Cools, Van Gorp & Opgenhaffen, 2022). Unlike other technological advances whether the choice to engage with them was always an option, AI poses a wider societal issue where that choice may no longer be possible, should the self-advancement of algorithmic decision making pose an overriding threat to humanity in terms of speed and capacity for action (Igna & Venturini, 2023). As such the ethical principles of AI are factors that all organisations now must contemplate so that the integration of ethical practice becomes a societal norm in terms of the use of AI in practice. Beyond an anthropological perspective, social ethics and the philosophies underpinning them all impact upon the capacity of organisational decision making and how AI may remain fully controllable and where the algorithms within which it operates may be constructively aligned with those affective attributes of humanity, that as a society, we would wish to promulgate, rather than any degree of negativity (Henin & Le Métayer, 2021). Whilst every organisational infrastructure operated by humans is designed on principles of altruism, equity and equality, the integration of AI poses several questions which necessitate critical reflexivity of the situated nature of their use within highly sensitive contexts such as healthcare, law, and education, all of which can have the potential for an inordinate impact on society as it is currently known (Cheng, Varshney & Liu, 2021). Perhaps then it is rather an issue with the design of AI rather than implementation, which ought to serve the hyperbole and hypothesising that surround it (Bareis & Jatzenbach, 2022). This chapter will also explore how the social implications of AI are being posited, often sensationalised as a threat to humanity, rather than being framed in something humanly designed that ought to remain within the control of its maker, transparent in terms of capacity to undertake complex decision making and which most importantly is accountable for every individual action made in terms of design and programming (Novelli, Taddeo & Floridi, 2023).

THE WIDENING GAPS OF SOCIETAL INEQUALITY

Geopolitically, there are several ethical debates around the role of AI (Palomeres et al, 2021). A collective sense of global responsibility necessitates ensuring not only accountability but a huge degree of reassurance that the use of AI in practice will not be detrimental to humanity in any way. In those developing countries where technological advances have not yet reached the stage of development of their Western counterparts, this poses a huge risk of adding further and widening gaps of societal inequality, where the impact of AI may still be felt but remain under the control of other nations (Haluza & Jungwirth, 2023). Being able to adapt to the use of emergent technology functionally still predominantly remains the preserve of developed nations, so from an ethical perspective, the use of AI as an adjunct to human experience rather than a replacement for it is essential if we are not to lose sight of global public wellbeing amidst global societal interest in novel approaches to technological development (Farrow, 2021; Floridi & Cowls, 2022).

GLOBAL ETHICS AND COLLECTIVE SOCIETAL RESPONSIBILITY

The irony of developing a metric framework of accountability for issues of ethical transparency, accountability, equity, and trust, is not lost on a world where the functional role of AI has far reached implications for address than those encountered in typical industrial, commercial, and educational contexts. In issues of human endeavour where predicting the future capacity and capability of AI as functionally autonomous, there are several issues of explanation which remain a challenge to justify in 21st Century developmental progress (Colaner, 2022). One of the main issues in terms of ontological and epistemological justification of AI is the lack of any apparent philosophical or theoretical underpinning for its use. Usually in the context of applied research, it is possible to provide a degree of constructive alignment, where ethical praxis is a primary and relatively predictable issue (Zhang et al, 2021). Global responsibility for a concept which has the potential to have universal impact, despite there not necessarily being a global capacity to support, sustain and ethically evaluate, impacts beyond one facet of human infrastructure and pervades them all (Khogali & Mekid, 2023). Perhaps most significantly it is the degree of agency that AI occupies, which is of greatest concern to humanity and our human tendencies to frame AI as insentient threats to humanity, which have caused the greatest concerns and misunderstandings of what the ethical implications of AI might be (Hwang & Park, 2020). Beyond the technological challenges of functional AI in relation to its capability development lies the justification of man to permit its widespread inception to the digital community. Formal policy and practice initiatives have been driven by global conferences, which in their earliest years focused largely on the fundamental positive impact that AI could bring, and which largely preceded the research literature which has provided an inferential insight into what the impact of widespread AI introduction might constitute for global civic futures on both a personal and professional level (Floridi & Cowls, 2022). Leading in this arena is the UNESCO Recommendation on the Ethics of Artificial Intelligence, which using an array of Delphi methodologies has drawn on the specific expertise of specialists in the field of AI to operationally define and frame the nature of ethical frameworks and praxes in the field ought to be. In theory, human attributes and characteristics are relatively understandable choices within the consensus of those with specialist expertise in AI. However, what is more concerning is how binary decision-making, without sentience or conscience, can become the preserve of man-made machines, which have no capacity for tacit discernment in relation to the binary decision-making processes that underpin the algorithms controlling them and enabling them to process a greater degree of digital information than any human has capacity for. The temporal fact that AI does not need to eat, sleep, or have any of the human 'baggage' that human capital is certain to have, ensures that progress can be made at an astonishing pace and to a level which may not have been anticipated before (Makridakis, 2017). As with any model of ethical praxis, key principles have been devised to ensure that the concepts of beneficence, non-maleficence, autonomy, justice, and explication are central to the use of ethical AI (Prem, 2023). Where the greatest challenges with this lie, though, is the fact that AI is not sentient, does not have a conscience, so in instances where automated decision making is advocated, the ethical use of AI has even greater ramifications, especially in relation to the justification of human decision making in its use (Floridi & Cowls, 2022; Mantello et al, 2023). The operational use of AI in practice is what has maintained a strategic focus on functional usage and the practicalities of system design (Peeters et al, 2021).

THE CULTURE AND CONTEXT OF AI ETHICS IMPLEMENTATION

Global cultural differences pose one of the greatest threats to the ethical management of AI, particularly in instances of competition (Humble, 2023). Not all use of AI will be altruistic and there are clear advantages to be gained in being able to win the race for supremacy in AI development and implementation (Qiao-Franco & Bode, 2023). Where specific ethical values are missing due to historical and local cultures then the justification of state intervention with AI may be lie beyond public questioning (Elliott, 2019). Across non-democratic countries, autocratic leaders may have a perceived benefit of asserting authority and surveillance with AI that has never been possible before (Zeng, 2020; Zuiderwijk, Chen & Salem, 2021; Young et al, 2021). It is in instances like this that human rights of privacy are destroyed, yet justified by the ideology that control of the state and state intervention is for human benefit. Any proposition to introduce global ethical governance and accountability frameworks must first consider how best these cultural differences can be reconciled amidst such a degree of diversity so that a universal set of principles can be agreed upon (Visivizi, 2021).

The whole concept of privacy is a relatively Westernized concept. Other nations value state intervention where collective control leads to individuals being responsible for their place and position in society (Döring, 2019) Not only does this link to ethics, but more significantly, in countries such as China, is an integral part of morality, where moral behaviour has been an instrumental focus of attention for thousands of years prior to the introduction of AI (Nichols, 2022). Liberalist Western democracies have presented the need for individual autonomy at all costs. The rise of AI implementation has raised new questions about just how possible universal regulation of such systems can be. With such differences in state infrastructure, it is virtually impossible to see how AI ethics, governance, and regulation can become operational under such differences in contextual and situational specificity. Where philosophy underpins the justification of human rights, then across different global stages, this can be radically different (Zajda & Vissing, 2022).

MECHANISMS OF ACCOUNTABILITY IN PROFESSIONAL PRACTICE

Technological emergence and machine learning continue to revolutionize societal life and will soon become existentially embedded as adjunct mechanisms of intellectual decision-making, upon which we become dependent (Bareis & Katzenbach, 2022). The ethical implications of this within health and medicine cannot be overlooked since AI is insentient. It may be capable of making active choices via strategically designed algorithmic programming, but it has no conscience with which to couple binary or even complex decision-making processes (Islam et al, 2022). Whilst scenarios such as this are usually the preserve of Hollywood movies, the implications for humanity, lie in the degree of control and algorithmic decision making that these machines are permitted (De Bruijn, Warnier & Janssen, 2022; Nader et al, 2021). Ethical complexity is even greater when we consider that any subjective or emotive intelligence can be removed from decisions where life and death can be at stake, for instance within policing, the military or indeed medical and surgical intervention (Miller, 2022). It is where autonomous AI is introduced that the situated context of its use must be contemplated, acknowledged, and accounted for (Alter, 2022). When faced with humanoid robots, which deliver AI this becomes even more of issue, since our cognitive capacity to perceive them as 'real' instead of the machines they are, is an issue (Finkel & Krämer, 2022). We have given non sentient objects, the characteristic of humanity, yet are surprised at our reaction to just how realistic they can appear (Sweeney, 2022). Since ethical practice is based on our capacity to recognise the potential risks that AI may pose to humanity. It is the metacognitive processes of meaning making which differentiates the highly nuanced characteristics of man from the decision making itself (Ganapini et al, 2023). Searching for meaning, in this sense is central to human consciousness and arguably more importantly conscience. Being able to bind algorithms to specific parameters of focused operational practice, is straightforward in terms of ethical praxis (He, 2022). Where it becomes steadily more contentious is in instances where the intellectual capacity of AI is released within parameters of practice which also incorporate social contexts and social interaction (Chen, Sun & Wang, 2022). From an economic perspective, it is AI's potential to impact positively on areas such as enhanced productivity, the elimination of human error and the potential for more specific surgical intervention, which offer most (Goralski and Tan, 2020). It is the transparency of decision making which is imperative to ensure that man always remains in control of ongoing algorithmic processing, since if AI is permitted to improve itself without oversight iteratively and reaches decision making capacity beyond man's knowledge and scope of ethical practice, then it can be hypothesized that the disconcertment characterizing Hollywood's portrayal of AI could indeed become an unwelcome reality (Brewer et al, 2022). This would entail the AI adding algorithmic decision-making processes into originally human-designed algorithms for iterative improvement, regardless of the ongoing need for ethical praxis. This potential also constitutes much of the hyperbole and media panic around just what AI might represent in terms of existential threat and how this might be best managed in the context of technological evolution (Harper, 2021).

ETHICAL EDUCATION AND THE FUTURE AGENCY OF AI IMPLEMENTATION

Since the progressive developmental work in AI operationalization and implementation forms the basis for future work in the field, the need to educate and provide an insight into the agentic power necessary to manage the ethical implications of AI has never been greater (Nyholm, 2020). Beyond the functional implications of introducing emergent technologies across society, the impact and meaning-making of AI on people's lives ought also to be considered so that mitigation of co-existing dangers, alongside the irrefutable benefit of AI, can be accounted for and organizations held accountable for in terms of formal governance processes (Smith, 2021). Education and skills training via the embedding of strategic pedagogical intervention across curricula will become a central mechanism of ensuring due regard for the ethical implications of AI and potentially a means of harnessing strategic frameworks which safeguard aspects of professional and workforce praxis, where AI may pose complex implications It is the widespread coverage of AI implementation which means that its use is no longer a proactive choice for society, rather something which has been progressively incorporated and at the same time exploited by those who wish to harness it for reckless and illegal activity (Dauvergne, 2021). In terms of corporate responsibility though, there remains active debate over whether, the military, for example, ought to be given intellectual and operational rights to AI for autonomous use in algorithmic decision making which lacks any bias and as such any conscience in relation to the potential outcome of it, when the primary objective of its mission is simply to reach the completion of a task (Shaw et al, 2019). Issues of data protection and the use of AI algorithms to collate specific information and identify all members of society pervade all use of the technology in practice. Where ethical issues are most apparent however is that AI has the potential to override the innate epistemic bias and positionality which provides the unique decision-making skill of every individual in terms of their rights, capacities, and capabilities (Araujo et al, 2020). Justification of AI within everyday society is frequently legitimised based on the accuracy with which technology can now make complex decisions from algorithmic processing, which outweighs the capacity, capability, and speed with which a human counterpart every could. In addition to this, we see a challenge to human existentialism in that any aspect of subjectivity raised by epistemic positionality and the consequent personal bias this perpetuates can be eliminated with AI. The complex ambiguity here is that from an ethical and moral perspective, since this technology is man-made, then the responsibility for what AI can do to humanity also has to be an embedded and integral part of AI design, justification, and evaluation, and the 21st Century must be educated to reflect this (Holmes et, 2021). Failing to do so could be catastrophic for the potential of what AI may progress to become and man's ability to maintain ultimate control of AI capacity and capability (Benbya, Davenport & Pachidi, 2020). As AI becomes further embedded into everyday society it is complacency which needs to be avoided as there is an educational and pedagogical responsibility to ensure that iterative generations of AI users, developers and entrepreneurs maintain absolute accountability for the emergent technology, which will inevitably be such a part of humanity's future. Ultimately, the situated and contextual nature of AI's use will determine how best algorithmic decision-making can be continually monitored to ensure that whilst society is progressively developed, ethical complexities of its use can be addressed at source and with ease.

THE EXISTENTIAL THREAT OF ARTIFICIAL GENERAL INTELLIGENCE (AGI)

Artificial General Intelligence (AGI) is the term applied to a theoretical version of AI which can surpass human intellect and undertake complex decision-making processes at speeds not possible in terms of cognitive function (Helm et al, 2020). Whether AI is an existential threat to humanity remains one of contention in the media, not least because those who invented it are now calling for a measured pause in its developmental progression and have released formal statements warning that AI could potentially pose a greater threat to humanity than nuclear weapons or further global pandemics. Whilst these statements are regarded as the hyperbole of the super-rich or super-invested. Whilst all scientists are aware of the need for ethical praxis in relation to technological advancement it is the routine use of AI which is causing greatest concern. Being clear evidence on the positive impact of it within fields such as medicine, in the context of drug discovery, health and education is imperative (Rajpurkar er al, 2022). Whilst AI use is purposeful and direct, the evolution of AI systems continues to astonish even those who have been instrumental in its invention (Samuel, 2023). Whether certain sectors of society should be given agency in relation to the use of AI is contentious, particularly the military, where exploitation of AI systems could pose an existential threat (Federspiel et al, 2023).

One of the commonest areas for concern, however, is the current use of AI chatbots such as ChatGTP, which are an active source of bias and the spread of potential misinformation (Najafali, 2023). Alongside this is the issue of whether human resources can be replaced by AI as a mechanism of economic savings and whether AI can produce written content, which can actively compete or surpass the capabilities of humans under any given circumstance (Alvero, 2023). In terms of explanation, it is the neural capacity of AI which demonstrates clear similarity to human neurological function. Deep learning is the process by which information is processed and learning takes place. By moving beyond the superficial mechanisms of data evaluation that initial computers could be programmed to undertake, it is the prospect of machine learning which can be developed to algorithmically perform reasoning and discernment, which is an issue, particularly in relation to the short time taken for developmental process with AI systems to be made (Zhang, Zhu & Su, 2023). Whilst presently AI is not sentient, larger debates exist around the notion of consciousness when AI develops significantly and has a far higher degree of sophistication in relation to its evolution.

DISCIPLINARY PERSPECTIVES IN SOCIAL SCIENCES WITH AI

Whilst the term simulation is now an integral part of our daily syntax, many Generative AI tools still remain human impersonators, rather than having any innate human capacity. The media hype surrounding the concept of robot senscience has led to a raft of Hollywood movies based on the premise of the latest technological beings becoming phenotypically human but still lacking the essence of humanity (Greenman, 2017). As with humanity, black and white binary decision making is disadvantageous on many levels but in instances where there are voluminous amounts of data to analyse, and this needs to be dealt with quickly, efficiently and with minimum scope for human error, then indeed technology may prove invaluable (Kuziemski & Misuraca, 2020). In terms of agency, simulated mannequins have served the purpose of becoming progressively more capable of appearing to be human and emulating human pathological conditions so that medical and health professionals can accommodate human factors in their pedagogic practice and permit people to practice first and scaffold their learning, so that risks and errors might be executed as part of the reflexive learning process informing newly designed curricula (McGue et al, 2021).

It is within the field of academic writing that Chat GPT has developed to the extent that to the discerning reader it is now difficult to distinguish between that text which is authored either via a Chat GPT system or a human (Dergaa et al, 2023). The real danger is that invalid information as well as that regarded as authentic, valid, and reliable can also be circulated alongside one another – it is only human intelligence at this stage which has the capacity to critically evaluate research and scholarship, so as a consequence, it may be that the accurate selection and retrieval of published literature for incorporation into academic citation and referencing is highlighted as a general flaw.

VIRTUE ETHICS AND ANTHROPOLOGICAL VIRTUE WITH AI

Criticisms that organisations harnessing ethical praxis in relation to environmental justice within the context of AI usage are not unfounded in terms of the potential processes and outcomes being adopted at the front academic institutions (Hickman & Petrin, 2021). What is necessary for address is the potential difference between the ideology of ethical responsibility and its practical implementation in work-based practice. One major concern is that if ethics is commodified and packaged as something tokenistically delivered by educators in abstraction from progressive technological emergence, that the tripartite relationship between technological advancement, power and social justice can effectively become meaningless and in some way diminished in terms of pragmatic impact and proactive conscientiousness (Burrell & Fourcade, 2021). Where knowledge comes from in terms of ongoing research of AI development and how AI ethics ought to be shaped therefore, is something stymied by standardized learning packages which are delivered (Birhane, 2021; Schiff, 2021). One outcome of this is the potential debate that rather than commodifying ethics and permitting them to exist in abstraction from the use of AI, is that as an anthropological virtue, they ought to be an embedded part of professional practice and intrinsic epistemic positionality, so that tacit assumption and concerns about deviation from acceptable practice can be identified as part of an ongoing process (Avnoon, Kotliar & Rivnai-Bahir, 2023).

CONCLUSION

Amidst the communities of practice that constitute expertise in AI on a personal and professional level, ethics has not been an historical element of operational praxis, which is attributable to relative need, rather than the need for proactive choice. Within the 21st Century progressive development of AI, though, ethics has become central to the capacity of the discipline of computing and technology to ensure social justice and a temporal regard for the future of humanity with AI playing an ever-increasing role across so many disciplines and societal infrastructures. This chapter has considered the emergent role of AI across societies, from education to spirituality and existentialism. Whilst it is impossible to conclusively predict what the future of AI across these infrastructures will be, what can be accounted for is human responsibility for the scope of its potential reach and impact. Education of existing and forthcoming generations of society will be instrumental in ensuring that the progressive implementation of AI across societies is subject to rigorous regulation and stringent regard for accountability and responsibility of use. Whilst there will always remain the opportunity for rogue non-state jeopardy in terms of AI misuse, the core principles of ethical AI use will be shaped and adapted to the sociocultural perspectives of members states for whom the ethics of AI is a priority.

Whether AI will ever fully autonomously and objectively override human decision making, remains a debate which both sensationalises and highlights the once unimaginable capacity of AI within the context of not only education but also medicine, health and the military and also the inevitable inequity that AI will exacerbate between the West and developing nations. How regulatory frameworks can be designed as a mechanism of consensus building across global society and its representatives remains an ongoing challenge. What is clear however is that ethical praxis must become instrumental rather than a conceptual commodity, which can be packaged to accompany education in computing, engineering, and technology over forthcoming decades. This chapter has illustrated how the progressive development from the use of AI in the manufacturing and industrial centres across the world represents an important opportunity to harness potential predictable complications and implications of AI use. To embed competence and AI literacy necessitates the active uptake of educational contexts to integrate AI literacy alongside core signature pedagogies such as Mathematics and English Language. The very possibility that AI can develop to have superhuman intelligence and far outpace humanity's intellect means embedding ethical contingency within all AI systems is imperative. When potential knowledge of the future remains entirely predictive and inferential it is these degrees of ethical contingency, which provide a haven for transparency and accountability, which ought to frame AI moral and ethical praxis in all educational situations, contexts and settings.

REFERENCES

Alter, S. (2022). Understanding artificial intelligence in the context of usage: Contributions and smartness of algorithmic capabilities in work systems. *International Journal of Information Management*, *67*, 102392. doi:10.1016/j.ijinfomgt.2021.102392

Alvero, R. (2023). ChatGPT: Rumors of human providers' demise have been greatly exaggerated. *Fertility and Sterility, 119*(6), 930–931. doi:10.1016/j.fertnstert.2023.03.010 PMID:36921837

Araujo, T., Helberger, N., Kruikemeier, S., & De Vreese, C. H. (2020). In AI we trust? Perceptions about automated decision-making by artificial intelligence. *AI & Society, 35*(3), 611–623. doi:10.1007/s00146-019-00931-w

Avnoon, N., Kotliar, D. M., & Rivnai-Bahir, S. (2023). Contextualizing the ethics of algorithms: A socio-professional approach. *New Media & Society*. doi:10.1177/14614448221145728

Bareis, J., & Katzenbach, C. (2022). Talking AI into being: The narratives and imaginaries of national AI strategies and their performative politics. *Science, Technology & Human Values, 47*(5), 855–881. doi:10.1177/01622439211030007

Benbya, H., Davenport, T. H., & Pachidi, S. (2020). Artificial intelligence in organizations: Current state and future opportunities. *MIS Quarterly Executive, 19*(4).

Birhane, A. (2021). The impossibility of automating ambiguity. *Artificial Life, 27*(1), 44–61. doi:10.1162/artl_a_00336 PMID:34529757

Burrell, J., & Fourcade, M. (2021). The society of algorithms. *Annual Review of Sociology, 47*(1), 213–237. doi:10.1146/annurev-soc-090820-020800

Chen, J., Sun, J., & Wang, G. (2022). From unmanned systems to autonomous intelligent systems. *Engineering (Beijing), 12*, 16–19. doi:10.1016/j.eng.2021.10.007

Cheng, L., Varshney, K. R., & Liu, H. (2021). Socially responsible AI algorithms: Issues, purposes, and challenges. *Journal of Artificial Intelligence Research, 71*, 1137–1181. doi:10.1613/jair.1.12814

Colaner, N. (2022). Is explainable artificial intelligence intrinsically valuable? *AI & Society*, 1–8.

Cools, H., Van Gorp, B., & Opgenhaffen, M. (2022). Where exactly between utopia and dystopia? A framing analysis of AI and automation in US newspapers. *Journalism*.

Dauvergne, P. (2021). The globalization of artificial intelligence: Consequences for the politics of environmentalism. *Globalizations, 18*(2), 285–299. doi:10.1080/14747731.2020.1785670

De Angelis, L., Baglivo, F., Arzilli, G., Privitera, G. P., Ferragina, P., Tozzi, A. E., & Rizzo, C. (2023). ChatGPT and the rise of large language models: The new AI-driven infodemic threat in public health. *Frontiers in Public Health, 11*, 1567. doi:10.3389/fpubh.2023.1166120 PMID:37181697

De Bruijn, H., Warnier, M., & Janssen, M. (2022). The perils and pitfalls of explainable AI: Strategies for explaining algorithmic decision-making. *Government Information Quarterly, 39*(2), 101666. doi:10.1016/j.giq.2021.101666

Dergaa, I., Chamari, K., Zmijewski, P., & Saad, H. B. (2023). From human writing to artificial intelligence generated text: Examining the prospects and potential threats of ChatGPT in academic writing. *Biology of Sport, 40*(2), 615–622. doi:10.5114/biolsport.2023.125623 PMID:37077800

Döring, H. (2019). Public perceptions of the proper role of the state. In *The State in Western Europe Retreat or Redefinition?* (pp. 12–31). Routledge. doi:10.4324/9781315037479-2

Elliott, A. (2019). *The culture of AI: Everyday life and the digital revolution*. Routledge. doi:10.4324/9781315387185

Farrow, E. (2021). Mindset matters: How mindset affects the ability of staff to anticipate and adapt to Artificial Intelligence (AI) future scenarios in organisational settings. *AI & Society, 36*(3), 895–909. doi:10.1007/s00146-020-01101-z PMID:33223620

Federspiel, F., Mitchell, R., Asokan, A., Umana, C., & McCoy, D. (2023). Threats by artificial intelligence to human health and human existence. *BMJ Global Health, 8*(5), e010435. doi:10.1136/bmjgh-2022-010435 PMID:37160371

Finkel, M., & Krämer, N. C. (2022). Humanoid robots–artificial. Human-like. Credible? Empirical comparisons of source credibility attributions between humans, humanoid robots, and non-human-like devices. *International Journal of Social Robotics, 14*(6), 1397–1411. doi:10.1007/s12369-022-00879-w

Floridi, L., & Cowls, J. (2022). A unified framework of five principles for AI in society. *Machine learning and the city: Applications in architecture and urban design*, 535-545

Ganapini, M. B., Campbell, M., Fabiano, F., Horesh, L., Lenchner, J., Loreggia, A., . . . Venable, K. B. (2023). Thinking fast and slow in AI: The role of metacognition. In *Machine Learning, Optimization, and Data Science: 8th International Conference, LOD 2022, Certosa di Pontignano, Italy, September 18–22, 2022, Revised Selected Papers, Part II* (pp. 502-509). Cham: Springer Nature Switzerland.

Goralski, M. A., & Tan, T. K. (2020). Artificial intelligence and sustainable development. *International Journal of Management Education, 18*(1), 100330. doi:10.1016/j.ijme.2019.100330

Greenman, C. (2017). Exploring the impact of artificial intelligence on the accounting profession. *Journal of Research in Business. Economics and Management, 8*(3), 1451.

Haluza, D., & Jungwirth, D. (2023). Artificial Intelligence and Ten Societal Megatrends: An Exploratory Study Using GPT-3. *Systems, 11*(3), 120. doi:10.3390/systems11030120

Harper, R. H. (2021). AI: The social future of intelligence. In *Routledge Handbook of Social Futures* (pp. 52–58). Routledge. doi:10.4324/9780429440717-4

He, Q., Zheng, H., Ma, X., Wang, L., Kong, H., & Zhu, Z. (2022). Artificial intelligence application in a renewable energy-driven desalination system: A critical review. *Energy and AI, 7*, 100123. doi:10.1016/j.egyai.2021.100123

Helm, J. M., Swiergosz, A. M., Haeberle, H. S., Karnuta, J. M., Schaffer, J. L., Krebs, V. E., Spitzer, A. I., & Ramkumar, P. N. (2020). Machine learning and artificial intelligence: Definitions, applications, and future directions. *Current Reviews in Musculoskeletal Medicine, 13*(1), 69–76. doi:10.1007/s12178-020-09600-8 PMID:31983042

Henin, C., & Le Métayer, D. (2021). Beyond explainability: Justifiability and contestability of algorithmic decision systems. *AI & Society*, 1–14.

Hickman, E., & Petrin, M. (2021). Trustworthy AI and corporate governance: The EU's ethics guidelines for trustworthy artificial intelligence from a company law perspective. *European Business Organization Law Review, 22*(4), 593–625. doi:10.1007/s40804-021-00224-0

Holmes, W., Porayska-Pomsta, K., Holstein, K., Sutherland, E., Baker, T., Shum, S. B., ... Koedinger, K. R. (2021). Ethics of AI in education: Towards a community-wide framework. *International Journal of Artificial Intelligence in Education*, 1–23.

Humble, K. (2023). Artificial Intelligence, International Law and the Race for Killer Robots in Modern Warfare. In *Artificial Intelligence, Social Harms and Human Rights* (pp. 57–76). Springer International Publishing. doi:10.1007/978-3-031-19149-7_3

Hwang, H., & Park, M. H. (2020). The Threat of AI and Our Response: The AI Charter of Ethics in South Korea. *Asian Journal of Innovation & Policy, 9*(1).

Igna, I., & Venturini, F. (2023). The determinants of AI innovation across European firms. *Research Policy, 52*(2), 104661. doi:10.1016/j.respol.2022.104661

Islam, S. R., Russell, I., Eberle, W., & Dicheva, D. (2022). Instilling conscience about bias and fairness in automated decisions. *Journal of Computing Sciences in Colleges*, *37*(8), 22–31.

Khogali, H. O., & Mekid, S. (2023). The blended future of automation and AI: Examining some long-term societal and ethical impact features. *Technology in Society*, *73*, 102232. doi:10.1016/j.techsoc.2023.102232

Kuziemski, M., & Misuraca, G. (2020). AI governance in the public sector: Three tales from the frontiers of automated decision-making in democratic settings. *Telecommunications Policy*, *44*(6), 101976. doi:10.1016/j.telpol.2020.101976 PMID:32313360

Larson, D. B., Harvey, H., Rubin, D. L., Irani, N., Justin, R. T., & Langlotz, C. P. (2021). Regulatory frameworks for development and evaluation of artificial intelligence–based diagnostic imaging algorithms: Summary and recommendations. *Journal of the American College of Radiology*, *18*(3), 413–424. doi:10.1016/j.jacr.2020.09.060 PMID:33096088

Madhav, A. S., & Tyagi, A. K. (2022). The world with future technologies (Post-COVID-19): open issues, challenges, and the road ahead. *Intelligent Interactive Multimedia Systems for e-Healthcare Applications*, 411-452.

Makridakis, S. (2017). The forthcoming Artificial Intelligence (AI) revolution: Its impact on society and firms. *Futures*, *90*, 46–60. doi:10.1016/j.futures.2017.03.006

Mantello, P., Ho, M. T., Nguyen, M. H., & Vuong, Q. H. (2023). Bosses without a heart: Socio-demographic and cross-cultural determinants of attitude toward Emotional AI in the workplace. *AI & Society*, *38*(1), 97–119. doi:10.1007/s00146-021-01290-1 PMID:34776651

McGue, S. R., Pelic, C. M., McCadden, A., Pelic, C. G., & Lewis, A. L. (2021). The use of simulation in teaching. *Psychiatria Clinica*, *44*(2), 159–171. PMID:34049640

Mele, C., & Russo-Spena, T. (2023). Artificial Intelligence in Services. Elgar Encyclopedia of Services, 356.

Mikalef, P., Conboy, K., Lundström, J. E., & Popovič, A. (2022). Thinking responsibly about responsible AI and 'the dark side'of AI. *European Journal of Information Systems*, *31*(3), 257–268. doi:10.1080/0960085X.2022.2026621

Miller, G. J. (2022, March). Artificial Intelligence Project Success Factors—Beyond the Ethical Principles. In *Information Technology for Management: Business and Social Issues: 16th Conference, ISM 2021, and FedCSIS-AIST 2021 Track, Held as Part of FedCSIS 2021, Virtual Event, September 2–5, 2021, Extended and Revised Selected Papers* (pp. 65-96). Cham: Springer International Publishing.

Mirbabaie, M., Brünker, F., Möllmann, N. R., & Stieglitz, S. (2022). The rise of artificial intelligence–understanding the AI identity threat at the workplace. *Electronic Markets, 32*(1), 1–27. doi:10.1007/s12525-021-00496-x

Nader, K., Toprac, P., Scott, S., & Baker, S. (2022). Public understanding of artificial intelligence through entertainment media. *AI & Society*, 1–14. PMID:35400854

Nichols, R. (2022). The cultural evolution of Chinese morality, and the essential value of multi-disciplinary research in understanding it. In The Routledge International Handbook of Morality, Cognition, and Emotion in China (pp. 19-37). Routledge. doi:10.4324/9781003281566-3

Novelli, C., Taddeo, M., & Floridi, L. (2023). Accountability in artificial intelligence: What it is and how it works. *AI & Society*, 1–12. doi:10.1007/s00146-023-01635-y

Owe, A., & Baum, S. D. (2021). Moral consideration of nonhumans in the ethics of artificial intelligence. *AI and Ethics, 1*(4), 517–528. doi:10.1007/s43681-021-00065-0

Palomares, I., Martínez-Cámara, E., Montes, R., García-Moral, P., Chiachio, M., Chiachio, J., Alonso, S., Melero, F. J., Molina, D., Fernández, B., Moral, C., Marchena, R., de Vargas, J. P., & Herrera, F. (2021). A panoramic view and swot analysis of artificial intelligence for achieving the sustainable development goals by 2030: Progress and prospects. *Applied Intelligence, 51*(9), 6497–6527. doi:10.1007/s10489-021-02264-y PMID:34764606

Prem, E. (2023). From ethical AI frameworks to tools: A review of approaches. *AI and Ethics, 3*(3), 1–18. doi:10.1007/s43681-023-00258-9

Qiao-Franco, G., & Bode, I. (2023). Weaponised artificial intelligence and Chinese practices of human–machine interaction. *The Chinese Journal of International Politics, 16*(1), 106–128. doi:10.1093/cjip/poac024

Samuel, J. (2023). *Response to the March 2023'Pause Giant AI Experiments: An Open Letter by Yoshua Bengio, signed by Stuart Russell, Elon Musk, Steve Wozniak, Yuval Noah Harari and others*. Academic Press.

Schiff, D. (2021). Out of the laboratory and into the classroom: The future of artificial intelligence in education. *AI & Society*, *36*(1), 331–348. doi:10.1007/s00146-020-01033-8 PMID:32836908

Shaw, J., Rudzicz, F., Jamieson, T., & Goldfarb, A. (2019). Artificial intelligence and the implementation challenge. *Journal of Medical Internet Research*, *21*(7), e13659. doi:10.2196/13659 PMID:31293245

Smith, H. (2021). Clinical AI: Opacity, accountability, responsibility and liability. *AI & Society*, *36*(2), 535–545. doi:10.1007/s00146-020-01019-6

Sweeney, P. (2022). Trusting social robots. *AI and Ethics*, 1–8. PMID:35634257

Visvizi, A. (2021). Artificial intelligence (AI): Explaining, querying, demystifying. *Artificial Intelligence and Its Contexts: Security, Business and Governance*, 13-26.

Yamin, M. M., Ullah, M., Ullah, H., & Katt, B. (2021). Weaponized AI for cyber attacks. *Journal of Information Security and Applications*, *57*, 102722. doi:10.1016/j.jisa.2020.102722

Young, A. T., Amara, D., Bhattacharya, A., & Wei, M. L. (2021). Patient and general public attitudes towards clinical artificial intelligence: A mixed methods systematic review. *The Lancet. Digital Health*, *3*(9), e599–e611. doi:10.1016/S2589-7500(21)00132-1 PMID:34446266

Zajda, J., & Vissing, Y. (Eds.). (2022). *Discourses of globalisation, ideology, and human rights* (Vol. 14). Springer. doi:10.1007/978-3-030-90590-3

Zeng, J. (2020). Artificial intelligence and China's authoritarian governance. *International Affairs*, *96*(6), 1441–1459. doi:10.1093/ia/iiaa172

Zhang, B., Zhu, J., & Su, H. (2023). Toward the third generation artificial intelligence. *Science China. Information Sciences*, *66*(2), 1–19. doi:10.1007/s11432-021-3449-x

Zhang, Y., Wu, M., Tian, G. Y., Zhang, G., & Lu, J. (2021). Ethics and privacy of artificial intelligence: Understandings from bibliometrics. *Knowledge-Based Systems*, *222*, 106994. doi:10.1016/j.knosys.2021.106994

Zuiderwijk, A., Chen, Y. C., & Salem, F. (2021). Implications of the use of artificial intelligence in public governance: A systematic literature review and a research agenda. *Government Information Quarterly*, *38*(3), 101577. doi:10.1016/j.giq.2021.101577

ADDITIONAL READING

Aung, Y. Y., Wong, D. C., & Ting, D. S. (2021). The promise of artificial intelligence: A review of the opportunities and challenges of artificial intelligence in healthcare. *British Medical Bulletin, 139*(1), 4–15. doi:10.1093/bmb/ldab016 PMID:34405854

Bistron, M., & Piotrowski, Z. (2021). Artificial intelligence applications in military systems and their influence on sense of security of citizens. *Electronics (Basel), 10*(7), 871. doi:10.3390/electronics10070871

Devagiri, J. S., Paheding, S., Niyaz, Q., Yang, X., & Smith, S. (2022). Augmented Reality and Artificial Intelligence in industry: Trends, tools, and future challenges. *Expert Systems with Applications, 207*, 118002. doi:10.1016/j.eswa.2022.118002

Haenlein, M., & Kaplan, A. (2019). A brief history of artificial intelligence: On the past, present, and future of artificial intelligence. *California Management Review, 61*(4), 5–14. doi:10.1177/0008125619864925

Hagendorff, T. (2021). Forbidden knowledge in machine learning reflections on the limits of research and publication. *AI & Society, 36*(3), 767–781. doi:10.1007/s00146-020-01045-4

Kaminski, M. E. (2023). Regulating the Risks of AI. *Forthcoming. Boston University Law Review. Boston University. School of Law*, 103.

Kaur, D., Uslu, S., Rittichier, K. J., & Durresi, A. (2022). Trustworthy artificial intelligence: A review. *ACM Computing Surveys, 55*(2), 1–38. doi:10.1145/3491209

Kazansky, B., & Milan, S. (2021). "Bodies not templates": Contesting dominant algorithmic imaginaries. *New Media & Society, 23*(2), 363–381. doi:10.1177/1461444820929316

Maibaum, A., Bischof, A., Hergesell, J., & Lipp, B. (2022). A critique of robotics in health care. *AI & Society, 37*(2), 1–11. doi:10.1007/s00146-021-01206-z

Medaglia, R., Gil-Garcia, J. R., & Pardo, T. A. (2023). Artificial intelligence in government: Taking stock and moving forward. *Social Science Computer Review, 41*(1), 123–140. doi:10.1177/08944393211034087

Shneiderman, B. (2020). Bridging the gap between ethics and practice: Guidelines for reliable, safe, and trustworthy human-centered AI systems. *ACM Transactions on Interactive Intelligent Systems, 10*(4), 1–31. doi:10.1145/3419764

KEY TERMS AND DEFINITIONS

Agency: Is the capacity for action or intervention producing a particular effect.

AI Safety: AI safety pertains to the interdisciplinary field which prevents the misuse, accidental or other consequences which could be the resultant outcome of an AI system.

Algorithm: An algorithm is a process or set of rules to be followed in decision-making or other problem-solving operations, especially by computing technology.

Epistemic Bias: The lens of subjective interpretation which influences systematic research practice due to failing to acknowledge or detail the ideals of human impartiality and value-freedom which may potentially be influencing it.

Existentialism: The philosophy of the nature of human existence as determined by capacity and capability for free will and free choice.

Hacking: The gaining of illegal, unlawful, or unofficially unauthorised access to data in within the context of computing and technology.

Reliability: The extent to which a research instrument can repeatedly provide the same results in temporally separated incidences of measurement.

Sentient/Sentience: Sentience is the capacity of a being to experience feelings and sensations.

Validity: Is the state of being officially true or legally acceptable.

Chapter 4
Democratizing Education AI and OpenAI Models for Global Access to Knowledge

Sevinj Isayeva
https://orcid.org/0000-0002-0342-1682
Süleyman Demirel University, Turkey

ABSTRACT

This chapter delves into an examination of the role of artificial intelligence models in the democratization of education. The central focus of the study revolves around the utilization of AI-supported technologies in education, with particular emphasis on enhancing the learning experience and ensuring accessibility to education and knowledge. Moreover, the chapter comprehensively addresses the advantages of employing AI technologies in the process of transitioning towards democratizing education, along with potential challenges encountered during the adaptation phase, aiming to comprehend their overall impact. Additionally, the chapter provides nuanced insights into various applications and usage fields for diverse AI technologies. In conclusion, it underscores that the effective and efficient deployment of these technologies is contingent upon a holistic consideration of ethical, regulatory, and social issues.

INTRODUCTION

Education stands as a critical phenomenon that allows individuals to explore their potential, access knowledge, and contribute to societal development. However, challenges such as ensuring equal access to education and democratically reaching

DOI: 10.4018/979-8-3693-1666-5.ch004

information persist as significant issues awaiting resolution in the present day. Economic constraints, geographical disparities, language barriers, and local resource deficiencies endure as the most prevalent obstacles to accessing education and information. In this context, democratizing education becomes the focal point of efforts to overcome existing barriers and ensure equal access to information (Bulathwela et al., 2021). The democratization of education is not limited to the democratic management of educational services, the democratization of the activities of educational institutions, or democratic regulations in the educational process (Bondarenko & Kozulin, 1991). The freedom to generate and disseminate knowledge among human communities globally constitutes an integral aspect of democratization within the realm of education (Raza & Sohaib Murad, 2008).

Increasing access to education and issues related to the democratization of education are primarily political and social matters, and their success heavily depends on the collaboration between technology and the environment where it operates. If these technologies are not appropriately and collaboratively designed or utilized with the correct infrastructure, it will inevitably lead to a deeper exacerbation of existing educational inequality worldwide (Bulathwela et al., 2021). Artificial intelligence technologies, vital in today's education, bring about revolutionary transformations in traditional teaching and learning methods. Providing more personalized experiences by AI tools enhances the efficiency of the educational process. It also facilitates the creation of more interactive learning environments and promotes inclusivity (Ivanashko et al., 2024). The use of biased artificial intelligence algorithms in decision-making processes, including education, poses a risk that it may contribute to the disadvantage of specific groups such as women, minorities, or individuals with low income, leading to the perpetuation of systemic inequalities. This problem needs to be considered and prevented (Farahani & Ghasemi, 2024).

In this context, this chapter aims to explore the role and impact of AI and Open AI models in the concept of democratizing education and global access to knowledge. The main objective of this chapter is to emphasize the urgent need for accessible education and knowledge. The chapter will initiate its discourse by meticulously addressing the extant challenges and disparities within the realm of education. Subsequently, it will expound upon the capacity of artificial intelligence and OpenAI models to effectively address these challenges and contribute to the democratization of education. The subsequent section will delve into a comprehensive examination of the implementations of artificial intelligence in education, meticulously scrutinizing their applications and intended objectives.

THE CONCEPT OF DEMOCRATIZING EDUCATION

Education, as a global fundamental need, stands out as one of the primary factors in developing countries (Tangonyire & Mayaki, 2024). As one of the fundamental needs on a global scale, education plays a crucial role in the development of countries (Tangonyire & Mayaki, 2024). It aligns with the values of democracy, which include inclusiveness, civic equality, civic participation, freedom of expression, and educational equality (Kucirkova & Leaton Gray, 2023). Democratic education provides a solid foundation for ensuring a society's citizens' civil and political freedoms. When citizens of a society are deprived of adequate education, their civil and political freedoms are jeopardized, and arguments against authoritarianism may weaken. In this context, it can be said that the full moral strength of democracy depends on democratic education (Gutmann, 1987). The historical and contemporary forms of democracy have played a pivotal role in shaping the concepts of public education and continue to do so (Provenzo & Renaud, 2009). This points to the two-way nature of the relationship between democracy and education.

Worldwide, international organizations recommend and encourage the democratization of education in the fight against discrimination and illiteracy, as well as in areas such as special education, education for migrants, the rights to education for minorities, adult education, and continuous education. Achieving democracy and equality in education requires special measures through educational policies to mitigate and overcome social inequalities. These measures include ensuring equal material conditions for education, providing educational materials, and improving student standards through social, organizational, and pedagogical measures based on the principle of solidarity. Additionally, efforts such as establishing school canteens, student dormitories, free transportation, scholarship opportunities, setting up pedagogical institutions for preschool education, and creating preparatory classes for preschool education are essential. Moreover, addressing challenging living conditions for students who lag may require additional efforts (Murati, 2015).

The democratization of education involves four major components: the democratization of educational activities, the democratization of educational content, the humanization of the functioning of educational establishments and extracurricular activities, and the democratization of education's interactions with other social spheres such as the economy, science, culture, media, and government bodies. The democratization of educational activities involves promoting diversity in teaching methods and encouraging individuality in educational activities. The democratization of the content of education encompasses the objective, free, complete, and multifaceted reflection of all subjects, with an emphasis on the integration of subjects to create a solid dialectical outlook (Bondarenko & Kozulin, 1991).

BARRIERS IN GLOBAL ACCESSING TO KNOWLEDGE AND EDUCATION

From a global perspective, accessing information encounters numerous impediments that hinder both the sharing and utilization of knowledge. Among these barriers, the deficiency in communication and interaction between knowledge sources and recipients emerges as a significant obstacle to global information access (Reige, 2005). In addition, there are various aspects to accessing information, such as the complexity of knowledge (Togola et al.,2019), challenges in planning and coordination across different time zones, and cultural differences (Martins et al., 2004). Inequalities in accessing education constitute one of the major barriers to obtaining knowledge and education. Scientific literature includes studies indicating the effects of individuals' socioeconomic backgrounds and educational progress, particularly on access to higher education (Czarnecki, 2017; Weng et al., 2021).

Nevertheless, gender discrimination also plays a pivotal role in shaping access to educational resources and curriculum, particularly in open and distance education settings (Qi et al., 2021). Dealing with the multifaceted nature of inequalities in accessing education and knowledge requires targeted interventions to address the challenges. In this regard, artificial intelligence technologies are considered to play a crucial role in eliminating issues of inequality.

FOUNDATIONS OF AI AND OPEN AI APPLICATION IN EDUCATION

Technological advancements such as big data, cloud computing, artificial neural networks, and machine learning have facilitated the creation of a machine capable of simulating human intelligence. Machines capable of perceiving, recognizing, learning, responding, and solving problems are referred to as artificial intelligence. Artificial intelligence, which holds strategic significance in education, is progressively becoming more prevalent and leading to a new era of innovation and transformation in many fields, including education. As a transformative force, artificial intelligence technology, offering new tools and applications with the potential to transform traditional teaching and learning methods, has broad applicability in education. Artificial intelligence plays a significant role in various aspects, such as enhancing productivity, improving learning outcomes, providing personalized instruction, offering instant feedback, and fostering student engagement (Adıguzel et al., 2023; Kamalov et al., 202; Zhai et al., 2021).

Personalized learning, one of the advantages of artificial intelligence technologies, enables students to learn subjects at their own pace and in a manner that suits their learning styles, thus allowing for better student outcomes. Through intelligent tutoring systems such as chatbots, automatic grading, and assessment, efficiency can be enhanced, and teachers can save time. At the same time, these systems can provide real-time support to students, detect gaps in understanding, and deliver targeted interventions to address misconceptions. Another salient characteristic of artificial intelligence applications that can profoundly influence education is the automation of administrative tasks. Automating administrative responsibilities, including grading, scheduling, and attendance tracking, aids in expediting these tasks for teachers and school administrators. Consequently, this allows educators to concentrate more on essential aspects such as lesson planning, instruction, and fostering student engagement (Harry, 2023; Snipes, 2023).

On the other hand, the rapid advancements in the field of artificial intelligence have brought forth various challenges, such as plagiarism and the generation of articles within minutes that are difficult to distinguish from human writing. This also indicates the ethical implications of using artificial intelligence. However, issues such as privacy and security concerns, cost, and lack of trust are among the significant matters that need to be addressed. In this context, Novelli et al. (2023) have discussed the issue of accountability in the use of artificial intelligence, identifying four accountability goals as compliance, reporting, oversight, and enforcement. Responsibility goals within artificial intelligence applications have different focuses. For instance, if responsibility is primarily aimed at compliance, it is possible to say that policymakers and designers should focus on creating artificial intelligence that complies with ethical, legal, and technical standards when forming educational policies. Despite the challenges of transitioning and adapting, artificial intelligence is expected to offer more opportunities compared to traditional technologies. In 2022, initially, discriminative artificial intelligence models, which statistically classify and aim to differentiate data, held prominence; however, later, generative artificial intelligence models designed to learn from data and generate new content and outputs, such as ChatGPT, ushered in significant changes in the public sphere. OpenAI's models such as GPT-4 are positioned for direct accessibility by the public due to their utilization of a straightforward natural language interface (Shah, 2023; Harry, 2023; Novelli et al., 2023; Tóth et al., 2022). The use of artificial intelligence in modern education is generally aimed at supporting learning, encompassing developments such as personalized education or dialogue education systems, exploratory learning, data mining in education, analysis of students' articles, intelligent agents, chatbots, education for special needs children, child-robot interaction, artificial intelligence-based assessment systems, and automatic test generation systems (Arslan, 2020).

The predominant reason for the feasibility of implementing artificial intelligence technologies in education lies in the swift developments within the field of information technology. Within the context of enhancing learning and decision-making processes, the application of artificial intelligence in education is articulated as the utilization of artificial intelligence technology, and application programs (Kavitha et al., 2023) and enables education to be made more accessible and inclusive, allowing students to access high-quality education (Harry, 2023).

It is worthwhile to recall Amara's Law, which elucidates how expectations regarding the impacts of technology shift as it matures and gains adoption (Fitzpatrick and Kelleher, 2018). This law, articulated by Roy Charles Amara, is formulated as follows: "We tend to overestimate the effect of a technology in the short run and underestimate the effect in the long run". Artificial intelligence is believed to have a largely positive impact on education, improving outcomes and assisting institutions in scaling quality education for their students. However, on the other hand, to fully leverage artificial intelligence, various regulatory, societal, and institutional concerns need to be addressed first. In this context, practical and ethical challenges also need to be resolved (Klutka et al., 2018).

OVERCOMING BARRIERS IN EDUCATION WITH AI AND OPENAI MODELS

Artificial intelligence technologies, emerging as powerful tools in overcoming barriers in education, provide innovative solutions for enhancing learning outcomes and addressing educational challenges. It is stated that artificial intelligence technologies offer opportunities for creating more personalized curricula, democratizing education worldwide, and essentially fostering a Renaissance in teaching and learning processes. In the academic literature, some studies highlight the dual nature of using artificial intelligence technologies in education (Bulathwela et al., 2021; Dalgıç et al., 2024; Farahani & Ghasemi, 2024; Li, 2023).

Examining the outcomes related to educational equity becomes crucial considering the advancements brought about by artificial intelligence (Demir & Demir, 2023a; 2023b; Li, 2023). While millions of students actively benefit from these technologies, it is also acknowledged that an equal number of students face challenges in accessing these advantages. If this trend continues, there is a concern that artificial intelligence in education may contribute to educational inequality (Bulathwela et al., 2021). In this context, the limited access to artificial intelligence-supported education programs emerges as a fact that needs to be considered, as it may lead to unequal skill development and job opportunities. Nevertheless, the lack of requisite skills among marginalized segments, including the elderly, low-income populations, and those with restricted access to education, to engage with AI technologies is a circumstance that may contribute to the expansion of the digital gap (Farahani & Ghasemi, 2024). On the other hand, Yao (2020) highlighted the importance of artificial intelligence for rural education in his study. He observed a significant improvement in both the quality and quantity of educational resources offered with the help of artificial intelligence in rural areas where attracting quality educators has historically been challenging as a significant agent of change. Dalgıç et al. (2024) concluded in their research on tourism education students that Chat GPT utilization affects learning outcomes. Additionally, the study results indicated that digital literacy plays a mediating role in ChatGPT usage, while individualized learning has a moderate effect. After all, it is a reality that must be considered that the use of ChatGPT has a destructive impact on the education system and scientific research. ChatGPT has been used and continues to be used to write summaries and even complete theses since its emergence. In addition, many authors have used this artificial intelligence bot to write portions of their articles and have also listed ChatGPT as an author. Naturally, this raises significant concerns about the future of education and research across different disciplines and fields, as well as the validity of conducted research and the value of academic degrees (De Angelis et al., 2023; Dalgıç et al., 2024). However, ChatGPT has some disadvantages, such as being trained on data only up to 2021 and lacking access to real-time data. Therefore, the answers it provides to questions may be irrelevant, incorrect, or outdated. On the other hand, the app's failure to provide references to the sources used for the response and its lack of critical analysis highlights the need for students and instructors to be more cautious with these texts. Nevertheless, ChatGPT's appearance in the scientific literature and earning four authorship credits in published works has sparked debate among journal editors, authors, and publishers regarding the appropriateness of citing ChatGPT as an author (Ivanov & Soliman, 2023).

AI APPLICATIONS IN EDUCATION

Examining the outcomes related to educational equity becomes crucial in light of the advancements brought about by artificial intelligence.

The rapid integration of artificial intelligence into social and business life profoundly affects these areas. In this context, it is an undeniable fact that the education system will be one of the fields most profoundly affected by the rapid development of artificial intelligence technologies (Dalgıç et al., 2024). Artificial Intelligence has been used in the field of education for over 60 years in the form of Machine Learning technology and continues to be utilized (Hardman, 2023). It is observed that artificial intelligence-supported applications are frequently utilized in the field of education, as in many other fields, and new technologies are continually being added to this repertoire every day. Globally, artificial intelligence programs in the field of education, such as "Thinkster Math", "Jill Watson", "Brainly",

"Nuance", and "Cognii", can be exemplified. "Thinkster Math" is an artificial intelligence-supported platform that creates personalized learning programs in the field of mathematics. On the other hand, "Jill Watson" was introduced as a virtual teaching assistant by the Georgia Institute of Technology in 2016. Brainly, as another application, serves as a social media site designed for classroom questions. "Nuance", yet another application, functions as speech recognition software capable of transcribing 160 words per minute, particularly beneficial for students experiencing difficulties in writing or with accessibility needs. "Cognii", designed for higher education institutions and corporate training organizations, is a virtual learning assistant (onlinedegrees.sandiego.edu). In addition, universities have developed artificial intelligence-supported technologies to provide support to students, offer information about the campus, guide on administrative matters, and answer questions. For instance, Georgia State University employs an artificial intelligence-supported chat robot named "Pounce" to assist with processes such as admissions, financial aid, and campus resources. Similarly, the University of California, Berkeley possesses an artificial support chatbot named Berkeley Chatbot, designed to answer questions from both students and prospective students. Likewise, Deakin University utilizes a chat robot named "Genie", aiming to assist prospective students regarding the information they need. Staffordshire University has developed a chatbot named Beacon, serving as a digital assistant for students. Furthermore, artificial intelligence-supported technologies can also assist students in areas such as mental health and learning difficulties (globaladmissions.com).

Another application of artificial intelligence technologies is the scoring of essays and assignments based on machine learning algorithms, focusing on factors such as grammar and coherence. This aims to provide quick feedback to students and save time for teachers. Examples of such tools include "Gradescope", and "E-rater". These tools utilize machine learning algorithms to analyze essays and provide scores based on various characteristics such as vocabulary usage, citation standards, sentence structure, and overall organization of the texts. The "OpenSimon" application developed by Carnegie Mellon University provides real-time and personalized feedback by analyzing student data based on both student performance and behavior (Hardman, 2023).

CONCLUSION

This study explores the potential contributions of artificial intelligence-supported technologies to democratizing education and access to knowledge, discussing how these technologies can be utilized for access to education. Artificial intelligence technologies can provide personalized learning experiences, enhance student engagement, and address various learning needs. This implies that artificial intelligence technologies have significant potential in advancing access to education (Zawacki-Richter et al., 2019). At the same time, artificial intelligence tools enable educational institutions to prepare personalized educational content and support programs for students, thereby promoting inclusivity. This can help in identifying and preventing individual learning challenges (Alasadi & Baiz, 2023). Increased access, improved learning outcomes, and reduced costs resulting in positive outcomes highlight the transformative potential of artificial intelligence in promoting educational accessibility (Huston et al., 2022). The importance of artificial intelligence applications in implementing practices aimed at reassessing pedagogical practices, integrating transformative learning approaches, and increasing student engagement is also emphasized in the scientific literature (Luitel & Pant, 2021). In this context, the potential of artificial intelligence to enable personalized learning experiences, create collaborative learning environments, and provide opportunities for educators' self-reflection comes to the forefront (Cochrane & Rhodes, 2013). The integration of artificial intelligence technologies into education highlights the importance of considering ethical and societal issues. Addressing ethical challenges is critical for ensuring the responsible and fair use of these technologies and for identifying their societal impacts. The literature emphasizes the significance of ethical rules and comprehensive ethical analyses for addressing ethical issues related to the use of artificial intelligence (Demir & Demir, 2023b; Jobin & Ienca, 2019).

Alongside highlighting the benefits of the widespread use of artificial intelligence technologies, the possible negative impacts are also discussed, addressing the subject from a comprehensive perspective. Furthermore, attention is drawn to the necessity of a regulatory, ethically grounded, and socially focused approach to enhance the effectiveness of these technologies. The success of efforts towards democratizing education is anticipated to depend not only on the use of technologies but also significantly on positive transformations in the overall structure of the education system and the adaptation of learning methods to these technologies.

This study contributes valuable insights to the literature by discussing how artificial intelligence (AI) technologies can contribute to the democratization process in education from a theoretical perspective. Particularly, it aims to encourage further in-depth research on the ethical and societal dimensions of using these technologies in the educational field. Additionally, the study focuses on the potential of OpenAI models to promote equality and justice in education by emphasizing their ability to provide global access to knowledge. It is believed that offering AI technologies to a wide range of users for free will increase access to educational materials for students and teachers with different levels of access to education.

While our study aims to shed light on the potential of artificial intelligence and OpenAI models in democratizing education and providing global access to knowledge, it is important to acknowledge certain limitations. Firstly, it should be noted that our study focuses on the theoretical and practical implications of artificial intelligence applications in education. However, it is crucial to consider the various technical, logistical, and socio-cultural challenges that may arise in the implementation of these technologies in different educational settings. Additionally, factors such as infrastructure limitations, digital divide issues, and cultural barriers may impact the effective adoption and usage of artificial intelligence technologies in diverse educational contexts. Furthermore, our study is based on existing research and scientific literature, which may result in methodological limitations. Despite our efforts to comprehensively examine the topic, there may be additional studies, perspectives, and developments that were not included in our review. Therefore, our conclusions are based on the current state of knowledge, and they may evolve as advancements in the field occur.

In conclusion, it is believed that this study, addressing the potential contributions of artificial intelligence-supported technologies to the democratization of education, will contribute to the existing discussions in this field, providing a significant theoretical and practical foundation. In this context, future research should focus on gaining a deeper understanding of the ethical and societal impacts of AI-supported educational models and ensuring their fair and equitable distribution to broader audiences.

REFERENCES

Adıgüzel, T., Kaya, M. H., & Cansu, F. K. (2023). Revolutionizing education with AI: Exploring the transformative potential of ChatGPT. *Contemporary Educational Technology, 15*(3), ep429. Advance online publication. doi:10.30935/cedtech/13152

Alasadi, E. A., & Baiz, C. R. (2023). Generative AI in education and research: Opportunities, concerns, and solutions. *Journal of Chemical Education, 100*(8), 2965–2971. doi:10.1021/acs.jchemed.3c00323

Arslan, K. (2020). Eğitimde yapay zekâ ve uygulamaları. *Batı Anadolu Eğitim Bilimleri Dergisi, 11*(1), 71-88. https://dergipark.org.tr/en/download/article-file/1174773

Bondarenko, Y. G., & Kozulin, A. V. (1991). The democratization of education: Basic principles. *Higher Education in Europe, 16*(1), 74–78. doi:10.1080/0379772910160109

Bulathwela, S., Pérez-Ortiz, M., Holloway, C., & Shawe-Taylor, J. (2021). Could AI democratize education? Socio-technical imaginaries of an edtech revolution. *35th Conference on Neural Information Processing Systems. 1-9.* 10.48550/arxiv.2112.02034

Cochrane, T., & Rhodes, D. (2013). iArchi [tech] ture: Developing a mobile social media framework for pedagogical transformation. *Australasian Journal of Educational Technology*, *29*(3). Advance online publication. doi:10.14742/ajet.191

Czarnecki, K. (2018). Less inequality through universal access? Socioeconomic background of tertiary entrants in Australia after the expansion of university participation. *Higher Education*, *76*(3), 501–518. doi:10.1007/s10734-017-0222-1

Dalgıç, A., Yaşar, E., & Demir, M. (2024). ChatGPT and learning outcomes in tourism education: The role of digital literacy and individualized learning. *Journal of Hospitality, Leisure, Sport and Tourism Education*, *34*, 100481. doi:10.1016/j.jhlste.2024.100481

De Angelis, L., Baglivo, F., Arzilli, G., Privitera, G. P., Ferragina, P., Tozzi, A. E., & Rizzo, C. (2023). ChatGPT and the rise of large language models: The new AI-driven infodemic threat in public health. *Frontiers in Public Health*, *11*, 1166120. doi:10.3389/fpubh.2023.1166120 PMID:37181697

Demir, M., & Demir, Ş. Ş. (2023). Is ChatGPT the right technology for service individualization and value co-creation? Evidence from the travel industry. *Journal of Travel & Tourism Marketing*, *40*(5), 383–398. doi:10.1080/10548408.2023.2255884

Demir, Ş. Ş., & Demir, M. (2023). Professionals' perspectives on ChatGPT in the tourism industry: Does it inspire awe or concern? *Journal of Tourism Theory and Research*, *9*(2), 61–77. doi:10.24288/jttr.1313481

Farahani, M., & Ghasemi, G. (2024). *Artificial intelligence and inequality: challenges and opportunities*. Qeios., doi:10.32388/7HWUZ2

FitzpatrickN.KelleherJ. (2018) On the Exactitude of Big Data: La Bêtise and Artificial Intelligence. *La Deluziana*, doi:10.21427/dfw8-m918

Gutmann, A. (1987). *Democratic education: With a New Preface and Epilogue*. Princeton University Press.

Hardman, P. (2023). *A Brief History of AI in Education: What we have learned in the last 60 years, and where we're going next.* https://drphilippahardman.substack.com/p/a-brief-history-of-ai-in- education?utm_source=substack&utm_medium=email&utm_content=share

Harry, A. (2023). Role of AI in Education. *Interdisciplinary Journal and Humanity*, *2*(3), 260–268. doi:10.58631/injurity.v2i3.52

Hutson, J., Jeevanjee, T., Vander Graaf, V., Lively, J., Weber, J., Weir, G., ... Edele, S. (2022). Artificial Intelligence and the Disruption of Higher Education: Strategies for Integrations across Disciplines. *Creative Education*, *13*(12), 3953–3980. Advance online publication. doi:10.4236/ce.2022.1312253

Ivanashko, O., Kozak, A., Knysh, T., & Honchar, K. (2024). The Role of Artificial Intelligence in Shaping the Future of Education: Opportunities and Challenges. *Futurity Education*, *4*(1), 126–146. doi:10.57125/FED.2024.03.25.08

Ivanov, S., & Soliman, M. (2023). Game of algorithms: ChatGPT implications for the future of tourism education and research. *Journal of Tourism Futures*, *9*(2), 214–221. doi:10.1108/JTF-02-2023-0038

Jobin, A., Ienca, M., & Vayena, E. (2019). The global landscape of AI ethics guidelines. *Nature Machine Intelligence*, *1*(9), 389–399. doi:10.1038/s42256-019-0088-2

Kamalov, F., Santandreu Calonge, D., & Gurrib, I. (2023). New era of artificial intelligence in education: Towards a sustainable multifaceted revolution. *Sustainability (Basel)*, *15*(16), 12451. doi:10.3390/su151612451

Kavitha, K. B., Pradeep Kumar, T.K., Nithiya, S., & Suguna, A. (2023). Implementation of Artificial Intelligence in Education. *International Research Journal of Computer Science, 10*(5), 104-108. . doi:10.26562/irjcs.2023.v1005.01

Klutka, J., Ackerly, N., & Magda, A. J. (2018). *Artificial intelligence in higher education: Current uses and future applications*. Learning House.

Kucirkova, N., & Leaton Gray, S. (2023). Beyond Personalization: Embracing Democratic Learning Within Artificially Intelligent Systems. *Educational Theory*, *73*(4), 469–489. doi:10.1111/edth.12590

Li, H. (2023). AI in Education: Bridging the Divide or Widening the Gap? Exploring Equity, Opportunities, and Challenges in the Digital Age. *Advances in Education. Humanities and Social Science Research*, *8*(1), 355–355. doi:10.56028/aehssr.8.1.355.2023

Martins, L. L., Gilson, L. L., & Maynard, M. T. (2004). Virtual teams: What do we know and where do we go from here? *Journal of Management*, *30*(6), 805–835. doi:10.1016/j.jm.2004.05.002

Murati, R. (2015). Conception and Definition of the Democratization of Education. *Journal of Education and Practice*, *6*(30), 173–183. https://files.eric.ed.gov/fulltext/EJ1081375.pdf

Novelli, C., Taddeo, M., & Floridi, L. (2023). Accountability in artificial intelligence: What it is and how it works. *AI & Society*, 1–12. doi:10.1007/s00146-023-01635-y

Provenzo, E. F., & Renaud, J. P. (Eds.). (2009). *Encyclopedia of the Social and Cultural Foundations of Education* (Vol. 1-3). Sage. doi:10.4135/9781412963992

Qi, B., Wang, X., & Sutton, P. (2021). Can Nighttime Satellite Imagery Inform Our Understanding of Education Inequality? *Remote Sensing (Basel)*, *13*(5), 843. doi:10.3390/rs13050843

Raza, A., & Sohaib Murad, H. (2008). Knowledge democracy and the implications to information access. *Multicultural Education & Technology Journal*, *2*(1), 37–46. doi:10.1108/17504970810867142

Riege, A. (2005). Three-dozen knowledge-sharing barriers managers must consider. *Journal of Knowledge Management*, *9*(3), 18–35. doi:10.1108/13673270510602746

Shah, P. (2023). *Embracing AI in Education*. John Wiley & Sons.

Snipes, S. (2023). Transforming Education With AI: Guide to Understanding and Using ChatGPT in the Classroom. Ai4 Press.

Tangonyire, R., & Mayaki, B. (2024). Social Media and its Democratizing Impact on Africa's Education: A Critique. *Chiedza. Journal of Arrupe Jesuit University*, *25*(1), 22–34.

Togola, A., Ahmed, S., & Jadaan, T. (2019). Barriers of knowledge transfer between globally distributed teams in ICT product development. *Proceedings of the 52nd Hawaii International Conference on System Sciences*. 5568-5577. 10.24251/HICSS.2019.670

Tóth, Z., Caruana, R., Gruber, T., & Loebbecke, C. (2022). The dawn of the AI robots: Towards a new framework of AI robot accountability. *Journal of Business Ethics*, *178*(4), 895–916. doi:10.1007/s10551-022-05050-z

Weng, Z., Tang, J., & Liu, K. (2021, October). The Impact of Free Preschool Education on Educational Inequality in China. In *2021 6th International Conference on Modern Management and Education Technology (MMET 2021)* (pp. 462-472). Atlantis Press. 10.2991/assehr.k.211011.085

Yao, W. (2020). Educational Equity in the age of artificial intelligence—taking the construction of rural teachers as an example. *The US-China Education Review: A*, *10*(4), 9-18.

Zawacki-Richter, O., Marín, V. I., Bond, M., & Gouverneur, F. (2019). Systematic review of research on artificial intelligence applications in higher education–where are the educators? *International Journal of Educational Technology in Higher Education*, *16*(1), 1–27. doi:10.1186/s41239-019-0171-0

Zhai, X., Chu, X., Chai, C. S., Jong, Y. S. M., Istenic, A., Spector, M., Liu, J. B., Yuan, J., & Li, Y. (2021). A Review of Artificial Intelligence (AI) in Education from 2010 to 2020. *Complexity*, *2021*, 1–18. Advance online publication. doi:10.1155/2021/8812542

ADDITIONAL READING

Simmons, A. B., & Chappell, S. G. (1988). Artificial intelligence-definition and practice. *IEEE Journal of Oceanic Engineering*, *13*(2), 14–42. doi:10.1109/48.551

KEY TERMS AND DEFINITIONS

Artificial Intelligence: It is expressed as the behavior exhibited by a machine (Simmons & Chappell, 1988).

Chat Generative Pre-Trained Transformer: The chatbot can be utilized for customer service, content generation, and language translation assignments, generating responses in multiple languages (Aydın & Karaarslan, 2022).

Open Artificial Intelligence: OpenAI could signify collaborative and replicable scientific endeavors and systems. For technologists, it might revolve around the unrestricted usage and dissemination of AI models, or possibly involve public engagement in algorithmic development (Ding, 2022). On the other hand, OpenAI is a non-profit research company engaged in artificial intelligence development and distribution (Fitria, 2023).

Chapter 5
How Artificial Intelligence in Tourist Guidance Education Is Changing the Game

Mahmut Demir
Isparta University of Applied Sciences, Turkey

ABSTRACT

This chapter explains the transformative impact of artificial intelligence (AI) on tourist guidance education, exploring the paradigm shift in teaching methodologies and industry practices. As AI technologies continue to advance, their integration into tourism education has revolutionized the way students acquire knowledge and skills essential for guiding travelers effectively. The chapter reviews incorporating AI-driven tools such as virtual reality simulations, chatbots, and machine learning algorithms into educational frameworks, fostering immersive and dynamic learning experiences. This chapter also underscores the economic implications, as AI-equipped guides contribute to the sustainability and competitiveness of tourist destinations.

INTRODUCTION

In an era marked by technological advancements, the fusion of artificial intelligence (AI) with the fabric of tourist guidance education stands as an intriguing frontier, reshaping the contours of knowledge dissemination (Demir, 2024; Demir et al., 2023). The allure of transformative narrative beckons as educators delve into the relationship between AI and educational institutions dedicated to training tourist guides (Demir & Demir, 2023c). Embarking on a journey through this paradigm shift, this chapter seeks to dissect the pivotal role played by AI in revolutionizing tourist

DOI: 10.4018/979-8-3693-1666-5.ch005

guidance education and transcending the conventional boundaries of pedagogical methodologies.

The complex structure of the tourism industry has been integrated with the dimensions of technology, which has always been on the agenda in how individuals engage with diverse education systems (Chatterjee & Bhattacharjee, 2020; Dalgıç et al., 2024). Technology has been integral in molding the contemporary tourist experience, from digitalizing tourist guidance education to innovation enthusiasts (Ali, 2023). Within this dynamic milieu, the forthcoming discourse will navigate the historical trajectory of technological interventions in tourism, setting the stage for an exploration into the transformative influence of AI on educational systems dedicated to shaping proficient tourist guides.

Central to this study is the profound impact of AI on tourist guidance education. Traditional methodologies characterized by static instructional paradigms are giving way to dynamic, AI-powered platforms that adapt to the evolving needs of both educators and learners. This inquiry will scrutinize the intersection of AI and tourist guidance education, unraveling how machine learning algorithms, data analytics, and immersive technologies reshape the educational landscape for those aspiring to guide travelers in an increasingly interconnected and AI-driven world. As the layers of this intricate relationship are unraveled, a comprehensive understanding of AI's transformative, game-changing role in tourist guidance education will be reviewed.

BACKGROUND

Current Tourist Guidance Education

Traditional methods in tourist guidance education have long been characterized by didactic instructional approaches deeply entrenched in historical and cultural narratives (Huang & Xia, 2016; Wachtel et al., 2021). The conventional model typically involves classroom-based lectures, reliance on static textbooks, and limited interactive engagements (Demir et al., 2023). Educators in this approach predominantly adopt a unidirectional flow of information, imparting knowledge without incorporating contemporary pedagogical advancements (Chokur & Al-Khafaji, 2023; Yaşar & Gafar, 2024). Traditional methods in tourist guidance education are static and should be more adaptable to the dynamic requirements of the modern tourism industry.

Challenges permeate the conventional approach to tourist guidance education, affecting both educators and learners (Yuan et al., 2014). Educators contend with the limitations imposed by outdated instructional materials and methodologies that need help to capture the multifaceted dimensions of tourist guidance (Ghany & Latif, 2012; Ülkü, 2023). The static nature of traditional resources hampers their ability to provide real-time insights into evolving cultural, historical, and geographical contexts (Ahmad et al., 2018; Arcodia et al.,2021). Concurrently, learners need help searching for comprehensive and interactive educational experiences. The absence of dynamic tools and immersive learning opportunities hinders their ability to develop the practical skills required in the field, creating discord between traditional instructional methods and the evolving demands of the tourism industry.

Recognizing the imperative for evolution within the educational environment, the importance of staying updated with the latest trends in technology is evident (Chandra et al., 2022; Dalgic et al., 2023). A proactive approach to integrating cutting-edge tools into educational frameworks is indispensable in the current environment, where technological advancements are reshaping the tourism industry. Embracing emerging technologies, including artificial intelligence (AI) and immersive platforms, is critical for aligning tourist guidance education with the contemporary demands of the field (Demir et al., 2022; Keçi & Qosja, 2021). Integrating these technologies not only enhances the educational experience but also equips educators and learners alike with the agility required to navigate the dynamic and evolving landscape of tourist guidance. This acknowledgment of the relationship between technological trends and educational practices serves as a foundational premise as we investigate the transformative impact of AI on tourist guidance education (Shi et al., 2022; Xu et al., 2022).

Rise of AI in Tourism Guidance Education

The ascent of artificial intelligence (AI) within tourism guidance education represents a pivotal juncture in the evolution of pedagogical methodologies (Adeyinka-Ojo et al., 2020; Morellato, 2014). Integrating AI into educational frameworks dedicated to preparing tourist guides reflects a strategic response to the dynamic landscape of the tourism industry. This rise is characterized by the infusion of AI technologies, such as machine learning algorithms and data analytics, into traditional instructional paradigms (Bilotta et al., 2021; Tuo et al., 2021). AI's role in tourism guidance education extends beyond augmenting teaching methods; it signifies a profound redefinition of knowledge dissemination within tourist guiding. The application of AI in tourism guidance education transcends theoretical constructs, finding tangible expression in innovative tools and platforms. AI-fueled immersive technologies offer simulated environments, replicating real-world scenarios, and providing learners with experiential training (Shi et al., 2022; Tuo et al., 2021). Language translation tools, underpinned by machine learning algorithms, facilitate effective cross-cultural communication, a skill imperative for proficient tourist guides. These applications not only cater to learners' diversifying needs (Kalbaska & Cantoni, 2022; Tolkach

& Pratt, 2021) but also underscore AI's adaptability in addressing the multifaceted challenges intrinsic to tourist guidance education.

The ascendancy of AI in tourism guidance education is underscored by its capacity to enhance the learning experience through dynamic adaptability. AI-powered platforms facilitate personalized learning journeys by adjusting to learners' pace and preferences (Keçi & Qosja, 2021; Mandalia, 2023). Incorporating AI into educational curricula for tourist guides equips them with a comprehensive understanding of cultural, historical, and geographical contexts and fosters critical thinking and problem-solving skills. As AI's influence continues to shape the educational environment (Benckendorff & Zehrer, 2017; Demir et al., 2023; Ivanov & Soliman, 2023), the ascent of AI in tourism guidance education emerges as a transformative force poised to redefine the competencies and capabilities expected of proficient tourist guides in an era dominated by technological innovation.

THE MAIN FOCUS OF THE CHAPTER

Integration of AI into Tourist Guidance Education

In tourist guidance education, the pervasive influence of artificial intelligence (AI) is profoundly altering pedagogical paradigms, ushering in transformative changes in instructional methodologies and learning outcomes (Basiri et al., 2018; Bulchand-Gidumal, 2022). The integration of AI has resulted in a seismic shift, redefining the contours of tourist guidance education. Specific applications such as virtual guides, interactive simulations, and language translation tools exemplify the operational facets of the guidance, imparting a nuanced understanding of tourist guidance principles and practices (Ivanova, 2019; Najbrt & Kapounova, 2015). Integrating these applications into the educational framework not only broadens the scope of learning but also imbues learners with practical skills essential for navigating the complexities of tourist guidance (Dhoundiyal & Mohanty, 2022).

Virtual guides represent AI's transformative impact on tourist guidance education (Jia et al., 2023). These sophisticated systems leverage machine learning algorithms and sensory inputs to simulate real-world scenarios, thus providing learners with immersive experiences (Hung et al., 2024; Lim & Aylett, 2009). The integration of interactive simulations further amplifies the pedagogical landscape, allowing students to engage dynamically with diverse tourism contexts. Language translation tools, underpinned by AI capabilities, can overcome linguistic barriers, facilitate effective communication and comprehension in multilingual settings, and are quintessential for contemporary tourist guides (Battour et al., 2023; Hammady et al., 2021).

The incorporation of AI into educational practices brings forth a panoply of advantages. The adaptability of AI-driven learning modules caters to individualized learning expectations, thus fostering an educational experience (Bogdanovych et al., 2010; Farrokhnia et al., 2023). Moreover, the analytical prowess of AI algorithms enables the extraction of actionable insights from vast datasets, augmenting the curriculum with real-time, industry-relevant information (Dhoundiyal & Mohanty, 2022; Skavronskaya et al., 2023). This correlation between technology and education empowers aspiring tourist guides with a comprehensive skill set, aligning them with the dynamic demands of the tourism sector.

AI's augmentative role in the learning experience for both students and educators is noteworthy. AI-infused educational modules provide personalized student feedback and assessments, promoting self-directed learning and skill mastery (Lo, 2023; Puig et al., 2020). Educators, in turn, benefit from AI-driven analytics that facilitate data-driven decision-making, enhancing instructional strategies, and optimizing educational outcomes (Adeyinka-Ojo et al., 2023; Lampoltshammer et al., 2023). The seamless integration of AI thus engenders a relationship between technology and pedagogy, fostering an environment conducive to continuous improvement and adaptability.

The examples and case studies in higher education substantiate the positive outcomes of AI integration in tourist guidance education. Instances where virtual guides significantly enhance the acquisition of practical skills and language translation tools mitigate communication challenges that underscore AI's tangible benefits (Demir & Demir, 2023a; Hsu, 2018; Wu & Yu, 2023). Moreover, the demonstrable success stories of educational institutions leveraging AI in their curricula further validate the efficacy of this paradigm shift, advocating for its broader adoption in the global pedagogical environment. As revealed through empirical evidence (e.g., Demir & Demir, 2023b; Hsu, 2018; Shi et al., 2022), AI and tourist guidance education epitomize a progressive trajectory toward enhanced learning outcomes and industry preparedness.

Challenges and Concerns With AI in Tourist Guidance Education

Integrating AI into tourist guidance education while heralding transformative possibilities is full of challenges and concerns (Demir & Demir, 2023b; Gupta et al., 2022). A critical aspect involves acknowledging the potential drawbacks associated with the incorporation of AI technologies. One of the primary challenges lies in ensuring equitable access to AI-driven educational tools, as disparities in technology infrastructure and resources may exacerbate existing educational inequalities. Adapting educators and learners to AI-powered platforms poses a challenge, as the learning curve may vary, impacting the efficacy of AI integration in different educational settings (Chaturvedi et al., 2023; Lin et al., 2023). Recognizing and addressing these challenges is essential for fostering an inclusive and effective integration of AI within tourist guidance education.

Ethical considerations are large in AI integration discourse, particularly concerning data privacy and transparency issues (Alyasiri et al., 2024; Chon & Hao, 2024). The use of AI in educational settings involves collecting and analyzing vast amounts of personal and sensitive data (Demir et al., 2022). Striking a balance between leveraging this data for individualized learning experiences and safeguarding individuals' privacy is complex. The potential impact of AI on employment in the tourism industry raises ethical concerns because the automation of certain tasks may lead to job displacement for traditional roles in tourist guidance (Dalgıç et al., 2024; Demir & Demir, 2023a). It is imperative to navigate these ethical considerations judiciously to ensure that the benefits of AI in education do not come at the expense of privacy or socioeconomic disparities.

Resistance and skepticism to AI in tourist guidance education may emanate from various sources. Educators and learners may need more clarification on the reliability and accuracy of AI-driven platforms, fearing potential misinformation or oversimplification of complex cultural and historical contexts (Deri et al., 2023; Kiryakova & Angelova, 2023). There may be resistance rooted in fear of job displacement, as the role of AI in automating certain aspects of tourist guidance may raise uncertainties about the future employment environment (Demir & Demir, 2023c). Addressing these concerns requires transparent communication, educational initiatives to demystify AI technologies, and collaborative efforts to ensure that AI complements rather than supplants the human element in tourist guidance education.

Future Trends and Innovations in Tourist Guidance Education

Emerging trends and innovations in artificial intelligence (AI) are increasingly shaping the trajectory of tourist guidance education. A salient development lies in the use of advanced AI algorithms for personalized learning experiences, allowing students to acquire a nuanced understanding of diverse tourist destinations (Drissi et al., 2024; Yang et al., 2023). Integrating natural language processing (NLP) mechanisms into educational platforms facilitates enhanced linguistic proficiency (Grassini, 2023; Saif et al., 2024), enabling future tourist guides to engage with a broad spectrum of global visitors.

Furthermore, the imminent incorporation of virtual reality (VR), augmented reality (AR), and mixed reality (MR) technologies into tourist guidance education is poised to revolutionize pedagogical methodologies (Ergen, 2020; Rangel-de Lázaro & Duart, 2023). These immersive technologies offer simulated environments, fostering experiential learning and giving aspirants a realistic preview of their future roles. The dynamic interplay of AI, VR, AR, and MR promises to cultivate a cohort of tourist guides adept at navigating the intricacies of diverse cultural environments (Dogru et al., 2023; Mandalia, 2023).

As AI technologies evolve, the potential ramifications for tourist guidance education extend beyond conventional classroom settings. E-learning modules driven by AI algorithms can dynamically adapt to individual learning styles, thereby ensuring optimal knowledge absorption (Kallou et al., 2023; Quiroz-Fabra et al., 2022). Additionally, the advent of predictive analytics in AI holds promise for tailoring educational content based on anticipated industry demands, thereby preemptively addressing evolving tourist preferences and trends (Adeyinka-Ojo et al., 2020; Bilotta et al., 2021; Demir et al., 2022).

CONCLUSION

In reviewing the current landscape of tourist guidance education, it is evident that traditional methodologies are gradually becoming transformative paradigms fueled by technological advancements. The pedagogical approach has historically been didactics, relying on textbooks and instructor-led classes. However, the emergent education system is characterized by a shift toward experiential learning, with a notable surge in demand for immersive, technology-driven educational modules (Pretorius, 2023; Soliman, 2022). This shift is emblematic of a broader trend in education, reflecting an acknowledgment of the need for dynamic, engaging formats that resonate with contemporary learners (Alvarez & Palmero, 2022; Brooks, 2023).

Artificial intelligence (AI) within tourist guidance education signifies a pivotal inflection point. Historically confined to automation and data analysis, AI has become an educational catalyst, leveraging machine learning algorithms to facilitate adaptive and individualized learning experiences (Demir et al., 2023). This evolution is emblematic of a paradigm shift in which the infusion of AI augments the pedagogical efficacy of tourist guidance education, transcending conventional boundaries (Balula et al., 2019; Stewart & Gorman, 2024).

The integration of AI in tourist guidance education is multifaceted, manifesting in various dimensions of the learning process. Natural language processing (NLP) algorithms contribute to linguistic proficiency, enabling aspirants to communicate effectively in diverse global contexts (Dalgıç et al., 2024; Skavronskaya et al. 2023). Moreover, virtual, augmented, and mixed-reality technologies afford immersive, simulated environments that foster experiential learning. Combining these elements not only enhances the comprehensiveness of educational content but also engenders a more intuitive and dynamic learning experience for prospective tourist guides (Demir & Demir, 2023a).

The benefits of integrating AI into tourist guide education need to be evaluated both in terms of academic learning outcomes and efficiency in achieving institutional goals. Personalized learning algorithms facilitate adaptive curricula by tailoring educational content to learners' needs and preferences (Demir et al., 2023; Shi et al., 2022). The dynamic nature of AI-driven educational platforms accommodates varying learning styles, thus optimizing knowledge acquisition (Balula et al., 2019; Xu et al., 2022). Furthermore, incorporating predictive analytics ensures that curricula remain attuned to evolving industry demands, equipping learners with anticipatory skills to navigate the complexities of the tourism sector (Deng & Benckendorff, 2022; Xu et al., 2022).

However, this transformative wave is not devoid of challenges and concerns (Koo et al., 2021; Yallop et al., 2023). Ethical considerations, privacy issues, and the potential for overreliance on AI-driven systems are salient concerns that warrant meticulous attention (Ivanov & Soliman, 2023; Limna & Kraiwanit, 2023). Striking a balance between technological integration and preserving the ethical tenets inherent to tourist guidance is imperative to preclude inadvertent repercussions. These challenges and concerns demonstrate the limitations of fully integrating AI into tourism guidance.

Looking ahead, the continued evolution of AI technologies is poised to shape future trends and innovations in tourist guidance education (Demir & Demir, 2023b). Predictive analytics will likely be more prominent in forecasting industry trends and guiding educational institutions in tailoring curricula to meet emerging demands (Avgeli et al., 2020; Femenia-Serra, 2018). As AI technologies advance, the synthesis of linguistic proficiency, immersive experiences, and predictive analytics promises to furnish a cadre of tourist guides uniquely adept at navigating the intricacies of an ever-evolving global tourism landscape. In conclusion, integrating AI into tourist guidance education represents a transformative trajectory that transcends conventional pedagogical norms. The benefits accrued and the imperative need to address ethical concerns position AI as an indispensable ally in shaping a cadre of tourist guides equipped to meet the challenges of an increasingly dynamic and interconnected global tourism industry.

Theoretical Implications

The theoretical implications of integrating AI into higher education institutions' tourist guidance education herald a paradigmatic shift in pedagogical frameworks. The benefits of AI-driven educational platforms underscore their potential for enhancing theoretical underpinnings. Individualized learning algorithms, an intrinsic facet of AI, offer theoretical enrichment by tailoring curricula to students' diverse needs and aptitudes. This adaptability ensures that theoretical foundations are fortified through individualized instruction, accommodating learning styles and preferences.

This innovative approach to education represents a departure from traditional methods, ushering in a new era in which intelligent systems play a pivotal role in shaping the skills and knowledge of future tourism professionals. By incorporating AI into tourism guidance education, researchers can delve into uncharted territory by examining the multifaceted impacts on learning outcomes, student engagement, and the overall efficacy of educational programs. This integration addresses a notable gap in the literature, where limited research has explored the intersection of AI and tourism guidance education. The conventional educational landscape often overlooks the potential benefits of AI in enhancing the learning experience for students pursuing careers in tourism. Filling this void in the literature becomes imperative as the tourism industry evolves, demanding a workforce with the latest technological skills and knowledge. Scholars can bridge this gap by elucidating the theoretical underpinnings of AI integration in tourism education and providing valuable insights into the transformative effects on pedagogical approaches and learning outcomes.

Furthermore, the theoretical implications of AI in tourism guidance education lay the foundation for future research endeavors. This integration is a reference point for scholars seeking to explore various facets of AI's impact on education, including curriculum development, adaptive learning technologies, and the evolving role of educators in a technologically driven environment. Researchers can build upon the existing knowledge base by establishing a theoretical framework, guiding future investigations into the nuanced dynamics between AI and tourism education.

However, the challenges and concerns introduced by the incorporation of AI in tourist guidance education necessitate a reevaluation of existing theoretical frameworks. Ethical considerations surrounding data privacy and algorithmic biases demand a theoretical lens that scrutinizes the intersection of AI and ethical imperatives. Theoretical exploration is imperative to devise frameworks that address the ethical dimensions of AI implementation, ensuring that the theoretical underpinnings align with the principles of fairness, transparency, and accountability.

Practical Implications

Integrating artificial intelligence (AI) into tourism guidance education has numerous practical implications for educators, students, and educational institutions. First, AI is a valuable tool for educators to enhance teaching methodologies and streamline administrative tasks. With AI-driven platforms, educators can create personalized learning experiences, adapt curriculum content based on student performance, and gain insights into individual learning patterns. This enables educators to focus more on facilitating meaningful student interactions and fostering a collaborative and engaging learning environment.

Incorporating AI into tourism guidance education provides students with a dynamic and adaptive learning experience. AI-powered tools can offer personalized recommendations, interactive simulations, and real-world scenarios that mimic the complexities of the tourism industry. This not only caters to diverse learning styles but also equips students with the practical skills and knowledge needed in the rapidly evolving field of tourism. Additionally, AI can assist in career guidance, helping students explore various job opportunities within the tourism sector and align their skills with industry demands.

Educational institutions benefit from the integration of AI by gaining efficiency in administrative tasks, resource allocation, and curriculum development. AI analytics can provide insights into student performance, enabling institutions to make data-driven decisions to enhance educational outcomes. Furthermore, AI-driven virtual assistants and chatbots can support administrative staff in addressing queries, facilitating smoother communication, and ensuring a more streamlined educational experience. This not only contributes to academic discourse but also serves as a roadmap for educators, policymakers, and industry stakeholders navigating the evolving landscape of tourism guidance education in an AI-infused era.

In conclusion, on the practical front, educational institutions are expected to optimize resources and enhance educational outcomes, contingent upon strategic measures to address challenges. However, from a negative perspective, integrating AI into tourism guidance education poses challenges and concerns. One primary concern is the potential job displacement of educators due to the automation of certain teaching tasks. There is also a risk of overreliance on AI, leading to a lack of human connection in education. In addition, ethical concerns regarding data privacy and the use of AI algorithms in decision-making processes may arise. Mitigating concerns related to data privacy and algorithmic biases requires the practical implementation of robust ethical frameworks and governance structures. Institutions must proactively address these concerns to uphold the integrity of the educational process. Students must acclimate to the practical nuances of AI-driven learning environments, necessitating adaptability and digital literacy to harness the full potential of AI tools. Striking a balance between the benefits of AI and the preservation of human-centric education is crucial to ensuring a holistic and ethical approach to integrating AI in tourism guidance education.

Limitations and Future Directions

Educational institutions navigating the integration of AI in tourist guidance education must contend with inherent limitations that demand strategic considerations for future development. One notable limitation lies in the potential exacerbation of educational inequalities. The accessibility of AI-driven platforms may depend on technological infrastructure, socioeconomic factors, and regional disparities, thereby perpetuating educational inequalities. Addressing this limitation requires a concerted effort to ensure equitable access to AI resources and foster inclusivity within the educational landscape.

In charting future directions, educational institutions should prioritize refining AI algorithms to mitigate biases and ensure ethical AI application. Furthermore, a more profound integration of experiential learning through virtual reality (VR), augmented reality (AR), and mixed reality (AR) technologies could enhance the practical dimension of tourist guidance education. Collaborative endeavors between academia and industry can also inform curriculum evolution, ensuring alignment with contemporary industry demands. Moreover, fostering a culture of continual learning adaptable to emerging AI technologies is imperative for both institutions and students. This future-oriented approach positions educational institutions to proactively navigate the evolving landscape of AI in tourist guidance education, fostering a dynamic and inclusive learning environment.

REFERENCES

Adeyinka-Ojo, S., Lee, S., Abdullah, S. K., & Teo, J. (2020). Hospitality and tourism education in an emerging digital economy. *Worldwide Hospitality and Tourism Themes, 12*(2), 113–125. doi:10.1108/WHATT-12-2019-0075

Ahmad, S. Z., Bakar, A. R. A., & Ahmad, N. (2018). An evaluation of teaching methods of entrepreneurship in hospitality and tourism programs. *International Journal of Management Education, 16*(1), 14–25. doi:10.1016/j.ijme.2017.11.002

Ali, F. (2023). Let the devil speak for itself: Should ChatGPT be allowed or banned in hospitality and tourism schools? *Journal of Global Hospitality and Tourism, 2*(1), 1–6. doi:10.5038/2771-5957.2.1.1016

Alvarez, A. J., & Palmero, H. (2022). The inner voices of students in asynchronous online learning approach. *International Journal of Social Sciences and Education Research, 8*(2), 148–154. doi:10.24289/ijsser.1065915

Alyasiri, O. M., Selvaraj, K., Younis, H. A., Sahib, T. M., Almasoodi, M. F., & Hayder, I. M. (2024). A Survey on the Potential of Artificial Intelligence Tools in Tourism Information Services. *Babylonian Journal of Artificial Intelligence, 2024*, 1–8. doi:10.58496/BJAI/2024/001

Arcodia, C., Abreu Novais, M., Cavlek, N., & Humpe, A. (2021). Educational tourism and experiential learning: Students' perceptions of field trips. *Tourism Review*, *76*(1), 241–254. doi:10.1108/TR-05-2019-0155

Avgeli, V., Dahlan, M. A., Bakir, A., & Wickens, E. (2020). 4IR Impacts on tourism education and industry. *Journal on Tourism & Sustainability*, *4*(1), 6–15.

Balula, A., Moreira, G., Moreira, A., Kastenholz, E., Eusébio, C., & Breda, Z. (2019). Digital transformation in tourism education. *Tourism in Southern and Eastern Europe*, *5*, 61–72. doi:10.20867/tosee.05.45

Basiri, A., Amirian, P., Winstanley, A., & Moore, T. (2018). Making tourist guidance systems more intelligent, adaptive and personalised using crowd sourced movement data. *Journal of Ambient Intelligence and Humanized Computing*, *9*(2), 413–427. doi:10.1007/s12652-017-0550-0

Battour, M., Mady, K., Salaheldeen, M., Elsotouhy, M., Elbendary, I., & Boğan, E. (2023). AI-enabled technologies to assist Muslim tourists in Halal-friendly tourism. *Journal of Islamic Marketing*, *14*(5), 1291–1309. doi:10.1108/JIMA-01-2022-0001

Benckendorff, P., & Zehrer, A. (2017). The future of teaching and learning in tourism. In *Handbook of teaching and learning in tourism* (pp. 609–626). Edward Elgar Publishing. doi:10.4337/9781784714802.00055

Bilotta, E., Bertacchini, F., Gabriele, L., Giglio, S., Pantano, P. S., & Romita, T. (2021). Industry 4.0 technologies in tourism education: Nurturing students to think with technology. *Journal of Hospitality, Leisure, Sport and Tourism Education*, *29*, 100275. Advance online publication. doi:10.1016/j.jhlste.2020.100275

Bogdanovych, A., Rodríguez-Aguilar, J. A., Simoff, S., & Cohen, A. (2010). Authentic interactive reenactment of cultural heritage with 3D virtual worlds and artificial intelligence. *Applied Artificial Intelligence*, *24*(6), 617–647. doi:10.1080/08839514.2010.492172

Brooks, R. M. (2023). Integrity Through Experience: Fostering a Culture of Academic Integrity Through an Experiential Learning Approach. In *Handbook of Academic Integrity* (pp. 287–303). Springer International Publishing. doi:10.1007/978-3-031-54144-5_94

Bulchand-Gidumal, J. (2022). Impact of artificial intelligence in travel, tourism, and hospitality. In *Handbook of e-Tourism* (pp. 1943–1962). Springer International Publishing. doi:10.1007/978-3-030-48652-5_110

Chandra, S., Ranjan, A., & Chowdhary, N. (2022). Online hospitality and tourism education-issues and challenges. *Tourism (Zagreb), 70*(2), 298–316. doi:10.37741/t.70.2.10

Chatterjee, S., & Bhattacharjee, K. K. (2020). Adoption of artificial intelligence in higher education: A quantitative analysis using structural equation modelling. *Education and Information Technologies, 25*(5), 3443–3463. doi:10.1007/s10639-020-10159-7

Chaturvedi, R., Verma, S., Ali, F., & Kumar, S. (2023). Reshaping Tourist Experience with AI-Enabled Technologies: A Comprehensive Review and Future Research Agenda. *International Journal of Human-Computer Interaction*, 1–17. doi:10.1080/10447318.2023.2238353

Chokur, M. F. S., & Al-Khafaji, S. J. N. (2023). The strategic use of events to revitalize cities: Najaf as a case study. *International Journal of Nonlinear Analysis and Applications, 14*(8), 265–282.

Chon, K. K. S., & Hao, F. (2024). Technological evolution in tourism: A Horizon 2050 perspective. *Tourism Review*. Advance online publication. doi:10.1108/TR-10-2023-0753

Dalgic, A., Demir, M., & Ergen, F. D. (2023). Does Perceived Vulnerability Mediate the Effect of Hotel Employees' Resilience on Mental Health Perceptions? *Tourism (Zagreb), 71*(1), 77–97. doi:10.37741/t.71.1.5

Dalgıç, A., Yaşar, E., & Demir, M. (2023). ChatGPT and learning outcomes in tourism education: The role of digital literacy and individualized learning. *Journal of Hospitality, Leisure, Sport and Tourism Education, 34*, 1–13. doi:10.1016/j.jhlste.2024.100481

Demir, M. (2024). Building Trust and Credibility: Ethical Use of AI in the Service Industry. In M. Demir & A. Dalgic (Eds.), *Revolutionizing the Service Industry With OpenAI Models* (pp. 243–267). IGI Global. doi:10.4018/979-8-3693-1239-1.ch010

Demir, M., & Demir, Ş. Ş. (2023b). Incorporating artificial intelligence into tourism education at universities: Opportunities and challenges. *Scientific Collection. InterConf*, (181), 106–114.

Demir, M., & Demir, Ş. Ş. (2023c). Is ChatGPT the right technology for service individualization and value co-creation? evidence from the travel industry. *Journal of Travel & Tourism Marketing, 40*(5), 383–398. doi:10.1080/10548408.2023.2255884

Demir, M., Demir, Ş. Ş., & Aktürk, O. (2023). The Effects of Distance Education Capabilities and Competencies on Learning Outcomes During COVID-19 in Higher Education Institutions. *Journal of Hospitality & Tourism Education*, 1–12. doi:10.1080/10963758.2023.2191966

Demir, M., Demir, Ş. Ş., & Yaşar, E. (2022). Big data and innovative organizational performance: Evidence from a moderated-mediated model. *Creativity and Innovation Management*, *31*(4), 696–709. doi:10.1111/caim.12525

Demir, Ş. Ş., & Demir, M. (2023a). Professionals' perspectives on ChatGPT in the tourism industry: Does it inspire awe or concern? *Journal of Tourism Theory and Research*, *9*(2), 61–77. doi:10.24288/jttr.1313481

Deng, R., & Benckendorff, P. (2022). Technology-enabled learning. In *Handbook of e-Tourism* (pp. 1687–1713). Springer International Publishing. doi:10.1007/978-3-030-48652-5_129

Deri, M. N., Zaazie, P., & Singh, A. (2023). Digital Future of the Hospitality Industry and Hospitality Education Globally. In *International Handbook of Skill, Education, Learning, and Research Development in Tourism and Hospitality* (pp. 1–23). Springer Nature Singapore.

Dhoundiyal, H., & Mohanty, P. (2022). Artificial intelligence and robotics driving Tourism 4.0: an exploration. In *Handbook of Technology Application in Tourism in Asia* (pp. 1265–1285). Springer Nature Singapore. doi:10.1007/978-981-16-2210-6_57

Dogru, T., Line, N., Hanks, L., Acikgoz, F., Abbott, J. A., Bakir, S., Berbekova, A., Bilgihan, A., Iskender, A., Kizildag, M., Lee, M., Lee, W., McGinley, S., Mody, M., Onder, I., Ozdemir, O., & Suess, C. (2023). The implications of generative artificial intelligence in academic research and higher education in tourism and hospitality. *Tourism Economics*. Advance online publication. doi:10.1177/13548166231204065

Drissi, S., Chefrour, A., Boussaha, K., & Zarzour, H. (2024). Exploring the effects of personalized recommendations on student's motivation and learning achievement in gamified mobile learning framework. *Education and Information Technologies*, 1–38. doi:10.1007/s10639-024-12477-6

Ergen, F. D. (2020). Artırılmış ve sanal gerçeklik teknolojilerinin Isparta ilinin kültürel miras alanlarında uygulanabilirliği üzerine bir literatür taraması. *Journal of Tourism Theory and Research*, *6*(1), 62–74. doi:10.24288/jttr.673593

Farrokhnia, M., Banihashem, S. K., Noroozi, O., & Wals, A. (2023). A SWOT analysis of ChatGPT: Implications for educational practice and research. *Innovations in Education and Teaching International*, *60*, 1–15. doi:10.1080/14703297.2023.2195846

Femenia-Serra, F. (2018). Smart tourism destinations and higher tourism education in Spain. Are we ready for this new management approach? In *Information and Communication Technologies in Tourism 2018: Proceedings of the International Conference in Jönköping, Sweden, January 24-26, 2018* (pp. 437-449). Springer International Publishing.

Ghany, S. Y. A., & Latif, M. M. A. (2012). English language preparation of tourism and hospitality undergraduates in Egypt: Does it meet their future workplace requirements? *Journal of Hospitality, Leisure, Sport and Tourism Education*, *11*(2), 93–100. doi:10.1016/j.jhlste.2012.05.001

Grassini, S. (2023). Shaping the future of education: Exploring the potential and consequences of AI and ChatGPT in educational settings. *Education Sciences*, *13*(7), 692. Advance online publication. doi:10.3390/educsci13070692

Gupta, S., Gupta, N., & Chauhan, P. (2022). Controlling the uncontrolled: Over tourism in hill stations of Northern India. *Journal of Positive School Psychology*, 6549–6568.

Hammady, R., Ma, M., Al-Kalha, Z., & Strathearn, C. (2021). A framework for constructing and evaluating the role of MR as a holographic virtual guide in museums. *Virtual Reality (Waltham Cross)*, *25*(4), 895–918. doi:10.1007/s10055-020-00497-9

Hsu, C. H. (2018). Tourism education on and beyond the horizon. *Tourism Management Perspectives*, *25*, 181–183. doi:10.1016/j.tmp.2017.11.022

Huang, Q., & Xia, L. (2016). Inspection of Spatial–Temporal Behavior of Backpackers in Beijing Based on Trajectory. *Wireless Personal Communications*, *87*(4), 1337–1356. doi:10.1007/s11277-015-3056-0

Hung, P. K., Liang, R. H., Ma, S. Y., & Kong, B. W. (2024). Exploring the experience of traveling to familiar places in VR: An empirical study using google earth VR. *International Journal of Human-Computer Interaction*, *40*(2), 255–277. doi:10.1080/10447318.2022.2114141

Ivanov, S., & Soliman, M. (2023). Game of algorithms: ChatGPT implications for the future of tourism education and research. *Journal of Tourism Futures*, *9*(2), 1–8. doi:10.1108/JTF-02-2023-0038

Ivanova, M. (2019). Robots, artificial intelligence, and service automation in travel agencies and tourist information centers. In Robots, Artificial Intelligence, And Service Automation In Travel, Tourism And Hospitality (pp. 221-237). Emerald Publishing Limited. doi:10.1108/978-1-78756-687-320191011

Jia, S., Chi, O. H., Martinez, S. D., & Lu, L. (2023). When "Old" Meets "New": Unlocking the Future of Innovative Technology Implementation in Heritage Tourism. *Journal of Hospitality & Tourism Research (Washington, D.C.)*. Advance online publication. doi:10.1177/10963480231205767

Kalbaska, N., & Cantoni, L. (2022). e-Learning in tourism education. In Handbook of e-Tourism (pp. 1667-1686). Cham: Springer International Publishing.

Kallou, S., Kikilia, A., Kalogiannakis, M., & Zacharis, N. Z. (2023). Emotional intelligence development: The implementation of transformative learning through digital technologies in tourism-a study protocol. *International Journal of Technology Enhanced Learning*, *15*(2), 180–194. doi:10.1504/IJTEL.2023.130112

Keçi, I., & Qosja, E. (2021). Tourism Education During the Pandemic: Is Distance Education a Solution? In Handbook of Research on the Impacts and Implications of COVID-19 on the Tourism Industry (pp. 863-884). IGI Global.

Kiryakova, G., & Angelova, N. (2023). ChatGPT—A Challenging Tool for the University Professors in Their Teaching Practice. *Education Sciences*, *13*(10), 1056. doi:10.3390/educsci13101056

Koo, C., Xiang, Z., Gretzel, U., & Sigala, M. (2021). Artificial intelligence (AI) and robotics in travel, hospitality and leisure. *Electronic Markets*, *31*(3), 473–476. doi:10.1007/s12525-021-00494-z PMID:35603226

Lampoltshammer, T. J., Wallinger, S., & Scholz, J. (2023). Bridging Disciplinary Divides through Computational Social Sciences and Transdisciplinarity in Tourism Education in Higher Educational Institutions: An Austrian Case Study. *Sustainability (Basel)*, *15*(10), 8133. Advance online publication. doi:10.3390/su15108133

Lim, M. Y., & Aylett, R. (2009). An emergent emotion model for an affective mobile guide with attitude. *Applied Artificial Intelligence*, *23*(9), 835–854. doi:10.1080/08839510903246518

Limna, P., & Kraiwanit, T. (2023). The role of chatgpt on customer service in the hospitality industry: An exploratory study of hospitality workers' experiences and perceptions. *Tourism and Hospitality Management*, *29*(4), 583–592. doi:10.20867/thm.29.4.9

Lin, W. R., Lee, S. S., & Huang, W. S. (2023). A scale for measuring tourists' technological competence. *Journal of Hospitality and Tourism Technology*, *14*(5), 802–814. doi:10.1108/JHTT-09-2021-0276

Lo, C. K. (2023). What Is the Impact of ChatGPT on Education? A Rapid Review of the Literature. *Education Sciences*, *13*(4), 410. doi:10.3390/educsci13040410

Mandalia, S. (2023). Tourism Education in the Digital Era: Navigating Innovation and Transformation. In *International Conference on Social Science and Education (ICoeSSE 2023)* (pp. 509-530). Atlantis Press. 10.2991/978-2-38476-142-5_48

Morellato, M. (2014). Digital competence in tourism education: Cooperative-experiential learning. *Journal of Teaching in Travel & Tourism*, *14*(2), 184–209. doi:10.1080/15313220.2014.907959

Najbrt, L., & Kapounova, J. (2015). Personalized Guide through Educational Exhibition: Fuzzy Expert System as Museum Exhibition "Virtual Guide". *Journal of Education and Human Development*, *4*(1), 159–170. doi:10.15640/jehd.v4n1a15

Pretorius, A. (2023). A Pedagogy to Support Learning Analytics: A Case for a Specific Higher Education Institution. In *Handbook of Research on AI and Machine Learning Applications in Customer Support and Analytics* (pp. 56–79). IGI Global. doi:10.4018/978-1-6684-7105-0.ch004

Puig, A., Rodríguez, I., Arcos, J. L., Rodríguez-Aguilar, J. A., Cebrián, S., Bogdanovych, A., Morera, N., Palomo, A., & Piqué, R. (2020). Lessons learned from supplementing archaeological museum exhibitions with virtual reality. *Virtual Reality (Waltham Cross)*, *24*(2), 343–358. doi:10.1007/s10055-019-00391-z

Quiroz-Fabra, J., Valencia-Arias, A., Londoño-Celis, W., & García-Pineda, V. (2022). Technological tools for knowledge apprehension and promotion in the cultural and heritage tourism sector: Systematic literature review. *Human Behavior and Emerging Technologies*, *2022*, 1–12. doi:10.1155/2022/2851044

Rangel-de Lázaro, G., & Duart, J. M. (2023). You Can Handle, You Can Teach It: Systematic Review on the Use of Extended Reality and Artificial Intelligence Technologies for Online Higher Education. *Sustainability (Basel)*, *15*(4), 3507. Advance online publication. doi:10.3390/su15043507

Saif, N., Khan, S. U., Shaheen, I., ALotaibi, F. A., Alnfiai, M. M., & Arif, M. (2024). Chat-GPT; validating Technology Acceptance Model (TAM) in education sector via ubiquitous learning mechanism. *Computers in Human Behavior*, *154*, 108097. Advance online publication. doi:10.1016/j.chb.2023.108097

Shi, J., Cai, L. A., & Wolfe, K. (2022). Advancing hospitality and tourism education and research through global crises. *Journal of Teaching in Travel & Tourism, 22*(3), 199–204. doi:10.1080/15313220.2022.2110550

Skavronskaya, L., Hadinejad, A., & Cotterell, D. (2023). Reversing the threat of artificial intelligence to opportunity: A discussion of ChatGPT in tourism education. *Journal of Teaching in Travel & Tourism, 23*(2), 253–258. doi:10.1080/15313220.2023.2196658

Soliman, M. (2022). Pedagogical Intelligence in Virtual Reality Environments. In *Learning with Technologies and Technologies in Learning: Experience, Trends and Challenges in Higher Education* (pp. 285–302). Springer International Publishing. doi:10.1007/978-3-031-04286-7_14

Stewart, J., & Gorman, C. (2024). Authentic Assessment and Embedding Sustainable Literacy and Technology Skills in Tourism Education. *Irish Journal of Academic Practice, 11*(2). https://arrow.tudublin.ie/ijap/vol11/iss2/10

Tolkach, D., & Pratt, S. (2021). Travel Professors: A YouTube channel about tourism education & research. *Journal of Hospitality, Leisure, Sport and Tourism Education, 28*, 100307. Advance online publication. doi:10.1016/j.jhlste.2021.100307 PMID:36569348

Tuo, Y., Ning, L., & Zhu, A. (2021). How artificial intelligence will change the future of tourism industry: The practice in China. In *Information and Communication Technologies in Tourism 2021: Proceedings of the ENTER 2021 eTourism Conference, January 19–22, 2021* (pp. 83-94). Springer International Publishing.

Ülkü, A. (2023). Artificial intelligence-based large language models and integrity of exams and assignments in higher education: The case of tourism courses. *Tourism & Management Studies, 19*(4), 21–34. doi:10.18089/tms.2023.190402

Wachtel, G., Schmöcker, J. D., Hadas, Y., Gao, Y., Nahum, O. E., & Ben-Moshe, B. (2021). Planning for tourist urban evacuation routes: A framework for improving the data collection and evacuation processes. *Environment and Planning. B, Urban Analytics and City Science, 48*(5), 1108–1125. doi:10.1177/2399808321994575

Wu, R., & Yu, Z. (2023). Do AI chatbots improve students learning outcomes? Evidence from a meta-analysis. *British Journal of Educational Technology*, 1–24. doi:10.1111/bjet.13334

Xu, J., Tavitiyaman, P., Kim, H. J., & Lo, S. K. J. (2022). Hospitality and tourism higher education in the post-COVID era: Is it time to change? *Journal of Hospitality & Tourism Education, 34*(4), 278–290. doi:10.1080/10963758.2022.2056044

Yallop, A. C., Gică, O. A., Moisescu, O. I., Coroş, M. M., & Séraphin, H. (2023). The digital traveller: Implications for data ethics and data governance in tourism and hospitality. *Journal of Consumer Marketing*, *40*(2), 155–170. doi:10.1108/JCM-12-2020-4278

Yang, Y., Shang, H., Jamal, N., & Ullah, F. (2023). Video resources recommendation for online tourism teaching in interactive network. *Mobile Networks and Applications*, *28*(3), 1–12. doi:10.1007/s11036-023-02193-9

Yaşar, E., & Gafar, B. Ü. (2024). Metaphorical perceptions of undergraduate tourism students towards the concepts of English and Professional English: The case of Türkiye-Spain. *Journal of Tourism Theory and Research*, *10*(1), 1–11. doi:10.24288/jttr.1269672

Yuan, H., Qian, Y., Yang, R., & Ren, M. (2014). Human mobility discovering and movement intention detection with GPS trajectories. *Decision Support Systems*, *63*, 39–51. doi:10.1016/j.dss.2013.09.010

ADDITIONAL READING

Carvalho, I., & Ivanov, S. (2024). ChatGPT for tourism: applications, benefits and risks. *Tourism Review*, *79*(2), 290-303.

Demir, M., Dalgıç, A., & Yaşar, E. (2022). How Perceived Overqualification Affects Task Performance and Proactive Behavior: The Role of Digital Competencies and Job Crafting. *International Journal of Hospitality & Tourism Administration*, 1–23. doi:10.1080/15256480.2022.2135665

Demir, M., Yaşar, E., & Demir, Ş. Ş. (2023). Digital transformation and human resources planning: The mediating role of innovation. *Journal of Hospitality and Tourism Technology*, *14*(1), 21–36. doi:10.1108/JHTT-04-2021-0105

Jia, S., Chi, O. H., Martinez, S. D., & Lu, L. (2023). When "Old" Meets "New": Unlocking the Future of Innovative Technology Implementation in Heritage Tourism. *Journal of Hospitality & Tourism Research (Washington, D.C.)*. Advance online publication. doi:10.1177/10963480231205767

Shin, H., & Kang, J. (2023). Bridging the gap of bibliometric analysis: The evolution, current state, and future directions of tourism research using ChatGPT. *Journal of Hospitality and Tourism Management*, *57*, 40–47. doi:10.1016/j.jhtm.2023.09.001

KEY TERMS AND DEFINITIONS

Artificial Intelligence (AI): Refers to developing and implementing computer systems that can perform tasks typically requiring human intelligence. This encompasses various subfields, including machine learning, computer vision, and natural language processing, aiming to simulate cognitive functions within machines.

Augmented Reality (AR): Integrates computer-generated content with the real-world environment, enhancing the user's perception by overlaying digital information onto their physical surroundings. AR applications provide an augmented view of reality, blending virtual elements seamlessly with the user's immediate surroundings.

ChatGPT: Is an instance of artificial intelligence, specifically a language model, developed by OpenAI. It leverages the GPT-3.5 architecture to generate human-like text responses conversationally. The model is trained on diverse internet text, allowing it to understand and generate contextually relevant and coherent responses.

Extended Reality (XR): Is an umbrella term encompassing virtual reality (VR), augmented reality (AR), and mixed reality (MR). XR technologies aim to extend human perception and interaction by merging the physical and virtual worlds, providing a spectrum of immersive experiences.

Mixed Reality (MR): Is a continuum combining virtual and augmented reality elements, allowing users to interact with digital and physical objects in a unified environment. MR experiences integrate virtual and real-world elements in real time, creating a dynamic and interactive user interface.

Natural Language Processing (NLP): Is a subfield of artificial intelligence that focuses on the interaction between computers and human language. NLP involves the development of algorithms and models to enable machines to understand, interpret, and generate human-like language, facilitating communication between humans and computers.

Tourist Guidance Education: Involves the instructional processes designed to impart knowledge and skills to individuals who guide and assist tourists. It encompasses a comprehensive approach to educating tourist guides, covering cultural, historical, and practical aspects to enhance their ability to facilitate meaningful and informed tourist experiences.

Tourist Guide: Is a trained professional who provides assistance, information, and interpretation to individuals or groups visiting various locations. This role involves conveying historical, cultural, and geographical knowledge to enhance the understanding and enjoyment of tourists during their explorations.

Virtual Reality (VR): Refers to a computer-generated environment that simulates a realistic experience, often through specialized hardware such as headsets. Users immersed in VR environments can interact with and navigate through computer-generated spaces, creating a sense of presence and immersion.

Chapter 6
Transforming Education With the Power of Artificial Intelligence:
Case Studies

E. Ivette Cota-Rivera
https://orcid.org/0009-0002-6240-9269
Universidad Politécnica de Baja California, Mexico

Martha Elena González Correa
https://orcid.org/0009-0000-6073-9585
Universidad Politécnica de Baja California, Mexico

Luis Antonio Bernal Marín
Universidad Politécnica de Baja California, Mexico

María Ysabel Marquez Montenegro
Universidad Politécnica de Baja California, Mexico

Abelardo Mercado Herrera
Universidad Politécnica de Baja California, Mexico

Martha Angelica Angelica Martinez Martinez
Universidad Politécnica de Baja California, Mexico

ABSTRACT

Artificial intelligence has had a significant impact on education, particularly owing to its ability to personalize students' learning experiences. AI-driven adaptive systems ensure that education aligns with each student's unique learning styles and abilities by analyzing their strengths and weaknesses, adapting content to their pace and specific needs. This encompasses a range of applications, from intelligent tutoring systems that provide real-time guidance to personalized content recommendations. In addition to fostering engagement and motivation, this approach enhances students' comprehension and retention. The learning process of university students is influenced

DOI: 10.4018/979-8-3693-1666-5.ch006

by numerous distractions, educators face the challenge of identifying pedagogical strategies that are both attractive and effective in achieving educational goals. This chapter explores the possibilities of AI in higher education and how it can enhance the creation of audiovisual materials, mentoring, and information dissemination for students and administrative staff.

INTRODUCTION

Education is undergoing a profound paradigm shift as the Fourth Industrial Revolution unfolds. Artificial Intelligence (AI) has played a pivotal role in transforming traditional models into personalized, data-driven, and adaptive approaches. The integration of AI has become a central driver for innovation, promising to reshape pedagogical approaches, administrative functions, student outcomes, and educational inclusivity. Furthermore, AI tools benefit not only students but also educators. The administrative workload of teachers has been reduced thanks to Natural Language Processing (NLP) algorithms, which assist in grading assignments and essays, as well as providing immediate feedback to students. Classroom management is streamlined through virtual platforms equipped with AI-driven chatbots that respond to student queries. This allows instructors to focus more on instruction and less on logistics, enabling educators to create a more user-friendly, enriched, and efficient teaching environment.

Artificial intelligence plays an increasingly significant role in assessing and evaluating student performance. Natural Language Processing (NLP) and machine learning have driven automatic essay scoring systems, ensuring consistent and efficient grading while providing students with immediate feedback on their performance. In standardized testing, AI-driven assessment tools provide more precise and comprehensive evaluations, adapting to individual skill levels, thus offering more accurate and comprehensive assessments. These advancements aim to create fairer and more reliable assessments to improve educational outcomes.

AI has the potential to bridge gaps in education by addressing issues of inclusivity and accessibility. Speech recognition technologies enable transcription services for students with hearing impairments, while AI-driven language translation tools break down language barriers, facilitating global collaboration and understanding. AI-guided interventions can identify and support students with learning disabilities, making education more inclusive and equitable. In the context of Animation and Visual Effects Engineering, AI is employed in the subject "Art History and Animation." AI structures topics and engages students through virtual tours and virtual reality (VR) resources, creating meaningful learning experiences by connecting prior knowledge with new information.

This chapter aims to demonstrate the utilization of tools provided by new technologies to facilitate meaningful learning, anchoring experiences to prior knowledge and integrating them into cognitive interaction, fostering sustained interest among students. AI systems are also utilized to create customized tutors for class-related inquiries, streamline administrative tasks, generate assessment tools, and provide personalized mentoring to students.

BACKGROUND

History And Evolution

The term "artificial intelligence" serves as an umbrella for various techniques such as machine learning, deep learning, and natural language processing. This chapter will analyze all possible artificial intelligence techniques that contribute to teaching methods within the traditional education paradigm. After conducting a thorough review and detailed analysis of scientific and professional papers, several relevant ones were found in the field of AI in education.

Goksel & Bozkurt (2019), in their research, presented the impact of AI on the role of teachers and educators in the future, such as personalized attention to students, allowing educators to concentrate on addressing the unique requirements of individual students by analyzing individual needs and educational preferences. Additionally, AI frees up valuable time for teachers to focus on teaching and mentoring students by automating tasks like grading and scheduling. Furthermore, AI plays a highly important role in the professional development of teachers as it provides valuable opportunities for them to improve their teaching methods and stay current with educational practices. Regarding student support, artificial intelligence allows teachers to offer specialized tools to students facing additional learning challenges. Finally, AI provides a wide variety of educational resources, fostering collaboration among educators and empowering them, thus creating an educational network full of resources.

In their study, Roll & Wylie (2016) identified the need for both evolutionary and revolutionary processes in the field of Artificial Intelligence in Education (AIED). Priority is given to balancing existing frameworks and enhancing the role of intelligent learning environments in education. The study aims to lead education in the 21st century and highlights the potential influence of these procedures on education over the next 25 years. This is done with the intention of spearheading education in the 21st century by considering current research approaches in AIED and making the necessary modifications to meet the ever-evolving needs of students and teachers.

In line with current society, education undergoes the collateral effects of technological transformation. It seems that artificial intelligence replaces certain tasks and facilitates the resolution of everyday problems, improving our time management, creating academic resources, information analysis, communications, and many other areas of the academic experience. However, this technological transformation, while revolutionizing and increasing processing speed, confronts us with the limitations of our species. It highlights that human intelligence is a scarce and very limited asset, capable of identifying problems, formulating questions, obtaining data, analyzing information, producing knowledge, and reaching a synthesis we can call wisdom. It depends on countless factors and does not always have a positive application in all aspects of humanity.

The transformation we are experiencing is of such importance that it is only comparable to when humans developed the ability to leave a written speech record. The complexity of written language goes hand in hand with the development of societies to the extent that the flourishing or decline of civilizations largely depends on their ability to read and write (Van Doren, 2022). And this knowledge was always elitist: it only spread to a few scribes, later clerics, as many fundamental matters depended on it, such as chronicles, records, orders, and accounting reports. Those who could master written language found a way to transcend socially, find wealth, and access power. The establishment of power is solidified in writing, validating and imposing the historical version of those who compile the record and, in turn, hold power.

As a technology, the ability to encode sounds into phonemes and words into ideograms is a milestone of human intelligence. In Mesopotamia, the first form of primitive writing was developed 8000 years before our era (Van Doren, 2022), which evolved into cuneiform writing around 3100 BCE. The Phoenicians are credited with the invention of a standardized alphabet 1100 years after our era. The Greeks developed vowels, resulting in the alphabet most similar to the one we currently use. Ancient Sumerian, Egyptian, Hebrew, and Chinese are not alphabetic scripts; they use thousands of different signs to represent sounds with various meanings (Van Doren, 2022).

The discussion of written languages in this chapter is relevant because written language reflects an abstraction capacity that allows the recording of one's own thoughts, ways of acting, and, in essence, allows the recording of thought. The Greeks were the ones who discovered that writing is a means to think in an orderly manner and build knowledge. Perhaps faced with the inescapable fact that we are constantly distracted, perpetually absorbed in concerns stemming from our modes of existence, it may be that - as humanity - we find it very challenging to embrace the changes and challenges posed by new technologies. To some extent, we mistrust progress, viewing the new with suspicion as a mechanism that could lead to exploitation or accentuate inequality and inequity.

Regarding the past, it is worth remembering that the acquisition of new technologies has been costly and slow, claiming the lives of thousands and, initially, as it is today, relying on forms of exploitation, not overlooking that it has been the privilege of a few. The democratization of access to new technologies is only true to the extent that one can access them, with everyone having the necessary tools and technology, along with the relevant training to use them. Otherwise, we will remain in technological obscurity and fall victim to our ignorance while new inequalities and technological gaps emerge.

Let us not lose sight of the fact that humans have generated knowledge for thousands of years. In this process, we have gained and lost portions of that knowledge, which has been employed for altruistic purposes and also for annihilation. Therefore, as humans think, record their thoughts, draw conclusions, correlate facts and effects, scientifically understand the natural world, and, of course, develop technologies, alongside all these processes, they define themselves, understand themselves, and recognize that they are part of a tumultuous, rhizomatic historical process that advances, retreats, and stagnates simultaneously. Perhaps an analysis of all this will help navigate the paradigm shifts that lie ahead.

PERSONALIZED LEARNING WITH AI

Personalized education supported by artificial intelligence has become a driving force for educational transformation, providing adaptive learning experiences that focus on the individualized requirements of students. The integration of artificial intelligence has become increasingly important in the educational domain, offering a more personalized and efficient approach to learning. Artificial intelligence can develop strategies for both teaching and creating educational resources that adapt precisely to the learning needs of each student. This is achieved by employing advanced algorithms and data analysis to understand the specific preferences, challenges, and progress of everyone.

AI can provide immediate feedback and make real-time adjustments that enable educators and students to identify areas for improvement. This fosters a more inclusive educational environment where individual differences are addressed, promoting the success of each student. In this context, personalized learning with artificial intelligence redefines the educational paradigm, enhancing educators' ability to address the specific needs of each student and providing students with the necessary tools to develop their maximum potential in an increasingly digitized world.

In the educational field, various artificial intelligence tools enhance learning and personalize student experiences. Among the main tools are:

Virtual Tutor

The virtual tutor is a computer-based learning system grounded in artificial intelligence, capable of providing the student with a personalized and adaptive learning environment (Carbonell, 1970). It can monitor the student's progress, provide feedback and suggestions, as well as structured and temporary support in developing new skills and acquiring new concepts. These systems can model students' psychological states, including motivation, emotion, knowledge, and previous knowledge, skills, and preferences (Lin et al., 2023).

According to Tong et al., AI can provide adaptive learning according to the individual circumstances of each student, Selecting the most suitable learning path that adjusts with the students' learning capabilities. Moreover, virtual tutors developed using AI offer high-quality support and can reduce costs generated by extracurricular tutoring. These virtual tutors are adaptive learning systems that prioritize independent learning and responding after class instead of focusing on traditional classroom teaching. They store extensive homework data and corresponding answers, continually accumulating additional homework consistent with the school's progress. Additionally, the combination of online courses and artificial intelligence provides a pleasant virtual school environment with the support of a virtual assistant, offering a course free from location and time restrictions, extending the learning process to any moment and place (Tong et al., 2019).

Adaptive Learning Systems

Adaptive learning is an instructional approach that leverages computerized systems to collect student performance data while interacting with educational content. It incorporates artificial intelligence and technology to personalize each student's learning experience. This data makes content delivery personalized, incorporating supplementary activities and targeted explanations based on identified areas that require reinforcement. This customization is facilitated by the system's ability to discern the individual strengths and weaknesses of each student, along with their preferred learning styles. Adaptive learning is a non-linear method in online instruction that tailors itself to the evolving needs of students as they navigate course content. It creates a personalized experience for learners by considering their prior knowledge. This concept is gaining prominence in the realm of online learning.

Enhancing this approach involves employing a structure that categorizes learners based on their distinct preferences and learning styles, suggesting content accordingly

(Ibrahim & Hamada, 2016). This is facilitated by technologies that dynamically adjust to the learner's proficiency level and the nature of course content, frequently utilizing artificial intelligence (Capuano & Caballé, 2020). Moreover, adaptive learning represents an individualized strategy, tailoring the learning experience to cater to individual needs and abilities (Shelle et al., 2018). Teachers can gather information about their students' progress, thanks to adaptive learning systems. With this data, they can suggest the best learning path tailored to their abilities and provide them with online materials to complete the learning curve. Additionally, the use of human-computer interaction technology associated with artificial intelligence becomes highly useful, especially when problems cannot be addressed in person. This technology can assist students in responding to online queries.

According to Orduño (2024) artificial intelligence (AI) systems possess significant potential to revolutionize the field of education. By utilizing AI algorithms and approaches, these applications can offer tailored and adaptable learning experiences. They adjust educational content and exercises according to the unique requirements of each learner, utilizing their capacity to analyze extensive datasets, identify patterns, and offer valuable insights into student performance. This, in turn, facilitates swift feedback, thereby enhancing the overall learning process.

Educational Virtual Assistants

Educational virtual assistants, also recognized as personal assistants within a Virtual Education Space (VES), represent intelligent entities that offer a context-aware interface for users (Todorov, 2018). Their utility extends to aiding students in time management, task prioritization, and motivation, proving especially beneficial for first-year students (Gubareva, 2020). Furthermore, these assistants find application in e-learning environments, facilitating access to courses, self-evaluation modules, and communication tools (Douidi, 2007). In secondary school settings, virtual teaching assistants can contribute to exam reviews, after-school tutoring, automated grading, and student performance reporting, although their design should emphasize support for teachers rather than displacement (Audras, 2022).

Numerous studies have delved into the integration of educational virtual assistants within e-learning environments. Douidi (2007) introduced AVUNET, an educational server incorporating self-evaluation and communication features. Todorov (2018) explored the role of personal assistants in a Virtual Education Space, emphasizing their contributions to the learning process. Geoffroy (2002) presented a virtual assistant for web-based training in engineering education, sharing responsibilities in training and evaluation with real assistants. Ivanova (2017) advocated for the incorporation of intelligent assistants in a VES designed for lifelong learning, highlight their role in expanding the learning space. Collectively, these studies underscore the considerable potential of educational virtual assistants in augmenting the overall learning experience.

Automated Assessment Systems

Automated Assessment Systems (AAS) are computer-based tools that evaluate and score student work with minimal human input (Rashid, 2016). They are used in various educational contexts, including programming assignments. Rashid (2016) presents a proposed framework of an Automatic Assessment System for learning object-oriented programming language, showing that the assessment system can help students in learning a programming language as well as reduce the lecturer's workload, essay scoring, Automated Essay Scores (AES), defined as the computer technology that evaluates and scores the written prose mainly used to overcome time, cost, reliability, and generalizability issues in writing assessment (Dikli, 2006), and cognitive testing (Stollery, 1996). AAS can help reduce the workload of educators and provide instant feedback to students (Rashid, 2016). They are particularly useful in online examination systems, where they can automatically assess student responses using algorithms for word frequency, keyword matching, and linguistic analysis, Kabir et al. (2020) propose a system with an automatically generated assessment technique. The performance of the system is evaluated with a large number of students, questions, as well as answers. The study found an absolute error of about 0.3% and a relative error of about 3.57%, which is deemed quite satisfactory (Kabir, 2020).

Interactive and Immersive Experiences

With the implementation of virtual reality and augmented reality in classroom education, the boundaries of traditional education have been expanded, enhancing the distribution of educational resources, even in remote regions (Tong et al., 2019). The incorporation of immersive and interactive experiences in education is an escalating trend, presenting substantial advantages for student engagement and learning. Kamal et al. (2019) underscores the pivotal role of these experiences in imparting job-related skills, particularly within the framework of Industry 4.0. They strongly argue that such immersive and interactive educational experiences represent the future of teaching and learning in the universities of their country. Building on this, O'Connor (2018) supports the idea that students immersed in virtual reality environments not only develop trust and camaraderie but also express a willingness to integrate VR applications into their own classrooms. Expanding on the potential of immersive media, including virtual reality, Dede (2009) and Gomez (2020) highlight the capacity of these technologies to enhance education by providing diverse perspectives, fostering situated learning, facilitating knowledge transfer, and creating vivid and emotionally resonant experiences. Collectively, these studies emphasize the transformative potential of interactive and immersive educational experiences, particularly in preparing students for the evolving demands of the future workforce. The dynamic fusion of technology and education emerges as a crucial component in cultivating well-rounded and future-ready learners.

AI-ENHANCED TEACHING

How can education be enhanced through Artificial Intelligence? Developers have created tools that facilitate the creation of lesson plans and content dosages, such as ChatGPT, which is a tool that works with predictive text capabilities, or generative artificial intelligences that, based on a prompt, can create diagrams, schematics, and even slide presentations, including 3D models. A SWOT analysis of ChatGPT reveals its potential to enhance education through personalized feedback, increased accessibility, and interactive conversations (Farrokhnia et al., 2023). However, its limitations, such as the inclusion of inaccurate and biased information, pose a threat to the quality of education (Zhu, 2023). Furthermore, a series of studies have explored the potential of ChatGPT in education. Cooper (2023) mentions that ChatGPT aligns with key themes in science education research in several ways, such as assisting in lesson planning, enhancing student engagement, and facilitating inquiry-based learning (Dalgıç et al., 2024). However, some ethical implications must be considered, such as how to critically evaluate AI-generated content. Educators should prioritize student privacy and data security when using AI tools in the classroom (Demir et al., 2023). However, improvement is not always about processing a larger volume of work or doing it faster, especially in the case of education. Improvement can refer to bringing something to a better state, or in a broader understanding, enhancing implies transcending an initially perfectible state to take something, in this case, education, to another state where it transcends its own limitations.

AI is increasingly permeating the education ecosystem by increasingly interacting and collaborating with students, building and maintaining social relationships, and offering personalized instruction. (Hyun et al., 2022)

Derived from the above, one must understand the challenges or limitations of current university education and identify which ones can be addressed using artificial intelligence. This involves researching available resources and applications, and in any case, designing learning activities oriented towards specific learning objectives.

Moreover, while AI applications differ from other technologies in that they explicitly aim to act as agents in the classroom environment by adaptively tapping into students' learning process, teachers face substantial pedagogical challenges in designing and facilitating how students interact, collaborate, and learn with AI in the classroom(...) (Hyun et al., 2022).

Let's start with the fact that even though a text-based AI can write an essay thousands of times faster than any human, it does not necessarily mean it does it better. AIs do not think; they predict. They use predictive algorithms. Therefore, what teachers, facilitators, or instructors can do better than AI at this moment is identify what is a problem in university education based on our experience in front of a group and pinpoint in which parts of the text an AI is mistaken, redundant, or inaccurate.

University students face significant difficulty in expressing their thoughts in writing. There is a trend in written communications, such as text messages, where language is becoming more limited. In immediate communications, emoticons, acronyms, and optional spelling are employed, among other aspects that undermine academic writing skills. This is concerning because the literacy skills of university students are declining, diminishing the professionalism and academic level of their texts. Moreover, this trend may escalate and, in turn, be reflected in AI systems that precisely feed on our knowledge and communications.

Keeping the above in mind and identifying the problem that young people face in expressing themselves clearly and orderly in writing, we need to analyze how they think and create reflections within the classrooms regarding the importance of thinking in an organized manner. We must implement teaching strategies that allow them to practice the ability to prioritize thoughts, argue, avoid jumping to conclusions, engage in dialectical discussions, gather information, and, above all, articulate their ideas in writing.

AI functions based on a prompt that must be clear and specific for the query result to be useful. Once the result is obtained, the so-called soft skills (a euphemism that understates their importance) that must come into play include the ability to critically read a text, discern information, and compare the importance and order of the ideas presented. This is a key skill. However, if we want to go further, we will have to teach students to critically correlate what they assert with all preexisting ideas, scientific facts, and, of course, verify the truthfulness of the statements made.

Figure 1. A Prompt Given to the Generative Text AI ChatGPT 3.5 for the Creation of an Exam for the Subject of Art History

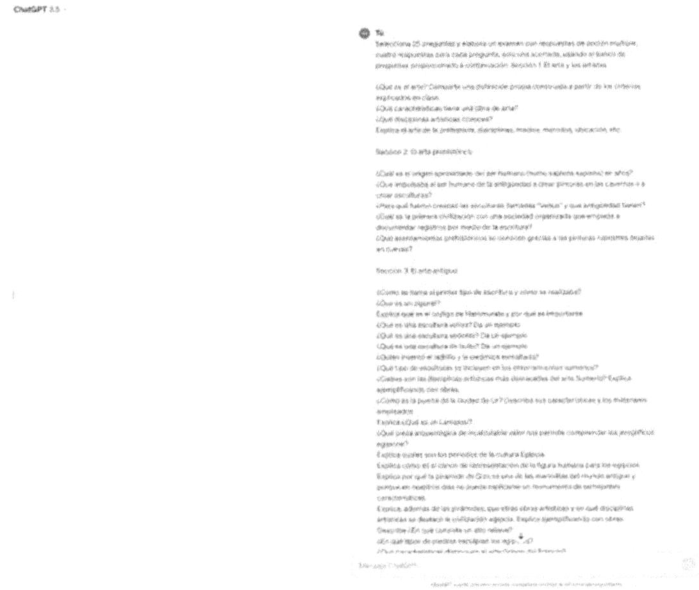

CASE STUDIES

The learning process of university students is influenced by numerous distractions. The competition for attention, while not a new phenomenon, has intensified today, largely due to the proliferation of audiovisual stimuli and the accessibility of devices with internet access. This has led to a substantial decrease in the attention span of university students. Therefore, educators face the challenge of identifying engaging pedagogical strategies that are also effective in achieving the academic objectives of their educational programs. AI engages in more autonomous, personalized, and active interaction with students. Interactions with AI are dynamic rather than static, reflecting upon the communication and interactions being exchanged within a learning process and context (Hyun et al., 2022).

In the specific context of Animation and Visual Effects Engineering, the subject "History of Art and Animation" is taught in the first training cycle. In this course, the implementation of artificial intelligence resources is utilized in two aspects: simplifying administrative tasks performed by the teacher as part of assignment duties, knowledge evaluation, and review of assessments; and engaging with the content interactively through augmented reality VR and immersive reality RX activities. Regarding the first aspect, which involves streamlining administrative

Figure 2. Example of a Prompt Requesting Corrections for a Text Generated by ChatGPT 3.5 and the Corresponding Correction

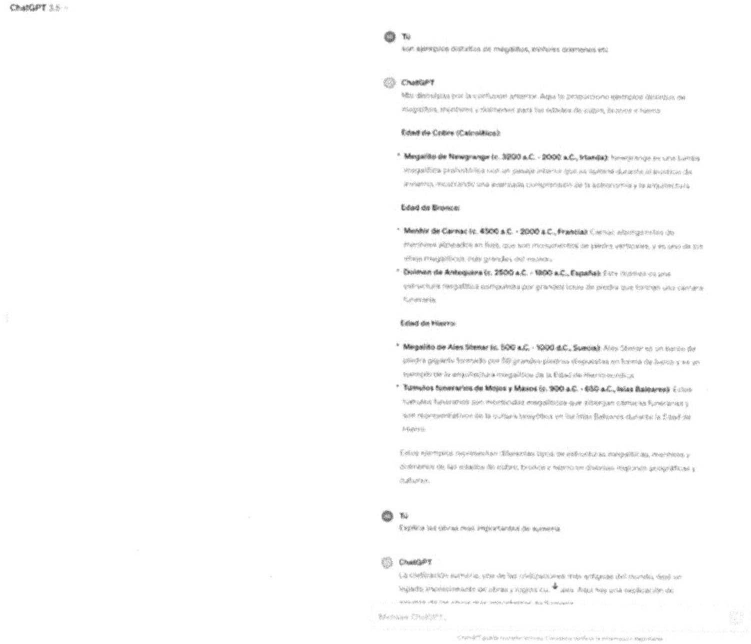

tasks, the generative AI ChatGPT 3 has been successfully used to develop study guides, questionnaires, topic sheets, syllabi, and exams, as shown in Figure 1.

The most important aspect when using this tool is to input a clear and well-defined prompt to yield the desired result. The guidance on topics should not only be specific but, once the text is generated, it should be reviewed. This is because the AI cannot prioritize the chosen content's importance. For instance, if requesting a list of the ten most important works of ancient art, the period in terms of dates, cultures, and other important parameters must be specified. Additionally, the results should be rigorously examined, as they are not always accurate, as seen in Figure 2.

Text-generating artificial intelligences are improvable. The results they provide must be thoroughly reviewed. In most cases, they are helpful if the results are verified. The availability of these tools has sparked the interest of students who use them to expand texts, generate correspondence, create reports, and complete assignments. The guidance we provide as educators is for them to pause and read the text carefully, identifying the central idea of the paragraph and determining whether this idea is being communicated clearly or, on the contrary, is buried in redundant statements.

For the drafting of internship reports, we request students that, if they use AI to generate texts, not to lose sight of the importance of the quality of the information

Figure 3. Activity with VR-Technology in the Art History Class

presented rather than the quantity. The hierarchy of ideas remains a key theme that should be reinforced in the classroom regarding the use of AI by students. Regarding the assistance that AIs can provide to teachers in dosing the topics, various interactive resources have been employed during the first unit of the subject program, which corresponds to the study of Ancient Art, with emphasis on specific topics such as the characteristics of archaeological sites, addressed through a virtual tour. In turn, available resources in virtual reality (VR) and virtual tours that provide access to the interior of the pyramids of Egypt (BBC News, 2019, 2m23s) and the 360-degree tour inside the Notre-Dame Cathedral (ODYSSEY VISUAL MEDIA, 2019, 1m31s) have been utilized, as shown in Figures 3 and 4.

As can be observed in Figures 3 and 4, students use simple prefabricated cardboard goggles to insert their mobile phones to play freely accessible videos available on the YouTube platform. These videos are adapted for the use of goggles that enable them to view 360-degree videos, providing the experience of an immersive tour within architectural spaces. The classroom activity involves watching the video and identifying the architectural elements explained during the class, articulating them.

This same activity fosters interest among students and encourages the exchange of ideas, discussion, questions, and generally promotes a deeper understanding of the topics studied. It has been observed that this activity increases students' interest in the history topics covered in class. Furthermore, it enables them to recall the contents explained in class. Technological resources have the benefit of recreating remote or inaccessible environments. Despite their limitations, they allow for capturing and maintaining students' attention, triggering what are known as meaningful learning experiences.

Figure 4. Students Observing the 360-degree Tour Inside Notre-Dame Cathedral

According to Moreira (2019), meaningful learning is the interaction between prior and new knowledge. Teaching strategies will be oriented towards considering the prior knowledge that the student possesses and facilitating learning experiences, in this case, accessible through new technologies and immersive - allowing the linking of prior knowledge with new information from these experiential learning opportunities, with the purpose of enabling the student to understand, explain, describe, and transfer their own experiences.

In meaningful learning, the learner is not a passive receiver; on the contrary, they must make use of the meanings they have already internalized to grasp the meanings of educational materials (Moreira, 2019).

The role of the student is not that of a passive recipient to certain stimuli; instead, it implies the active reorganization of their learning, connecting experiences with pre-existing knowledge, and consequently enhancing their understanding in a lasting manner. The proposal we put forth is to leverage the tools provided by new technologies to facilitate meaningful learning through discovery, anchoring these experiences with prior knowledge, integrating them into cognitive interaction. As anticipated, these types of experiences are attractive, satisfying, and foster sustained interest for students.

Critical thinking is of particular importance to meet some of those new demands, as students must be able to read complex texts in order to distinguish between credible and untrustworthy sources, and between fact and fiction. Creativity is also key to the development of new solutions that cannot be invented by computers

Figure 5. Augmented Reality Filters Infographic. Author: Martha Elena González Correa

yet, including solutions that are enhanced by AI and the use of robots. Besides the economic argument that complex innovation skills are less easy to automate, they also contribute to human well-being and to the good functioning of democratic societies. This is also true for socio-emotional skills such as persistence, communication or collaboration. (Stéphan et al., 2020).

As part of the work undertaken in the Meta Centro Santander Bootcamp RX scholarship program for women, an augmented reality experience was designed to enhance the learning of students in the Art History and Animation subject. The need was identified for students to distinguish the characteristic features belonging to certain periods in art history, including pictorial production, major artists, attire from each era, themes, and symbolism employed in certain paintings. In Figure 5, the infographic is shown through which augmented reality filters can be accessed via QR codes.

With this in mind, an augmented reality experience was designed, using generative AI to identify a list of suggested paintings and elements by historical period that

Figure 6. RX Technology Activity in Art History Class. Students Utilizing the Augmented Reality Filter for Marie Antoinette's Attire and Wig

are identifiable, recognizable, and emblematic. Subsequently, the learning activity was crafted using augmented reality. The learning objective involves a meticulous observation, from which the student identifies the multidisciplinary elements that make up a work of art to achieve a comprehensive appreciation of the artwork that allows an understanding of the historical context from which it originates. As

Figure 7. Students Utilizing the Augmented Reality Filter for Attire, Dress of the Infanta Margarita

Figure 8. Professor Testing the Augmented Reality Filter for Attire, Elizabethan Ruff

depicted in Figures 6, 7, and 8, students enthusiastically participate in these learning experiences.

For users, in this case, students, wearing different elements of clothing through an augmented reality filter serves as a mnemonic resource that aids in the identification of different historical periods and retention of these key contents. Once the content of the learning activity was defined and the level of immersion was established, the required software for designing the experience was chosen. In this case, the Spark AR platform was used, and 3D body filters were edited with images of clothing from each era depicted in selected historical paintings for this purpose. The chosen periods are the Renaissance, Baroque, and Rococo.

As a result of this activity, students demonstrated improved performance in academic assessments for the subject, as they could more accurately identify which clothing element belonged to which period. Therefore, we can conclude that these types of resources, in addition to being attractive to students, enable them to enhance their academic performance. Artificial intelligence applications can yield positive results, provided that teachers take the time to structure the activity considering its objectives and adapting it to achieve certain anticipated outcomes.

THE IMPACT OF EDTECH ON EDUCATION

Edtech innovation refers to the collaboration of developers to innovate, adapt, and implement new products and services to improve teaching and learning. The individuals and organizations that develop these tools, such as teachers, students, participants, researchers, and investors, use their knowledge, experiences, and skills together to benefit the advancement of new technologies (Huges, 2019). The digital era and the digital economy are trends of a modern world that require the adaptation and modernization of the educational system, whose main purpose is to prepare students for professional life with knowledge of digital tools. The purpose of digital transformation in education is to create an effective way of teaching that meets all the needs of a digital economy and ensures maximum use of the potential of such tools in a virtual classroom. Digital technologies that are important from an educational point of view implement telecommunication, technologies for the generation of communication systems, artificial intelligence technologies that process large amounts of information also known as BigData, augmented and virtual reality, databases located in information clouds, among others (Bhutoria, 2022).

There is only one way to teach is an outdated way of thinking that has been criticized in recent years, as studies and information on student learning progress evolves, the old mentality has demonstrated a lack of ability to meet individual student needs (Zmyzgova, 2020).

In recent decades, we have seen a boom in transformation worldwide and technology due to factors such as services, needs, and logistics, among other things. Development companies in the educational environment frequently encounter problems in advancing the incorporation of artificial intelligence into teaching tools due to the lack of important information which would have the function of teaching the algorithms of said artificial intelligence to provide support in teaching strategies to the teacher and personalize the study contents to the students (Chaudhry & Kazim, 2022). The formation of new implementation requirements and contents of the educational process, especially in terms of its customization, creating an individual development of educational routes and providing a practically oriented educational experience that simulates the introduction of different forms of digital education through systems adaptive, blended learning, case studies, mobile learning, gamification, project activities, etc. These trends are taking over the educational market and changing it. For new technologies in the educational field to be more effective, it is necessary to develop reliable indicators that help with the logic of cognitive processes and the fundamental impact on learning results (Alam & Mohanty, 2022).

The personalization of education allows us to recognize and analyze the student's specific needs so that they can develop their skills, comply with teaching methods, and achieve educational goals through learning methods that adapt to the individual. This personalization is created through redirecting, reviewing and reconstructing information and adapting it to capture the student's attention, facilitating the absorption and retention of the information. This individual and personalized learning method helps eliminate the learning difficulties of students with neurological problems, who suffer from discrimination with the current classroom teaching method, boosting their intellect and productivity (Bhutoria, 2022). One of the most important problems in using artificial intelligence is ensuring access to quality education throughout the student's life. It should be noted that equity and inclusivity are basic moral principles for implementing goals in a sustainable development field and are designed to cover all segments of the population with digital education. Currently, artificial intelligence tools are designed to overcome gender inequalities, access to education and people with disabilities.

ETHICAL CONSIDERATIONS

First Approaches in the Construction of a Regulatory Framework for the Ethical Use and Disclosure of Artificial Intelligence in Mexico

The National Alliance of Artificial Intelligence (ANIA) (https://www.alejandralagunes.mx/inteligencia-artificial) announced on August 22 of the current year, at the Senate of the Republic, its collaboration with UNESCO to develop an initial diagnosis of artificial intelligence in Mexico. This diagnosis will serve as a basis for future actions and marks Mexico's entry into the group of over 50 nations working with UNESCO's Readiness Assessment Methodology (RAM). This effort aims to understand and harness AI in an ethical and effective manner in Mexico. In this context, on September 22, 2023, the analysis session "Cybersecurity and Risk Management" was held, organized by the Senate of the Republic in conjunction with experts, professors, and academics. The objective was to assess the potential risks associated with new technologies and based on the analysis, establish a robust regulation for the field of Artificial Intelligence (AI). This initiative seeks the Mexican State to enact legislation that ensures the security of personal data, equitable access to information and telecommunications technologies, as well as safe, free, and universal access to the Internet.

During this forum, Senator Alejandra Lagunes (PVEM) and Senator Gustavo Madero (GP) pointed out that a critical aspect requiring appropriate legislation is user security against potential crimes that may arise through the malicious use of AI tools. Furthermore, the fundamental purpose is to ensure that the realization of these rights do not result in an increase of the existing inequalities, as the technological gap between different users could widen (Canal del Congreso, 2023). While Mexico makes significant efforts to embrace the era of artificial intelligence, it is in the diagnosis and knowledge dissemination stage, evaluating the risks and potential impacts that a technology threatening to take over many jobs involving mechanical tasks may bring. On the other hand, there are risks associated with the use of personal data and, in a very specific aspect, hyper-surveillance and control of personal data.

When we speak of pervasiveness, we refer to the degree of penetration of this technology into all layers of activities, services, industries, and government, both in the public and private sectors, at the individual and collective levels. Considering the human being as the focal point, and in expanding waves from the individual to society, we observe different spheres of data collection and interaction with automated systems, from which it is not always possible to escape. To illustrate this, we can trace an arc that ranges from devices inserted into our bodies (prosthetics and augmentation cyborg trends for smart humans) to those used on our bodies. Body devices (prosthetics, wearables) encompass sensitive and personal data, some entirely involuntary, likely subject to more stringent regulation than other data types (Mantenga, 2022, p. 15).

The authors propose the establishment of an ethical observatory for AI in education to address the ethical implications of AI in the educational context. They suggest that this observatory would contribute to developing ethical guidelines and regulations for AI in education (Vivar & Peñalvo, 2023). The authors emphasize the need to ensure that the development and implementation of AI in education do not compromise human values or diversity or create new inequalities. They highlight the importance of incorporating ethical principles into the design of AI tools for education.

CHALLENGES AND FUTURE DIRECTIONS

Initiating a reflection on the future challenges and directions that must be taken regarding the use of artificial intelligence tools, we understand that it is crucial to educate thoughtful individuals who are aware of their value and their ability to influence the adaptation of these technologies for use in a noble and dignified purpose. The prominent presence of Artificial Intelligence in various sectors of society in Mexico and Latin America has sparked intense debates and transformations, with education being one of the most impacted sectors in recent years. This phenomenon has led to the generation of profound debates, reforms in public policies, and ethical reflections around technology integration in the educational field. Given the fundamental role of education in stimulating economic productivity and competitiveness, educational policies are placed at the epicenter of the economic growth framework (Tuomi, I., 2020). While we acknowledge that our region has faced needs in various sectors since the pandemic's beginning, education is high on the list, particularly in higher

Figure 9. Towards a New Era of Digital Agendas
Source: Comisión Económica para América Latina y el Caribe (2021)

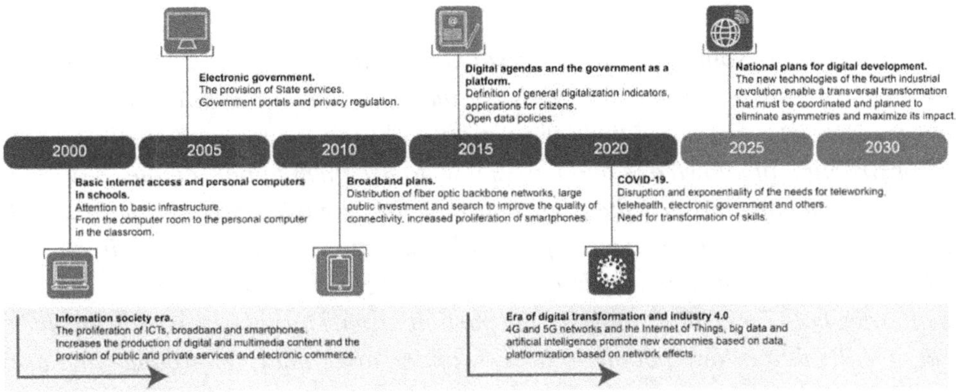

education. With a little more than two years of universities being forced to offer online classes, it created new gaps and further increased those that already existed (ProFuturo and OEI, 2023).

This global event accelerated the use of digital technologies, which have grown exponentially, and their use has become globalized. This has become an important topic on international digital agendas, along with Artificial Intelligence, and in Mexico, it has not been the exception (Figure 9). Faced with this globalization, anyone in the world has access to the network at hand, generating a growing influence on our lives. Against this backdrop, the importance and need for digital policies become more evident, as it is not only about capitalizing on the opportunities that arise with technological advancement but also about mitigating potential negative impacts on various aspects of society. Consequently, economic reactivation and recovery strategies must place digital initiatives in a central position, recognizing their crucial role in building a more resilient economic and social future (CEPAL, 2021).

This poses new challenges and social phenomena for society that can be addressed through education. Proposing a reflection on future challenges and the directions that should be taken regarding the use of artificial intelligence tools, we understand that it is critical to educate individuals who can think critically, are aware of their value, and possess the ability to influence the appropriateness of these technologies for noble and dignified purposes. This should guide humanity in overcoming contemporary challenges such as climate issues, armed conflicts, ideologies, inequality, and many others (CEPAL, 2021). Alternatively, we can instruct and accompany individuals in the process of transcending an era of technological disadvantages, backwardness, impoverishment of work, and collective ignorance. This involves reminding them of human dignity and the value of human work and seeking strategies to harness the best that AIs can offer us. This encompasses the concept of digital citizenship.

A digital citizen is someone who understands the functioning and principles that govern the digital environment, analyzes the place and role that technologies occupy in society, evaluates their impact on daily life, understands their role in the construction of knowledge and knows how to use them to participate. A digital citizen is someone who has the ability to navigate complex digital contexts and understand their social, economic, political, educational and labor implications. A digital citizen is someone who knows how to make thoughtful and creative use of the Internet, both for critical analysis and participation. Digital Citizenship involves a set of skills that allows people to access, understand, analyze, produce and use the digital environment in a critical, ethical and creative way (UNESCO 2020).

We are far from achieving this model of a digital citizen. We can rely on artificial intelligence to accomplish this goal, but it should not be the sole dependency, as it aligns with the predictions of some authors who anticipate that AI could replace teachers in education. According to Kai-Fu Lee, "Personalized homework and AI-assisted grading can improve education, but human teachers are still necessary for conversation practice and instilling moral values" (Chanel. Aprendemos Juntos 2030, 2020, 05m16s). Training teachers to incorporate AI into their classes can help them save up to 40 or 50% of their time, enabling a focus on developing moral aspects, values, teamwork, empathy, and creativity among students. AI can aid individuals with physical and cognitive disabilities, personalizing each student's homework based on their abilities, qualifications, and aspirations, potentially revolutionizing the education system. AI technology can optimize students' understanding of a subject, leading to improved grades and personalized learning experiences (Chanel. Aprendemos Juntos 2030, 2020, 05m16s). We need to shift from training repetitive robots to nurturing creative and empathetic humans, preparing university students to be critical, creative, strategic, compassionate, and empathetic thinkers. Education should prioritize teaching young people teamwork, communication, collaboration, love, empathy, and trust, preparing them for future jobs that require strategic, compassionate, and empathetic individuals (Chanel. Aprendemos Juntos 2030, 2020, 05m16s). While many universities are already implementing the use of AI as a tool for education, it is not yet clear which aspects will have more developmental importance by the year 2030—whether to utilize AI as a general learning tool for young people or to cater to specific groups, such as students with special needs (ProFuturo y OEI 2023).

The global panorama of AI is ambiguous; while some believe that developing new technologies based on AI could significantly benefit the educational system, others argue that the state prefers to support the industrial and private sectors. There is also skepticism regarding the state's growing involvement in AI development in both sectors, with this need being covered by the private sector. Looking ahead, the future of Artificial Intelligence in education in Mexico is expected to evolve further, leveraging technologies like machine learning and virtual reality to provide even more immersive learning experiences. Collaboration between the education sector, government, and the technology industry will be essential to ensure these innovations' effective and ethical deployment. In conclusion, the future of Artificial Intelligence in education in Mexico offers an exciting panorama full of possibilities. If implemented carefully and ethically, AI can transform education, making it more accessible, personalized, and effective for all students.

REFERENCES

Alam, A. (2022). Employing adaptive learning and intelligent tutoring robots for virtual classrooms and smart campuses: Reforming education in the age of artificial intelligence. *Advanced Computing and Intelligent Technologies Proceedings of ICACIT, 2022*, 395–406.

Alam, A., & Mohanty, A. (2022). Business models, business strategies, and innovations in EdTech companies: integration of learning analytics and artificial intelligence in higher education. In *2022 IEEE 6th Conference on Information and Communication Technology (CICT)* (pp. 1-6). IEEE. 10.1109/CICT56698.2022.9997887

Aprendemos Juntos 2030. (2020). *V. Completa. Las claves educativas en la era de la inteligencia artificial.* https://www.youtube.com/watch?v=18QBF0LifbY

Audras, D., Zhao, A., Isgar, C., & Tang, Y. (2022). *Virtual teaching assistants: A survey of a novel teaching technology. International Journal of Chinese Education, 11*(2).

BBC News. (2019) In 360: *Notre-Dame cathedral before the fire - BBC News.* Youtube. https://www.youtube.com/watch?v=mOuvAJRknXk&t=22s

Bhutoria, A. (2022). Personalized education and artificial intelligence in the United States, China, and India: A systematic review using a human-in-the-loop model. *Computers and Education: Artificial Intelligence*, *3*, 100068. doi:10.1016/j.caeai.2022.100068

Calvo, H., & Ruiz, J. (2024). *Sociedad Mexicana de Inteligencia Artificial.* SMIA. https://smia.mx/

Canal del Congreso. (n.d.). *Impulsan regulación de Inteligencia Artificial.* https://www.canaldelcongreso.gob.mx/noticias/17075/Impulsanr egulaciondeInteligenciaArtificial

Capuano, N., & Caballé, S. (2020). Adaptive learning technologies. *AI Magazine*, *41*(2), 96–98. doi:10.1609/aimag.v41i2.5317

Carbonell, J. R. (1970). AI in CAI: An artificial-intelligence approach to computer-assisted instruction. *IEEE Transactions on Man-Machine Systems*, *11*(4), 190–202. doi:10.1109/TMMS.1970.299942

Chaudhry, M. A., & Kazim, E. (2022). Artificial Intelligence in Education (AIEd): A high-level academic and industry note 2021. *AI and Ethics*, *2*(1), 1–9. doi:10.1007/s43681-021-00074-z PMID:34790953

Comisión Económica para América Latina y el Caribe (CEPAL). (2021). Tecnologías digitales para un nuevo futuro (LC/TS.2021/43). Academic Press.

Cooper, G. (2023). Examining science education in chatgpt: An exploratory study of generative artificial intelligence. *Journal of Science Education and Technology*, *32*(3), 444–452. doi:10.1007/s10956-023-10039-y

Dalgıç, A., Yaşar, E., & Demir, M. (2024). ChatGPT and learning outcomes in tourism education: The role of digital literacy and individualized learning. *Journal of Hospitality, Leisure, Sport and Tourism Education*, *34*, 100481. doi:10.1016/j.jhlste.2024.100481

Dede, C. (2009). Immersive interfaces for engagement and learning. *Science*, *323*(5910), 66–69. doi:10.1126/science.1167311 PMID:19119219

Demir, Ş. Ş., & Demir, M. (2023). Professionals' perspectives on ChatGPT in the tourism industry: Does it inspire awe or concern? *Journal of Tourism Theory and Research*, *9*(2), 61–76. doi:10.24288/jttr.1313481

Dikli, S. (2006). An overview of automated scoring of essays. *The Journal of Technology, Learning, and Assessment*, *5*(1).

Douidi, L., Djoudi, M., & Khentout, C. (2007). Users assistants for e-learning environment over the web. *Journal of Computational Science*, *3*(3), 122–129. doi:10.3844/jcssp.2007.122.129

Farrokhnia, M., Banihashem, S. K., Noroozi, O., & Wals, A. (2023). A SWOT analysis of ChatGPT: Implications for educational practice and research. *Innovations in Education and Teaching International*, 1–15.

Fernandez, E. (2024). *Impulsan regulación de la inteligencia artificial.* Canal del Congreso. https://www.canaldelcongreso.gob.mx/noticias/17075/ImpulsanregulaciondeInteligenciaArtificial

Flores-Vivar, J. M., & García-Peñalvo, F. J. (2023). Reflexiones sobre la ética, potencialidades y retos de la Inteligencia Artificial en el marco de la Educación de Calidad (ODS4). *Comunicar, 31*(74). Advance online publication. doi:10.3916/C74-2023-03

Geoffroy, F., Aimeur, E., & Gillet, D. (2002). *A virtual Assistant for Web-Based Training in engineering education. In International Conference on Intelligent Tutoring Systems* (pp. 301-310). Springer Berlin Heidelberg. 10.1007/3-540-47987-2_34

Gomez, L. I. (2020). *Immersive virtual reality for learning experiences. Radical Solutions and eLearning: Practical Innovations and Online Educational Technology*, 183-198.

Gubareva, R., & Lopes, R. P. (2020). Virtual Assistants for Learning: A Systematic Literature Review. *CSEDU*, (1), 97–103. doi:10.5220/0009417600970103

Hughes, J. (2019). Learning across boundaries: Educator and startup involvement in the educational technology innovation ecosystem. *Contemporary Issues in Technology & Teacher Education, 19*(1), 62–96.

Ibrahim, M. S., & Hamada, M. (2016). Adaptive learning framework. In *2016 15th International Conference on Information Technology Based Higher Education and Training (ITHET)* (pp. 1-5). IEEE. 10.1109/ITHET.2016.7760738

Ivanova, V., Toskova, A., Stoyanova-Doycheva, A., Stoyanov, S., & Veselinova, M. (2017, September). Lifelong learning in Virtual education space with intelligent assistants. In *Proceedings of the 8th Balkan Conference in Informatics* (pp. 1-6). 10.1145/3136273.3136287

Kabir, S., Hossain, M. P., Mallik, K., Rahman, M., Islam, M. J., & Khatun, A. (2019). An Extensive Online Examination System With Automatic Assessment Technique. *GUB Journal of Science and Engineering, 6*(01), 54–59. doi:10.3329/gubjse.v6i1.52051

Kim, J., Lee, H., & Cho, Y. H. (2022). Learning design to support student-AI collaboration: Perspectives of leading teachers for AI in education. *Education and Information Technologies, 27*(5), 6069–6104. doi:10.1007/s10639-021-10831-6

Lagunes, A. (2024) *Hacia un Diagnóstico de la Inteligencia Artificial en México: Implementación Ética y Responsable ANIA-UNESCO*. Senadora Alejandra Lagunes. https://www.alejandralagunes.mx/inteligencia-artificial

Lin, C. C., Huang, A. Y., & Lu, O. H. (2023). Artificial intelligence in intelligent tutoring systems toward sustainable education: A systematic review. *Smart Learning Environments*, *10*(1), 41–50. doi:10.1186/s40561-023-00260-y

Mantegna, M. (2022). *No soy un robot: construyendo un marco ético accionable para analizar las dimensiones de impacto de la inteligencia artificial*. Academic Press.

Moreira, M. (2000). Aprendizaje significativo. *Recuperado el, 8*, 149-181.

Mustafa Kamal, N. N., Mohd Adnan, A. H., Yusof, A. A., Ahmad, M. K., & Mohd Kamal, M. A. (2019). Immersive interactive educational experiences–adopting Education 5.0, Industry 4.0 learning technologies for Malaysian Universities. In *Proceedings of the International Invention, Innovative & Creative (InIIC) Conference, Series* (pp. 190-196). Academic Press.

O'Connor, E. A., & Worman, T. (2019). Designing for interactivity, while scaffolding student entry, within immersive virtual reality environments. *Journal of Educational Technology Systems*, *47*(3), 292–317. doi:10.1177/0047239518817545

Odyssey Visual Media. (2019) *Abu Simbel Egypt Virtual Tour | VR 360° Travel Experience* Youtube. https://www.youtube.com/watch?v=_4kBntxPUic&t=2s

ProFuturo y OEI (2023). *El futuro de la Inteligencia Artificial en educación en América Latina*. Academic Press.

Rashid, N. A., Lim, L. W., Eng, O. S., Ping, T. H., Zainol, Z., & Majid, O. (2016). A framework of an automatic assessment system for learning programming. *Advanced Computer and Communication Engineering Technology Proceedings of ICOCOE, 2015*, 967–977.

Shelle, G., Earnesty, D., Pilkenton, A., & Powell, E. (2018). Adaptive learning: An innovative method for online teaching and learning. *Journal of Extension*, *56*(5), 17. doi:10.34068/joe.56.05.17

Todorov, J., Valkanov, V., Stoyanov, S., Daskalov, B., Popchev, I., & Orozova, D. (2018). Personal assistants in a virtual education space. *Practical issues of intelligent innovations*, 131-153.

Tong, M. S., Zheng, H. Q., & Wan, G. C. (2019). Improvement of Education Method by Using Artificial Intelligence Technology. In *2019 IEEE International Conference on Engineering, Technology and Education (TALE)* (pp. 1-5). IEEE. 10.1109/TALE48000.2019.9225891

Tuomi, I. (2020). The Impact of Artificial Intelligence on Learning, Teaching, and Education. Policies for the future. *European Union.*

UNESCO. (2020). *La ciudadanía digital como política pública en educación en América Latina.* Oficina Regional de Ciencias para América Latina y el Caribe.

Van Doren, C. (2022). *Breve Historia del Saber.* Booket Paidós.

Vincent-Lancrin, S., & Van der Vlies, R. (2020). *Trustworthy artificial intelligence (AI) in education: Promises and challenges.* Academic Press.

Vivar, J. M. F., & Peñalvo, F. J. G. (2023). Reflexiones sobre la ética, potencialidades y retos de la Inteligencia Artificial en el marco de la Educación de Calidad (ODS4). *Comunicar: Revista científica iberoamericana de comunicación y educación*, (74), 37-47.

Zhu, C., Sun, M., Luo, J., Li, T., & Wang, M. (2023). How to harness the potential of ChatGPT in education? *Knowledge Management & E-Learning, 15*(2), 133.

Zmyzgova, T. R., Polyakova, E. N., & Karpov, E. K. (2020). Digital transformation of education and artificial intelligence. In *2nd International Scientific and Practical Conference "Modern Management Trends and the Digital Economy: from Regional Development to Global Economic Growth" (MTDE 2020)* (pp. 824-829). Atlantis Press. 10.2991/aebmr.k.200502.134

ADDITIONAL READING

Chiu, M. C., Hwang, G. J., Hsia, L. H., & Shyu, F. M. (2022). Artificial intelligence-supported art education: A deep learning-based system for promoting university students' artwork appreciation and painting outcomes. *Interactive Learning Environments*, 1–19. doi:10.1080/10494820.2022.2129392

Mateas, M. (2002). *Interactive Drama, Art and Artificial Intelligence.* Carnegie Mellon University.

KEY TERMS AND DEFINITIONS

Artificial Intelligence (AI): A scientific discipline that creates computer programs that perform operations comparable to those carried out by the human mind, such as learning or logical reasoning.

Artificial Intelligence for Education (AIED): The application of artificial intelligence computer systems to optimize the teaching-learning process.

Augmented Reality: The combination of technologies that, through peripheral devices, allows the visualization of graphic elements using technology. These intangible, digital elements can be 2D graphics, 3D models, texts, and the user can interact with them. Augmented reality elements enable incorporating these virtual elements into a real environment.

Deep Learning: A set of machine learning algorithms that attempt to model high-level abstractions in data using computational architectures that support multiple and iterative non-linear transformations of data expressed in matrix or tensor form.

Generative Artificial Intelligence: A type of Artificial Intelligence system that generates text, multimedia images, and other visual files such as videos and 3D models based on a prompt.

Machine Learning (ML): A subfield of Artificial Intelligence that involves the development of systems with autonomous learning. Machine learning implies that computers accumulate experience and improve their performance using data.

Meaningful Learning: The learning process in which new knowledge is linked to the individual's existing knowledge, giving the new learning significance.

Natural Language Processing (NLP): A field within computational disciplines that focuses on the interactions between computers and human natural language. It aims to enhance communication between people and machines.

Virtual Reality (VR): A simulated digital environment created by a computer that gives the user the sensation of being immersed in it using peripheral devices such as VR glasses or headsets.

Chapter 7
The Technological Transformation of Social Science Education: An Overview

Jonai Wabwire
Kisii University, Kenya

ABSTRACT

The chapter explores the evolution of higher education in the social sciences, tracking its transition from traditional classroom settings to artificial intelligence (AI)-driven learning environments that define the contemporary educational landscape. Historically, social science education relied on traditional pedagogical methods. While these methods served as effective means of disseminating knowledge, they also presented limitations. The advent of technology, particularly the internet and learning management systems (LMS), began to supplement these traditional approaches, paving the way for a gradual shift. The rise of artificial intelligence marked a pivotal moment in this transformation. AI, encompassing machine learning, natural language processing, and data analytics, revolutionized social science education by enabling personalized learning experiences. This chapter examines the contemporary landscape of AI-driven learning environments in social science education. While this technological evolution offers exciting possibilities, it raises challenges and ethical considerations.

DOI: 10.4018/979-8-3693-1666-5.ch007

INTRODUCTION

Higher education has witnessed a profound transformation in recent decades, driven by rapid technological advancements and artificial intelligence (AI) proliferation. Nowhere is this transformation more evident than in the realm of social science education. Traditional pedagogical methods, once the cornerstone of social science instruction, are giving way to innovative AI-driven learning environments that reshape how students learn, educators teach, and researchers conduct their work. This chapter provides a comprehensive overview of the evolution of higher education in the social sciences, tracking its trajectory from traditional classrooms to the dynamic and data-driven AI-powered landscape that characterizes the present.

The discipline of social studies has had a precarious relationship with technology, simultaneously touting its potential benefits and critiquing its limitations in facilitating social studies practice. The integration of technology tools and resources into instruction has been accompanied by an interest in the power of technology to affect changes in social, civic, and economic functioning. Some of these impacts have benefited the construction of global connections among diverse people spread all over the globe. At the same time, other components of technology diffusion have highlighted and accentuated inequities in access and quality of exposure. Historically, we have many examples of the simultaneous predictions of the utopia of technological progress (Hudson, 1997) and cautionary views that question the value and worth of technology (Postman, 2000; Stoll, 1999).

Social science educators and researchers have been fascinated by the potential of technology to make our lives more enjoyable, efficient, and productive. In social studies, the application of technology to ameliorate work products has become firmly entrenched in the curriculum, based on the premise that technology-based products can promote integrative learning, exploration of ethical and social policies, and active engagement in authentic activities. However, many schools have not kept pace with the techno culture, either as an instruction tool or as a focus of investigation and exploration (Berson, Lee, & Stuckart, 2001). Furthermore, the mere act of placing a computer in the classroom does not seed reform. Students may access data and receive up-to-date information from top researchers in any specialty area; however, effectiveness requires more than facilitated access to knowledge.

As white (1997b) puts it, Technology is merely a "means to an end." It necessitates a broader understanding of its role and application by educators and learners in the social sciences. Technology is a dynamic resource and tool that continues to develop over time and subsequently has acquired an increasingly prominent role in society. Although the prohibitive cost of technology had initially inhibited widespread access for students in many schools, observations of the activities of children and youth today continue to bear witness to a generation immersed in computer technology for recreational purposes and more reliant on this global medium for information and social interaction. This sentiment is echoed by Berson (2002), who claimed that most youths are technology fanatics. Technology has facilitated access to vast resources in social sciences. Yet the promise of technology has not only been the ability to access information but also the opportunity to "command the inherited knowledge of the ages" (Ayers, 1999). It is the connections between remote pieces of information that can amplify patterns of thinking that were previously overlooked. This amplification is intensified by disseminating acquired insights to others across remote distances. As archives of past knowledge expand, the focus turns to creating new associations and interpretations that may further enhance our understanding and contribute to the field's richness. This process necessitates recognizing that we only identify a sampling of the nearly infinite hypotheses possible through alternative combinations of knowledge. However, in an environment with an endless assortment of content, it is critical to evolve a discerning ability to grasp the complexity of information and justify the rationale for how we structure and analyze information and synthesize its meaning (Berson & Berson, 2003). Multiple voices, perspectives, events, and implications are possible in this techno-environment, but what of the impact on teaching and learning?

Educational reform must take root in the classroom setting with informed and active participation by educators in modifying the teaching and learning process. In 1996, Berson examined the existing literature on the use and effectiveness of technology in social studies and observed that "computers (in social studies classrooms) have served the primary function of facilitating students' access to content and have been relegated to being an appendage to traditional classroom materials" (p. 495). Little empirical evidence existed to support computer integration in social studies, and most experiences were based on anecdotal information to substantiate the positive benefits of technology. Subsequently, a body of research has accumulated that examines specific constructs in social studies (Whitworth & Berson, 2003). Social Education, a journal of the National Council for the Social Studies, introduced a regular feature in 1996 that presented Web-based resources for social studies educators (Risinger, 1996; Risinger, 2002).

Over the past decade, the conceptualization of technology in social studies has evolved from a theoretical integration of a collection of tools to a constructivist orientation for advocating technology integration. Additionally, Web-based instruction (Donlan, 1999; Fontana, 1997) and the facilitation of multicultural awareness through telecommunications (Fabos & Young, 1999) have achieved prominence. Johnson and Rector (1997) also reinforced the importance of the Internet in social studies for developing and involving citizens in an information age. Nonetheless, Diem (2000) contends that the "promise of technology is not so much its cutting-edge advances as its innovative and imaginative applications" (p. 494); however, social studies classrooms have been especially reticent in applying uses of technology to instruction (Pahl, 1996). Shaver (1999) similarly notes that technology has little potential for stimulating instructional reform within social studies, especially in a context that has been relatively devoid of thoughtful deliberation and careful attention to instructional details. This chapter intends to accumulate the collective knowledge of educational technology in social studies and assess its relative effect on teaching and learning over time. As we reflect on the evolution of the field, it is important to note that the rapid proliferation of new technologies necessitates recognition of the adolescence of the past discourse and the need for a reflective perspective that does not merely track the integration of new technological developments, but also reflects on the future trends toward innovation and diffusion of emerging applications in the social studies.

BACKGROUND

Traditional Pedagogy In Social Science Education

Before delving into the technological revolution, it is essential to understand the foundations of social science education. Historically, social science education relied on traditional classroom settings, lectures, textbooks, and peer discussions. While these methods served as effective means of disseminating knowledge, they also presented limitations, such as limited interactivity, standardization, and a one-size-fits-all approach to learning (Brown, et al., 2015: McIver, et al., 2016: Nilson, 2016). Learning is a fundamental element of education and plays a vital role in the development of a state (Hafeez et al., 2020). The most important challenge in the educational process is the selection of suitable and effective teaching methods to make the learning process useful and to develop the critical thinking skills in the learners (Senthamarai, 2018; Tavoosy & Jelveh, 2019). Two important factors to develop the critical thinking skills among the learners are (i) strategy adopted by the instructor (ii) dynamic engagement of learners in learning process (Nelson, 2017). In the teaching-learning process, the instructor must act as a guider instead of knowledge transfer (Molbaek, 2018). According to (Palis & Quiros, 2014) some important principles for useful learning are (i) learning becomes useful when new knowledge is connected with previous knowledge (ii) The students apply previous knowledge to construct new knowledge (iii) The learning must consist of the strategies to increase the cognitive skills of the learners (iv) All the learners must be engaged in the learning process (v) The learning process must increase the motivation and confidence of the learners. Traditional pedagogy in social science education represents a time-tested and enduring approach to teaching fundamental subjects like history, geography, sociology, political science, and economics. It embodies a structured and teacher-centric method that has been prevalent for generations (Brown, et al., 2015). Traditional pedagogy in social science education emphasizes the transmission of established knowledge, typically through lectures, textbooks, and standardized assessments. This introduction provides an overview of traditional pedagogy in the context of social science education, setting the stage for a deeper exploration of its characteristics and implications as shown below:

Lecture Method: It is the oldest procedure of teaching. It is widely used in schools and colleges. It is a good method and covers a wide range of topics in higher-level classes, but its success depends on the personality and ability of students. The lecture method motivates students, gives an overview of a large topic, makes an important matter understandable, provides background of a topic or introduces the topic, helps the students to use their time wisely, explains the major concepts of a lesson, etc. The traditional lecture method is a one-way conversation in which the instructor delivers the information before the audience (Gholami et al., 2016). After the lecture, the educators give notes and assign some tasks as homework (Gregorius, 2017). In traditional lecture teaching methods, no learner feedback session is conducted (Almanasef et al., 2020). Generally, very little conversation happens between the learners and instructors (Sarıhan et al., 2016). The learners receive a passive strategy of learning (Maqbool et al., 2018). Among the merits of lecture methods is that they establish face-to-face contact. It develops attention span. Students develop listening and note-taking skills. Students can prepare the notes. It is an easy method for novice teachers. On the other hand, the lecture method is monotonous and tiring, and sometimes it becomes boring. It brings a lot of burden and reading to the teacher. It is not an interactive method (Cohen, et al 2010).

Source Method: The "source method" of teaching typically refers to an educational approach emphasizing primary sources, which are original documents or artifacts from a particular period or context. There are three types of sources in this method: i) Material resource: This entails using Ideas, machines, and weapons in instruction by the educator. ii) Oral resources: Songs, folk stories, traditions, customs are used by the educator. iii) Written and printed resources: Records, reports, letters are presented in during the instruction process (Nilson, 2016).

The source method is an activity-oriented method. It is generally used in social studies. Generally, sources mean a person, books, documents, pictures, or actual objects that can provide information for learning. It is learning directly from the actual sources. For example, for social studies, it can be a contract with the bank – or studying the sample of stone collected from the moon or an object found in any ancient place can also be studied. One can also take students to museums to find the objects to study. Steps Followed while using the source method include: i) Demonstration or presentation by the teacher. ii) Locate related reading material and assign reading to the study. iii) Problem-solving by students with group discussion among the students. The advantages of Sources Method include;

i) provides direct, firsthand experience. ii) develops a sense of reality. iii) creates a motivating and interesting ambiance in the class. iv) develops data collection, thinking skills, and observation skills. v) makes the subject meaningful.

Discussion Method: The word discussion means exchanging views and debate. Here, about Welty (1989), the discussion can be among the students as a whole group. The educator could use the discussion method in social science when sharing information and ideas from a large group; it has also been used when one needs to solve a problem or do thinking and analytical activity in the class. The method helps obtain information and ideas from many students (Ahmad, 2013; Welty, 1989). Helps in checking or evaluating students' progress.

Problem-Solving Method: Problem-solving is the ability to systematically identify and solve problems by applying appropriate skills. Problem-solving is a process—an ongoing activity in which we take what we know to discover what we don't know. It involves overcoming obstacles by generating hypotheses, testing those predictions, and arriving at satisfactory solutions. Problem-solving involves three basic functions: i) Seeking information ii) Generating new knowledge, iii) Making decisions.

Problem-solving is, and should be, a real part of the curriculum. It presupposes that students can take on some of the responsibility for their own learning and take personal action to solve problems, resolve conflicts, discuss alternatives, and focus on thinking as a vital curriculum element. It provides students with opportunities to use their newly acquired knowledge in meaningful, real-life activities and assists them in working at higher levels of thinking. Students are presented with problems requiring them to find a scientific or technological solution. It is a student-centered strategy requiring students to participate in the learning process actively. Problem-solving is a teaching strategy that employs the scientific method in searching for information.

Project Method: The project method is a direct outcome of pragmatism, especially of John Dewey's educational philosophy. Pragmatism believes in reality. It is scientific and empirical. It is based on the principle of learning by doing. The Project-Based teaching-learning strategy is a learner-centered instructional approach that is based on three constructivist learning principles (i) learners are engaged actively, (ii) the learning process is context-specific, (iii) Goals are achieved by sharing the knowledge between the learners (Kubiatko & Vaculová, 2011). Project-based learning is also called inquiry-based learning, where the course content is provided by questions and problems related to the real-world context (Al-Balushi & Al-Aamri,2014) that leads to useful learning practices (Kwon et al., 2014). The project-based learning strategy connects with other inquiry-based and problem-based learning strategies. These learning strategies mainly focus on sharing knowledge in the group (Anazifa

& Djukri, 2017). The freedom of work and challenges that the learners face in the project-based learning are the key elements for the active involvement of the learners and to develop the higher order thinking skills (Kolmos &Graaff, 2014). In project-based learning strategy, higher order thinking skills and cognitive skills are judged by solving the real-life problems (Brassler & Dettmers, 2017).

Dialogical Method: Dialog is a means to transform social relations in the classroom and to raise awareness about relations in society at large. In a problem-posing participatory format, the teacher and students transform learning into a collaborative process to illuminate and act on reality. Dialogic teaching is an approach which harnesses the power of talk to stimulate and extend pupils thinking, advancing their learning and understanding. It is mainly built on 'talk' – both the teachers and the pupils.

Co-operative Learning Strategies: Cooperative Learning, sometimes called small-group learning, is an instructional strategy in which small groups of students work together on a common task. The task can be as simple as solving a multi-step math problem together, or as complex as developing a design for a new kind of school. In some cases, each group member is individually accountable for part of the task; in other cases, group members work together without formal role assignments.

According to David Johnson and Roger Johnson (1999), five basic elements allow successful small-group learning: i) Positive interdependence: Students feel responsible for their own and the group's efforts. ii) Face-to-face interaction: Students encourage and support one another; the environment encourages discussion and eye contact. iii) Individual and group accountability: Each student is responsible for doing their part; the group is accountable for meeting its goal. iv) Group behaviors: Group members gain direct instruction in the interpersonal, social, and collaborative skills needed to work with others. v) Group processing: Group members analyze their own and the group's ability to work together.

Cooperative learning changes students' and teachers' roles in classrooms. The ownership of teaching and learning is shared by groups of students and is no longer the sole responsibility of the teacher. All share the authority to set goals, assess, learn, and facilitate learning. Students have more opportunities to actively participate in their learning, question and challenge each other, share and discuss their ideas, and internalize their learning. Along with improving academic learning, cooperative learning helps students engage in thoughtful discourse and examine different perspectives, and it has been proven to increase students' self-esteem, motivation, and empathy.

Role Play and Dramatization Method: Role playing, socio drama or creative dramas present a specific situation for study and discussion. There is no prepared script. It is unrehearsed, speaking parts are not memorized and minimum properties are used. Role play is a way of bringing real-life situations into the classroom. A role, in other words, they pretend to be different people. They pretend to be doing something different: role $ and a situation. In role-play, students improvise. The situation is fixed, but they make up exactly as they go.

Assignment Method: Assignments require learner's engagement and a final tangible product that enables you to assess what your students know and don't know. They represent one of the most common ways to assess learning. They can be either low-stakes [formative assessment] or high-stakes [summative assessment], so the number and type of assignments will depend upon your course design, learning outcomes, and course enrollment numbers.

Reflective Learning Strategies: In the last few decades, reflective learning has come into the education spotlight. Reflective learning involves students thinking about what they have read, done, or learned, relating the lesson hand to their own lives and making meaning out of their material. It's more than just memorizing some facts, formulas, or dates.

Brain-Based Learning: Brain-based learning involves understanding how the brain works best. The brain is very complex and brain-based research is still in the developing stages. Each learners brain is unique and the most effective teaching method varies based on each student's learning capacities. Active participation, student-centered learning, and differentiated instruction are at the core of this theory. Most teachers are already incorporating these practices in one form or another, into their classrooms. According to brain-based learning, students learn best when they are immersed into the subject area. According to this theory, exposing the students to as much of the subject matter, having them actively participate, and surrounding them with as many manipulatives as possible, creates the best environment for successful learning. Each student learns differently, and it is the teacher's job to provide the best opportunity for each individual to experience success. This can be accomplished through reading, hands-on activities, field trips, or creative expression. Another key component of brain-based learning is active processing. This involves connecting learning to a prior experience. Students will better grasp a concept if it is connected to something they have already learned. When students can relate concepts to a life experience or past knowledge, the brain is better able to comprehend. Brain-based learning also suggests the importance of balancing stress and comfort. It suggests students should be in a state of relaxed alertness. Teachers should create an environment that stimulates the brain, while eliminating fear. When students are challenged or slightly stressed, the brain functions better. Too much stress and the brain completely shut down from learning.

Investigative Case-Based Learning: The use of teaching cases is as old as storytelling itself. It is instruction by the use of narratives - stories - about individuals facing decisions or dilemmas. Learners engage with the characters and circumstances of the story. They work to identify problems and connect the story's meaning to their own lives. It is a variant of PBL (problem-based learning) that encourages students to develop questions that can be explored further by reasonable investigative approaches. Students then gather data and information to test their hypotheses. They produce materials that can be used to persuade others of their findings. Students employ various methods and resources, including traditional laboratory and field techniques, software simulations and models, data sets, internet-based tools and information retrieval methods.

Discovery Learning: Discovery learning is a technique of inquiry-based learning and is considered a constructivist-based approach to education. It is supported by the work of learning theorists and psychologists Jean Piaget, Jerome Bruner, and Seymour Papert. Although this form of instruction has great popularity, there is some debate in the literature concerning its efficacy. Jerome Bruner is often credited with originating discovery learning in the 1960s, but his ideas are very similar to those of earlier writers (e.g. John Dewey). Bruner argues that "Practice in discovering for oneself teaches one to acquire information in a way that makes that information more readily viable in problem solving" (Bruner, 1961). This philosophy later became the discovery learning movement of the 1960s. The mantra of this philosophical movement suggests that we should 'learn by doing'. In 1991, The Grauer School, a private secondary school in California, was founded with the motto, "Learn by Discovery", and integrated a series of world-wide expeditions into their program for high school graduation.

Textbook Method of Teaching: A textbook is a collection of a selected topic or course's knowledge, concepts, and principles. It's usually written by one or more teachers, college professors, or education experts who are authorities in a specific field. Most textbooks are accompanied by teacher guides, providing supplemental teaching materials, ideas, and activities throughout the academic year.

Socratic Teaching Method: The oldest and still the most powerful teaching tactic for fostering critical thinking is Socratic teaching. In Socratic teaching, educators focus on giving students questions, not answers. We model an inquiring, probing mind by continually probing into the subject with questions. Fortunately, the abilities we gain by focusing on the elements of reasoning in a disciplined and self-assessing way, and the logical relationships that result from such disciplined thought, prepare us for Socratic questioning. Each of the elements represents a dimension into which one can delve in questioning a person. We can question goals and purposes. We can probe into the nature of the question, problem, or issue that is on the floor. We can inquire into whether or not we have relevant data and information. We can consider alternative interpretations of the data and information. We can analyze key concepts and ideas. We can question assumptions being made. We can ask students to trace out the implications and consequences of what they are saying. We can consider alternative points of view. All of these, and more, are the proper focus of the Socratic questioner.

Storytelling Method: Learners have an innate love of stories. Stories create magic and a sense of wonder at the world. Stories teach us about life, about ourselves and others. Storytelling is a unique way for students to develop an understanding, respect, and appreciation for other cultures, and it can promote a positive attitude toward people from different lands, races, and religions. There are several ways in which storytelling can enhance intercultural understanding and communication. Stories allow learners to explore their cultural roots, experience diverse cultures, empathize with unfamiliar people/places/situations, offer insights into different traditions and values, etc. Stories reveal universal truths about the world. Through stories, we see how very different people share the same life experiences and how human nature can transcend culture.

Socialized Recitation Method: A socialized recitation technique or discussion method is one wherein "learners are discussing, questioning, reporting, and working in natural ways. The educator is a guide, counselor, advisor, contributor, and director in the best sense of the word, trying to get learners to discover things by themselves rather than to have them by merely listening to them." It is a technique of teaching in which a friendly spirit of cooperation prevails (Brown et al., 2015; McIver et al., 2016; Nilson, 2016). Learners discuss social, economic, cultural, political, and moral problems and discover their meaning and significance.

TECHNOLOGICAL ADVANCEMENTS IN SOCIAL SCIENCE EDUCATION

Educational reform must take root in the classroom setting with informed and active participation by educators in modifying the teaching and learning process. In 1996, Berson examined the existing literature on the use and effectiveness of technology in social studies and observed that "computers (in social studies classrooms) have served the primary function of facilitating students' access to content and have been relegated to being an appendage to traditional classroom materials" (p. 495). Little empirical evidence existed to support computer integration in the social studies, and most experiences were based on anecdotal information to substantiate the positive benefits of technology. Over the past decade the conceptualization of technology in the social studies has evolved from a theoretical integration of a collection of tools to a constructivist orientation for advocating technology integration. Additionally, Web-based instruction (Donlan, 1999; Fontana, 1997) and the facilitation of multicultural awareness through telecommunications (Fabos & Young, 1999) have achieved prominence. Johnson and Rector (1997) also reinforced the importance of the Internet in social studies for developing and involving citizens in an information age. Nonetheless, Diem (2000) contends that the "promise of technology is not so much its cutting-edge advances as its innovative and imaginative applications" (p. 494); however, social studies classrooms have been especially reticent in applying uses of technology to instruction (Pahl, 1996). Shaver (1999) similarly notes that technology has little potential for stimulating instructional reform within social studies, especially in a context that has been relatively devoid of thoughtful deliberation and careful attention to instructional details.

Technology as a Useful Tool in the Social Sciences

Numerous researchers claim that technology has not appreciably changed social studies instruction (Diem, 2002; Glenn, 2002; Martorella, 1997; White, 1997a), despite anecdotal assurances of substantial progress over time. We have experienced the initial euphoria of the promise of technology, followed by a pessimistic disillusionment and, subsequently, a new pragmatic perspective on its potential. Hardware and software have continued to evolve with greater power and versatility. Drill and practice programs are now accompanied by interactive software, and innovations in hypermedia, telecommunication, and peripheral devices allow teachers to develop lessons "that enhance student skills in information retrieval, the presentation of data, the comparison and evaluation of different perspectives, and critical reflection and decision making" (Rose & Fernlund, 1997, p. 160). Although software companies continue to generate new titles, classics such as Carmen Sandiego and Oregon Trail remain popular in classrooms. Many teachers continue to rely on productivity tools, such as word processing programs, data graphing, timeline generators, and spreadsheets, while reference products also maintain widespread use. Software has gained increased visual appeal as advances in programming and larger memory capacity have led to the expansive use of graphics to capture the attention of a visually oriented youth audience. This phenomenon is exemplified in simulations that provide rich learning environments and allow students to engage in activities that would be otherwise out of their reach (Harper, Hedberg, Corderoy, & Wright, 2000).

In addition to software options, the Internet has especially gained prominence as a communication tool and resource for information available worldwide (Berson, Cruz, Duplass, & Johnston, 2004). Technology has been conceptualized as a tool to achieve goals specific to social studies. Proponents have noted its usefulness in actively engaging students in learning with the opportunity for instruction that is multidisciplinary, inquiry-oriented, student-centered, and multisensory (Eaton, 1999; Frye & Frager, 1996). Specialized areas that previously received sparse treatment in textbooks and supplementary materials can now be explored in-depth through online resources that combine updated information with appealing visuals

(Berson, 2000b). Current events and evolving areas of interest in social studies can be more easily explored with online access to information (Berson & Berson, 1999). Technology can facilitate an instructional partnership in the social studies classroom, creating venues where students' creativity and competency can be developed with various resources (Saye, 1998). Moreover, there is a growing body of knowledge on using e-mail, the World Wide Web, and Web page construction to foster global understanding and cultural insights while engaging students in various educational telecollaboration activities (Ady, 1999; Harris, 1999). Similarly, WebQuests (Donlan, 1999) and simulations (Frye & Frager, 1996) have encouraged students to explore historical and contemporary perspectives while constructing their learning with a visually stimulating and interactive tool. The lessons often rely on Web links and other technology to promote students' research, analysis, and critical thinking skills.

However, the tool-based approach is limited in reflecting what may soon be obsolete and often lacks a broader connection to educational objectives and curriculum. The promise of profound change as traditional classrooms are replaced with interactive cyber-environments—a limitless world of resources that incites students to become efficient information processors—may describe a utopia, but not reality. The innovative use of technology has not incited a transformation of curriculum and instruction. Still, it has provided experiential learning that broadens students' understanding of nations, cultures, and languages (Gragert, 2000). Curriculum directors have increasingly sought assistance in aligning digital content with the curricula, often necessitating expensive modifications to software collections to coordinate with state standards and testing (Hoff, 1999). Although teachers are generally interested in acquiring technology, this is perhaps the easiest step in the expensive and demanding process of integrating technology into teaching and learning. The decision-making process requires sound pedagogical judgment on the educational benefits, appropriateness, and logistical feasibility of computer-based learning (Harris, 1999). Educators may erroneously focus the experience of students and model in their classroom teaching the use of technology as a tool to access information and knowledge as developed by others, but they may simultaneously fail to evolve skills in critically and creatively constructing ideas and thoughts that may transform the function of society (Berson, 2000a; 127).

Constructing Knowledge and Inquiry Through the Retrieval and Analysis of Documents

An educated citizen is not necessarily an individual who has been exposed and formally instructed in every possible mode of accessing information. Given the development of new modes of information retrieval, this is not even a fathomable task. Instead, it is more critical for educated citizens to be engaged in any activity that requires them to be critical thinkers, problem solvers, creative visionaries, and accurate appraisers of benefits and risks. Constructivist practice is associated with collaborative student-initiated tasks in which the teacher models the use of a diverse array of resources and equipment to process information in a meaningful context that relates learning to students' prior knowledge and experiences. This authentic model of problem solving relies on engagement in a social context that can be facilitated through cooperative learning situations. Students have been particularly enamored by the role of researcher and archivist (Carr, 1999) as memorization tasks are replaced by analysis activities. The Web and CD-ROM activities have offered these new possibilities for sharing and using information (Bass & Rosenweig, 2000).

Digital materials are often utilized to structure inquiry learning processes that engage students in research, analysis, and interpretation of primary sources to understand the complexity of the past and the intricacies of social knowledge. The constructivist movement assumes that problem-centered instruction can be achieved through an engaged approach to learning. Student inquiry and problem solving can be facilitated through electronic technologies; however, inquiry based instruction has languished as student use of technology overshadowed teachers' understanding of these resources. Although technology may expose students to alternative perspectives and seed empathic responses, students often rely on simplified models of thinking unless they can utilize metacognitive strategies that require the application of existing knowledge to novel situations to build more complex associations. Focused instruction to orient learners to the process of making linkages between the specifics of the problem and broader knowledge can be facilitated with electronic resources (Saye & Brush, 1999). Conceptual understanding is reflected in students who exceed the mechanics of reading and writing. They act like scientists, think like mathematicians, and see connections among events today and in the past (Dockterman, 2002).

Technology and Authentic Learning in Social Sciences

The transition from print resources to the widespread availability of primary source documents on the World Wide Web has promulgated the dissemination and access to source information. The choices for social science researchers have been expanded as card catalogs and archival records have been augmented by search engines and Boolean logic (Anderson, 1999). Yet some also lament that the increased expansiveness of readily available resources is reliant on the discretion of research institutions and governmental organizations to select pertinent material, resulting in a significant underrepresentation of the extensive volume of information that is available in repositories worldwide. Although many activities of social scientists can be simulated through the Web, educators and students need an understanding that cyberspace may augment research by providing an alternative venue in which to locate information critical to a research project, but it is not a replacement. The experience of clicking on a primary source online cannot replicate the sensations associated with holding a coveted resource after seeking it out, touching the paper, examining the ink used, observing the details on the binding, and smelling the age of the document. Achieving a balance between online and traditional readings may be helpful in navigating the adaptation process for integrating advanced technologies into classroom instruction and learning (de Syon, 2000). Students may need encouragement to utilize print resources in conjunction with Internet material so that they do not overlook important aspects in their research and have quality information to gauge the credibility of information encountered online.

Additionally, although some (Cantu, 2000a) contend that the Internet facilitates access to historical resources and minimizes the role of the teacher as informational gatekeeper, there is a risk that intellectual curiosity will wane in the mass of information. Without adequate critical thinking and analysis skills, communities of learners may wallow in the midst of dubious material that is easily accessible and succumb to mental passivity when it becomes too much of a bother to seek out esoteric resources that are invaluable to the learning process. Multiple responses to the availability of online resources have been noted, including those who reject the Web as an information source, those who indiscriminately tout the wonders of online resources, and those who are optimistically cautious that the development of students' critical evaluation and search skills can overcome the weakness associated with cyber-resources (Ehman, 2002). Faculty who promote a prohibition against the use of electronic sources by students often desire a preservation of the nostalgic process of discovering resources in the library through searches that may necessitate creative reconceptualization of topics, drawing linkages and associations as an unexpected find takes place when the eye glimpses a book on the shelf that was not part of the original search but nonetheless offers important insight into the topic. The cost-benefit assessment often leads opponents of online resources to observe that few useful pages of information are acquired after students devote enormous amounts of time on the Web, when a library search may have yielded many more nonelectronic resources with less time allotment. Moreover, the volatility of material on the Web combined with the difficulty of finding verifiable information necessitates the guidance of teachers who can assist students in the process of becoming active learners in an online environment.

Proponents of online sources note that by simulating the activities of social scientists, students can be challenged to critically evaluate information. Activities that are enhanced by technology are based on recognition that desired skills can be achieved by the opportunity to utilize knowledge and information in a simulated context with real world applicability (Cox, 1997). Student achievement as measured by the goals and objectives of social studies learning standards can be promoted through technology integration (Danker, 2000; Johnson & Rector, 1997). The process of accessing and interpreting information optimizes individual's capacity for effective citizenship (Berson & Berson, 2003). The ability to manage the barrage of information facilitates informed decision making. Moreover, examination of the complex interrelationship between science, technology, and society reveals imbalances in power and inequities in the diffusion of knowledge. "The Web offers an exciting and authentic arena in which students can learn to become critical consumers of information" (Bass & Rosenweig, 2000, p. 5). Multimedia technology has enhanced the access to diverse resources that enrich the learning experience and provide an opportunity for students to not only visually examine archives of information, but also to engage in creative searches of resources so that patterns can be explored, information can be manipulated, connections can be discovered, and students can synthesize resources with their expressive capabilities to transform their connection to the material. What often has been overlooked in this process is the necessary step of instructing students to acquire a set of progressive skills that may guide their use of online resources, including technology skills, search techniques for accessing databases, and criteria for evaluating the content, presentation, and value of the information found.

Another authentic learning activity is the class field trip. Computers cannot replicate the "tactile, olfactory, visual, and dialogical experience of an actual field trip" (Bellan & Scheurman, 1998, p. 38), but they do provide an opportunity to counter the potential pitfalls associated with real life excursions outside the school setting. Virtual field trips offer a cost-effective means of exposing students to places and people around the world. They also are helpful when they precede actual field trips. The virtual trip can prepare students in advance by exposing them to the sites and sounds associated with a historical place. However, there are limitations to electronic field trips when used in isolation. Ill-prepared students can aimlessly surf the Web, achieving only a cursory overview of information. Educators also are cautioned that virtual field trips lose their educational value when they are primarily used as a means to entertain students without regard for achieving curriculum objectives. Conversely, authentic learning is enhanced when the virtual field trip is used as a resource to develop students' prior knowledge and facilitate question formation. Necessary elements include a comprehensive information gathering process that is accompanied by advance preparation and subsequent follow up by the teacher.

Digitally Enhanced Writing and Electronic Dialogue

Writing and discussion enable students to be active participants in the learning process. The exchange of ideas allows students to evolve their skills in articulating information and extending their understanding of concepts. The digital media has expanded the possibilities to create new learning opportunities that require connecting with others at a geographic distance through written communication. Electronic interactions foster connections between content and literacy skills while simultaneously promoting guided dialogue. This online dialogue involves students in constructing discussion, practicing public communication skills, and creating public projects, such as Web pages. The formation of e-mail learning communities has facilitated the connection between diverse groups of individuals and highlighted their commonalties while promoting understanding of their cultural diversity (Baugh & Baugh, 1997). Merryfield (2000) has applied electronic technologies in social studies teacher education and noted that threaded discussions enhance culturally diverse learning communities by expanding worldviews and changing patterns of voice and dominance in the interactions. Although electronic technologies facilitate meaningful discussions in which controversial and sensitive issues such as prejudice, privilege, and discrimination are explored in depth, cross-cultural learning is simultaneously hampered by the loss of vital contextual cues (i.e., body language, facial expressions, etc.) that uniquely define face to-face communication (Fabos & Young, 1999).

Bridging the gap between face-to-face interaction and threaded discussions is the use of tele collaboration to bring together geographically distant communities that also may represent cultural diverse settings (Sembor, 1997). In this era of globalization, the Internet provides social studies teachers the opportunity to expose their students to multiple perspective and contexts beyond the textbook through participation in many tele collaborative projects. These interactions can extend to authentic living history projects, in which artifacts and resources, which are stored and maintained within online collections and virtual community museums, are analyzed. Additionally, digital learning activities are especially well suited for motivating students with a variety of learning styles. Cantu (1999) suggested that an Internet-based model works well with teaching strategies in the history classroom that incorporate Howard Gardner's theory of multiple intelligences. The resources of the World Wide Web offer access to information and learning experiences that serve as a pedagogical platform for multiple intelligence lessons, including verbal linguistic products and interpersonal interaction through e-mail, class chat rooms, and Web site development. Technology facilitates a multisensory approach that accommodates varying learning styles through rich and diverse online materials and experiences. By structuring instruction to appeal to different learning styles, students can be engaged and motivated for extended periods of time, and educators can enjoy the flexibility of offering a new way to bring relevant first-hand experiences into social studies content.

Portable Technology

Technology in the social studies has potential as an instructional tool in teaching students both content and processing skills. Nonetheless, initiatives have often lacked the perspective of children who are helping to forge the technology landscape through their ambitious participation in this global medium. Portable devices offer the opportunity to fully engage children and youth with direct applications of the technology in applied contexts. Among these technologies are handheld devices, digital cameras, and mobile phones. Additionally, the evolving area of wireless computing offers the potential of inspiring different educational experiences that are free of the traditional constraints of the classroom or lab setting. The technologies used in handheld devices have evolved during the last decade, while digital cameras and cell phones have emerged from technology that is over a quarter-century old. These tools have increasingly become affordable for consumers and schools. For example, in the digital camera market, approximately one-third of cameras sold in 2001 were digital (7 million), and analysts predicted digital cameras to outsell film cameras by 2010. T5his has come to pass. In the year 2023 film cameras are part of our history. Flash memory card readers, Bluetooth, sender and other technologies have significantly simplified transfer of images from camera to computer or printer. The operating systems of both the PC and Macintosh now include multimedia programs that facilitate digital storytelling.

Similarly, handheld technology offers a means to maintain the physical structure of the classroom while enhancing content delivery and student productivity. Since learning is not restricted to a lab setting, handhelds allow versatility for application in authentic contexts. This is especially true when the handheld technology is designed explicitly for use by teachers and students in the classroom setup. Beyond organizational skills within the classroom, students can use the handheld for survey and data collection, notation on field trips, networked communication, collaborative writing, and tracking of chronological events (Whitworth, Owings Swan, & Berson, 2002). The devices offer value, utility, and portability. Through the effective and appropriate use of handheld technology, early implementers are anticipating a paradigm shift in how technology is integrated into the teaching and learning process in a constantly changing world. Teachers will be able to spend more time teaching students to be critical thinkers, effective communicators, and responsible citizens. Additionally, by using handheld technologies built specifically for education, less time will likely be spent adapting the technology for use in the classroom. By sending students into their world with portable technology in hand, teachers provide opportunities for children and youth to bring their lives into the classroom, creating a rich, authentic authoring space. Writing notes, developing timelines, and arranging pictures as artifacts within a digital space allow students to explore events from multiple perspectives.

As an extension or adaptation, students might create digital movies about an event, place or individual, using the various portable technologies to capture scenes, artifacts, and observation notes that would be woven together to tell a particular story. In an era of increasing educational accountability, new innovations in education must be linked to content standards in order to succeed. Current national standards in social studies lend themselves to work with portable technologies. The National Social Studies Standards (1994) designed by the National Council for the Social Studies specify that students are to "analyze and explain the ways that groups, societies, and cultures address human needs and concerns; and demonstrate the value of cultural diversity, as well as cohesion, within and across groups." Additional standards require students to "articulate personal connections to time, place, and social/cultural systems; identify, describe, and express appreciation for the influences of various historical and contemporary cultures on an individual's daily life; and analyze the role of perceptions, attitudes, values, and beliefs in the development of personal identity." There are strong potential connections in all the areas of social science education as educators focus on the common goal of enhancing and enriching social studies curricula by building from the base of quality pedagogic practice.

Artificial Intelligence in The Social Science Education

Just as the classroom teacher's role has evolved from "sage on the stage" to "guide on the side," a similar shift in the role of artificial intelligence in education has been recommended, replacing computer-directed learning with software that supports the learning processes of students engaged in collaborative critical inquiry (Suthers et al., 2001). Students using technology that is void of software that enables rich explorations and investigations are often simply learning the same material as those students not using technology and are often learning it similarly. Even with systems that provide cognitive tools and open environments for exploration, students could still construct knowledge to satisfy some machine expectation instead of the knowledge specific to the intended problem situation (Balacheff, 1993). Concerning artificial intelligence (AI), we are still far from achieving humans' versatile cognitive skills. Therefore, research will continue along several paths—each with its ardent proponents (Wagman, 1997). We anticipate a convergence with these paths in the next decade. The proponents of cognitive tutors are already realizing the importance of building open learning environments supporting explorations into their integrated tutoring systems (Anderson, Corbett, Koedinger, & Pelletier, 1995). Educational technology is gradually moving away from being a distinct object of attention to an integrated tool used in the teaching and learning of social studies. Studies such as those undertaken by Nathan, Koedinger, and Tabachneck (2000) on teachers' knowledge and beliefs emphasize enhanced programs of teacher preparation and the development of theoretically and empirically rooted approaches to classroom instruction.

AI applications are new and exciting technologies in today's educational environments. The impact of these technologies is not limited to education but is felt in all areas of social life (Holt, 2018). While Reinhart (2018) states that 85% of Americans use at least one AI-assisted technology daily, Chiu (2021) says that the influence of innovative AI applications everywhere significantly affects society and future generations. At this point, it is important for individuals to understand the structure of their society surrounded by AI and to grow up knowing how to use these technologies effectively and ethically. Social studies, which aims to prepare individuals as active citizens of today and the future, will play an essential role. In social studies, hands-on activities can be designed where students interact with AI technologies and discover their working principles and social effects. At this point, social studies teachers can direct students to interact with various AI technologies. For example, in a scenario where chatbots are used, the teacher can organize classroom learning activities requiring students to use them themselves. In addition, after a short training, students can develop their chatbots through non-coding programs such as Mobilemonkey, Botsify, and MindBehind and present them in the classroom. Through these hands-on activities, students can better learn the basic working principles of chatbot technology and concepts such as natural language processing and understanding specific to chatbots. Fostering hands-on experiences is an essential element in social studies education. Real-time application of hands-on experiential learning activities and AI pedagogies in the social studies classroom proves critically important in improving technical skills, creativity, critical thinking, and problem-solving skills essential for AI success (Southworth et al., 2023). Ng et al. (2021) stated that AI learning originally started with university-level computer science education, which is challenging for social science students and requires advanced programming competencies. Still, with the emergence of age-appropriate hardware and software such as chatbots or translation applications, young students have the chance to use AI technologies while acquiring AI literacy. At this point, social studies teachers can benefit from these age-appropriate AI technologies while teaching AI literacy.

Although the necessity of teaching AI to students has been widely discussed in recent years (Su, Zhong, and Ng, 2022), bringing this literacy to individuals through education has become an important issue (Laupichler et al., 2022), attempts to promote AI literacy for citizens are in adequate (Kong, Cheung, & Zhang, 2021). In addition, awareness of the potential role of social studies in this regard is quite weak. However, considering the increasing importance of AI technologies and their possible future effects, it is possible to say that AI literacy may become an important citizenship qualification of our age. Social studies can play an important role in teaching this literacy, which is currently seen as a sub-type of digital literacy (Yang, 2022) but is likely to become an independent and important citizenship qualification. At this point, it can be suggested that social studies educators conduct theoretical and applied studies that point out the relationship between AI literacy and social studies. These studies will help the development of new perspectives on the subject, revealing the potential role of social studies in teaching AI literacy and encouraging social studies educators to work on this subject.

CHALLENGES AND ETHICAL CONSIDERATIONS IN THE SOCIAL SCIENCE EDUCATION

Social science education is faced with several ethical challenges today. Critical decisions must be made to ensure personal freedoms are protected and data is used appropriately in social education. Which ethical issues are the most important in applying technology in social science education? Here are the top five according to (Ali, et al. 2019; Almeida, et al. 2021):

Misuse of Personal Information: One of the primary ethical dilemmas in our technologically empowered age revolves around how instructors and students use personal information. We constantly provide personal details as we browse internet sites, make online references, enter our information on websites, engage with different scholars online, and participate in social media. Various organizations often gather information to hyper-personalize our online experiences, but to what extent is that information impeding our right to privacy? Personal information is the new gold, as the saying goes.

Misinformation and Deep Fakes: One thing that became evident during the 2016 and 2020 U.S. presidential elections was the potential of misinformation to gain a wider support base. The effect created polarization that has had wide-reaching effects on global academic environments. In contrast to how information was accessed prior to the internet, we are constantly flooded with real-time events and news as it breaks. Celebrities and political figures can disseminate opinions on social media without fact-checking, which is then aggregated and further spread despite its accuracy—or inaccuracy. Information no longer undergoes the strenuous validation process that we formerly used to publish newspapers and books. This affects social sciences as some information is sometimes used to inform the scholarship. Similarly, video was believed to tell a story undeniably rooted in truth. But deep fake technology now allows such a sophisticated manipulation of digital imagery that people appear to be saying and doing things that never happened. The potential for privacy invasion and misuse of identity is very high with the use of this technology.

Lack of Oversight and Acceptance of Responsibility: Most companies operate with a hybrid stack, comprised of a blend of third-party and owned technology. As a result, there is often some confusion about where responsibility lies when it comes to governance, use of big data, cybersecurity concerns and managing personally identifiable information. Whose responsibility is it *really* to ensure data is protected? If you engage a third party for software that processes payments, do you bear any responsibility if credit card details are breached? The fact is that it's everyone's job. Players in the social science scholarship need to adopt a perspective where all collective parties share responsibility. Similarly, many experts lobby for a global approach to governance, arguing that local policing is resulting in fractured policy making and a widespread mismanagement of data. Similar to climate change, we need to band together if we truly want to see improvement.

Use of AI in the social science academy: Artificial intelligence certainly offers great scholarship potential. But, at what point do AI systems cross an ethical line into dangerous territory? Brey, (1998) provides the following answers:

- Facial recognition: Use of software to find individuals can quickly become a less-than-ethical problem. According to the NY Times, facial recognition has various concerns, such as misuse, racial bias and restriction of personal freedoms. The ability to track movements and activity quickly morphs into a lack of privacy. Facial recognition also isn't foolproof and can create bias in certain situations.
- Replacement of jobs: While this is anticipated to a certain degree, AI is meant to increase automation of low-level tasks in many situations so that human resources can be used on more strategic initiatives and complicated job duties. The large-scale elimination of jobs has many workers concerned about job security, but AI is more likely to create jobs.
- Health tracking: The pandemic brought contact tracing into the mainstream. Is it ethical to track the health status of people and how will that impact our limitations on them?
- Bias in AI technology: Technology is built by programmers and inherits the bias of its creators because humans inherently have bias. "Technology is inherently flawed. Does it even matter who developed the algorithms? AI systems learn to make decisions based on training and coding data, which can be tainted by human bias or reflect historical or social inequities," according to Forbes. Leading AI developer Google has even experienced an issue where AI software believes male nurses and female historians do not exist.

Autonomous Technology: Self-driving cars, robotic weapons and drones for service are no longer a thing of the future—they are a thing of the present and they come with ethical dilemmas. Robotic machines in place of human soldiers is a very real possibility, along with self-driving cars and package delivery via unmanned drone. Autonomous technology packs a punch when it comes to business potential, but there is significant concern that comes with allowing programmed technology to operate seemingly without needed oversight. It's a frequently mentioned ethical concern that we trust our technology too much without fully understanding it.

CONCLUSION

Criticisms of the education system have reflected that students continue to receive an archaic education while attending school in the 21st century. Although the social studies has existed as a discrete discipline for many years, traditional, teacher, and textbook-centered methods of instruction dominate the classroom learning experience (Dunn, 2000). Technology has typically been assimilated into existing roles and functions of social studies instruction, and little in the way of transformations of teaching and learning occurred during the formative period of its use (Cuban, Kirkpatrick, & Peck, 2001). New developments are contributing to a dynamic modification of technology integration in which the classroom becomes a site of active learning and thinking, fostered by the technological resources available. Yet this encouraging approach to the use of technology is still based on anecdotal experience, and needs further time for the educational impact to be assessed for its influence in facilitating inquiry-based learning, encouraging constructivist pedagogies, and disseminating an exchange of knowledge representations across regional settings. In educational settings, effectiveness must also take into account the facilitation of students' learning. When social studies students put impressive pictures into a report and cite the latest information, the experience does not necessarily equate with the ability to formulate an original thought, engage in critical analysis, or avoid problematic cyber-activity. Direct instruction in online procedures to promote safe and effective educational outcomes has often been overlooked (Berson & Berson, 1999; Berson, Berson, & Ralston, 1999). The investment in the creation of technologically competent students necessitates modifications in the social studies curricula so that tasks are combined to facilitate students' utilization of their critical analysis skills to uncover bias and discriminate between quality information and tainted data (Berson & Berson, 2003). How much progress has been made since 1996 in integrating technology into instruction? The World Wide Web, in particular, has expanded as a resource for the social studies classroom. However, the promise of the increased access to information has not been harnessed for purposes of optimizing its educational application. There is still a need for exemplary models that demonstrate innovative applications as well as guidelines for creative use and infusion of technology into instruction. Martorella (1997) warned of the "rapid obsolescence of both our technology and our discourse related to it" (p. 512). The life span of technology is brief, although education institutions have attempted to extend the usability of their limited resources.

The discipline of social studies has often disregarded its unique position to not only enhance education with advances in technological resources, but also to reflect on the impact of technology on our society. We have not yet identified what is beneficial, effective, or informative about the current use of technology in education (Berson, Lee, & Stuckart, 2001). We have lacked universal constructs regarding the integration of technology into the social studies and struggled to identify a theoretical basis to guide the selection and application of technology in the classroom. The current marginalization of computers as a means to facilitate students' access to content does not take into account the potential role of technology in developing students' process of inquiry. Students may encounter online information that lacks authenticity, accuracy, and importance. Preparation of students to accommodate the challenges of online interaction necessitates more than mere technical proficiency. The expertise of a well-trained educator is crucial for evolving a disciplined inquiry of social problems by students (Saye & Brush, 1999). This process includes recognition of the impact of technology on the development of society. Criteria for effective citizenship have changed due to the influence of technology, and the demands on students' learning and teacher instruction have been altered by the expansive access to information and subsequent processing required of technology-driven forms of knowledge. Concern about the social consequences of technology have driven some to suggest de-emphasizing technology in education (Postman, 2000; Stoll, 1999), while others have argued that effective instruction (particularly social studies education) must include a range of computer technology skills (Martorella, 1997). Yet the field of social studies cannot ignore the influence of technology on our society and is obligated to at least consider its political, sociological, psychological, historical, geographic, and economic effects.

The required shift in pedagogical style and perspective will only be accomplished by modifications in the training of social studies teachers with technology that provides a framework for integrating it with instructional practices to improve teaching and learning. Moreover, this training will not be forthcoming unless social studies teacher educators have empirical evidence of effectiveness to guide their reconceptualization and implementation of best practice. Empirically validated research focusing on the effects of technology in social studies classrooms is needed. The literature lacks longitudinal perspectives on technology and its impact on students or instructional performance in the field. There is a void of metacognitive studies, and many articles continue to be impressionistic or rely on data that tend to involve short-term analyses of single concepts. Technology is at an exciting crossroad. The adolescence of technology integration into the social studies has been tumultuous. Some educators have made a stronger connection with computers and their curricular application, touting the opportunity to enrich students' learning and critical skill development. Others have cringed at the influence asserted by a tool whose power is largely.

REFERENCES

Ady, J. K. (1999). Computer-mediated communication in a high school global education curriculum: A brochure project. *Social Studies*, *90*(4), 159–163. doi:10.1080/00377999909602408

Ahmad, C. (2013). *The Effectiveness of Small Group Discussion Method in Teaching Reading*. Perpustakaan.upi.edu.

Ali, S. A., Payne, B. H., Williams, R., Park, H. W., & Breazeal, C. (2019). *Constructionism, ethics,and creativity: developing primary and middle school artificial intelligence education*. Paper presented at International Workshop on Education in Artificial Intelligence (EDUAI), Palo Alto, CA, USA.

Almeida, D., Shmarko, K., & Lomas, E. (2021). The ethics of facial recognition technologies, surveillance, and accountability in an age of artificial intelligence: A comparative analysis of US, EU, and UK regulatory frameworks. *AI and Ethics*. Advance online publication. doi:10.1007/s43681-021-00077-w PMID:34790955

Anazifa, R. D., & Djukri, D. (2017). Project-Based Learning and Problem-Based Learning: Are They Effective to Improve Student's Thinking Skills? *Jurnal Pendidikan IPA Indonesia*, *6*(2), 346–355. doi:10.15294/jpii.v6i2.11100

Anderson, D. L. (1999). Heuristics for educational use and evaluation of electronic information: A case of searching for shaker history on the World Wide Web. *Journal of the Association for History & Computing*, *2*(2). http://www.mcel.pacificu.edu/JAHC/JAHCII2/INDEX.html

Anderson, T., & Dron, J. (2011). Three generations of distance education pedagogy. *International Review of Research in Open and Distance Learning*, *12*(3), 80–97. doi:10.19173/irrodl.v12i3.890

Ayers, E. L. (1999). *History in hypertext*. Retrieved August 24, 1999 from: http://jefferson.village.virginia.edu/vcdh/Ayers.OAH.html

Balacheff, N. (1993). Artificial intelligence and real thinking. In C. Keitel & K. Ruthven (Eds.), *Learning from computers: Mathematics education and technology* (pp. 131–158). Springer-Verlag. doi:10.1007/978-3-642-78542-9_6

Bass, R., & Rosenweig, R. (2000). *Rewriting the history and social studies classroom needs, frameworks, dangers, and proposals*. White Papers on the Future of Technology in Education: U.S. Department of Education. Available: https://www.air.org/forum/Bass.pdf

Bates, A. W. (2019). *Teaching in a Digital Age: Guidelines for designing teaching and learning for a digital age*. Tony Bates Associates Ltd.

Baugh, I. W., & Baugh, J. G. (1997). Global classrooms: E-mail learning communities. *Learning and Leading with Technology, 25*(3), 38–41.

Becker, H. J. (1999). Internet usage by teachers: Conditions of professional use and teacher-directed student use. In *Teaching, Learning, & Computing: 1998 National Survey, Report* (Vol. 1). Center for Research on Information Technology & Organizations, University of California, Irvine.

Bellan, J. M., & Scheurman, G. (1998). Actual and virtual reality: Making the most of field trips. *Social Education, 62*(1), 35–40.

Berson, I. R., & Berson, M. J. (2003). Digital literacy for cyber safety, digital awareness, and media literacy. *Social Education, 67*(3), 164–168.

Berson, M. J. (1996). Effectiveness of computer technology in the social studies: A literature review. *Journal of Research on Computing in Education, 28*(4), 486–499. doi:10.1080/08886504.1996.10782179

Berson, M. J. (2000a). Rethinking research and pedagogy in the social studies: The creation of caring connections through technology and advocacy. *Theory and Research in Social Education, 28*(1), 121–131. doi:10.1080/00933104.2000.10505900

Berson, M. J. (2000b). The Caribbean online: Exploration through Internet resources. *Social Education, 64*(2), 101–104.

Berson, M. J. (2002). Reflecting on technology in the social studies: Past, present, and future perspectives. *The International Social Studies Forum, 2*(2), 159–161.

Berson, M. J., & Berson, I. R. (1999). Coming to terms with Mother Nature: Using the Web to educate children about natural disasters. *Social Studies and the Young Learner, 12*(1), 19–21.

Berson, M. J., Berson, I. R., & Ralston, M. E. (1999). Threshing out the myths and facts of Internet safety: A response to "Separating wheat from chaff.". *Social Education, 63*(3), 60–61.

Berson, M. J., Cruz, B., Duplass, J., & Johnston, H. (2004). *Social studies on the Internet* (2nd ed.). Merrill/Prentice Hall.

Berson, M. J., Mason, C. L., Heinecke, W. F., & Coutts, C. B. (2001). An examination of beliefs and practices of social studies methods faculty. *The International Social Studies Forum, 1*(2), 89–105.

Bolick, C. M. (2002). Digital history TIP: Preservice social studies teachers' experiences in a technology-rich field initiative. *Journal of Computing in Teacher Education, 19*(2), 54–60.

Bower, M., Kennedy, G. E., Dalgarno, B., Lee, M. J., & Kenney, J. (2015). Design and implementation factors in blended synchronous learning environments: Outcomes from a cross-case analysis. *Computers & Education, 86*, 1–17. doi:10.1016/j.compedu.2015.03.006

Brassler, M., & Dettmers, J. (2017). How to enhance interdisciplinary competence interdisciplinary problem-based learning versus interdisciplinary project-based learning. *The Interdisciplinary Journal of Problem-Based Learning, 11*(2), 1–12. doi:10.7771/1541-5015.1686

Braun, J. (1997). Past, possibilities, and potholes on the information superhighway. *Social Education, 61*(3), 49–153.

Braun, J. A. (2002). Social studies education and technology: A rock and roll perspective. *The International Social Studies Forum, 2*(2), 167–169.

Brey, P. (1998). The Politics of Computer Systems and the Ethics of Design. In J. van den Hoven (Ed.), *Computer Ethics: Philosophical Enquiry*. Rotterdam University Press.

Brown, A. H., & Green, T. D. (2015). *The essentials of instructional design: Connecting fundamental principles with process and practice*. Routledge. doi:10.4324/9781315757438

Cantu, D. A. (1999). An Internet-based multiple intelligences model for teaching high school history. *Journal of the Association for History & Computing, 2*(3). http://mcel.pacificu.edu/jahc/jahcII3/ index.html

Cantu, D. A. (2000a). Teaching pre-columbian and colonial American history on the Web. *Journal of the Association for History & Computing*, *3*(1). http://mcel.pacificu.edu/JAHC/JAHCIII1/index.html

Cantu, D. A. (2000b). Technology integration in preservice history teacher education. *Journal of the Association for History & Computing*, *3*(2). http://mcel.pacificu.edu/JAHC/JAHCIII2/index.html

Carr, F. L. (1999). Using the World Wide Web as a teaching tool in an introduction to American history: Some technical and ethical difficulties. *Journal of the Association for History & Computing*, *2*(3). http://mcel.pacificu.edu/jahc/jahcII3/index.html

Chiu, K. F. C. (2021). A holistic approach to the design of artificial intelligence (AI) education for K-12schools. *TechTrends*, *65*(5), 796–807. doi:10.1007/s11528-021-00637-1

Cohen, L., Manion, L., Morrison, K., & Wyse, D. (2010). *A guide to teaching practice*. Rutledge. doi:10.4324/9780203848623

Corbett, J. R. (1995). Cognitive tutors: Lessons learned. *Journal of the Learning Sciences*, *4*(2), 167–207. doi:10.1207/s15327809jls0402_2

Cox, A. C. (1997). Using the stock market game in the social studies classroom. *Social Education*, *61*(6), 347–350.

Cuban, L., Kirkpatrick, H., & Peck, C. (2001). High access and low use of technologies in high school classrooms: Explaining an apparent paradox. *American Educational Research Journal*, *38*(4), 813–834. doi:10.3102/00028312038004813

Danker, A. (2000). Linking technology with social studies learning standards. *Social Studies*, *91*(6), 253–256. doi:10.1080/00377990009602474

De Syon, G. (2000). Teaching the space program with the World Wide Web: Challenges and rewards of assigning online readings. *Journal of the Association for History & Computing*, *3*(1). http:// mcel.pacificu.edu/JAHC/JAHCIII1/index.html

Demir, Ş. Ş., & Demir, M. (2023). Professionals' perspectives on ChatGPT in the tourism industry: Does it inspire awe or concern? *Journal of Tourism Theory and Research*, *9*(2), 61–77. doi:10.24288/jttr.1313481

Diem, R. (2000). Can it make a difference? Technology and social studies. *Theory and Research in Social Education*, *28*(4), 493–501. doi:10.1080/00933104.2000.10505920

Diem, R. A. (2002). It was twenty years ago today: Prospects for infusing technology in the social studies. *The International Social Studies Forum*, *2*(2), 171–173.

Dockterman, D. (2002). *Weaving technology into your teaching*. Tom Snyder Productions, Inc.

Donlan, L. (1999). Come dream with us: Online projects teach more than technology. *Learning and Leading with Technology*, *26*(7), 42–45.

Dunn, M. A. (2000). Closing the book on social studies: Four classroom teachers go beyond the text. *Social Studies*, *91*(3), 132–136. doi:10.1080/00377990009602456

Eaton, J. S. (1999). The social studies classroom on the eve of the cyber century. *Social Education*, *63*(3), 139–141.

Ehman, L. H. (2002). Why haven't secondary social studies teachers adopted information technologies? *The International Social Studies Forum*, *2*(2), 175–178.

Fabos, B., & Young, M. D. (1999). Telecommunications in the classroom: Rhetoric versus reality. *Review of Educational Research*, *69*(3), 217–259. doi:10.3102/00346543069003217

Fontana, L. A. (1997). Online learning opportunities: Implications for the social studies. In P. H. Martorella (Ed.), *Interactive technologies and the social studies: Emerging issues and applications* (pp. 1–25). State University of New York Press.

Frye, B., & Frager, A. M. (1996). Civilization, colonization, SimCity: Simulations for the social studies classroom. *Learning and Leading with Technology*, *24*(2), 21–23, 32.

Garrison, D. R., & Kanuka, H. (2004). Blended learning: Uncovering its transformative potential in higher education. *The Internet and Higher Education*, *7*(2), 95–105. doi:10.1016/j.iheduc.2004.02.001

Gholami, M., Moghadam, P. K., Mohammadipoor, F., Tarahi, M. J., Sak, M., Toulabi, T., & Pour, A. H. H. (2016). Comparing the effects of problem-based learning and the traditional lecture method on critical thinking skills and metacognitive awareness in nursing students in a critical care nursing course. *Nurse Education Today*, *45*, 16–21. doi:10.1016/j.nedt.2016.06.007 PMID:27429398

Glenn, A. D. (2002). Thirty years and some of the same issues. *The International Social Studies Forum*, *2*(2), 179–181.

Gragert, E. H. (2000, Sept). Expanding international education through the Internet: No longer limited to the global studies and language curriculum. *White Paper from the Secretary's Conference on Educational Technology, U.S. Department of Education*: Washington, DC. Available: https://www.ed.gov/Technology/techconf/2000/ed_gragert.pdf

Gregorius, R. M. (2017). Performance of underprepared students in traditional versus animation-based flipped-classroom settings. *Chemistry Education Research and Practice, 18*(4), 841–848. doi:10.1039/C7RP00130D

Harper, B., Hedberg, J., Corderoy, B., & Wright, R. (2000). Employing cognitive tools within interactive multimedia applications. In S. P. Lajoie (Ed.), *Computers as cognitive tools: No more walls* (pp. 227–245). Erlbaum.

Harris, J. (1999). First steps to telecollaboration. *Learning and Leading with Technology, 27*(3), 54-57.

Hattie, J. (2009). *Visible learning: A synthesis of over 800 meta-analyses relating to achievement*. Routledge.

Holt, M. (2018). Artificial intelligence in modern society. *Integrated Studies*, 138. https://digitalcommons.murraystate.edu/bis437/138

Hudson, D. (1997). *Rewired: A brief and opinionated net history*. Macmillan Technical Publishing.

Johnson, C., & Rector, J. (1997). The Internet ten: Using the Internet to meet social studies curriculum standards. *Social Education, 61*(3), 167–169.

Keiper, T., Harwood, A., & Larson, B. E. (2000, Fall). Preservice teachers' perceptions of infusing computer technology onto social studies instruction. *Theory and Research in Social Education, 28*(4), 566–579. doi:10.1080/00933104.2000.10505924

Kolmos, A., & de Graaff, E. (2014). Problem-based and project-based learning in engineering education. Cambridge Handbook of Engineering Education Research, 141-161.

Kong, S. C., Cheung, W. M. Y., & Zhang, G. (2022). Evaluating an AI literacy programme for empoweringand developing concepts, literacy and ethical awareness in senior secondary students. *Education and Information Technologies*. Advance online publication. doi:10.1007/s10639-022-11408-7

Kubiatko, M., & Vaculová, I. (2011). Project-based learning: Characteristic and the experiences with application in the science subjects. *Energy Education Science and Technology, Part B. Social and Educational Studies, 3*(1), 65–74.

Kwon, S. M., Wardrip, P. S., & Gomez, L. M. (2014). Co-design of interdisciplinary projects as a mechanism for school capacity growth. *Improving Schools, 17*(1), 54–71. doi:10.1177/1365480213519517

Laupichler, M. C., Aster, A., Schirch, J., & Raupach, T. (2022). Artificial intelligence literacy in higher and adult education: A scoping literature review. *Computers and Education: Artificial Intelligence, 3*, 100101. doi:10.1016/j.caeai.2022.100101

Lee, M. J., & Stuckart, D. W. (2001). Promise and practice of computer technologies in the social studies: A critical analysis. In W. B. Stanley (Ed.), *Critical issues in social studies research for the 21st century* (pp. 209–229). Information Age Publishing.

Maqbool, S., Ismail, S. A. M. B. M., Maqbool, S., & Hassan, S. U. (2018). Effects of Traditional Lecture Method and Multi-Sensory Approach on ELT Learners at Graduate Level. International. *Journal of Academic Research in Progressive Education and Development*, *7*(4), 488–505.

Martorella, P. H. (1997). Technology and social studies—or: Which way to the sleeping giant? *Theory and Research in Social Education, 25*(4), 511–514. doi:10.1080/00933104.1997.10505828

Mason, C., Berson, M., Diem, R., Hicks, D., Lee, J., & Dralle, T. (2000). Guidelines for using technology to prepare social studies teachers. *Contemporary Issues in Technology & Teacher Education, 1*(1), 107–116.

Mason, C. L., & Berson, M. J. (2000). Computer-mediated communication in elementary social studies methods. *Theory and Research in Social Education, 28*(4), 527–545. doi:10.1080/00933104.2000.10505922

Merryfield, M. M. (2000, Fall). Using electronic technologies to promote equity and cultural diversity in social studies education. *Theory and Research in Social Education, 28*(4), 502–526. doi:10.1080/00933104.2000.10505921

Nathan, M. J., Koedinger, K. R., & Tabachneck, H. J. M. (2000). Teachers' and researchers' beliefs of early algebra development. *Journal of Mathematics Education Research, 31*(2), 168–190. doi:10.2307/749750

National Council for the Social Studies Curriculum Standards Task Force. (1994). *Expectations of excellence: Curriculum standards for social studies (Bulletin 89).* National Council for the Social Studies.

Ng, D. T. K., Leung, J. K. L., Chu, S. K. W., & Qiao, M. S. (2021). Conceptualizing AI literacy: An exploratory review. *Computers and Education: Artificial Intelligence, 2*, 100041. doi:10.1016/j.caeai.2021.100041

Nilson, L. (2016). *Teaching at its best: A research-based resource for college instructors*. Jossey Bass.

Oblinger, D. G., & Oblinger, J. L. (2005). *Educating the Net Generation*. EDUCAUSE.

Pahl, R. H. (1996). Digital technology and social studies. In B. G. Massialas & R. F. Allen (Eds.), *Crucial Issues in teaching social studies K– 12* (pp. 341–386). Wadsworth.

Postman, N. (2000). Will our children only inherit the wind? *Theory and Research in Social Education, 28*(4), 580–586. doi:10.1080/00933104.2000.10505925

Reinhart, R. J. (2018). *Most Americans already using artificial intelligence products*. https://perma.cc/RVY5-WP9WS

Risinger, C. F. (1996). Webbing the social studies: Using Internet and World Wide Web resources in social studies instruction. *Social Education, 60*(2), 111–112.

Risinger, C. F. (2002). Technology, the social studies, an educational change. *The International Social Studies Forum, 2*(2), 187–190.

Rose, S. A., & Fernlund, P. M. (1997). Using technology for powerful social studies learning. *Social Education, 61*(3), 160–166.

Rose, S. A., & Winterfeldt, H. F. (1998). Waking the sleeping giant: A learning community in social studies methods and technology. *Social Education, 62*(3), 151–152.

Sarıhan, A., Oray, N. C., Güllüpınar, B., Yanturali, S., Atilla, R., & Musal, B. (2016). The comparison of the efficiency of traditional lectures to video-supported lectures within the training of the Emergency Medicine residents. *Turkish Journal of Emergency Medicine, 16*(3), 107–111. doi:10.1016/j.tjem.2016.07.002 PMID:27857987

Saye, J. W. (1998). Creating time to develop student thinking: Team teaching with technology. *Social Education, 62*(6), 356–362.

Saye, J. W., & Brush, T. (1999). Student engagement with social issues in a multimedia-supported learning environment. *Theory and Research in Social Education, 27*(4), 472–504. doi:10.1080/00933104.1999.10505891

Sembor, E. C. (1997). Citizenship, diversity, and distance learning: Video conferencing in Connecticut. *Social Education, 61*(3), 154–159.

Shaver, J. P. (1999). Electronic technology and the future of social studies in elementary and secondary schools. *Journal of Education, 181*(3), 13–41. doi:10.1177/002205749918100303

Siemens, G. (2005). Connectivism: A learning theory for the digital age. *International Journal of Instructional Technology and Distance Learning*, *2*(1), 3–10.

Siemens, G., & Long, P. (2011). Penetrating the fog: Analytics in learning and education. *EDUCAUSE Review*, *46*(5), 30–32.

Southworth, J., Migliaccio, K., Glover, J., Glover, J. N., Reed, D., McCarty, C., Brendemuhl, J., & Thomas, A. (2023). Developing a model for AI Across the curriculum: Transforming the higher education landscape via innovation in AI literacy. *Computers and Education: Artificial Intelligence*, *4*, 100127. doi:10.1016/j.caeai.2023.100127

Steinbauer, G., Kandlhofer, M., Chklovski, T., Heintz, F., & Koenig, S. (2021). A differentiated discussion about AI education K-12. *Kunstliche Intelligenz*, *35*(2), 131–137. doi:10.1007/s13218-021-00724-8 PMID:34007103

Stoll, C. (1999). *High-tech heretic*. Doubleday.

Su, J., Zhong, Y., & Ng, D. T. K. (2022). A meta-review of literature on educational approaches for teaching at the K -12 levels in the Asia-Pacific region. *Computer and Education: Artificial Intelligence*, *3*, 100065. doi:10.1016/j.caeai.2022.100065

Suthers, D., Connelly, J., Lesgold, A., Paolucci, M., Erdosne, E., Toth, J., & Weiner, A. (2001). Representational and advisory guidance for students learning scientific inquiry. In K. D. Forbus & P. J. Feltovich (Eds.), *Smart machines in education* (pp. 7–35). American Association for Artificial Intelligence.

Wagman, M. (1997). *Cognitive science and the symbolic operations of human and artificial intelligence: theory and research into the intellective processes*. Praeger Publishers.

Welty, W. M. (1989). Discussion Method Teaching. *Change*, *21*(July/August), 40–49. doi:10.1080/00091383.1989.9939866

White, C. S. (1997a). Information technology in U.S. social studies classrooms: Potentials and realities. Washington DC: Office of Educational Research and Improvement. (ERIC Document Reproduction Service No. ED 421 415)

White, C. S. (1997b). Technology and social studies: An introduction. *Social Education*, *61*(3), 147–148.

Whitworth, S. A., & Berson, M. J. (2003). Computer technology in the social studies: An examination of the effectiveness literature (1996–2001). *Contemporary Issues in Technology & Teacher Education, 2*(4). http://www.citejournal.org/vol2/iss4/socialstudies/ article1 .cfm

Whitworth, S. A., Owings Swan, K., & Berson, M. J. (2002). Handheld computing in the social studies. *Social Education, 66*(3), 174–179.

Wiley, D. (2017). What is open pedagogy? In E. Mays (Ed.), *A Guide to Making Open Textbooks with Students* (pp. 9–16). Rebus Community.

Zhu, M., Sari, A., & Lee, M. H. (2018). The impact of flipped classroom design on student performance and perceptions in the learning of mathematics in higher education: A meta-analysis. *Educational Technology Research and Development, 66*(2), 427–453.

ADDITIONAL READING

Ali, F. (2023). Let the devil speak for itself: Should ChatGPT be allowed or banned in hospitality and tourism schools? *Journal of Global Hospitality and Tourism, 2*(1), 1–6. doi:10.5038/2771-5957.2.1.1016

Chiu, T. K., Moorhouse, B. L., Chai, C. S., & Ismailov, M. (2023). Teacher support and student motivation to learn with Artificial Intelligence (AI) based chatbot. *Interactive Learning Environments*, 1–17. doi:10.1080/10494820.2023.2172044

Cooper, G. (2023). Examining science education in ChatGPT: An exploratory study of generative artificial intelligence. *Journal of Science Education and Technology, 32*(3), 444–452. doi:10.1007/s10956-023-10039-y

Dalgıç, A., Yaşar, E., & Demir, M. (2024). ChatGPT and learning outcomes in tourism education: The role of digital literacy and individualized learning. *Journal of Hospitality, Leisure, Sport and Tourism Education, 34*, 1–13. doi:10.1016/j.jhlste.2024.100481

Dimitriadou, E., & Lanitis, A. (2023). A critical evaluation, challenges, and future perspectives of using artificial intelligence and emerging technologies in smart classrooms. *Smart Learning Environments, 10*(1), 1–26. doi:10.1186/s40561-023-00231-3

Farrokhnia, M., Banihashem, S. K., Noroozi, O., & Wals, A. (2024). A SWOT analysis of ChatGPT: Implications for educational practice and research. *Innovations in Education and Teaching International*, *61*(3), 460–474. doi:10.1080/14703297.2023.2195846

KEY TERMS AND DEFINITIONS

Artificial Intelligence (AI): Artificial intelligence (AI) is a rapidly growing field of technology that is changing the way we interact with machines. AI is the ability of a computer or machine to think and learn like a human being. It has become an integral part of our lives, from self-driving cars to voice-activated home assistants.

Authentic Learning: This refers to the process of making what your students learn meaningful by engaging them in relevant and real-world learning.

Autonomous Technology: This is technology that can function and execute tasks without being controlled by a human. The key tools here are the Autonomous devices. Robots, both functional and humanoids, drones and vehicles are a few examples of autonomous devices.

Electronic Dialogue: Refers to any conversation between instructors and leaners held via our electronic devices.

Mixed-Mode Learning: This refers to combining traditional face-to-face learning with learning at a distance in a structured program. The Web may enhance learning during study by one or both of these modes. Mixed Mode is also known as Blended Learning and Distributed Learning.

Pedagogical Transformation: Also referred to as Transformative pedagogy. It involves engaged learning. It is democratic. It utilizes ideas from Pablo Freire, such as dialogic education rather than "banking education."

Social Science Education: This describes any branch of science that focuses on studying society, the interactions of people or organizations is in the field of social science. Examples that fit this criterion are anthropology, sociology, communication, economics, psychology and political science.

Technological Transformation: This refers to the complete overhaul of an organization's technology systems encompassing network architecture, hardware, software and how data is stored and accessed and affecting all of people, process and technology.

Traditional Pedagogy: Traditional pedagogy refers predominantly to the face-to-face teaching environment and the conceptual frameworks around how people learn in that particular space. Over the past few decades, conventional pedagogy has evolved to include other modalities; specifically, the online environment. Most of the pedagogical practices used in the traditional face-to-face classroom can be applied effectively to other modes of teaching like an online, hybrid, or blended learning environments and vice versa.

Chapter 8
AI and OpenAI in Education: Unveiling the Future of Learning and Teaching

Krishna Kumari R.
https://orcid.org/0000-0002-1802-628X
Career Development Centre, College of Engineering and Technology, Srm Institute of Science and Technology, India

Snehalatha M.
SRM Institute of Science and Technology, India

ABSTRACT

In the ever-evolving landscape of education, the rise of artificial intelligence (AI) and the advent of OpenAI models have ushered in transformative possibilities. This chapter serves as an in-depth exploration, illuminating the core principles of AI and the inner workings of OpenAI models. It unveils the dynamic applications of AI within educational contexts, from personalized learning to administrative streamlining. The chapter commences by unraveling the foundational principles of AI, including machine learning and deep learning, demystifying these technologies that hold immense potential for education. It subsequently delves into the functioning of OpenAI models, shedding light on their architecture, natural language processing capabilities, and their practical utility in the educational domain. This chapter, thus, equips educators, policymakers, researchers, and the broader educational community with the essential knowledge to harness the extraordinary potential of AI for the betterment of learners.

DOI: 10.4018/979-8-3693-1666-5.ch008

INTRODUCTION

The modern educational landscape is undergoing a profound transformation, fueled by the relentless march of technology. At its forefront are two powerful forces: artificial intelligence (AI) and innovative models like OpenAI. These technologies are not only reshaping teaching and learning methods but also fundamentally altering how educational institutions are administered (Dalgıç et al., 2024). In the past, education was often perceived as a static and uniform process, with educators relying on standardized approaches, learners following fixed curricula, and administrators managing institutions with traditional methodologies. However, we now stand amidst an educational revolution characterized by dynamism, adaptability, and personalized learning experiences. This shift towards individualized education empowers learners, engaging them more deeply in learning. Additionally, AI and OpenAI models enable educators to tailor instruction to meet each student's unique needs and preferences, moving away from the one-size-fits-all approach of the past. Moreover, these technologies enhance administrative processes within educational institutions, facilitating data-driven decision-making and optimizing resource allocation. As we navigate this transformative era, we must remain mindful of ethical considerations, ensuring that AI is deployed responsibly and equitably. Ultimately, this revolution promises to unlock new possibilities for education, empowering learners and educators alike to thrive in an ever-evolving educational landscape.

The potential of Artificial Intelligence (AI) to transform education has captured significant scholarly attention in recent years (Bahroun et al., 2023). Research has explored a vast array of AI applications within educational settings, with a focus on personalized learning (Chan & Tsi, 2023), intelligent tutoring systems (Holstein et al., 2020), automated assessment (Druga et al., 2022), and even the use of generative AI for content creation (Bozkurt et al., 2023; Lim et al., 2023). Studies by Bahroun et al. (2023) and Yildirim et al. (2021) offer comprehensive reviews of the field, highlighting the potential for AI to personalize learning experiences, improve student outcomes, and reimagine educational practices altogether. However, the integration of AI in education is not without its challenges. A critical analysis by Bearman et al. (2023) examines the various discourses surrounding AI in higher education, raising important questions about its potential impact on faculty roles and educational philosophy. Similarly, Popenici (2023) emphasizes the need for a critical approach to AI implementation, advocating for a judicious use that prioritizes educational values. Ethical considerations surrounding AI in education are also emerging as a key area of research. Holmes et al. (2023) investigate stakeholder perspectives on the ethics of AI in distance learning, highlighting concerns about data privacy and potential biases within algorithms. Michel-Villarreal et al. (2023) delve specifically into the ethical implications of generative AI tools like ChatGPT, urging educators to develop frameworks for responsible integration.

The evolving nature of AI necessitates continuous exploration of its role in education (Dalgıç et al., 2024). Works by Roll and Wylie (2016) and Holmes and Tuomi (2022) provide valuable insights into the historical development and current state of the art in AI for education. Looking ahead, Karam (2023) explores the potential for AI to reform higher education, while Fullan et al. (2023) examine the challenges and opportunities AI presents for school leadership. While some, like Chan and Tsi (2023), raise concerns about AI replacing teachers, the dominant perspective favors a collaborative approach. Molenaar (2022) suggests a move towards "hybrid human-AI learning technologies," where AI augments and supports educators rather than supplanting them. This sentiment is echoed by Mills et al. (2023), who emphasize the importance of open educational practices in navigating the evolving landscape of AI-powered education. Thus, the research landscape on AI in education is rich and multifaceted. Studies (e.g., Demir & Demir 2023a; 2023b) explore the vast potential of AI for personalized learning, intelligent tutoring, and content creation. However, critical voices also highlight the need to address ethical considerations, potential biases, and the impact on educators' roles. As AI evolves, ongoing research will be crucial to ensure its responsible and effective integration into educational practices, fostering a future where human and machine intelligence work together to empower learners.

This chapter serves as an inclusive foundational guide, meticulously tailored to meet the diverse needs of its audience. Whether you're an educator dedicated to fostering a more engaging learning environment, a policymaker shaping the future of education, a researcher exploring the intersections of technology and pedagogy, or a member of the broader educational community eager for knowledge, this chapter aims to equip you with essential insights into the role of AI and OpenAI models in education. At its core, this chapter embarks on a journey of enlightenment, delving deep into the fundamental principles, mechanisms, and ethical considerations surrounding AI and OpenAI in education. We aspire to provide you with the knowledge necessary to effectively leverage the tremendous potential of AI, transforming it from an abstract concept into a tangible tool for enriching education. Throughout this exploration, we will uncover myriad ways AI enhances the educational experience, from facilitating personalized learning paths and intelligent feedback systems to enabling data-driven decision-making in education administration. Amidst these opportunities, ethical considerations emerge as critical guides, ensuring that the ethical use of AI remains a cornerstone of educational progress, fostering a future where technology enhances, rather than detracts from, the educational journey. Through this chapter, we aim to facilitate a deeper understanding of the symbiotic relationship between education and technology, ultimately enabling readers to embrace AI as an ally in improving teaching, more engaged learning, and more efficient educational management. By the end of this journey, you will possess the insights and tools needed to navigate the ever-evolving intersection of AI and education, contributing to the ongoing evolution of our educational landscape.

This chapter's aim is to foster a profound understanding of the symbiotic relationship between education and technology. We strive to empower readers to perceive AI as a valuable ally in advancing teaching practices, enhancing learning engagement, and optimizing educational management. By the conclusion of this journey, you will not only gain deep insights into the interplay between AI and education but also acquire the necessary tools to navigate the dynamic intersection of these fields. Armed with knowledge and understanding, you will be poised to contribute meaningfully to the ongoing evolution of our educational landscape, shaping a future where technology serves as a catalyst for transformative educational experiences.

BACKGROUND: AI IN EDUCATION: FUNDAMENTALS AND PRINCIPLES

Understanding AI

Definition and Core Principles of Artificial Intelligence

Artificial Intelligence (AI) is a multifaceted domain within computer science aimed at engineering systems capable of executing tasks that traditionally necessitate human intelligence. These tasks span problem-solving, learning, reasoning, and perception, constituting the bedrock of AI's functionality. At its essence, AI endeavors to replicate and, in many cases, surpass human cognitive abilities through computational means.

The core principles of AI encapsulate a spectrum of capabilities:

Learning: Fundamentally, AI systems possess the capacity to learn from data and adapt their behavior in response to changing environments. This learning process underpins advancements in machine learning (ML) and deep learning (DL), enabling algorithms to refine their performance over time through exposure to data and feedback mechanisms.

Reasoning: AI employs logical and statistical reasoning to make decisions and solve intricate problems. Whether through deductive reasoning from established premises or probabilistic inference to navigate uncertainty, AI systems demonstrate the ability to engage in sophisticated cognitive processes.

Perception: The perceptual capabilities of AI enable it to interpret and interact with its environment through various modalities. Technologies such as computer vision, speech recognition, and natural language processing equip AI systems with the capacity to comprehend and respond to complex stimuli from the world around them.

Problem-Solving: AI excels in addressing challenges across diverse domains, spanning from classic intellectual games like chess to real-world applications such as medical diagnosis and climate modeling. Its prowess in problem-solving lies in its capacity to navigate complex decision spaces and derive optimal solutions.

Autonomy: One of AI's defining attributes is its autonomy, allowing systems to operate independently and make decisions sans continuous human intervention. This autonomy empowers AI to execute tasks efficiently and effectively in dynamic environments.

Interaction: AI facilitates seamless interaction with humans and other systems through natural language interfaces, conversational agents, or other communication modalities. This capacity for interaction fosters collaboration and enhances the usability of AI-driven solutions in various contexts.

Machine Learning, Deep Learning, and Neural Networks

Machine Learning (ML), a subset of AI, focuses on developing systems capable of learning from data to make predictions or decisions without explicit programming. ML encompasses diverse approaches, including supervised, unsupervised, and reinforcement learning, each tailored to specific learning paradigms.

Deep Learning (DL) emerges as a subfield of ML, leveraging neural networks with multiple layers (deep neural networks) to process and learn from vast datasets. DL architectures, such as convolutional neural networks (CNNs) for image analysis and recurrent neural networks (RNNs) for sequential data, have demonstrated remarkable proficiency in handling complex tasks with unparalleled accuracy.

Neural Networks serve as the foundational building blocks of deep learning, mimicking the structure and function of biological neural networks. Comprising interconnected nodes (neurons) organized into layers, neural networks exhibit hierarchical processing capabilities, enabling them to extract intricate patterns and representations from input data.

AI's Potential to Revolutionize Education

The transformative potential of AI in education extends across various dimensions:

- Personalization: AI facilitates the customization of educational content and experiences to suit the unique needs and preferences of individual learners, thereby enhancing engagement and optimizing learning outcomes.

Figure 1. AI and OpenAI in Education

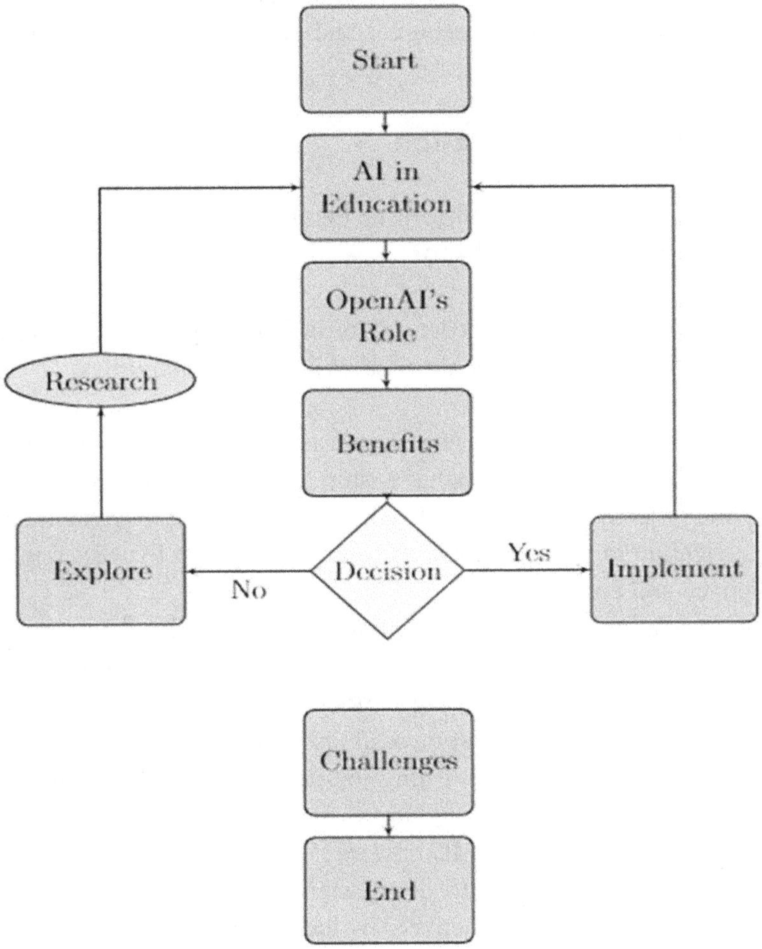

- Data-Driven Insights: By analyzing extensive educational datasets, AI furnishes educators and institutions with actionable insights into student performance, learning trajectories, and instructional efficacy, informing evidence-based decision-making and targeted interventions.
- Efficiency: AI-driven automation streamlines administrative tasks, grading processes, and resource allocation, affording educators more time and bandwidth to focus on pedagogical endeavors and student support.
- Accessibility: Through adaptive learning technologies and assistive tools, AI fosters inclusive educational environments, catering to diverse learner populations and mitigating barriers to participation and achievement.

- Global Access: AI-powered platforms and online learning ecosystems extend the reach of education beyond geographical boundaries, democratizing access to high-quality educational resources and opportunities for lifelong learning on a global scale.

Machine Learning in Education

An In-Depth Exploration of Machine Learning's Role in Personalized Education

Machine learning (ML) stands as a cornerstone in achieving personalized education, revolutionizing traditional approaches with its adaptive capabilities:

- Adaptive Learning: ML algorithms serve as the backbone of adaptive learning systems, meticulously assessing a student's current knowledge, learning style, and progress. Leveraging this data, these algorithms dynamically tailor the curriculum to meet each learner's needs, ensuring they are appropriately challenged and engaged.
- Recommendation Systems: Similar to the personalized recommendations on platforms like Netflix and Amazon, educational platforms harness ML to curate personalized course suggestions, resources, and learning materials based on a student's historical data and preferences. This approach fosters a more intuitive and tailored learning journey, enhancing student satisfaction and retention.
- Early Warning Systems: ML-powered early warning systems analyze students' performance data to detect signs of struggle or risk of dropout. Educators can intervene proactively by identifying these indicators early on, providing targeted support and interventions to prevent issues from escalating and bolster student success.

Adaptive Learning Systems and Intelligent Tutoring

Adaptive Learning Systems represent a paradigm shift in education, leveraging AI and ML to deliver tailored content and assessments to individual learners:

- Assessment: Regular assessments form the backbone of adaptive learning systems, enabling the platform to accurately gauge a student's current knowledge level and learning trajectory.
- Personalization: These systems dynamically adjust learning paths in response to a student's performance, offering additional explanations or presenting

more challenging material as needed. This personalized approach ensures that students are neither overwhelmed nor under-challenged, fostering optimal learning outcomes.

- Feedback: Adaptive learning systems provide immediate and constructive feedback, empowering students to address misconceptions and refine their skills in real-time. This timely feedback loop enhances learning efficacy and student engagement.

Intelligent Tutoring Systems (ITS) epitomize the pinnacle of personalized education, leveraging AI to simulate the role of a human tutor:

- Personalized Guidance: ITS offer individualized tutoring and guidance, adapting their approach to cater to each student's unique learning needs and preferences.
- Real-Time Feedback: These systems provide instantaneous feedback and support, enabling students to receive personalized assistance and guidance as they navigate complex concepts and tasks.
- Subject Coverage: ITS span a diverse array of subjects, from mathematics to language learning, offering tailored support across various educational domains.

Use Cases and Successful Implementations

AI and machine learning have garnered considerable success across diverse educational contexts:

- Language Learning: Apps like Duolingo leverage AI to personalize lessons based on individual progress, facilitating immersive and effective language acquisition experiences.
- Mathematics Education: Platforms such as Khan Academy utilize AI to offer tailored exercises and explanations, enabling students to master mathematical concepts at their own pace.
- Higher Education: Universities harness AI for enrollment predictions, student support services, and initiatives to improve graduation rates, fostering student success and institutional efficiency.
- Special Education: AI tools, including text-to-speech and speech recognition technologies, assist students with disabilities in accessing educational content and participating in learning activities, promoting inclusivity and accessibility.

- EdTech Startups: Many startups have emerged, offering AI-based solutions for educators, including plagiarism detection, essay scoring, and automated grading, streamlining administrative tasks and enhancing instructional efficiency.

Thus, AI and machine learning drive a paradigm shift in education, enabling personalized learning experiences, data-driven insights, and more efficient educational processes. Adaptive learning systems and intelligent tutoring represent cutting-edge innovations at the forefront of this transformation, empowering students with tailored education experiences. At the same time, AI-driven tools enhance the accessibility and efficacy of education for learners worldwide.

DECIPHERING OPENAI MODELS

Introduction to OpenAI

OpenAI and Its Mission

OpenAI was established with a profound mission to ensure the safe and beneficial development of artificial general intelligence (AGI). AGI represents a future where machines attain human-level intelligence, enabling them to perform complex tasks autonomously. Central to OpenAI's mission is the principle that the benefits of AGI should be accessible to all of humanity. The organization is committed to preventing any harmful or unfair use of AGI and prioritizes safety in its development and deployment. OpenAI adopts a cooperative orientation, actively seeking collaboration with other research and policy institutions. This emphasis on global collaboration underscores OpenAI's commitment to addressing the societal challenges posed by AGI collaboratively and inclusively.

Overview of Prominent OpenAI Models

GPT-3, the third iteration of the Generative Pre-trained Transformer, is one of OpenAI's flagship models. It's renowned for its capacity to generate human-like text. With a staggering 175 billion parameters, GPT-3 can understand context, answer questions, translate languages, and perform various natural language processing tasks. GPT-3's versatility stems from its pre-trained nature and fine-tuning capacity, which makes it adaptable for diverse applications. Beyond GPT-3, OpenAI has also developed other models with unique capabilities and applications. For instance, models like DALL·E can generate images from textual descriptions, while CLIP

Figure 2. Deciphering OpenAI Models

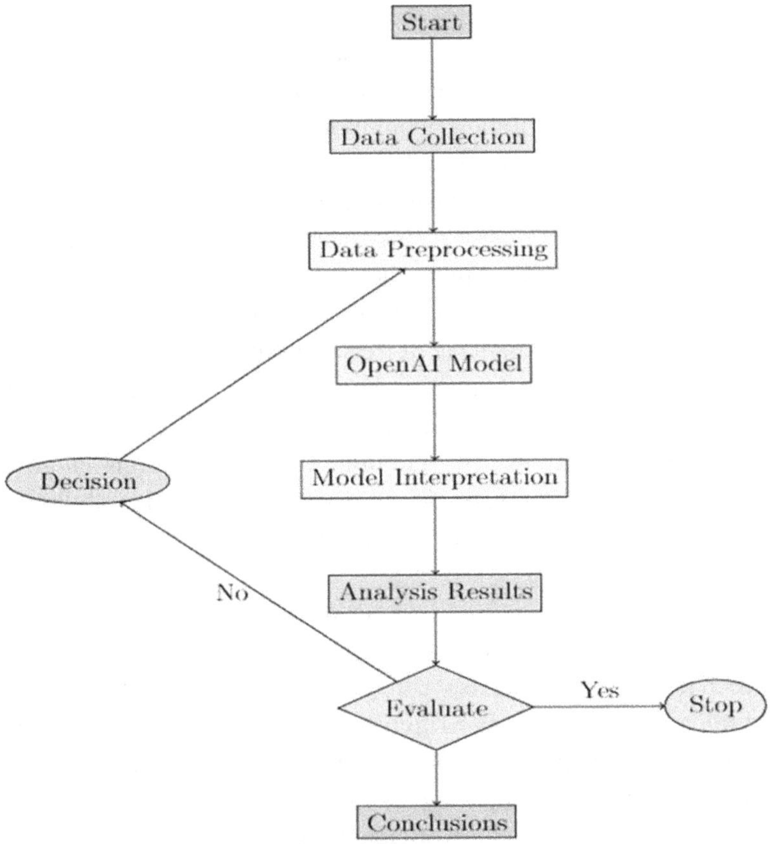

can understand and interact with both text and images. These models collectively represent a significant leap in AI capabilities.

Real-World Applications and Impact in Educational Contexts

OpenAI models have had a profound impact on the field of education. Their applications are wide-ranging and transformative:

Automated Content Generation: OpenAI models like GPT-3 can play a pivotal role in automating the generation of educational materials. Teachers and content creators can leverage these models to produce lesson plans, quizzes, explanations, and even textbooks. This not only saves a substantial amount of time but also ensures the consistency and quality of educational content. Lesson plans can be tailored to the specific needs of students, quizzes can be diverse and comprehensive, and explanations can simplify complex topics, making learning more accessible and effective.

Tutoring and Q&A: AI-powered chatbots and virtual assistants, powered by OpenAI models, can provide personalized tutoring and answer students' questions. This is particularly valuable in remote or online learning, where students may not have immediate access to a teacher. These AI-based systems can adapt to each student's unique learning needs, offering explanations of complex concepts in a manner that's tailored to individual understanding. This personalized support extends educational access beyond traditional classroom hours.

Language Learning: OpenAI models can significantly contribute to language learning. They can generate language exercises, assist in text translation, and help students with pronunciation and language comprehension. Language exercises can range from grammar correction to vocabulary quizzes, offering diverse practice opportunities. Translation services facilitate learning foreign languages, and pronunciation guidance helps learners improve their language skills. Language learning apps and platforms can integrate these features, enhancing their offerings and user experience.

Accessibility: AI models can be leveraged to develop tools that enhance the accessibility of educational content, particularly for individuals with disabilities. Text-to-speech technology converts written text into spoken words, allowing those with visual impairments to access written content effectively. Speech recognition, on the other hand, transforms spoken language into text, providing valuable support to individuals with auditory impairments. These technologies make educational materials more inclusive and enable a broader range of learners to access and engage with the content.

Research Assistance: Researchers across various fields can benefit from OpenAI models in their work. AI can assist in summarizing lengthy research papers, making it easier to identify key findings and concepts. It can also generate hypotheses by processing existing literature, offering valuable directions for further research. In addition, AI can aid in creating literature reviews by identifying relevant studies and summarizing their findings. These applications streamline the research process, enhancing productivity and the quality of research outcomes.

Automated Grading: OpenAI models are also instrumental in automating the grading of assignments and exams. This is particularly beneficial in large classes or for standardized tests. Educators save significant time that would otherwise be spent on manual grading. AI provides consistent and objective grading, reducing the potential for bias in assessment. Moreover, automated grading offers rapid feedback to students, which is crucial for their learning and progress.

How OpenAI Models Function

An Insight Into the Architecture and Functioning of OpenAI Models

OpenAI models, such as GPT-3, function based on the transformer architecture, a breakthrough in deep learning. Transformers are neural networks designed for processing data sequences, making them exceptionally suited for human language tasks. Transformers rely on attention mechanisms, which allow them to weigh the importance of different words or tokens within a text. This mechanism helps understand the context and relationships between words, enabling the model to generate coherent, contextually relevant responses. In terms of functioning, OpenAI models go through a two-step process: pre-training and fine-tuning. Pre-training involves exposing the model to a massive corpus of text, where it learns grammar, facts, reasoning abilities, and language structure. Fine-tuning then adapts the pre-trained model to specific tasks or applications, allowing it to become specialized in various domains, including education.

The large number of parameters in models like GPT-3 (175 billion in the case of GPT-3) is crucial to their capabilities. These parameters capture intricate patterns in language, facilitating understanding and generation of text.

The Role of Natural Language Processing (NLP)

Natural Language Processing (NLP) is a subfield of artificial intelligence that deals with the interaction between computers and human language. OpenAI models are at the forefront of NLP research and application. NLP techniques employed by OpenAI models include:

- Tokenization: OpenAI models break down text into smaller units called tokens. Tokens can represent words, subwords, or even characters. This tokenization is vital for processing language effectively.
- Text Generation: OpenAI models are capable of generating human-like text. They can take context and input and produce coherent, contextually relevant text, whether it's answering questions, creating content, or engaging in conversations.
- Language Understanding: These models understand the semantics, syntax, and nuances of language, which is fundamental for answering questions, providing explanations, and engaging in natural, human-like interactions.
- Language Translation: OpenAI models can perform language translation tasks with high accuracy. They can translate text from one language to another,

which is valuable for language learning and international collaboration in education.

- Text Summarization: OpenAI models can generate concise summaries of longer texts, making it easier for students and researchers to digest complex content.

These NLP capabilities have far-reaching applications in educational scenarios, from assisting with language learning to facilitating research, automated grading, and personalized tutoring. In conclusion, OpenAI models like GPT-3 and their underlying transformer architecture, as well as their proficiency in NLP, are revolutionizing education by providing tools for content generation, tutoring, accessibility, research assistance, and more. Their contributions to the education field demonstrate AI's potential to augment and transform traditional learning environments.

AI IN PRACTICE: ENHANCING TEACHING AND LEARNING

Personalized Learning

The Potential of AI in Tailoring Educational Experiences

Adaptive Learning: AI systems can dynamically adjust the pace and content of learning to match the unique needs of each student. For example, a student who struggles with a particular concept can receive additional practice and explanations until they achieve mastery, while a more advanced learner can move on to more challenging material. This adaptability is difficult to achieve through traditional classroom instruction alone.

Data-Driven Insights: AI's ability to process and analyze large volumes of data can provide educators with valuable insights into student performance. By identifying patterns in student behavior and learning styles, teachers can develop more effective teaching strategies. This data can also help pinpoint areas where individual students may require additional support.

Content Personalization: AI can recommend educational content that aligns with a student's interests and learning preferences. For example, an AI-driven language learning platform might recommend articles or videos related to a student's favorite topics, making learning more engaging and relevant.

Adaptive Assessments and Customized Learning Paths

Tailor Questions: Adaptive assessments utilize AI algorithms to present questions or tasks that are appropriate for a student's current skill level. As the student progresses, the system adjusts the difficulty of questions in real-time. This ensures that students are consistently challenged without becoming frustrated or overwhelmed.

Continuous Feedback: AI-powered assessment tools can provide instant, detailed feedback on student performance. This immediate feedback helps students identify their mistakes, understand concepts better, and make corrections. Educators can also use this information to adapt their teaching strategies.

Customized Learning Paths: Based on the results of assessments, AI can suggest personalized learning paths. For instance, if a student demonstrates proficiency in one area but struggles with another, the system can recommend additional practice or supplementary resources to address specific weaknesses.

Efficiency: Adaptive assessments save educators time. Since the system automatically adapts the questions and evaluates responses, teachers can focus on providing additional support or intervention where needed.

Benefits and Considerations in Implementing Personalized Learning

Benefits:

- Improved Learning Outcomes: Personalized learning can significantly improve learning outcomes. When students receive content and support tailored to their needs, they are more likely to succeed.
- Increased Engagement: Customized learning experiences make education more engaging. Students are more motivated when the content is relevant to their interests and abilities.
- Efficiency: AI automates many educational processes, saving educators time and resources. This efficiency allows teachers to focus on individualized instruction.
- Data-Driven Insights: The data generated by AI systems can help schools and educators make informed decisions about curriculum and teaching strategies.

Considerations:

- Data Privacy: The use of AI in education involves the collection and analysis of student data. This raises concerns about data privacy, especially in the context of K-12 and higher education institutions.

- Equity: Ensuring all students have equal access to personalized learning resources can be challenging. Not all schools or students may have access to the necessary technology.
- Teacher Training: Implementing personalized learning often requires professional development for educators. They need training to use AI tools and interpret data effectively.
- Ethical Considerations: Decisions about student progress, interventions, and assessments should be made ethically and not solely based on AI recommendations. Ethical guidelines for AI in education are crucial.

AI-Driven Educational Tools

An Exploration of AI-Powered Tools and Platforms for Educators

AI-powered tools and platforms for educators are diversifying and enhancing the teaching and learning experience:

Smart Content Creation: AI tools like OpenAI's GPT-3 can generate educational content, lesson plans, quizzes, and explanations. This automation frees up educators' time and ensures high-quality content.

Grading Automation: AI can automate the grading of assignments and exams. Tools like Turnitin and Gradescope can evaluate written work, while platforms like Coursera use AI to grade quizzes and exams. Grading automation is particularly useful for large classes or online education.

Virtual Assistants: AI-driven virtual assistants, such as chatbots, help educators with administrative tasks like scheduling and communication. They can also provide instant responses to common student questions, reducing the workload on educators and improving student support.

Content Recommendation: AI can recommend educational materials, such as books, articles, or resources, based on the individual interests and needs of both educators and students. This ensures that learning resources are highly relevant and engaging.

Case Studies of AI-Enhanced Classrooms and Digital Resources

Numerous case studies demonstrate the effectiveness of AI-enhanced classrooms and digital resources:

Khan Academy: This popular online platform uses AI to offer personalized math education. Students receive tailored exercises and lessons based on their performance. As a result, Khan Academy has seen significant improvements in student outcomes.

ScribeSense: ScribeSense uses AI to grade handwritten assignments and exams. This automation dramatically reduces the time educators spend on grading, allowing them to allocate more time to teaching and providing personalized feedback.

IBM Watson for Education: IBM's AI system, Watson, supports educators by providing insights into student performance. It helps identify at-risk students and recommends appropriate interventions to improve learning outcomes.

Duolingo: The language learning app Duolingo employs AI to offer personalized language exercises and lessons. This makes language acquisition more effective and engaging, as the app adapts to individual learning progress.

EdTech Startups: Many startups harness AI to create innovative educational tools, including plagiarism detection systems, automated essay scoring, and personalized tutoring platforms. These tools are transforming the education landscape by enhancing efficiency and learning outcomes.

Thus, AI-driven personalized learning and educational tools are at the forefront of educational transformation. They offer a range of benefits, including improved learning outcomes, increased engagement, and enhanced efficiency. However, it is essential to address considerations like data privacy, equity, teacher training, and ethical decision-making to ensure that AI's integration into education is both effective and responsible. AI-powered tools and platforms significantly impact education, and their potential for further growth is substantial.

Artificial Intelligence (AI) integration revolutionizes how we teach and learn in today's ever-evolving educational landscape. The following algorithm is a simplified representation of how AI can provide personalized feedback to students based on their understanding and engagement levels.

Components of the Algorithm

The primary objective of this algorithm is to demonstrate how AI can enhance the educational experience by providing tailored feedback to students. In traditional teaching, instructors often have limited time and resources to provide individualized feedback to each student. AI can fill this gap by automating the process and delivering personalized insights to learners.

Let's delve into the components of the algorithm and their roles:

1. *StudentClass:* The StudentClass represents an individual student. It has a constructor that takes the student's name as input. It initializes students' understanding and engagement levels with random values between 0.0 and 1.0. The receive feedback method generates feedback for the student based on their understanding and engagement levels. If the students' understanding is high (greater than or equal to 0.7), they receive praise for their excellent grasp

Table 1. AI-Driven Educational Tools

Tool	Description	Benefit
Virtual Tutors	AI-powered tutors that provide personalized instruction and feedback to students.	Adapts to individual learning pace and identifies areas needing improvement.
Intelligent Content Recommendations	Systems that suggest learning materials based on a student's progress, interests, and goals.	Creates a more personalized learning path and exposes students to relevant content.
Automated Assessment Systems	AI-powered tools that grade essays, quizzes, and other assignments.	Saves teachers time on grading and provides students with faster feedback.
Gamified Learning Platforms	Educational games that use AI to adapt difficulty and offer rewards based on student performance.	Makes learning more engaging and motivates students to progress.
Chatbots	AI-powered chatbots that answer student questions and provide support.	Offers 24/7 assistance and can answer basic questions, freeing up teachers for more complex topics.

of the topic. If not, they are encouraged to review the material. Similarly, high engagement results in commendation, while lower engagement suggests the need for increased involvement.

2. *TeacherClass:* The TeacherClass represents the teacher or educator. It takes a list of students as input. The provide_feedback method iterates through the list of students and collects feedback for each student using the StudentClass. The feedback for each student is stored in FeedbackList, which is returned as the output.
3. *Main:* The Main function is the entry point of the algorithm. It takes the names of students as input. It creates instances of students based on their names, invokes the TeacherClass to provide feedback for each student, and finally, prints the feedback for review.

How the Algorithm Works

This algorithm is implemented in the Python programming language, a versatile and widely used language in AI and education technology. Python's ease of use and rich ecosystem of libraries make it a popular choice for AI-related applications in the education sector. The running time of this algorithm can vary based on factors such as the number of students and the complexity of the AI logic involved. In general, the algorithm's time complexity is linear, as it iterates through the list of students to provide feedback. The specific execution time would depend on the hardware and environment in which it is run. Python's efficiency and speed ensure that the algorithm operates within a reasonable timeframe, making it a practical tool for educators.

The algorithm simulates a scenario where a teacher uses AI to provide feedback to students. Here's a step-by-step breakdown of its operation:

- Input: The algorithm takes as input the names of students. These names are typically provided by an educational institution.
- Creating Student Instances: For each student name, an instance of the StudentClass is created. Within each instance, the student's understanding and engagement levels are randomly assigned.
- Generating Feedback: The TeacherClass is responsible for collecting feedback for each student. It iterates through the list of student instances, invoking the receive_feedback method for each student to obtain personalized feedback.
- Displaying Feedback: The algorithm concludes by displaying the individualized feedback for each student. This feedback can be used by students to assess their performance and identify areas for improvement.

The "AI-Enhanced Teaching and Learning" algorithm exemplifies how AI can be harnessed to improve the educational experience. By providing personalized feedback to students, it empowers them to enhance their understanding and engagement with the learning material. As AI continues to advance, its role in education is set to grow, offering new possibilities for both educators and learners. In summary, this algorithm serves as a simplified model of the potential applications of AI in education and underscores the importance of personalized feedback in the learning process.

ETHICAL CONSIDERATIONS AND THE FUTURE OF AI IN EDUCATION

Ethical AI in Education

Addressing Ethical Concerns in AI-Powered Education

As AI becomes more integrated into education, addressing ethical concerns is of paramount importance. Key ethical considerations include:

- Data Privacy: Educational institutions and technology providers must ensure the privacy of student data. Data should be protected from breaches and unauthorized access, and students should have control over their personal information.

Figure 3. Components of the Algorithm

```
Algorithm 1 AI-Enhanced Teaching and Learning
  Input: Number of students, Student names
  Output: AI-enhanced teaching and learning
  procedure STUDENTCLASS(Name)
    Input: Name
    Output: Feedback for the student
    Understanding ← Random value between 0.0 and 1.0
    Engagement ← Random value between 0.0 and 1.0 if
  Understanding ≥ 0.7 then
      Feedback ← "Your understanding of the topic is excellent." else
      Feedback ← "You may want to review the material to improve
  your understanding."
    if Engagement ≥ 0.7 then
      Feedback ← Feedback+"Yourhighlevelofengagementisimpressive." else
    Feedback ← Feedback+"Increasingyourengagementwillbenefityourlearning."
   Return Feedback
end procedure
procedure TEACHERCLASS(Students)
   Input: Students
   Output: Feedback for each student
   FeedbackList ← [] for each Student in Students do
     FeedbackList.append(STUDENTCLASS(Student))

   Return FeedbackList
end procedure
procedure MAIN
   Input: StudentNames
   Output: None
   Students ← [] for each Name in StudentNames do
     Students.append(STUDENTCLASS(Name))

   FeedbackList ← TEACHERCLASS(Students) for each Feedback in
FeedbackList do
     Print(Feedback)

end procedure
```

- Bias and Fairness: AI algorithms should be designed and trained to avoid bias and discrimination. Fairness in AI means ensuring that it does not disadvantage any group of students based on their background or characteristics.
- Accountability and Transparency: There should be clear lines of accountability in AI systems. It should be transparent how decisions are made, and students and educators should be able to understand the reasoning behind AI-generated recommendations or actions.
- Informed Consent: Students and their parents or guardians should be informed about the use of AI in their education, and they should provide informed consent. They should understand how AI is used and its implications.

Ensuring Data Privacy, Transparency, and Fairness

- Data Privacy: Institutions must have robust data privacy policies in place. This includes encryption, secure storage, and the use of data only for educational purposes. Consent should be obtained for data collection, and students should be able to access and delete their data.
- Transparency: AI systems should be designed with transparency in mind. Educators and students should be able to understand how recommendations are generated and how AI influences decision-making.
- Fairness and Bias Mitigation: Developers should proactively work to eliminate bias in AI systems. This involves carefully selecting training data, conducting fairness audits, and refining algorithms to ensure that no student group is unfairly disadvantaged.

Ethical Guidelines and Regulations for AI Use in Educational Settings

Ethical guidelines and regulations are crucial to ensure that AI is used responsibly in educational settings. These should be based on principles of fairness, transparency, and privacy. Key considerations include:

- International Standards: Collaboration on international standards for AI in education can help ensure that ethical guidelines are upheld globally.
- Oversight and Regulation: Governments and education authorities should establish regulatory bodies to oversee AI use in education and enforce ethical guidelines.
- Education and Training: Educators, administrators, and AI developers should be educated on the ethical considerations and implications of AI use in education.
- Ethical Impact Assessments: Institutions and technology providers should conduct ethical impact assessments to evaluate the potential ethical consequences of AI systems before implementation.

The Future of AI in Education

A Glimpse into the Future: AI's Potential to Revolutionize Education

The future of AI in education is promising, with the potential to revolutionize learning in the following ways:

Table 2. The Future of AI in Education

Feature	Description	Potential Impact
Hyper-Personalized Learning	AI tutors that create individualized learning paths based on a student's strengths, weaknesses, and learning style.	Students learn at their own pace and master concepts more effectively.
Immersive Learning Experiences	AI-powered VR and AR simulations that bring complex subjects to life.	Increased engagement and deeper understanding of abstract concepts.
Real-time Feedback and Intervention	AI analyzes student performance data to identify areas of struggle and provide immediate support.	Early intervention to prevent learning gaps and improve overall achievement.
Automated Curriculum Development	AI generates and tailors lesson plans based on learning objectives and student data.	Teachers save time on lesson planning and focus on delivering engaging instruction.
AI-powered Assistive Technologies	AI personalizes learning for students with disabilities, providing tailored instruction and support.	Greater access to education and improved learning outcomes for all students.

- Personalized Learning: AI will continue to refine its ability to offer highly personalized learning experiences, tailoring content and assessments to individual students, optimizing their learning journeys.
- Collaborative Learning: AI will support collaborative learning by providing tools for group projects, communication, and knowledge sharing among students worldwide. This will create global classrooms where students from different countries can work together.
- Emerging Technologies: Advancements in AI, augmented reality (AR), virtual reality (VR), and mixed reality will create immersive learning experiences, allowing students to explore historical events, conduct virtual science experiments, and engage in realistic simulations.
- Assistive Technology: AI-powered assistive technology will empower students with disabilities, offering features like real-time language translation, speech recognition, and text-to-speech, enabling a more inclusive education environment.

Collaborative Learning and Global Classrooms

Collaborative Learning facilitated by Artificial Intelligence (AI) is poised to revolutionize education and promote the development of Global Classrooms, where students from diverse backgrounds can work together seamlessly. This transformation has several significant implications:

A. Cultural Exchange

Collaborative learning powered by AI allows students from different countries to participate in joint educational activities, projects, and discussions. This virtual mingling of cultures provides students with unique opportunities for cultural exchange and understanding. Here's a more detailed look at how this works:

- Cross-Border Collaboration: Students can collaborate on projects, research, and assignments, regardless of their geographical locations. This interaction exposes them to diverse perspectives and ways of thinking, enriching their educational experience.
- Global Dialogues: AI tools can facilitate global dialogues where students discuss local customs, traditions, and worldviews. They can discuss cultural differences and similarities, fostering a deeper appreciation for global diversity.
- Cultural Competence: Interacting with peers from different cultural backgrounds encourages students to become culturally competent. They develop sensitivity to cultural nuances, learning to respect and embrace differences.

B. Language Learning

Language barriers can be a significant obstacle to effective global collaboration. However, AI-powered translation and language learning tools are bridging this gap, making it easier for students to communicate and collaborate in a multilingual environment:

- Real-Time Translation: AI-driven translation tools enable real-time language translation during virtual discussions and collaborative work. Students can communicate in their native languages, and AI ensures everyone can understand each other.
- Language Learning Assistance: AI can also serve as a language learning aid. It provides language lessons, vocabulary, and pronunciation guidance, making it easier for students to become multilingual.
- Global Communication: Students are no longer limited by language proficiency. AI empowers them to communicate globally, connect with peers worldwide, and access a broader pool of knowledge.

C. Cultural Understanding

Exposure to different cultures and viewpoints in collaborative learning promotes cultural understanding and empathy. This is crucial in preparing students for a more interconnected world:

- Empathy and Tolerance: Students naturally develop empathy and tolerance as they engage with peers from diverse backgrounds. They gain insights into the challenges and opportunities faced by individuals worldwide.
- Global Citizenship: Collaborative learning fosters a sense of global citizenship. Students become aware of global issues, such as climate change, poverty, and human rights, and are inspired to act.
- Breaking Stereotypes: Interacting with peers from various countries dispels stereotypes and misconceptions. Students realize that the world is complex and multifaceted, and people from different backgrounds share common values and goals.

D. Interdisciplinary Learning

Collaborative projects, facilitated by AI, naturally encourage interdisciplinary learning. Students from diverse educational backgrounds can work together to tackle complex problems:

- Problem-Solving Teams: AI can assemble teams of students with varied skills and expertise. For instance, a team could include students with backgrounds in engineering, economics, and environmental science, all working together on a sustainability project.
- Holistic Approaches: Interdisciplinary collaboration encourages students to adopt holistic approaches to problem-solving. They consider economic, environmental, social, and technological aspects essential to addressing real-world challenges.
- Real-World Preparedness: This type of collaborative learning prepares students for the real world, where solving complex problems often requires input from multiple disciplines. It's an excellent foundation for future careers and research.

Thus, Collaborative Learning facilitated by AI in Global Classrooms brings many opportunities. It promotes cultural exchange, breaks language barriers, fosters cultural understanding, and encourages interdisciplinary learning. These transformative experiences make students better equipped to thrive in our interconnected and diverse world. This approach prepares them academically and for the global challenges and opportunities of the 21st century.

Emerging Trends and Opportunities in the Field

Several emerging trends and opportunities will shape the future of AI in education:

- AI-Enhanced Assessments: AI-driven assessments will provide richer insights into student performance, enabling more effective interventions and tailored learning experiences.
- AI-Enhanced Tutoring: Virtual tutors and chatbots will become more sophisticated, providing students instant, personalized assistance and feedback.
- Professional Development: Opportunities for educators to develop AI literacy and effectively integrate AI tools into their teaching will expand.
- Education for All: AI has the potential to reach underserved populations, offering quality education to remote and disadvantaged communities.
- Lifelong Learning: AI will support lifelong learning, allowing individuals to upskill and adapt to a rapidly changing job market continuously.

Overall, the future of AI in education is marked by great potential, but it also requires careful consideration of ethical guidelines and regulations. AI will enable personalized learning, collaborative global classrooms, and integrating emerging technologies for more effective and inclusive education. By addressing ethical concerns and embracing AI's opportunities, education can become more engaging, effective, and accessible for students worldwide.

CONCLUSION

Throughout this chapter, we've embarked on a transformative journey into the realm of Artificial Intelligence (AI) and its profound implications for education. Delving into the foundational principles of AI and exploring the practical applications of OpenAI models, we've glimpsed the potential to reshape the educational landscape fundamentally. As we draw this exploration to a close, it's imperative to reflect on the key insights garnered, issue a compelling call to action, and envision a future where AI and OpenAI models serve as cornerstones in crafting innovative, inclusive, and student-centered learning environments. As we conclude, let's reflect on the key takeaways, issue a compelling call to action, and envision a future where AI and

OpenAI models play a central role in creating innovative, inclusive, and student-centered learning environments.

Key Takeaways

- AI, driven by deep learning and neural networks, has the power to revolutionize education by offering personalized learning experiences and enhancing the role of educators through automation and data-driven insights.
- Adaptive assessments and customized learning paths empower students by providing tailored support, ultimately leading to improved learning outcomes and increased engagement.
- AI-driven educational tools, such as smart content creation, grading automation, and virtual assistants, streamline administrative tasks and enable educators to focus on personalized instruction.
- Addressing ethical concerns, ensuring data privacy, and establishing clear guidelines are crucial in integrating AI into education.
- The future of AI in education holds the promise of global classrooms, immersive experiences, and lifelong learning, but ethical considerations must be at the forefront of this evolution.

A Compelling Call to Action

To educators, policymakers, and the educational community, the call to action is clear:

- Embrace AI as an Enabler: Recognize AI as a transformative force that can unlock the potential of each learner. Embrace its ability to provide personalized and engaging educational experiences.
- Champion Ethical Practices: Uphold ethical standards and principles in the use of AI. Prioritize data privacy, transparency, and fairness in every AI-driven initiative.
- Invest in Teacher Training: Equip educators with the knowledge and skills needed to harness the power of AI. Provide professional development opportunities to ensure they can effectively integrate AI into their teaching practices.
- Collaborate and Share Knowledge: Foster collaboration among educational institutions, tech developers, and policymakers. Share knowledge, best practices, and resources to advance the field of AI in education collectively.
- Ensure Inclusivity: Strive for inclusive AI solutions that provide equal access and support to all students, regardless of their background or abilities.

A Vision of the Future

In the not-so-distant future, we envision a world where AI and OpenAI models play a central role in education:

- Personalized Learning: Each student's educational journey is uniquely tailored, ensuring that their individual needs and interests are met. AI-driven assessments and content recommendations guide students toward success.
- Global Classrooms: AI breaks down geographical and cultural barriers, allowing students from diverse backgrounds to collaborate on projects and learn from one another. This fosters cultural exchange and a deeper understanding of global issues.
- Immersive Learning: Emerging technologies, such as augmented and virtual reality, transport students to new dimensions of understanding. History becomes an immersive experience, science experiments are vivid, and simulations are realistic.
- Empowered Teachers: Educators are liberated from administrative burdens, enabling them to provide students more individualized support and mentorship.
- Lifelong Learning: AI supports lifelong learning, allowing individuals to continually acquire new skills and knowledge as the job market evolves.

The future of education, driven by AI, is a dynamic and inclusive ecosystem that equips learners with the skills and knowledge they need to thrive in a rapidly changing world. By embracing AI as a powerful tool for transformation and committing to ethical standards, we can create an educational experience that is accessible, engaging, and effective for all, shaping a brighter future for education and for the generations to come.

REFERENCES

Bahroun, Z., Anane, C., Ahmed, V., & Zacca, A. (2023). Transforming education: A comprehensive review of generative artificial intelligence in educational settings through bibliometric and content analysis. *Sustainability (Basel), 15*(17), 12983. doi:10.3390/su151712983

Bearman, M., Ryan, J., & Ajjawi, R. (2023). Discourses of artificial intelligence in higher education: A critical literature review. *Higher Education, 86*(2), 369–385. doi:10.1007/s10734-022-00937-2

Bozkurt, A., Junhong, X., Lambert, S., Pazurek, A., Crompton, H., Koseoglu, S., ... Romero-Hall, E. (2023). Speculative futures on ChatGPT and generative artificial intelligence (AI): A collective reflection from the educational landscape. *Asian Journal of Distance Education, 18*(1), 53–130.

Chan, C. K. Y., & Tsi, L. H. (2023). The AI Revolution in Education: Will AI Replace or Assist Teachers in Higher Education? *arXiv preprint arXiv:2305.01185.*

Dalgıç, A., Yaşar, E., & Demir, M. (2024). ChatGPT and learning outcomes in tourism education: The role of digital literacy and individualized learning. *Journal of Hospitality, Leisure, Sport and Tourism Education, 34*, 100481. doi:10.1016/j.jhlste.2024.100481

Demir, M., & Demir, Ş. Ş. (2023a). Is ChatGPT the right technology for service individualization and value co-creation? Evidence from the travel industry. *Journal of Travel & Tourism Marketing, 40*(5), 383–398. doi:10.1080/10548408.2023.2255884

Demir, Ş. Ş., & Demir, M. (2023b). Professionals' perspectives on ChatGPT in the tourism industry: Does it inspire awe or concern? *Journal of Tourism Theory and Research, 9*(2), 61–77. doi:10.24288/jttr.1313481

Druga, S., Otero, N., & Ko, A. J. (2022, July). The landscape of teaching resources for ai education. In *Proceedings of the 27th ACM Conference on on Innovation and Technology in Computer Science Education* Vol. 1 (pp. 96-102). 10.1145/3502718.3524782

Fullan, M., Azorín, C., Harris, A., & Jones, M. (2023). Artificial intelligence and school leadership: Challenges, opportunities and implications. *School Leadership & Management*, 1–8. doi:10.1080/13632434.2023.2246856

Holmes, W., Iniesto, F., Anastopoulou, S., & Boticario, J. G. (2023). Stakeholder Perspectives on the Ethics of AI in Distance-Based Higher Education. *International Review of Research in Open and Distance Learning, 24*(2), 96–117. doi:10.19173/irrodl.v24i2.6089

Holmes, W., & Tuomi, I. (2022). State of the art and practice in AI in education. *European Journal of Education, 57*(4), 542–570. doi:10.1111/ejed.12533

Holstein, K., Aleven, V., & Rummel, N. (2020). A conceptual framework for human–AI hybrid adaptivity in education. *Artificial Intelligence in Education: 21st International Conference, AIED 2020, Ifrane, Morocco, July 6–10, 2020 Proceedings, 21*(Part I), 240–254.

Karam, J. (2023). Reforming Higher Education Through AI. In *Governance in Higher Education: Global Reform and Trends in the MENA Region* (pp. 275–306). Springer Nature Switzerland. doi:10.1007/978-3-031-40586-0_12

Kengam, J. (2020). Artificial intelligence in education. *Research Gate*, *18*, 1–4.

Kim, N. J., & Kim, M. K. (2022, March). Teacher's perceptions of using an artificial intelligence-based educational tool for scientific writing. *Frontiers in Education*, *7*, 755914. doi:10.3389/feduc.2022.755914

Lim, W. M., Gunasekara, A., Pallant, J. L., Pallant, J. I., & Pechenkina, E. (2023). Generative AI and the future of education: Ragnarök or reformation? A paradoxical perspective from management educators. *International Journal of Management Education*, *21*(2), 1–12. doi:10.1016/j.ijme.2023.100790

Michel-Villarreal, R., Vilalta-Perdomo, E., Salinas-Navarro, D. E., Thierry-Aguilera, R., & Gerardou, F. S. (2023). Challenges and opportunities of generative AI for higher education as explained by ChatGPT. *Education Sciences*, *13*(9), 856–868. doi:10.3390/educsci13090856

Mills, A., Bali, M., & Eaton, L. (2023). How do we respond to generative AI in education? Open educational practices give us a framework for an ongoing process. *Journal of Applied Learning and Teaching*, *6*(1), 16–30.

Molenaar, I. (2022). Towards hybrid human-AI learning technologies. *European Journal of Education*, *57*(4), 632–645. doi:10.1111/ejed.12527

Peters, M. A., Jackson, L., Papastephanou, M., Jandrić, P., Lazaroiu, G., Evers, C. W., Cope, B., Kalantzis, M., Araya, D., Tesar, M., Mika, C., Chen, L., Wang, C., Sturm, S., Rider, S., & Fuller, S. (2023). AI and the future of humanity: ChatGPT-4, philosophy and education–Critical responses. *Educational Philosophy and Theory*, 1–35. doi:10.1080/00131857.2023.2213437

Popenici, S. (2023). The critique of AI as a foundation for judicious use in higher education. *Journal of Applied Learning and Teaching*, *6*(2), 1–12.

Roll, I., & Wylie, R. (2016). Evolution and revolution in artificial intelligence in education. *International Journal of Artificial Intelligence in Education*, *26*(2), 582–599. doi:10.1007/s40593-016-0110-3

Sah, G. K., Gupta, D. K., & Yadav, A. P. (2024). Analysis of ChatGPT and the future of artificial intelligence: Its effect on teaching and learning. *Journal of AI. Robotics & Workplace Automation*, *3*(1), 64–80.

Walczak, K., & Cellary, W. (2023). Challenges for higher education in the era of widespread access to Generative AI. *Economics and Business Review*, *9*(2), 71–100. doi:10.18559/ebr.2023.2.743

Yildirim, Y., Arslan, E. A., Yildirim, K., & Bisen, I. (2021). Reimagining education with artificial intelligence. *Eurasian Journal of Higher Education*, *2*(4), 32–46. doi:10.31039/ejohe.2021.4.52

ADDITIONAL READING

Brown, T. B., Mann, B., Ryder, N., Subbiah, M., Kaplan, J., Dhariwal, P., & Amodei, D. (2020). *Language models are few-shot learners*. arXiv preprint.

Chen, L., Chen, P., & Lin, Z. (2020). Artificial intelligence in education: A review. *IEEE Access : Practical Innovations, Open Solutions*, *8*, 75264–75278. doi:10.1109/ACCESS.2020.2988510

Demir, M. (2024). Building Trust and Credibility: Ethical Use of AI in the Service Industry. In M. Demir & A. Dalgic (Eds.), *Revolutionizing the Service Industry With OpenAI Models* (pp. 243–267). IGI Global., doi:10.4018/979-8-3693-1239-1.ch010

Dignum, V. (2018). Ethics in artificial intelligence: Introduction to the special issue. *Ethics and Information Technology*, *20*(1), 1–3. doi:10.1007/s10676-018-9450-z

Goodfellow, I., Bengio, Y., & Courville, A. (2016). *Deep Learning*. MIT Press.

Hirschberg, J., & Manning, C. D. (2015). Advances in natural language processing. *Science*, *349*(6245), 261–266. doi:10.1126/science.aaa8685 PMID:26185244

Schmidhuber, J. (2015). Deep learning in neural networks: An overview. *Neural Networks*, *61*, 85–117. doi:10.1016/j.neunet.2014.09.003 PMID:25462637

VanLehn, K. (2011). The relative effectiveness of human tutoring, intelligent tutoring, and other tutoring systems. *Educational Psychologist*, *46*(4), 197–221. doi:10.1080/00461520.2011.611369

Wang, F., & Hannafin, M. J. (2005). Design-based research and technology-enhanced learning environments. *Educational Technology Research and Development*, *53*(4), 5–23. doi:10.1007/BF02504682

Zawacki-Richter, O., Marín, V. I., Bond, M., & Gouverneur, F. (2019). Systematic review of research on artificial intelligence applications in higher education – Where are the educators? *International Journal of Educational Technology in Higher Education, 16*(1), 39–48. doi:10.1186/s41239-019-0171-0

KEY TERMS AND DEFINITIONS

Adaptive Learning Systems: Systems that use AI to dynamically adjust the difficulty and type of content based on the learner's performance and engagement.

Artificial Intelligence (AI): The simulation of human intelligence processes by machines, especially computer systems. These processes include learning, reasoning, problem-solving, perception, and language understanding.

Deep Learning: A subset of machine learning involving neural networks with many layers (deep neural networks) that can learn from large amounts of data.

Ethical AI: The practice of designing and deploying AI systems that are fair, transparent, and accountable, ensuring they do not harm individuals or society.

Grading Automation: The use of AI algorithms to assess and grade student work, such as essays, quizzes, and exams, automatically.

Intelligent Tutoring Systems (ITS): Computer systems that provide immediate and customized instruction or feedback to learners, usually without human intervention.

Machine Learning (ML): A subset of AI that uses algorithms and statistical models to enable computers to perform tasks without explicit instructions by relying on patterns and inference.

Natural Language Processing (NLP): A branch of AI that focuses on the interaction between computers and humans through natural language. It enables machines to understand, interpret, and generate human language.

Neural Networks: A series of algorithms that attempt to recognize underlying relationships in a data set through a process miming how the human brain operates.

OpenAI: An AI research and Deployment Company known for developing powerful AI models like GPT-3, capable of understanding and generating human-like text.

Personalized Learning: An educational approach that aims to customize learning for each student's strengths, needs, skills, and interests. It provides tailored learning experiences that support individual learning paths.

Smart Content Creation: The use of AI to generate educational materials, such as summaries, flashcards, and quizzes tailored to the curriculum and learning needs.

Chapter 9
Can the Potential Contributions of ChatGPT in Tourism Education Be Realized?

Emre Yaşar
https://orcid.org/0000-0003-1573-0930
Isparta University of Applied Sciences, Turkey

ABSTRACT

This study fully addresses the effects of ChatGPT on tourism students from the perspective of academic tourism. When the research results are evaluated comprehensively, it is determined that academics have negative and positive opinions about the effects of ChatGPT on their students. It is seen that ChatGPT increases students' learning performance and digital literacy. However, there are also some opposing views on learning performance. It is stated that it is difficult for students to internalize information using ChatGPT; therefore, learning performance will be negatively affected. Similarly, it is thought that students' critical and analytical skills will be negatively affected by ChatGPT. Other positive effects of ChatGPT on students include raising their awareness of innovation and time management, providing information diversity, and supporting personal development and language learning. The adverse impact of ChatGPT on students includes making them lazy, weakening their researcher identities, losing motivation, and decreasing their evaluation skills.

INTRODUCTION

DOI: 10.4018/979-8-3693-1666-5.ch009

Artificial intelligence and its various applications have permeated virtually every aspect of modern society (Demir & Demir, 2023b; Gill et al., 2024). Among these applications, ChatGPT has emerged as a prominent tool since its introduction in late 2022 (Dwivedi et al., 2023). ChatGPT leverages artificial intelligence and natural language processing techniques to facilitate interactive conversations (Elbanna & Armstrong, 2024). ChatGPT is distinguished by its ability to create diverse content types, including text, images, and voice, and respond to queries in a manner that is similar to human interaction (Kasneci et al., 2023). This capability to emulate human speech and behavior has spurred a surge in demand for ChatGPT-generated content across various domains (Duong et al., 2023). Moreover, the persuasiveness and effectiveness of the content produced by ChatGPT have piqued the interest of businesses and individuals across diverse sectors, driving widespread adoption (Demir & Demir, 2023a).

The field of education is witnessing the transformative impact of artificial intelligence applications like ChatGPT (Demir et al., 2023; Mhlanga, 2023). ChatGPT's ability to tailor responses to students' individual needs and enhance the research experience has rendered it increasingly valuable (Mogavi et al., 2024). Its adaptability within the educational context further underscores its utility (Rahman & Watanobe, 2023). ChatGPT serves diverse purposes for students, including homework assistance, exam preparation, personal tutoring, and language learning support (Adeshola & Adepoju, 2023). By swiftly delivering targeted content, ChatGPT has become a favored tool among students and educators in the educational domain (Montenegro-Rueda et al., 2023). Moreover, the learning process facilitated by ChatGPT fosters the generation of innovative ideas, thereby supporting intellectual development (Habibi et al., 2023). Consequently, ChatGPT emerges as a disruptive force reshaping the education landscape (Hong, 2023).

In addition to its positive contributions to education, ChatGPT also has some negative effects. ChatGPT has been criticized for not having up-to-date information after 2021 (Lo, 2023). The possibility that the content produced by ChatGPT may be inaccurate or incomplete is also frequently emphasized (Michel-Villarreal et al., 2023). In addition, the negative impact of ChatGPT on students' critical thinking and problem-solving skills is also a concern (Demir & Demir, 2023c). The fact that ChatGPT has positive and negative aspects on students requires research on the subject in different branches within the field of education. One of these branches is tourism education.

The studies examining the impact of ChatGPT on tourism education have predominantly focused on elucidating its potential effects and applications. The purpose of many of these studies is to explore the possible use of ChatGPT in tourism education through interactions with it (Ali, 2023; Dogru et al., 2023; Iskender, 2023; Ivanov & Soliman, 2023; Ülkü, 2023; Yiğit, 2023). Others have delved into its influence on students' learning outcomes (Dalgıç et al., 2024), critical thinking abilities (Demir & Demir, 2023c), and academic performance (Emam, 2023) within the tourism field. Some researchers have also examined the efficacy of ChatGPT in assisting students in the tourism field during exams (Göktaş, 2023). Additionally, Skavronskaya et al. (2023) have provided theoretical insights into the potential applications of ChatGPT in tourism education. Although these studies offer valuable theoretical perspectives, there remains a gap in understanding the practical effectiveness and applicability of ChatGPT in tourism education, particularly from the student's perspective. Therefore, this research aims to comprehensively evaluate the potential impacts of ChatGPT on tourism students by analyzing existing literature findings. By doing so, this study seeks to contribute to a deeper understanding of the practical implications of ChatGPT for tourism education and provide diverse insights into its potential contributions.

BACKGROUND

ChatGPT and Education

ChatGPT has been frequently used in the field of education recently. The perceived ease and motivation towards the use of ChatGPT improve students' attitudes positively (Tiwari et al., 2023). Fulfilling many functions in a short time through ChatGPT in the field of education also influences both students and instructors to use ChatGPT. For this reason, the use of ChatGPT in education, especially for students, is increasing daily (Rejeb et al., 2024). However, the fact that ChatGPT also has negative effects in education prevents the formation of a consensus. For this reason, researchers from different fields are trying to evaluate the potential contributions and drawbacks of ChatGPT in the field of education together.

Memaria and Doleck (2023) highlight two significant contributions of ChatGPT in education: personalizing the learning process and providing timely feedback. ChatGPT can tailor the learning experience to suit individual student needs and preferences, enhancing accessibility and simplifying the learning process. Additionally, ChatGPT's rapid feedback mechanisms facilitate uninterrupted and expedited learning progression. However, it is essential to acknowledge the potential drawbacks associated with ChatGPT in education, such as limitations in data quality, possible misuse, and instances where genuine learning may be hindered.

The utilization of ChatGPT enables students to comprehend any text more effortlessly and efficiently. By leveraging ChatGPT, students can promptly articulate their thoughts on a subject in written form. Moreover, ChatGPT facilitates the scanning of information sources, enabling students to save valuable time while uncovering overlooked points and information. Consequently, students can attain a deeper understanding of the relevant subject matter. However, it is crucial to acknowledge the potential for ChatGPT to generate biased content in educational contexts. There exists a risk of unfairness in creating content that pertains to specific groups or events, potentially leading students towards discriminatory attitudes (Kasneci et al., 2023). Thus, educators must exercise caution and vigilance when incorporating ChatGPT into educational practices to mitigate the risk of bias and discrimination.

Mogavi et al. (2023) highlight that ChatGPT is extensively utilized in higher education and delineate its potential contributions to schooling. These contributions encompass various aspects such as content creation and organization, content summarization, personalized learning support, assistance in language learning, and accessibility for every student. Additionally, ChatGPT positively impacts career preparation, communication skills development, and problem-solving skills enhancement. With ChatGPT, students can swiftly generate and refine the content of articles or research, facilitating content summarization tasks. Moreover, the accessibility of ChatGPT enables students to create a personalized learning environment and access assistance at any time. Furthermore, students can leverage ChatGPT for career-related guidance, soliciting suggestions to address any gaps in their career development endeavors.

ChatGPT allows students to refine and diversify their learning techniques (Mhlanga, 2023). Using ChatGPT, students can engage in a more creative learning process, departing from traditional educational methods and environments. The conversational nature of ChatGPT fosters a deeper understanding and retention of topics learned, contributing to more enduring learning outcomes (Gill et al., 2024). Additionally, students can utilize ChatGPT to brainstorm ideas and explore different facets of a subject, enhancing their comprehension (Rospigliosi, 2023). ChatGPT is a valuable resource for students to seek clarification on various aspects of a topic, enabling them to address any questions or uncertainties. However, it is essential to acknowledge that the generation of erroneous information by ChatGPT during the learning process poses a potential risk of disrupting students' learning experiences. Therefore, careful supervision and critical evaluation of the information provided by ChatGPT are necessary to mitigate this risk and ensure the accuracy and effectiveness of the learning process.

The integration of ChatGPT in education has facilitated the improvement of students' collaboration and the strengthening of teamwork dynamics (Dwivedi et al., 2023). Through ChatGPT, students can track their progress and evaluate their learning processes, enabling them to identify and address any deficiencies effectively (Rejeb et al., 2024). ChatGPT also offers concrete examples of subjects, which accelerates students' understanding of the material. Moreover, ChatGPT serves as a valuable tool for language learning, allowing students to create language practice exercises and homework tailored to their needs (Elbanna & Armstrong, 2024). However, it is important to recognize potential drawbacks associated with the use of ChatGPT in education. Tlili et al. (2023) highlight concerns regarding the increased incidence of plagiarism among students using ChatGPT and the potential negative impact on the learning process, particularly in the context of homework assignments. These challenges underscore the importance of promoting ethical behavior and academic integrity among students while utilizing ChatGPT as an educational resource.

Farrokhnia et al. (2023) identified the opportunities and weaknesses created by ChatGPT in education. According to this research, ChatGPT increases access to information in the field of education, accelerates personal learning, facilitates complex learning, and reduces instructors' workload. On the other hand, the weaknesses of ChatGPT are ChatGPT's lack of deep understanding and comprehension of the subject matter, the quality of responses, the possibility of bias and discrimination, and the lack of critical and analytical thinking skills. A similar study was conducted by Baidoo-Anu and Ansah (2023). In this study, the potential positive contributions of ChatGPT in education are explained as personalized tutoring, language translation, and interactive and adaptive learning. The possible disadvantages of ChatGPT in education are privacy and security issues, limited comprehension ability, and not being a substitute for human interaction. Loos et al. (2023) state that ChatGPT improves students' learning process, but ChatGPT lacks empathy and emotion and is not good enough for contextual understanding.

ChatGPT is seen as important because it is possible to realize similar potential contributions of ChatGPT to general education in tourism education (Ivanov & Soliman, 2023). In studies examining the impact of ChatGPT in tourism education, potential positive contributions and disadvantages are recognized. Notably, students' performance increases with the use of ChatGPT in tourism education (Emam, 2023). With the inclusion of ChatGPT in the tourism education system, students' learning outcomes and digital literacy improve positively (Dalgıç et al., 2024). Ali (2023) evaluates the positive contributions of ChatGPT in tourism education under five headings. These are providing automated customer simulations, language training, personalized learning, virtual reality experience, and industry knowledge.

ChatGPT is seen as important because it is possible to realize similar potential contributions of ChatGPT to general education in tourism education (Ivanov & Soliman, 2023). In studies examining the impact of ChatGPT in tourism education, potential positive contributions and disadvantages are recognized. It is noteworthy that students' performance increases with the use of ChatGPT in tourism education (Emam, 2023). With the inclusion of ChatGPT in the tourism education system, students' learning outcomes and digital literacy improve positively (Dalgıç et al., 2024). Ali (2023) evaluates the positive contributions of ChatGPT in tourism education under five headings. These are: providing automated customer simulations, language training, personalized learning, virtual reality experience, and industry knowledge.

The integration of ChatGPT in tourism education offers several benefits, including the opportunity for students to engage in automated customer simulations, language training, and virtual reality experiences tailored to the hospitality and tourism industry (Ali, 2023). Through automated customer simulations, students can simulate various customer behaviors encountered in hospitality settings, allowing them to apply their knowledge and skills in customer service and behavior management. Additionally, ChatGPT can support language education initiatives by providing language practice exercises and conversational experiences relevant to tourism contexts.

Moreover, ChatGPT can create virtual reality scenarios specific to accommodation areas, offering students immersive learning experiences that enhance their understanding of hospitality operations and guest interactions (Ali, 2023). However, it's important to acknowledge that while ChatGPT presents numerous advantages, there are also notable drawbacks, as highlighted by Ivanov and Soliman (2023). These disadvantages include limitations in accessing real-time information, potential gaps in responses to specific queries, the risk of generating fake references in generated texts, and the provision of superficial answers. Furthermore, Demir and Demir (2023c) raise concerns about the potential negative impact of ChatGPT on students' critical thinking and analytical skills in tourism education. Educators need to consider these drawbacks and implement strategies to mitigate their effects while leveraging the benefits of ChatGPT to enhance learning outcomes in tourism education.

MAIN FOCUS OF THE CHAPTER

Research Method

It is known from the literature review that ChatGPT has positive and negative outcomes for tourism students. However, there is a lack of research in which these results are evaluated and discussed more comprehensively. This study aims to fill this gap in the literature. This study fully addresses the effects of ChatGPT on tourism students from the perspective of tourism academics. Since it is necessary to obtain comprehensive information about the impact of ChatGPT on tourism students from the standpoint of tourism academics, a qualitative research method was applied in this study. With the qualitative research method, the thoughts and feelings of individuals about any subject are learned comprehensively (Creswell, 2013).

In this study, the semi-structured interview technique, which is a qualitative research method, was utilized to learn the thoughts of tourism academics about the effects of ChatGPT on their students. The semi-structured interview technique starts with questions prepared by the researchers and can continue according to the answers obtained (Brinkmann, 2014). In this context, an interview form was created. The interview form includes three demographic questions and five questions to learn the effects of ChatGPT on students. These questions were inspired by the studies of Dalgıç et al. (2024), Demir and Demir (2023c), and Emam (2023) to learn the opinions of tourism academics about the effects of ChatGPT on tourism students. The first four questions concern tourism academics' potential contributions to ChatGPT to students. The fifth question was created to learn about the negativities of ChatGPT on students. The questions in the interview form are as follows;

1. How can ChatGPT affect the learning performance of tourism students?
2. How can ChatGPT affect tourism students' critical and analytical thinking skills?
3. How can ChatGPT affect tourism students' digital literacy?
4. Apart from learning performance, critical and analytical thinking, and digital literacy, what kind of contributions can ChatGPT make to tourism students?
5. What negativities can ChatGPT cause for tourism students?

Sample and Data Collection

Purposive sampling was used in the study. In purposive sampling, participants are included in line with specific criteria that are appropriate for the research (Bernard, 2017). In this study, there are some criteria for selecting the participants. The academics included in the study are from the field of tourism. Another criterion for including academics in the study is that they have used ChatGPT at least once. Academics who did not use ChatGPT were not included in the study. Within these criteria, interviews were conducted with eight tourism academics. In the qualitative research method, there is no need to increase the number of participants when the interviews continue within an inevitable repetition, and the researcher is convinced that they have reached sufficient data saturation (Miles & Huberman, 1994). Marshall (1996) emphasizes that the interviews should be ended when the participants' responses become repetitive. Creswell (2013) explains that 5-25 participants are sufficient in interviews. Within the scope of this information, the interviews were completed with eight participants.

An online interview form via Google Forms was selected for conducting interviews in this study. This decision was motivated by eliciting participants' views in a manner that allowed for flexibility and minimized time constraints and pressure. Furthermore, the online format ensured that participants were not influenced by the researcher's presence, thus enabling them to express their thoughts freely and honestly. The online interview form was distributed to participants over two days,

Table 1. Demographic Characteristics of the Participants

Participant	Gender	Department	Title
P1	Female	Gastronomy And Culinary Arts	Assistant Professor D.
P2	Female	Tourism Management	Research Assistant
P3	Male	Tourism Guidance	Research Assistant
P4	Male	Tourism Management	Lecturer
P5	Female	Tourism Management	Research Assistant
P6	Male	Tourism Guidance	Lecturer
P7	Female	Tourism Guidance	Associate Professor
P8	Male	Tourism Management	Lecturer

from February 27, 2024, to February 28, 2024. Before participating in the interviews, participants were provided with information about the research topic. It's important to note that participation in the interviews was entirely voluntary, and individuals chose to participate in the research at their discretion.

The responses collected from the interviews were analyzed using thematic analysis, following the framework outlined by Braun and Clarke (2006). Thematic analysis involves identifying patterns, themes, and codes within the data, aligning them with existing literature, and drawing meaningful conclusions. The analysis process in this study involved several stages. First, the data were carefully reviewed to understand the content. Next, preliminary codes were assigned to data segments to capture key ideas and concepts. These initial codes were then organized into recurring themes from the dataset. The themes were further refined and defined, and appropriate names were assigned to represent their content accurately. Throughout the analysis, rigor and validity were ensured through scrutiny and review by two independent academics with expertise in the research topic.

Demographic characteristics of the participants are shown in Table 1. Four of the participants were male, and four were female. There were participants from three different departments. The titles of the participants vary between research assistant and associate professor.

Results

Upon analyzing the responses obtained from participants, five main themes emerged in the study. These main themes encompassed the effect of ChatGPT on learning performance, critical and analytical skills, digital literacy, other effects on students, and negative effects. The main theme concerning the effect of ChatGPT on learning performance focused on participants' perspectives regarding its influence on the

Table 2. The Effect of ChatGPT on Learning Performance

Main Theme	Sub Themes	Sub Codes
The Effect of ChatGPT on Learning Performance	ChatGPT Positively Impacts Students' Learning Performance	Accessing accurate information with ChatGPT
		Conduct detailed research in a short time with ChatGPT
		ChatGPT is creative and fun
		ChatGPT provides motivation
		ChatGPT guides the learning process
	ChatGPT Negatively Impacts Students' Learning Performance	It is difficult to internalize information with ChatGPT

academic progress of tourism students. Subsequently, Table 2 outlines the sub-themes and corresponding codes associated with the effect of ChatGPT on learning performance.

The majority of participants (seven individuals) expressed a positive outlook on the potential contribution of ChatGPT to the learning performance of tourism students. Participants cited several reasons to support this perspective. Firstly, it was anticipated that ChatGPT would facilitate more accessible access to accurate information for students. P3 remarked, *"It can enhance student performance because students can quickly conduct comprehensive research. Obtaining detailed information quickly through other means is challenging, but they can achieve this with ChatGPT."* Additionally, it was underscored that ChatGPT adds a creative and enjoyable dimension to the learning process for students. P5 mentioned, *"ChatGPT has the potential to boost students' learning performance because it makes the learning process enjoyable."* P6 noted that ChatGPT could be a motivational tool for students during the learning process. He stated, *"The presence of ChatGPT may motivate students to engage with technology, thereby positively impacting learning performance."* Moreover, participants highlighted that ChatGPT's ability to guide learning and encourage personalized learning positively influences learning performance. P8 elaborated, *"ChatGPT can assume a guiding role akin to that of a teacher in the learning process. It can assist students with challenging topics and provide the information they seek, ultimately enhancing learning performance."*

P2 thinks the belief that ChatGPT will exert a detrimental influence on students' learning performance. She argues that while ChatGPT enables students to access information easily and quickly, it does so superficially. P2 emphasizes that this superficial information acquisition may hinder students' ability to internalize and comprehend the material effectively. She articulated, *"It may have a negative impact.*

Table 3. The Effect of ChatGPT on Critical and Analytical Skills

<table>
<tr><th>Main Theme</th><th>Sub Themes</th><th>Sub Codes</th></tr>
<tr><td rowspan="3">The Effect of ChatGPT on Critical and Analytical Skills</td><td rowspan="2">ChatGPT Negatively Affects Students' Critical and Analytical Skills</td><td>ChatGPT prevents discussing ideas</td></tr>
<tr><td>ChatGPT does it all</td></tr>
<tr><td>ChatGPT Positively Affects Students' Critical and Analytical Skills</td><td>ChatGPT provides access to information in different languages and contents</td></tr>
</table>

While it allows easy access to information and learning, the lack of in-depth research from various sources could impede internalization."

The main theme of the effect of ChatGPT on critical and analytical skills includes the participants' thoughts on the impact of ChatGPT on tourism students' critical and analytical skills. Table 3 shows the sub-themes and codes related to the effect of ChatGPT on critical and analytical skills.

Participants highlight two primary reasons for the negative impact of ChatGPT on students' critical and analytical skills. Firstly, they note that ChatGPT diminishes opportunities for students to engage in discussions and express their thoughts, reducing brainstorming activities. As a result, students may experience a decline in their critical and analytical abilities. P3 remarked, *"It might adversely affect analytical skills. Typically, students rely on ChatGPT to complete assignments and tasks they would otherwise design themselves through independent thinking. When everything is readily available without questioning via ChatGPT, critical thinking is sidelined."* P7 stated, *"ChatGPT could hinder students' critical and analytical thinking abilities. Since ChatGPT handles most tasks, students may become complacent."*

Another reason for the negative impact of ChatGPT on critical and analytical skills is its capability to handle a wide range of tasks. Students often rely on ChatGPT to complete various academic endeavors such as research topics, exams, or assignments. Consequently, students may become less inclined to engage in critical thinking and creative activities. P5 highlighted this concern, *"It has a negative impact because ChatGPT already provides answers to everything in some form."*

P1 and P8 think ChatGPT will improve students' critical and analytical skills. These opinions are because students access information in different languages and contents through ChatGPT. Students can learn concepts, ideas, and information they are unaware of under normal conditions through ChatGPT. This improves students' critical and analytical skills. P8 stated, *''I think that accessing information written in various languages about the subjects to be learned in their language will contribute positively to developing their understanding and thinking skills.''*

Table 4. The Effect of ChatGPT on Digital Literacy

Main Theme	Sub Themes	Sub Codes
The Effect of ChatGPT on Digital Literacy	ChatGPT Positively Affects Students' Digital Literacy	Students' existing digital skills and literacy improve with the use of ChatGPT

The main theme of the effect of ChatGPT on digital literacy includes the participants' thoughts on the effect of ChatGPT on the digital literacy of tourism students. Table 4 shows the sub-themes and codes related to the effect of ChatGPT on digital literacy.

Participants concur that ChatGPT will positively impact students' digital literacy. They argue that utilizing artificial intelligence tools like ChatGPT requires a baseline level of digital proficiency, which students can develop through engaging with such applications. As students use ChatGPT, their digital skills are expected to improve gradually. P3 articulated this perspective, "*It can positively impact digital literacy. Students must possess a certain level of digital competence to utilize ChatGPT effectively. This competence is likely to increase over time through ChatGPT.*" Similarly, P5 remarked, "*It has a positive effect. It enhances learning and the utilization of tools such as artificial intelligence.*"

The main theme of other effects of ChatGPT on students includes the participants' thoughts on other potential effects of ChatGPT on tourism students. Table 5 shows the sub-themes and codes related to the other effects of ChatGPT on students.

Participants expressed varied perspectives on the additional positive effects of ChatGPT on students. They highlighted that students' awareness of innovation may improve through the utilization of ChatGPT, as it enables access to diverse information and fosters technological engagement. For instance, P1 remarked, "*Students may engage in various entrepreneurial endeavors in the future, aligning their professional growth with technological advancements. Their awareness of innovation in tourism is enhanced.*" Additionally, ChatGPT facilitates time management by expediting

Table 5. The Other Effects of ChatGPT on Students

Main Theme	Sub Themes
Other Effects of ChatGPT on Students	Innovation awareness improves
	Provides effective time management
	Provides support in language learning
	Provides personal development
	Provides diversity of information

Table 6. The Negative Effects of ChatGPT on Students

Main Theme	Sub Themes
The Negative Effects of ChatGPT on Students	Makes students lazy
	Causes vision loss
	Researcher identities are weakened
	Their ability to use different options is weakened

research processes, as noted by P5: *"It offers a time-saving advantage by providing concise information. Students can utilize ChatGPT for foreign language acquisition."* Furthermore, P3 mentioned, *"Students can leverage ChatGPT for language learning."* By broadening their knowledge base through ChatGPT, students may also enhance their personal development, as highlighted by P8: *"Accessing information from around the globe, even in languages prevalent in specific regions, positively impacts personal growth."*

The main theme of the negative effects of ChatGPT on students includes the participants' opinions on the negative effects of ChatGPT on tourism students. Table 6 shows the sub-themes and codes related to the negative effects of ChatGPT on students.

Participants expressed concerns that the use of ChatGPT might lead to student laziness. They highlighted that ChatGPT's ability to provide diverse information quickly may discourage students from exploring alternative learning channels, potentially fostering a dependence on the platform. As articulated by P4, *"Relying solely on ChatGPT may deter them from utilizing other resources. Limiting research and learning to a single platform could breed laziness."* Moreover, participants noted that excessive reliance on ChatGPT may stifle students' creativity, particularly among those content with the information provided by the tool. P2 elaborated, *"Tourism students, who typically learn about nature and historical culture through firsthand experiences and travel, may be negatively impacted by ChatGPT. It may facilitate learning of textual information while discouraging exploration and creative ideation."*

Students who perceive ChatGPT as a quick solution for research may witness a decline in their motivation to conduct comprehensive inquiries. Students might sacrifice thoroughness by favoring ChatGPT for its convenience, reducing their inclination towards in-depth research. As expressed by P8, *"The swift access to resources via ChatGPT could erode students' dedication to research."* Moreover, students who rely solely on ChatGPT without consulting other sources may struggle to evaluate and compare information effectively. P6 highlighted, *"Overreliance on ChatGPT for research may limit students' exposure to diverse information outlets. Although ChatGPT streamlines information retrieval, it might inadvertently encourage a narrow approach to sourcing, potentially impeding students' capacity to explore alternative avenues."*

SOLUTIONS AND RECOMMENDATIONS

There is a prevailing consensus among participants regarding the positive impact of ChatGPT on the learning performance of tourism students. A key factor supporting this viewpoint is ChatGPT's ability to deliver information to students swiftly. With ChatGPT, students can access desired content and research outcomes promptly, maximizing learning within minimal time. This notion is corroborated by several researchers (Kasneci et al., 2023; Rahman & Watanobe, 2023). Another factor contributing to enhanced learning performance with ChatGPT is the creative and enjoyable learning process it facilitates. Through interactive learning experiences, students deviate from conventional learning paradigms, making the learning journey more engaging. Kostka and Toncelli (2023) contend that ChatGPT fosters a creative and enjoyable learning atmosphere. By providing an innovative and interactive learning environment, ChatGPT enhances the overall learning experience (Zafrullah et al., 2023), thereby bolstering learning performance.

Furthermore, ChatGPT's role as a companion akin to a teacher throughout the learning process, offering personalized learning environments, positively influences learning performance. Furnishing a distinctive learning milieu arguably constitutes ChatGPT's most salient feature in education (Memaria & Doleck, 2023). ChatGPT aids students through personalized learning support, guiding them through deficiencies, strengths, or errors. Scholars such as Ali (2023) and Farrokhnia et al. (2023) underscore personal learning as ChatGPT's primary contribution to education. Emam (2023) asserts that ChatGPT generally enhances the performance of tourism students.

However, some participants express concerns that ChatGPT may adversely impact learning performance. According to this perspective, internalizing information obtained through ChatGPT poses challenges. Students might fail to internalize information acquired effortlessly through ChatGPT-driven research, leading to a superficial learning process. Ivanov and Soliman (2023) also highlight a similar drawback, suggesting that the learning process with ChatGPT tends to be simplistic. Therefore, it is imperative for students to verify and internalize information obtained from ChatGPT (Xu et al., 2024). Failure to authenticate information from ChatGPT may result in shallow internalization or misinformation (Wieser et al., 2023), potentially hampering students' learning performance.

Different views prevail on the effects of ChatGPT on students' critical and analytical abilities. Participants who think that ChatGPT will negatively affect critical and analytical skills think that ChatGPT reduces the discussion environment and originality because ChatGPT does everything. As a result, there is a learning process dominated by one type of thinking. Students can go through the learning process without reflecting and sharing their thoughts. This weakens critical and analytical skills. This view is also supported by Demir and Demir (2023c). According to the authors, ChatGPT provides convenience in terms of access to information but negatively affects students' critical thinking and analytical skills. Hasanein and Sobaih (2023) argue a similar view and emphasize that students' critical thinking and discussions will be negatively affected with ChatGPT. Therefore, the integration of ChatGPT into the education system should be completed in time. Students' critical thinking skills may be damaged in an education system where ChatGPT is suddenly dominated and used (Liu et al., 2023).

The fact that ChatGPT provides access to information in different languages and contexts is thought to affect students' critical and analytical skills positively. Participants focus on the fact that the richness of ChatGPT in terms of content will add diversity to students' thinking. Gill et al. (2024) state that students can brainstorm with ChatGPT because new ideas will increase. ChatGPT can positively affect critical thinking and problem solving as it presents different information and opinions with the topic that students are interested in (Essel et al., 2024).

There is a consensus that ChatGPT will positively improve students' digital literacy. Participants believed that students' digital literacy would improve using ChatGPT. This finding is consistent with the literature. Dalgıç et al. (2024) stated that tourism students' ChatGPT learning outcomes positively affect digital literacy. As students become interested in ChatGPT, they start to use it more. With the increase in the use of ChatGPT, the level of digital literacy also increases (Kasneci et al., 2023). Tran and Tran (2023) also state that digital literacy improves with the use of ChatGPT.

According to the participants, other positive effects of ChatGPT on students are developing innovation awareness, time management, support in language learning, personal development and diversity of knowledge. With the use of ChatGPT, different thoughts are learned. Thanks to these different thoughts, the innovative aspect develops (Habibi et al., 2023). Students can use their time efficiently by using ChatGPT. Because they can increase their knowledge and complete their work in a short time. Students can benefit from ChatGPT in language learning processes. ChatGPT can help in learning grammar rules and developing writing techniques (Baskara, 2023; Hong, 2023). ChatGPT supports students to complete their deficiencies by supporting their development (Rejeb et al., 2024).

The potential negative effects of ChatGPT on students focus on different issues. According to the participants, students are expected to experience laziness with the use of ChatGPT. It is convenient for students to do their homework and research easily with ChatGPT. ChatGPT offers the opportunity to do many things with little effort. This situation does not only cause laziness. It also causes students to weaken their researcher identity. Students lose the research process and motivation and gain the habit of using ChatGPT. With ChatGPT, students surrender to ChatGPT by not using their evaluation skills. They act by making decisions in line with ChatGPT suggestions or content. This situation weakens students' vision and ability to evaluate different options.

Theoretical Implications

When examining the research on ChatGPT and its implications for tourism education, it becomes apparent that there is a dearth of studies focusing on the effects of ChatGPT, specifically on tourism students (Dalgıç et al., 2024; Demir & Demir, 2023c; Emam, 2023). Instead, existing research predominantly centers around assessing the efficacy of ChatGPT through the lens of conversation theory. This study offers a theoretical contribution by evaluating the impacts of ChatGPT on tourism students from the perspective of tourism academics. This shift is crucial as previous research has primarily centered on the experiences of tourism students, necessitating a broader evaluation from the educators' standpoint.

Furthermore, a strong belief exists that ChatGPT will positively influence students' learning performance and digital literacy. The potential for ChatGPT to enhance students' learning processes is evident, promising a more efficient and effective educational experience. However, concerns arise regarding the negative impact of ChatGPT on students' critical and analytical skills. The comprehensiveness of ChatGPT's capabilities may inadvertently diminish students' inclination to question and engage in discussions, potentially impeding their development in these crucial areas.

Additionally, participants posit various positive contributions of ChatGPT, including fostering innovation awareness, aiding in time management, facilitating language learning, promoting personal development, and broadening access to diverse information. Despite these benefits, ChatGPT is also expected to negatively affect students, such as fostering laziness, eroding their research identities, diminishing motivation, and impairing evaluation skills.

In sum, this study sheds light on the multifaceted impacts of ChatGPT on tourism education, underscoring its potential benefits and drawbacks. By offering insights from the perspective of tourism academics, this study enriches our understanding of the complex dynamics at play when integrating ChatGPT into educational contexts.

Practical Implications

With this study, it is possible to have an idea about the positive and negative effects of ChatGPT on students. In cases where students are directed to ChatGPT in the learning process, there may be results such as increased learning performance and improved digital literacy. There may be positive results, such as increasing students' innovative thinking, effective time management, and personal development. However, students' critical and analytical skills are likely to be negatively affected by the use of ChatGPT. As students get used to the ease of ChatGPT, their motivation may decrease, and they may become lazy. For this reason, in directing students to artificial intelligence applications such as ChatGPT, only positive contributions should not be focused on. ChatGPT may be an easy-to-access and simple-to-use application for students, but it does not consistently produce positive student outputs. In line with this information, it can be stated that students should be guided with caution in the process of using ChatGPT.

Future Research Directions

This study was conducted to determine the potential effects of ChatGPT on tourism students from the perspective of tourism academics. Similar research can be performed for academics from different fields in future research. The views of academics and students can be compared. This research was conducted with a qualitative research method. Research can be completed in which both qualitative and quantitative methods can be used together. Research can be performed on different positive and negative features of ChatGPT.

CONCLUSION

When the research results are evaluated comprehensively, it is determined that academics have negative and positive opinions about the effects of ChatGPT on their students. It is seen that ChatGPT increases students' learning performance and digital literacy. However, there are also some opposing views on learning performance. It is stated that it is difficult for students to internalize information using ChatGPT; therefore, learning performance will be negatively affected. Similarly, it is thought that students' critical and analytical skills will be negatively affected by ChatGPT. Students do not question, discuss, or avoid expressing their thoughts while using artificial intelligence applications such as ChatGPT.

Other positive effects of ChatGPT on students include raising their awareness of innovation and time management, providing information diversity, and supporting personal development and language learning. The adverse impact of ChatGPT on students includes making them lazy, weakening their researcher identities, losing motivation, and decreasing their evaluation skills. As a result, it is seen that the effects of ChatGPT on students are not only positive or negative. What is important is the duration of ChatGPT use. It is not necessary to have ChatGPT do everything. If its proportional use can be realized, the negatives of ChatGPT will inevitably decrease, and the positive aspects will increase.

REFERENCES

Adeshola, I., & Adepoju, A. P. (2023). The opportunities and challenges of ChatGPT in education. *Interactive Learning Environments*, 1–14. doi:10.1080/10494820.2023.2253858

Ali, F. (2023). Let the devil speak for itself: Should ChatGPT be allowed or banned in hospitality and tourism schools? *Journal of Global Hospitality and Tourism*, *2*(1), 1–6. doi:10.5038/2771-5957.2.1.1016

Baidoo-Anu, D., & Ansah, L. O. (2023). Education in the era of generative artificial intelligence (AI): Understanding the potential benefits of ChatGPT in promoting teaching and learning. *Journal of AI*, *7*(1), 52–62. doi:10.61969/jai.1337500

Baskara, R. (2023). Exploring the implications of ChatGPT for language learning in higher education. *Indonesian Journal of English Language Teaching and Applied Linguistics*, *7*(2), 343–358.

Bernard, H. R. (2017). *Research methods in anthropology: Qualitative and quantitative approaches*. Rowman & Littlefield.

Braun, V., & Clarke, V. (2006). Using thematic analysis in psychology. *Qualitative Research in Psychology*, *3*(2), 77–101. doi:10.1191/1478088706qp063oa

Brinkmann, S. (2014). Unstructured and semi-structured interviewing. The Oxford handbook of qualitative research, 2, 277-299.

Creswell, J. W. (2013). *Qualitative inquiry and research design: Choosing among five approaches*. Sage publications.

Dalgıç, A., Yaşar, E., & Demir, M. (2024). ChatGPT and learning outcomes in tourism education: The role of digital literacy and individualized learning. *Journal of Hospitality, Leisure, Sport and Tourism Education*, *34*, 100481. doi:10.1016/j.jhlste.2024.100481

Demir, M., & Demir, Ş. Ş. (2023b). Is ChatGPT the right technology for service individualization and value co-creation? evidence from the travel industry. *Journal of Travel & Tourism Marketing*, *40*(5), 383–398. doi:10.1080/10548408.2023.2255884

Demir, M., & Demir, Ş. Ş. (2023c). Reflection of artificial intelligence applications on students' critical and analytical abilities. *Scientific Collection. InterConf*, (184), 459–467.

Demir, M., Demir, Ş. Ş., & Aktürk, O. (2023). The Effects of Distance Education Capabilities and Competencies on Learning Outcomes During COVID-19 in Higher Education Institutions. *Journal of Hospitality & Tourism Education*, 1–12. doi:10.1080/10963758.2023.2191966

Demir, Ş. Ş., & Demir, M. (2023a). Professionals' perspectives on ChatGPT in the tourism industry: Does it inspire awe or concern? *Journal of Tourism Theory and Research*, *9*(2), 61–76. doi:10.24288/jttr.1313481

Dogru, T., Line, N., Hanks, L., Acikgoz, F., Abbott, J. A., Bakir, S., Berbekova, A., Bilgihan, A., Iskender, A., Kizildag, M., Lee, M., Lee, W., McGinley, S., Mody, M., Onder, I., Ozdemir, O., & Suess, C. (2023). The implications of generative artificial intelligence in academic research and higher education in tourism and hospitality. *Tourism Economics*. Advance online publication. doi:10.1177/13548166231204065

Duong, C. D., Bui, D. T., Pham, H. T., & Vu, A. T. (2023). How effort expectancy and performance expectancy interact to trigger higher education students' uses of ChatGPT for learning. Interactive Technology and Smart Education. doi:10.1108/ITSE-05-2023-0096

Dwivedi, Y. K., Kshetri, N., Hughes, L., Slade, E. L., Jeyaraj, A., Kar, A. K., Baabdullah, A. M., Koohang, A., Raghavan, V., Ahuja, M., Albanna, H., Albashrawi, M. A., Al-Busaidi, A. S., Balakrishnan, J., Barlette, Y., Basu, S., Bose, I., Brooks, L., Buhalis, D., ... Wright, R. (2023). "So what if ChatGPT wrote it?" Multidisciplinary perspectives on opportunities, challenges and implications of generative conversational AI for research, practice and policy. *International Journal of Information Management*, *71*, 102642. doi:10.1016/j.ijinfomgt.2023.102642

Elbanna, S., & Armstrong, L. (2024). Exploring the integration of ChatGPT in education: Adapting for the future. *Management & Sustainability: An Arab Review*, *3*(1), 16–29. doi:10.1108/MSAR-03-2023-0016

Emam, R. M. (2023). *The effect of using Chat GPT technology as one of the applications of artificial intelligence in tourism education for students of tourism and hotels institutes by using task Technology fit model*. doi:10.21608/mfth.2023.327915

Essel, H. B., Vlachopoulos, D., Essuman, A. B., & Amankwa, J. O. (2024). ChatGPT effects on cognitive skills of undergraduate students: Receiving instant responses from AI-based conversational large language models (LLMs). *Computers and Education: Artificial Intelligence*, *6*, 100198. doi:10.1016/j.caeai.2023.100198

Farrokhnia, M., Banihashem, S. K., Noroozi, O., & Wals, A. (2023). A SWOT analysis of ChatGPT: Implications for educational practice and research. *Innovations in Education and Teaching International*, 1–15. doi:10.1080/14703297.2023.2195846

Gill, S. S., Xu, M., Patros, P., Wu, H., Kaur, R., Kaur, K., Fuller, S., Singh, M., Arora, P., Parlikad, A. K., Stankovski, V., Abraham, A., Ghosh, S. K., Lutfiyya, H., Kanhere, S. S., Bahsoon, R., Rana, O., Dustdar, S., Sakellariou, R., ... Buyya, R. (2024). Transformative effects of ChatGPT on modern education: Emerging Era of AI Chatbots. *Internet of Things and Cyber-Physical Systems*, *4*, 19–23. doi:10.1016/j.iotcps.2023.06.002

Göktaş, L. S. (2023). ChatGPT Uzaktan Eğitim Sınavlarında Başarılı Olabilir Mi? Turizm Alanında Doğruluk ve Doğrulama Üzerine Bir Araştırma (Can ChatGPT Succeed. *Journal of Tourism & Gastronomy Studies*, *11*(2), 892–905. doi:10.21325/jotags.2023.1224

Habibi, A., Muhaimin, M., Danibao, B. K., Wibowo, Y. G., Wahyuni, S., & Octavia, A. (2023). ChatGPT in higher education learning: Acceptance and use. *Computers and Education: Artificial Intelligence*, *5*, 100190. doi:10.1016/j.caeai.2023.100190

Hasanein, A. M., & Sobaih, A. E. E. (2023). Drivers and Consequences of ChatGPT Use in Higher Education: Key Stakeholder Perspectives. *European Journal of Investigation in Health, Psychology and Education*, *13*(11), 2599–2614. doi:10.3390/ejihpe13110181 PMID:37998071

Hong, W. C. H. (2023). The impact of ChatGPT on foreign language teaching and learning: Opportunities in education and research. *Journal of Educational Technology and Innovation*, *5*(1), 1–9. doi:10.61414/jeti.v5i1.103

Iskender, A. (2023). Holy or unholy? Interview with open AI's ChatGPT. *European Journal of Tourism Research*, *34*, 3414–3414. doi:10.54055/ejtr.v34i.3169

Ivanov, S., & Soliman, M. (2023). Game of algorithms: ChatGPT implications for the future of tourism education and research. *Journal of Tourism Futures*, *9*(2), 214–221. doi:10.1108/JTF-02-2023-0038

Kasneci, E., Seßler, K., Küchemann, S., Bannert, M., Dementieva, D., Fischer, F., Gasser, U., Groh, G., Günnemann, S., Hüllermeier, E., Krusche, S., Kutyniok, G., Michaeli, T., Nerdel, C., Pfeffer, J., Poquet, O., Sailer, M., Schmidt, A., Seidel, T., ... Kasneci, G. (2023). ChatGPT for good? On opportunities and challenges of large language models for education. *Learning and Individual Differences*, *103*, 102274. doi:10.1016/j.lindif.2023.102274

Kostka, I., & Toncelli, R. (2023). Exploring applications of ChatGPT to English language teaching: Opportunities, challenges, and recommendations. *TESL-EJ, 27*(3), 1–19. doi:10.55593/ej.27107int

Liu, M., Ren, Y., Nyagoga, L. M., Stonier, F., Wu, Z., & Yu, L. (2023). Future of education in the era of generative artificial intelligence: Consensus among Chinese scholars on applications of ChatGPT in schools. *Future in Educational Research, 1*(1), 72–101. doi:10.1002/fer3.10

Lo, C. K. (2023). What is the impact of ChatGPT on education? A rapid review of the literature. *Education Sciences, 13*(4), 410. doi:10.3390/educsci13040410

Loos, E., Gröpler, J., & Goudeau, M. L. S. (2023). Using ChatGPT in Education: Human Reflection on ChatGPT's Self-Reflection. *Societies (Basel, Switzerland), 13*(8), 196. doi:10.3390/soc13080196

Marshall, M. N. (1996). Sampling for qualitative research. *Family Practice, 13*(6), 522–526. doi:10.1093/fampra/13.6.522 PMID:9023528

Memarian, B., & Doleck, T. (2023). ChatGPT in education: Methods, potentials and limitations. *Computers in Human Behavior: Artificial Humans, 100022*(2), 100022. Advance online publication. doi:10.1016/j.chbah.2023.100022

Mhlanga, D. (2023). Open AI in education, the responsible and ethical use of ChatGPT towards lifelong learning. *Education, the Responsible and Ethical Use of ChatGPT Towards Lifelong Learning,* 1-19.

Michel-Villarreal, R., Vilalta-Perdomo, E., Salinas-Navarro, D. E., Thierry-Aguilera, R., & Gerardou, F. S. (2023). Challenges and opportunities of generative AI for higher education as explained by ChatGPT. *Education Sciences, 13*(9), 856. doi:10.3390/educsci13090856

Miles, M. B., & Huberman, A. M. (1994). Qualitative data analysis: An expanded sourcebook. *Sage (Atlanta, Ga.).*

Mogavi, R. H., Deng, C., Kim, J. J., Zhou, P., Kwon, Y. D., Metwally, A. H. S., ... Hui, P. (2024). ChatGPT in education: A blessing or a curse? A qualitative study exploring early adopters' utilization and perceptions. *Computers in Human Behavior: Artificial Humans, 2*(1), 100027. doi:10.1016/j.chbah.2023.100027

Montenegro-Rueda, M., Fernández-Cerero, J., Fernández-Batanero, J. M., & López-Meneses, E. (2023). Impact of the implementation of ChatGPT in education: A systematic review. *Computers, 12*(8), 153. doi:10.3390/computers12080153

Rahman, M. M., & Watanobe, Y. (2023). ChatGPT for education and research: Opportunities, threats, and strategies. *Applied Sciences (Basel, Switzerland)*, *13*(9), 5783. doi:10.3390/app13095783

Rejeb, A., Rejeb, K., Appolloni, A., Treiblmaier, H., & Iranmanesh, M. (2024). Exploring the impact of ChatGPT on education: A web mining and machine learning approach. *International Journal of Management Education*, *22*(1), 100932. doi:10.1016/j.ijme.2024.100932

Rospigliosi, P. (2023). Artificial intelligence in teaching and learning: What questions should we ask of ChatGPT? *Interactive Learning Environments*, *31*(1), 1–3. doi:10.1080/10494820.2023.2180191

Skavronskaya, L., Hadinejad, A., & Cotterell, D. (2023). Reversing the threat of artificial intelligence to opportunity: A discussion of ChatGPT in tourism education. *Journal of Teaching in Travel & Tourism*, *23*(2), 253–258. doi:10.1080/15313220.2023.2196658

Tiwari, C. K., Bhat, M. A., Khan, S. T., Subramaniam, R., & Khan, M. A. I. (2023). What drives students toward ChatGPT? An investigation of the factors influencing adoption and usage of ChatGPT. Interactive Technology and Smart Education. doi:10.1108/ITSE-04-2023-0061

Tlili, A., Shehata, B., Adarkwah, M. A., Bozkurt, A., Hickey, D. T., Huang, R., & Agyemang, B. (2023). What if the devil is my guardian angel: ChatGPT as a case study of using chatbots in education. *Smart Learning Environments*, *10*(1), 15. doi:10.1186/s40561-023-00237-x

Tran, T. N., & Tran, H. P. (2023, November). Exploring the role of ChatGPT in developing critical digital literacies in language learning: a qualitative study. *Proceedings of the AsiaCALL International Conference*, *4*, 1-17. 10.54855/paic.2341

Ülkü, A. (2023). Artificial intelligence-based large language models and integrity of exams and assignments in higher education: The case of tourism courses. *Tourism & Management Studies*, *19*(4), 21–34. doi:10.18089/tms.2023.190402

Wieser, M., Schöffmann, K., Stefanics, D., Bollin, A., & Pasterk, S. (2023, October). Investigating the Role of ChatGPT in Supporting Text-Based Programming Education for Students and Teachers. In *International Conference on Informatics in Schools: Situation, Evolution, and Perspectives* (pp. 40-53). Cham: Springer Nature Switzerland. 10.1007/978-3-031-44900-0_4

Xu, X., Su, Y., Zhang, Y., Wu, Y., & Xu, X. (2024). Understanding learners' perceptions of ChatGPT: A thematic analysis of peer interviews among undergraduates and postgraduates in China. *Heliyon*, *10*(4), 1–13. doi:10.1016/j.heliyon.2024.e26239 PMID:38420484

Yiğit, S. (2023). Yapay Zekâ Gastronomi Eğitimine Katkı Sunabilir Mi? ChatGPT Örneği. *Journal of Tourism & Gastronomy Studies.*, *11*(3), 1970–1982.

Zafrullah, Z., Hakim, M. L., & Angga, M. (2023). ChatGPT open AI: Analysis of mathematics education students learning interest. *Journal of Technology Global*, *1*(01), 1–10.

ADDITIONAL READING

Dalgıç, A., Yaşar, E., & Demir, M. (2024). ChatGPT and learning outcomes in tourism education: The role of digital literacy and individualized learning. *Journal of Hospitality, Leisure, Sport and Tourism Education*, *34*, 100481. doi:10.1016/j.jhlste.2024.100481

Demir, M. (2024). Building Trust and Credibility: Ethical Use of AI in the Service Industry. In M. Demir & A. Dalgic (Eds.), *Revolutionizing the Service Industry With OpenAI Models* (pp. 243–267). IGI Global., doi:10.4018/979-8-3693-1239-1.ch010

Demir, M., Demir, Ş. Ş., & Aktürk, O. (2023). The Effects of Distance Education Capabilities and Competencies on Learning Outcomes During COVID-19 in Higher Education Institutions. *Journal of Hospitality & Tourism Education*, 1–12. doi:10.1080/10963758.2023.2191966

Demir, Ş. Ş. (2024). Innovations With ChatGPT in the Tourism Industry: Current Challenges and Opportunities. In M. Demir & A. Dalgic (Eds.), *Revolutionizing the Service Industry With OpenAI Models* (pp. 29–51). IGI Global. doi:10.4018/979-8-3693-1239-1.ch002

Fianu, E., Amankwah-Sarfo, F., Affum, E. K., & Brown-Acquaye, W. L. (2024). Investigating the Service Quality of Chatbots on Telecom Service Providers' Websites and Apps. In M. Demir & A. Dalgic (Eds.), *Revolutionizing the Service Industry With OpenAI Models* (pp. 1–28). IGI Global. doi:10.4018/979-8-3693-1239-1.ch001

Fianu, E., Amankwah-Sarfo, F., & Ofori, M. (2024). Examining the Task - Technology Fit of ChatGPT for Healthcare Services. In M. Demir & A. Dalgic (Eds.), *Revolutionizing the Service Industry With OpenAI Models* (pp. 192–218). IGI Global. doi:10.4018/979-8-3693-1239-1.ch008

Yaşar, E., Yayla, E., & Alakuş, N. A. (2024). Artificial Intelligence-Supported Travel Agencies: Analysis of ChatGPT Usage and Future Perspectives. In M. Demir & A. Dalgic (Eds.), *Revolutionizing the Service Industry With OpenAI Models* (pp. 87–113). IGI Global. doi:10.4018/979-8-3693-1239-1.ch004

KEY TERMS AND DEFINITIONS

Artificial Intelligence: It is an artificial operating system that exhibits human-like behavior.

ChatGPT: It is an artificial intelligence supported chat robot.

Critical and Analytical Skills: It is the individual's deep thinking.

Digital Literacy: It is the ability to use and understand digital technologies.

Learning Performance: It is the outcome that an individual obtains from the learning process.

Chapter 10
The Impact of NBA Implementation Across Engineering Disciplines:
Innovative Approaches

S. Saravanan
https://orcid.org/0000-0001-8255-2623
Department of Electrical and Electronics Engineering, B.V. Raju Institute of Technology, Narsapur, India

J. Chandrasekar
Department of Social Work, Madras School of Social Work, Chennai, India

S. Satheesh Kumar
Department of Business Administration, Panimalar Engineering College, Chennai, India

Pavan Patel
Department of HRM & SM, Siva Sivani Institute of Management, Hyderabad, India

J. Maria Shanthi
Department of Artificial Intelligence and Machine Learning, J.B. Institute of Engineering and Technology, Hyderabad, India

Sampath Boopathi
https://orcid.org/0000-0002-2065-6539
Mechanical Engineering, Muthayammal Engineering College, Namakkal, India

ABSTRACT

NBA principles and technologies have significantly impacted engineering disciplines, leading to social changes and reshaping industries. NBA-inspired innovations have influenced materials science, data analytics, public health, urban design, and entertainment experiences. The study examines equity, access, and ethical dimensions of NBA-driven engineering innovations, focusing on data privacy, algorithmic bias,

DOI: 10.4018/979-8-3693-1666-5.ch010

and commodification of athlete performance. The goal is to foster inclusivity, equity, and sustainable development, fostering collaboration between the sports industry and engineering disciplines. This approach emphasizes the transformative power of sports-driven innovation in engineering for societal betterment.

INTRODUCTION

The NBA's integration of principles and technologies into engineering disciplines has revolutionized the industry, causing significant social changes and reshaping industries beyond sports. This introduction provides a comprehensive overview of the impact of NBA implementation across engineering disciplines. The NBA, a global sports powerhouse, is a hub for innovation and technological advancement. Its influence extends beyond the court to engineering fields, influencing various aspects of modern life. NBA-driven innovations optimize athlete performance and enhance spectator experiences, revolutionizing industries and promoting societal well-being (Venkatasubramanian et al., 2024).

Sports engineering is a dynamic field with a rich tapestry of interdisciplinary research and technological innovation. Collaborations between sports scientists, engineers, and athletes have led to groundbreaking advancements in biomechanics, materials science, and data analytics, driving the evolution of sports technology and pushing human performance boundaries. The NBA's influence in engineering has led to significant advancements in mechanical engineering, enhancing the design and optimization of athletic equipment like high-performance footwear and state-of-the-art basketball hoops. These innovations not only improve athlete safety and performance but also contribute to materials science, paving the way for other industries (Poornima, 2019).

Integrating data analytics into sports performance has significantly improved teams' analysis and optimization of player performance. Advanced tracking systems and algorithms provide valuable insights into player movement, fatigue patterns, and strategic gameplay. These data-driven approaches not only aid in informed decision-making but also aid researchers in understanding human movement and performance. NBA-inspired innovations have led to significant social changes beyond the sports arena. In public health, fitness tracking devices and personalized training programs promote active lifestyles. In urban planning and design, sports science insights have informed recreational spaces and infrastructure design, enhancing community engagement and quality of life (Pare, 2023).

NBA principles have transformed fan engagement with sports content, blurring the lines between virtual and physical experiences. Technology-driven innovations, such as immersive augmented reality and interactive fan engagement platforms, bring fans closer to the action and foster deeper connections with their favorite teams and players. The integration of NBA-driven engineering innovations into society requires a focus on equity and accessibility, ensuring that the benefits are accessible to all. This can be achieved through prioritizing inclusivity, ethical considerations, and responsible innovation, thereby promoting a more equitable and sustainable future (Vasudevan & SudalaiMuthu, 2020).

The intersection of NBA implementation and engineering disciplines is crucial for understanding the transformative power of professional sports and technological innovation. The NBA, a global leader in professional sports, drives innovation and pushes boundaries of human achievement. Engineering disciplines, including mechanical, materials, data analytics, and urban planning, each contribute unique ways to society. Sports engineering is a dynamic field where scientists, engineers, and athletes collaborate to optimize performance and advance technology. The NBA, focusing on athleticism, strategy, and spectacle, drives the evolution of sports technology and inspires breakthroughs in engineering disciplines. The NBA's influence extends to high-performance athletic equipment design and advanced data analytics tools, influencing modern engineering practice (Zhen et al., 2023).

Sports engineering is an interdisciplinary field that involves various disciplines. Biomechanics researchers study human movement to improve performance and prevent injuries, materials scientists develop advanced materials for sports equipment durability, and data scientists use machine learning algorithms and statistical models to analyze player performance data for coaches and teams. The NBA's implementation and engineering disciplines are intertwined, fostering a symbiotic relationship between sports innovation and technological advancement. The NBA serves as a testing ground for innovative engineering solutions, pushing boundaries and driving continuous innovation. As technology evolves, the sports industry and engineering disciplines can collaborate, leading to transformative changes beyond professional sports(Poornima, 2019).

NBA-driven engineering innovations have significant societal implications, promoting active lifestyles, wellness initiatives, urban design, and entertainment experiences. By understanding and harnessing the transformative power of sports technology, engineers and researchers can address pressing societal challenges and create a more equitable and sustainable future for all. The NBA implementation and engineering disciplines are a convergent field of innovation, collaboration, and societal impact. By fostering responsible innovation and interdisciplinary cooperation, sports technology can transform society and shape the future of engineering and engineering(Mane, 2015).

This chapter explores the profound impact of sports-driven innovations on societal dynamics, highlighting their multifaceted significance and their profound

Figure 1. NBA Influences on Engineering Disciplines

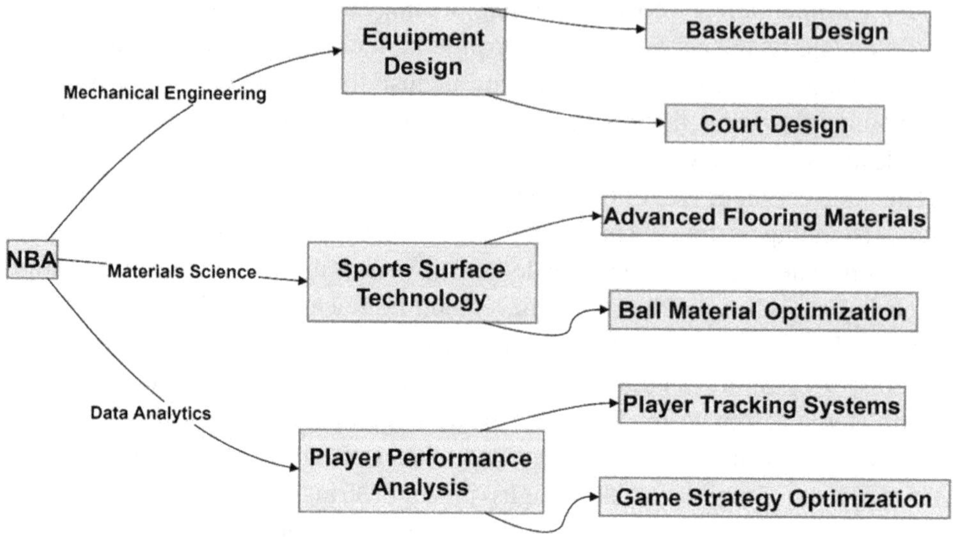

impact on various aspects of modern society, aiming to provide a comprehensive understanding of their implications.

NBA INFLUENCE ON ENGINEERING DISCIPLINES

The NBA has significantly influenced various engineering disciplines, as depicted in Figure 1.

Effects of NBA-Inspired Technologies and Methodologies

The study explores the impact of NBA-inspired technologies and methodologies on various engineering fields, highlighting the connection between professional sports and advanced engineering. The NBA's innovation and technological prowess extend beyond the basketball court, revealing the multifaceted effects of NBA-inspired innovations on various engineering disciplines. NBA-inspired technologies have significantly impacted mechanical engineering in designing and optimizing athletic equipment (Venkatasubramanian et al., 2024). High-performance basketball shoes and advanced hoops are engineered for traction, stability, and precision. Advancements in sports biomechanics have also led to developing specialized equipment tailored to athletes' unique needs, enhancing performance and safety (Viswanadhan & Rao, 2005).

The NBA's focus on performance and durability has led to advancements in materials science, resulting in the development of high-performance materials for athletic equipment. Engineers have created specialized composites and polymers with enhanced strength, flexibility, and impact resistance. This research has also led to breakthroughs in sports apparel and protective gear, improving comfort, performance, and injury prevention for athletes. Advanced data analytics in the NBA has revolutionized player performance analysis and optimization. Engineers and data scientists use sophisticated tracking systems and algorithms to analyze vast player movement data, providing insights into individual and team performance. This information informs coaching decisions, player development strategies, and game tactics, ultimately improving performance and competitive advantage (Aithal & Aithal, 2020).

Biomechanical engineering is crucial for understanding human movement and optimizing athletic performance. Like motion capture systems and wearable sensors, NBA-inspired technologies allow biomechanical engineers to study basketball players' biomechanics in detail. They can identify inefficiencies and develop personalized training programs by analyzing running mechanics, jumping kinetics, and shooting techniques. This research has broader implications for sports science and rehabilitation medicine, benefiting athletes across disciplines (Yenugu, 2022).

NBA arenas influence urban planning and design, shaping urban landscapes, contributing to economic development, and community identity. Architects and urban planners use NBA design principles to create vibrant, inclusive, and functional public spaces that foster community engagement. Sustainable design practices in NBA arena construction set a precedent for environmentally conscious urban development, promoting sustainability and resilience in urban environments. NBA-inspired technologies and methodologies have significantly impacted various engineering fields, including mechanical engineering, materials science, data analytics, and urban planning. This influence drives innovation and pushes technological advancement boundaries. Analyzing these impacts provides valuable insights into the dynamic intersection of professional sports and engineering disciplines, with societal progress and well-being implications.

NBA implementation

Disciplines such as mechanical engineering, computer science, and biomechanics have been significantly influenced by NBA implementation, leveraging the league's advancements in technology, data analytics, and athlete performance tracking to drive innovation and push the boundaries of their respective fields. Here, we explore how each discipline has been impacted and transformed by the NBA's influence (Moharir et al., 2022).

Mechanical Engineering: In the realm of mechanical engineering, NBA implementation has spurred innovation in the design and optimization of athletic equipment. Basketball shoes, in particular, have evolved significantly, with engineers leveraging insights from NBA athletes to develop footwear that enhances traction, stability, and comfort. Advanced materials such as high-performance foams and specialized rubber compounds are meticulously engineered to provide the necessary support and responsiveness demanded by professional basketball players. Furthermore, NBA-inspired innovations have extended to other aspects of athletic equipment, including basketball hoops and training apparatus, where mechanical engineers apply principles of durability, precision, and safety to enhance the overall player experience (Mahadevan et al., 2013).

Computer Science: Computer science has been revolutionized by NBA implementation through advancements in data analytics, machine learning, and computer vision technologies. NBA teams utilize sophisticated tracking systems and player performance analysis software to collect vast amounts of data on player movement, shooting efficiency, and defensive strategies. Computer scientists and data analysts leverage this data to develop predictive models, optimize player performance, and gain strategic insights into game dynamics. Machine learning algorithms are trained on historical game data to identify patterns and trends, enabling coaches to make data-driven decisions and gain a competitive edge on the court. Moreover, computer vision technologies enable real-time analysis of player movements and game events, providing valuable feedback for coaches and players alike (Sreedhar et al., 2024; Tirlangi et al., 2024).

Biomechanics: Biomechanics, the study of human movement and mechanics, has been profoundly influenced by NBA implementation, with researchers leveraging advanced motion capture systems and wearable sensors to analyze the biomechanics of basketball players. Biomechanical engineers gain insights into athletic performance and injury prevention by studying factors such as running mechanics, jumping kinetics, and shooting techniques. NBA athletes serve as invaluable subjects for biomechanical research, allowing researchers to quantify and analyze the mechanics of elite-level athleticism. Moreover, insights from biomechanical studies in basketball have broader implications for sports science and rehabilitation medicine, informing training protocols and injury prevention strategies across various athletic disciplines (Boopathi & Kumar, 2024; Hussain et al., 2023).

NBA implementation has significantly influenced fields like mechanical engineering, computer science, biomechanics, athletic equipment design, data analytics, and biomechanical research, driving innovation and pushing boundaries. It also influences scientific inquiry and technological advancement, shaping the future of sports technology and performance optimization.

SPORTS ENGINEERING LANDSCAPE

Sports engineering is an interdisciplinary field that combines scientific disciplines, technological innovations, and practical applications to improve athletic performance, safety, and spectator experiences. It is at the intersection of sports science, engineering, and technology, driving innovation across various sports disciplines. Biomechanics is a crucial aspect of sports engineering, focusing on human movement and mechanics. It allows researchers to quantify and analyze athletic performance mechanics like running mechanics, jumping kinetics, and throwing techniques. By applying physics and engineering principles, biomechanical engineers aim to optimize performance, prevent injuries, and improve sports efficiency and effectiveness (Zhen et al., 2023).

Materials science is pivotal in sports engineering, driving innovation in athletic equipment design and construction. Engineers and materials scientists create specialized materials and composites with enhanced properties for competitive sports (Madan et al., 2024; Singh Madan et al., 2024). These innovations, from lightweight carbon fiber composites in bicycle frames to impact-resistant polymers in football helmets, have transformed the design and performance of athletic equipment across various sports disciplines. Data analytics and sports technology are revolutionizing the sports engineering industry by enabling athletes, coaches, and teams to collect and analyze vast amounts of data on player movement, performance metrics, and game dynamics. This data-driven approach allows for informed decisions, identifying strengths and weaknesses, and optimizing training regimens to maximize performance and gain a competitive edge (Mane, 2015).

Sports engineering involves the design and construction of sports facilities and venues, involving architects, engineers, and urban planners to create innovative and sustainable spaces for athletic competition and spectator experiences. Sports engineers use design, construction, and sustainability principles to enhance safety, accessibility, and enjoyment for athletes and spectators (G. Upadhyaya et al., 2021a). Sports engineering is a field that integrates scientific inquiry, technological innovation, and practical application to enhance athletic performance, safety, and spectator experiences, driving innovation and shaping the future of sports technology and performance optimization.

Figure 2 visualizes the interconnectedness of various aspects within the sports engineering landscape, highlighting the flow from biomechanics to data analytics, materials science, equipment design, performance optimization, facilities design, and finally, spectator experience. Each component plays a crucial role in enhancing athletic performance, safety, and overall sports experience.

Figure 2. Interconnectedness of Sports Engineering and Biomechanics to Data Analytics

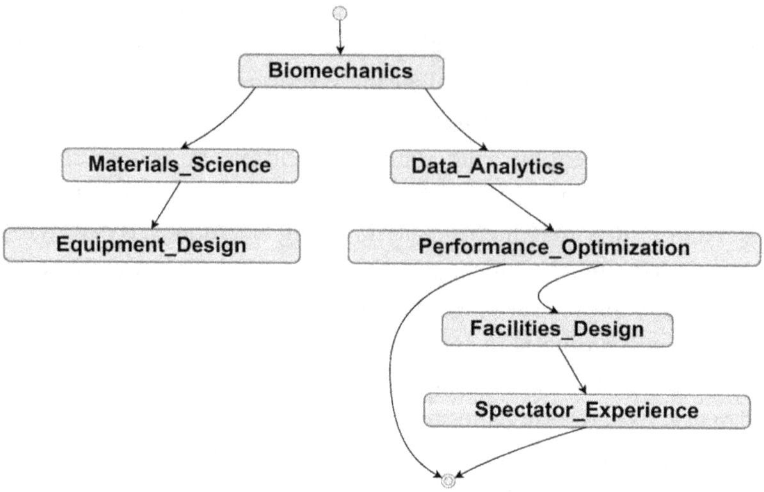

Landscape of Sports Engineering and Technological Advancements

The history of sports engineering is marked by innovation and technological advancements aimed at improving athletic performance, safety, and spectator experiences, with key milestones and advancements shaping the modern landscape. Sports engineering has its roots in ancient civilizations, where basic athletic equipment and facilities were developed for competition and recreation. It gained prominence in the late 19th and early 20th centuries due to advancements in materials science, biomechanics, and industrial manufacturing processes (Mane, 2015).

The modern bicycle revolutionized transportation and sports equipment design by introducing lightweight materials like aluminum and carbon fiber. This led to faster, more durable, and efficient bicycles, enhancing competitive cycling performance and paving the way for advancements in sports equipment. The mid-20th century saw the emergence of biomechanics as a scientific discipline in athletics, revolutionizing our understanding of human movement and mechanics. Biomechanical analysis led to new training methods, equipment design, and injury prevention strategies. High-speed cameras, motion capture systems, and force plate technology further enhanced the study of movement patterns and kinetics, providing valuable insights for optimizing athletic performance (Venkatesh & King, 2021).

The 20th century saw significant advancements in materials science, particularly in developing synthetic materials like polyester, nylon, and elastomers, which significantly improved the comfort, durability, and performance of athletic apparel and footwear. In recent decades, the convergence of technology and sports has led to unprecedented advancements in sports engineering. The proliferation of data analytics, wearable sensors, and advanced tracking systems has transformed the way athletes, coaches, and teams approach training, strategy, and performance optimization. Real-time data analysis enables coaches to monitor athlete performance, identify areas for improvement, and tailor training regimens to individual needs, leading to enhanced performance and reduced risk of injury.

Sports engineering is rapidly evolving due to technological advancements, research, and innovation. It involves the development of smart fabrics, wearable technology, and sustainable sports facilities. Sports engineers are at the forefront of shaping the future of sports technology and performance optimization, contributing to sports science and promoting physical activity, health, and well-being.

Role of Interdisciplinary Collaboration in Pushing the Boundaries of Sports Innovation

The study highlights the importance of interdisciplinary collaboration in sports innovation, highlighting its multifaceted process of combining expertise from various fields like engineering, biomechanics, materials science, computer science, and sports medicine to tackle complex challenges and unlock new frontiers in athletic performance, equipment design, and sports technology. One of the key benefits of interdisciplinary collaboration is the diversity of perspectives and expertise it brings to the table. By bringing together individuals with different backgrounds and skill sets, interdisciplinary teams can approach problems from multiple angles, fostering creativity, innovation, and out-of-the-box thinking. Engineers work alongside biomechanists to analyze movement patterns and optimize equipment design, while data scientists leverage advanced analytics to extract insights from vast amounts of performance data. This collaborative approach enables teams to develop holistic solutions that address the multifaceted nature of sports innovation (Mane, 2015; Saha et al., 2023a; G. Upadhyaya et al., 2021a). Moreover, interdisciplinary collaboration fosters knowledge exchange and cross-pollination of ideas between disciplines. Engineers draw inspiration from biomechanical research to inform athletic equipment design, while biomechanists leverage engineering principles to develop advanced motion capture systems and biomechanical models. This cross-disciplinary exchange of ideas stimulates innovation and drives advancements that would not be possible within the confines of a single discipline (Durairaj et al., 2023; Paul et al., 2024).

Another important aspect of interdisciplinary collaboration is its ability to bridge the gap between research and application. By bringing together researchers, practitioners, and industry partners, interdisciplinary teams can translate scientific

Figure 3. Societal Impacts of NBA-related Technologies and Methodologies

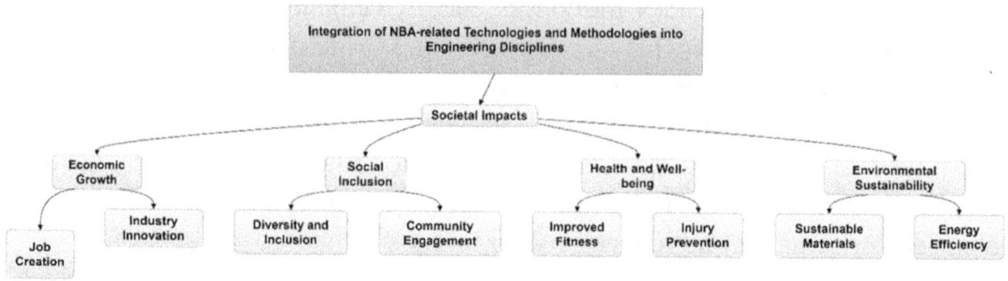

discoveries into practical solutions that have real-world impact. For example, advancements in biomechanics research can inform the design of personalized training programs and injury prevention strategies for athletes, while innovations in materials science can lead to the development of lightweight, high-performance sports equipment. Furthermore, interdisciplinary collaboration fosters a culture of continuous learning and professional growth. By working alongside experts from different fields, individuals have the opportunity to expand their skill sets, broaden their knowledge base, and gain exposure to new methodologies and techniques. This cross-disciplinary training not only enhances individual capabilities but also cultivates a collaborative mindset that is essential for tackling complex challenges and driving innovation in sports engineering and technology (Mane, 2015; Saha et al., 2023b). Interdisciplinary collaboration is crucial for sports innovation, fostering creativity, knowledge exchange, and practical application. It drives advancements in athletic performance, equipment design, and sports technology, shaping the future of sports science and engineering.

SOCIAL CHANGES AND IMPACTS

Figure 3 illustrates the potential societal impacts of NBA-related technologies and methodologies in engineering disciplines, including economic growth, social inclusion, health, and environmental sustainability. It highlights job creation, diversity, improved fitness, injury prevention, industry innovation, community engagement, sustainable materials, and energy efficiency.

Social Changes Catalyzed by NBA-Related Innovations

The NBA's integration of NBA-related innovations into engineering disciplines has led to significant social changes, transforming the field beyond sports. The

NBA's leadership in professional sports has led to advancements in technology, data analytics, and athlete performance tracking, influencing various engineering fields.

One of the most profound social changes catalyzed by the integration of NBA-related innovations is the promotion of active lifestyles and wellness initiatives. By leveraging advancements in sports technology and athlete performance tracking, engineers and researchers have developed innovative fitness tracking devices, personalized training programs, and health monitoring tools that empower individuals to take control of their physical well-being. These technologies not only encourage regular exercise and physical activity but also promote health awareness and disease prevention, leading to improved overall health outcomes and reduced healthcare costs for individuals and communities(Alexander, 2021; G. Upadhyaya & others, 2021a). Furthermore, the integration of NBA-related innovations into engineering disciplines has led to advancements in urban planning and design, with implications for community health and well-being. NBA arenas and sports facilities serve as focal points for social interaction, cultural exchange, and community engagement, contributing to the vitality and vibrancy of urban environments. Architects, engineers, and urban planners draw inspiration from NBA arena design principles to create inclusive, accessible, and sustainable public spaces that foster community cohesion, promote physical activity, and enhance quality of life for residents (Reddy et al., 2023; Sreedhar et al., 2024).

Moreover, the integration of data analytics and sports technology into engineering disciplines has revolutionized how cities are designed, managed, and optimized. By leveraging insights from NBA-inspired technologies, engineers and urban planners can analyze patterns of human movement, traffic flow, and public behavior to inform urban design decisions, transportation planning, and infrastructure development. This data-driven approach enables cities to improve efficiency, reduce congestion, and enhance the overall livability and sustainability of urban environments (Mane, 2015).

Additionally, the integration of NBA-related innovations into engineering disciplines has sparked advancements in entertainment experiences and digital media, with implications for cultural enrichment and economic development. NBA-inspired technologies, such as augmented reality experiences, interactive fan engagement platforms, and immersive sports content, have transformed how fans engage with sports content and interact with their favorite teams and players. These innovations not only enhance the spectator experience but also create new opportunities for revenue generation, brand promotion, and fan loyalty, driving economic growth and cultural enrichment in communities around the world (Venkatasubramanian et al., 2024).

The integration of NBA-related innovations into engineering disciplines has led to significant social changes, impacting health, urban development, entertainment, and economic prosperity. Engineers and researchers are driving innovation in technology, data analytics, and athlete performance tracking, shaping the future of sports science, engineering, and societal well-being. Collaboration and innovation can create a more equitable, sustainable, and vibrant future.

Advancements in Sports Technology

Sports technology advancements have significantly impacted various aspects of society, including health, urban planning, and entertainment experiences. Engineers and researchers have utilized sports innovations to improve quality of life and societal well-being (Balasubramani & Chiplunkar, 2017; Jadhav et al., 2020; Sawant, 2016).

- Health and Wellness: Advancements in sports technology have played a pivotal role in promoting health and wellness by enabling individuals to lead more active and healthy lifestyles. Fitness tracking devices, wearable sensors, and mobile apps equipped with sophisticated analytics allow individuals to monitor their physical activity, track fitness goals, and measure key health metrics in real time. These technologies provide valuable insights into exercise habits, sleep patterns, and overall well-being, empowering users to make informed decisions about their health and fitness. Additionally, virtual coaching platforms and personalized training programs leverage data-driven approaches to optimize workout routines, enhance performance, and prevent injuries, promoting long-term health and wellness for individuals of all ages and fitness levels (Sreedhar et al., 2024; A. N. Upadhyaya et al., 2024).
- Urban Planning: Advancements in sports technology have also influenced urban planning and design, shaping the built environment to promote physical activity, social interaction, and community engagement. The design of sports facilities, parks, and recreational spaces incorporates principles of accessibility, inclusivity, and sustainability to create vibrant and dynamic urban environments. For example, pedestrian-friendly infrastructure, green spaces, and multipurpose sports facilities encourage active transportation, outdoor recreation, and social gatherings, fostering a sense of community and enhancing quality of life for residents. Moreover, data analytics and urban modeling tools enable planners to analyze patterns of human behavior, traffic flow, and public usage to inform land use decisions, transportation planning, and infrastructure development, leading to more efficient, resilient, and livable cities (Maguluri et al., 2023; Sonia et al., 2024).
- Entertainment Experiences: Advancements in sports technology have transformed entertainment experiences, blurring the lines between physical and digital interactions and creating immersive and interactive fan experiences. Virtual reality (VR) and augmented reality (AR) technologies enable fans to engage with sports content in innovative and immersive

ways, from experiencing live games from the perspective of their favorite athletes to interacting with digital avatars of players and coaches in virtual training environments. Interactive fan engagement platforms and social media integrations allow fans to connect with each other, share experiences, and participate in real-time discussions, enhancing the sense of community and camaraderie among fans around the world. Moreover, advancements in digital media and content creation have led to the proliferation of streaming services, e-sports competitions, and interactive gaming experiences, providing fans with unprecedented access to sports content and driving new opportunities for revenue generation, brand promotion, and fan engagement in the entertainment industry (Revathi et al., 2024).

Advancements in sports technology have significantly impacted health, wellness, urban planning, entertainment, and societal well-being. Engineers and researchers are pushing the boundaries of sports technology through innovation and collaboration, shaping the future of society and enhancing urban environments and cultural experiences.

EQUITY AND ACCESS CONSIDERATIONS:

NBA-driven engineering innovations require addressing equity, accessibility, and inclusivity to ensure the benefits are accessible to all individuals and communities, regardless of socioeconomic status, race, gender, or geographic location. Strategies promoting equity and preventing the widening of existing disparities are crucial as NBA-inspired technologies continue to drive innovation in engineering disciplines (Bhat et al., 2022).

Figure 4 visualizes the various equity and access considerations in NBA-driven engineering innovations. It highlights strategies such as promoting equal opportunities, community engagement, diversity and inclusion initiatives, cultural sensitivity, gender equity programs, women in STEM initiatives, rural access strategies, and urban accessibility projects. These considerations aim to ensure that the benefits of NBA-inspired technologies are accessible to all individuals and communities, irrespective of socioeconomic status, race, gender, or geographic location (Prasad & Bhar, 2010).

Equitable Access to Technology

The NBA-driven engineering innovations need a comprehensive approach to address equity, accessibility, and inclusivity. This includes equitable technology access,

Figure 4. Various Equity and Access Considerations in NBA-driven Engineering Innovations

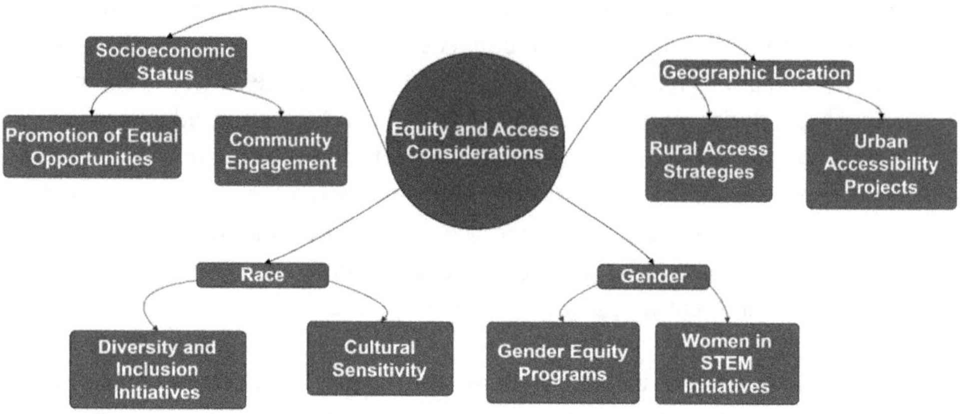

inclusive design, community engagement, and policy advocacy. By prioritizing equity and social justice, engineers and researchers can ensure the benefits of innovation are shared equitably, preventing marginalized communities from being left behind (Mane, 2015; Prasad & Bhar, 2010).

- Ensure that NBA-driven engineering innovations, such as sports performance tracking systems and athlete training tools, are accessible to individuals and communities across diverse socioeconomic backgrounds. This may involve providing subsidies, grants, or financial assistance programs to make technology more affordable and accessible to underserved populations.
- Collaborate with community organizations, schools, and recreational centers to offer technology training programs and educational initiatives that empower individuals to leverage sports technology for health, fitness, and personal development. By providing resources and support, marginalized communities can benefit from the transformative power of sports technology and engineering innovations.

Inclusive Design and Representation

- Emphasize inclusive design principles in the development of NBA-inspired technologies to ensure that products and solutions are accessible and usable by individuals with diverse abilities, backgrounds, and preferences. This may involve incorporating features such as customizable interfaces, language localization, and accessibility options to accommodate a wide range of users.

- Prioritize diversity and representation in the design and development process to ensure that the needs and perspectives of marginalized communities are considered and addressed. Engage with diverse stakeholders, including athletes, coaches, and community leaders, to gather feedback and insights that inform the design of inclusive and culturally sensitive products and solutions.

Community Engagement and Empowerment

- Foster partnerships with community organizations, grassroots initiatives, and local stakeholders to co-create solutions that address the unique challenges and needs of marginalized communities. By involving community members in the design, implementation, and evaluation process, engineers and researchers can ensure that solutions are contextually relevant, culturally appropriate, and sustainable in the long term.
- Empower individuals and communities to take ownership of NBA-driven engineering innovations through education, training, and capacity-building initiatives. Provide opportunities for skill development, mentorship, and entrepreneurship to enable individuals to leverage sports technology for personal and community empowerment, economic development, and social change.

Policy and Advocacy

- Advocate for policies and regulations that promote equity, accessibility, and inclusivity in the development and deployment of NBA-driven engineering innovations. This may involve advocating for government funding, incentives, or mandates to support equitable access to technology and resources, as well as regulations that protect privacy, data security, and digital rights for all users.
- Collaborate with policymakers, industry stakeholders, and advocacy groups to develop and implement guidelines, standards, and best practices for inclusive design, responsible innovation, and ethical use of sports technology. By working together to establish norms and expectations, we can create a more equitable and inclusive ecosystem for NBA-driven engineering innovations.

ETHICAL DIMENSIONS AND CHALLENGES

The adoption of NBA-inspired technologies in engineering raises ethical dilemmas, such as data privacy, algorithmic bias, and commodification of athlete performance.

As engineers and researchers continue to develop and implement these innovations, it is crucial to critically examine these ethical dimensions and address potential risks and concerns (Venkatesh & King, 2021).

Data Privacy and Security

- NBA-inspired technologies, such as athlete performance tracking systems and fan engagement platforms, rely on collecting and analyzing vast amounts of personal data, including biometric information, location data, and behavioral patterns. This raises concerns about data privacy and security, as sensitive information about athletes and fans may be vulnerable to misuse, unauthorized access, or breaches.
- Engineers and researchers must prioritize data protection measures, such as encryption, anonymization, and secure storage protocols, to safeguard the privacy and security of user data. Additionally, transparent data governance policies and informed consent processes should be implemented to ensure that individuals have control over how their data is collected, used, and shared.

Algorithmic Bias and Fairness

- The use of algorithms and machine learning models in NBA-inspired technologies introduces the risk of algorithmic bias, where decisions and predictions may be influenced by biased or incomplete data, leading to unfair outcomes or discrimination. For example, algorithms used to analyze player performance data may inadvertently reinforce existing biases or stereotypes, impacting player evaluations, coaching decisions, and talent recruitment processes.
- Engineers and researchers must implement measures to mitigate algorithmic bias and promote fairness and equity in decision-making processes. This may involve auditing algorithms for bias, diversifying training datasets, and incorporating fairness metrics into algorithmic design and evaluation. Additionally, transparency and accountability mechanisms should be established to ensure that algorithmic decisions are explainable and accountable to stakeholders.

Commodification of Athlete Performance

- The adoption of NBA-inspired technologies in engineering raises concerns about the commodification of athlete performance, where athletes' skills and abilities are quantified, monetized, and exploited for commercial gain.

Technologies such as player tracking systems and performance analytics enable teams, coaches, and sponsors to assess and evaluate athletes' performance in unprecedented detail, potentially leading to increased pressure to perform and heightened scrutiny of athletes' physical and mental well-being(Saravanan et al., 2022).

- Engineers and researchers must consider the ethical implications of commodifying athlete performance and strive to strike a balance between performance optimization and athlete well-being. This may involve implementing safeguards to protect athletes' rights and interests, such as ensuring informed consent, providing access to performance data, and promoting athlete autonomy and agency in decision-making processes(Das et al., 2024; Durairaj et al., 2023; Sharma et al., 2024).

The adoption of NBA-inspired technologies in engineering raises ethical dilemmas, such as data privacy, algorithmic bias, and commodification of athlete performance. As engineers and researchers continue to develop and implement these innovations, it is crucial to critically examine these ethical dimensions and address potential risks and concerns.

FUTURE OUTLOOK AND OPPORTUNITIES

NBA-driven engineering innovations hold great potential for societal impact and collaboration between sports and engineering disciplines, with potential developments revealing key growth areas and opportunities (Prasad & Bhar, 2010; G. Upadhyaya et al., 2021b, 2021a).

Figure 5 highlights the future opportunities of NBA-driven engineering innovations, including societal impact, economic growth, technological advancements, social integration, interdisciplinary research, industry partnerships, job creation, revenue generation, community engagement, diversity, and inclusion. It highlights specific areas of focus such as biomechanics, sports technology, manufacturing, product development, data analytics, equipment innovation, and protective gear advancement.

Enhanced Performance and Training

Future innovations in NBA-driven engineering are likely to focus on further enhancing athlete performance and training methodologies. This could involve the development of advanced wearable technologies, such as smart fabrics and biometric sensors, to provide real-time feedback on player biomechanics, physiological responses, and injury risk factors. Collaborations between sports scientists, engineers, and

Figure 5. The Future Opportunities of NBA-Driven Engineering Innovations

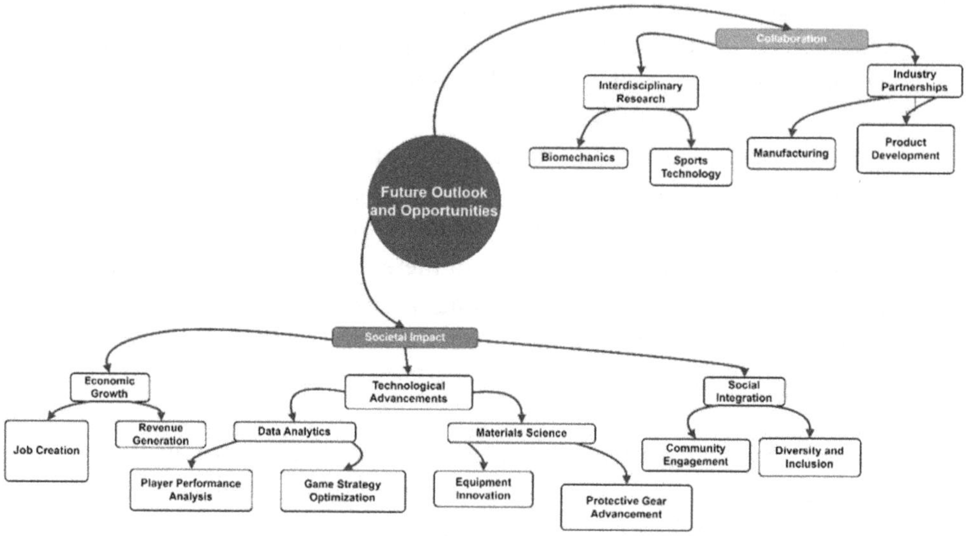

coaches will be crucial in translating these technological advancements into practical training strategies that optimize athlete performance while minimizing the risk of injury(Agrawal et al., 2023; Prabhuswamy et al., 2024; Sharma et al., 2024).

Fan Engagement and Immersive Experiences

The future of NBA-driven engineering innovations will also see advancements in fan engagement and immersive experiences. Augmented reality (AR), virtual reality (VR), and mixed reality (MR) technologies will enable fans to experience games and events in entirely new ways, from interactive live streams to virtual courtside seats. Engineers and content creators will collaborate with the sports industry to develop immersive experiences that blur the lines between physical and digital worlds, creating deeper connections between fans, athletes, and teams.

Health and Wellness Solutions

NBA-driven engineering innovations will increasingly focus on promoting health and wellness, both for athletes and fans. This could involve the development of personalized health monitoring systems, telemedicine platforms, and digital coaching services that empower individuals to take control of their well-being. Collaborations between sports organizations, healthcare providers, and technology companies will drive the development and adoption of these solutions, improving access to healthcare and promoting healthy lifestyles among athletes and fans alike.

Social Impact and Community Development

The societal impact of NBA-driven engineering innovations will extend beyond the realm of sports, addressing pressing social challenges and driving positive change in communities around the world. Opportunities for collaboration between the sports industry and engineering disciplines include initiatives focused on promoting inclusivity, diversity, and accessibility in sports, such as the development of adaptive sports equipment, barrier-free facilities, and sports programs for underserved populations. By working together, engineers, policymakers, and community leaders can harness the power of sports to foster social cohesion, empowerment, and sustainable development (Kumara et al., 2023).

NBA-driven engineering innovations offer promising opportunities for collaboration and societal impact. By leveraging technology, data analytics, and materials science, engineers and researchers can drive positive changes in performance, fan engagement, health, and community development. Strategic partnerships and interdisciplinary collaboration can address social challenges, creating a more inclusive, healthy, and sustainable future for all.

CONCLUSION

NBA-driven engineering innovations have the potential to bring positive social change, but they also present ethical challenges. The study highlights the importance of responsible innovation and interdisciplinary cooperation in harnessing the transformative power of sports technology. NBA-inspired technologies have impacted various aspects of society, such as enhancing athletic performance, fan engagement, and health and wellness. However, ethical issues like data privacy, algorithmic bias, and commodification of athlete performance persist. Therefore, it is crucial for engineers and researchers to prioritize responsible innovation, ensuring ethical, transparent, and equitable technological development.

Interdisciplinary cooperation is crucial in driving positive social change through sports technology. By bringing together experts from various fields, such as engineering, sports science, medicine, and social science, we can address social challenges, promote inclusivity, and foster community engagement. These initiatives prioritize diversity, equity, and inclusion, aiming to create a more equitable, healthy, and sustainable future. Responsible innovation and interdisciplinary cooperation are essential for harnessing the transformative power of sports technology, paving the way for a future where sports technology drives athletic excellence, social progress, and well-being for individuals and communities worldwide.

REFERENCES

Agrawal, A. V., Pitchai, R., Senthamaraikannan, C., Balaji, N. A., Sajithra, S., & Boopathi, S. (2023). Digital Education System During the COVID-19 Pandemic. In Using Assistive Technology for Inclusive Learning in K-12 Classrooms (pp. 104–126). IGI Global. doi:10.4018/978-1-6684-6424-3.ch005

Aithal, P., & Aithal, S. (2020). Implementation strategies of higher education part of national education policy 2020 of India towards achieving its objectives. *International Journal of Management, Technology, and Social Sciences*, *5*(2), 283–325. doi:10.47992/IJMTS.2581.6012.0119

Alexander, J. S. (2021). Implementing Outcome Based Education (OBE): Case Studies in a College and School Setting. *Social Action*, 71.

Balasubramani, R., & Chiplunkar, N. N. (2017). Attainment of programme outcomes through course outcomes in outcome based education: A case study. *Journal of Engineering Education Transformations*, *31*(2), 26–30.

Bhat, R., Kamath, C. R., Mathias, K. A., & Mulimani, P. (2022). Practical Implementation of Outcome-Based Education Practices in the Indian Engineering Institutes–Approach An Objective Based Investigation. *Journal of Engineering Education Transformations*, *36*(1). Advance online publication. doi:10.16920/jeet/2022/v36i1/22133

Boopathi, S., & Kumar, P. (2024). Advanced bioprinting processes using additive manufacturing technologies: Revolutionizing tissue engineering. *3D Printing Technologies: Digital Manufacturing, Artificial Intelligence, Industry 4.0*, 95.

Das, S., Lekhya, G., Shreya, K., Shekinah, K. L., Babu, K. K., & Boopathi, S. (2024). Fostering Sustainability Education Through Cross-Disciplinary Collaborations and Research Partnerships: Interdisciplinary Synergy. In Facilitating Global Collaboration and Knowledge Sharing in Higher Education With Generative AI (pp. 60–88). IGI Global.

Durairaj, M., Jayakumar, S., Karpagavalli, V., Maheswari, B. U., Boopathi, S., & ... (2023). Utilization of Digital Tools in the Indian Higher Education System During Health Crises. In *Multidisciplinary Approaches to Organizational Governance During Health Crises* (pp. 1–21). IGI Global. doi:10.4018/978-1-7998-9213-7.ch001

Hussain, Z., Babe, M., Saravanan, S., Srimathy, G., Roopa, H., & Boopathi, S. (2023). Optimizing Biomass-to-Biofuel Conversion: IoT and AI Integration for Enhanced Efficiency and Sustainability. In Circular Economy Implementation for Sustainability in the Built Environment (pp. 191–214). IGI Global.

Jadhav, M. R., Kakade, A. B., Jagtap, S. R., & Patil, M. S. (2020). Impact assessment of outcome based approach in engineering education in India. *Procedia Computer Science*, *172*, 791–796. doi:10.1016/j.procs.2020.05.113

Kumara, V., & Sharma, M. D., Samson Isaac, J., Saravanan, S., Suganthi, D., & Boopathi, S. (2023). An AI-Integrated Green Power Monitoring System: Empowering Small and Medium Enterprises. In Advances in Environmental Engineering and Green Technologies (pp. 218–244). IGI Global. doi:10.4018/979-8-3693-0338-2.ch013

Madan, B. S., Viraj Dravid, S., Deenadayalan, G., Rathod, P., Arumugam, G., & Boopathi, S. (2024). Innovations and Applications of Engineered Cementitious Composites and Alternative Materials: Reimagining Construction. In Advances in Chemical and Materials Engineering (pp. 53–86). IGI Global. doi:10.4018/978-1-6684-8182-0.ch003

Maguluri, L. P., Arularasan, A., & Boopathi, S. (2023). Assessing Security Concerns for AI-Based Drones in Smart Cities. In Effective AI, Blockchain, and E-Governance Applications for Knowledge Discovery and Management (pp. 27–47). IGI Global. doi:10.4018/978-1-6684-9151-5.ch002

Mahadevan, R., Shivaprakash, N., Khobragade, N., Raju, K., & Rao, V. N. (2013). Implementing a sustainable methodology for assessment of course outcomes and program outcomes in an Indian Engineering institute. *Proceedings of 2013 IEEE International Conference on Teaching, Assessment and Learning for Engineering (TALE)*, 51–54. 10.1109/TALE.2013.6654398

Mane, S. D. (2015). NBA and NAAC Accreditation of UG Engineering Programmes/ Colleges in India: A Review. *International Journal of Scientific Engineering and Applied Science*, *1*(6), 2395–3470.

Moharir, M., Agavekar, R., Bhore, P., Kadam, H., & Bewoor, A. (2022). Effective Implementation of Peer Review as an Active Learning Technique to Attain Course Outcome: A Case Study. *Journal of Engineering Education Transformations, 36*(Special Issue 1).

Pare, S. K. (2023). Outcome-based Education: Calculating Attainment of Programme Outcome through Course Outcome. *Universities Handbook–34th Edition, 61*, 60.

Paul, A., Thilagham, K., KG, J., Reddy, P. R., Sathyamurthy, R., & Boopathi, S. (2024). Multi-criteria Optimization on Friction Stir Welding of Aluminum Composite (AA5052-H32/B4C) using Titanium Nitride Coated Tool. Engineering Research Express.

Poornima, S. N. (2019). Outcome based education, need for the hour-NBA. *Int. J. Adv. Res. Ideas Innov. Technol*, *5*(2), 1030–1033.

Prabhuswamy, M., Tripathi, R., Vijayakumar, M., Thulasimani, T., Sundharesalingam, P., & Sampath, B. (2024). A Study on the Complex Nature of Higher Education Leadership: An Innovative Approach. In *Challenges of Globalization and Inclusivity in Academic Research* (pp. 202–223). IGI Global. doi:10.4018/979-8-3693-1371-8.ch013

Prasad, G., & Bhar, C. (2010). Accreditation system for technical education programmes in India: A critical review. *European Journal of Engineering Education*, *35*(2), 187–213. doi:10.1080/03043790903497294

Reddy, M. A., Reddy, B. M., Mukund, C., Venneti, K., Preethi, D., & Boopathi, S. (2023). Social Health Protection During the COVID-Pandemic Using IoT. In *The COVID-19 Pandemic and the Digitalization of Diplomacy* (pp. 204–235). IGI Global. doi:10.4018/978-1-7998-8394-4.ch009

Revathi, S., Babu, M., Rajkumar, N., Meti, V. K. V., Kandavalli, S. R., & Boopathi, S. (2024). Unleashing the Future Potential of 4D Printing: Exploring Applications in Wearable Technology, Robotics, Energy, Transportation, and Fashion. In Human-Centered Approaches in Industry 5.0: Human-Machine Interaction, Virtual Reality Training, and Customer Sentiment Analysis (pp. 131–153). IGI Global.

Saha, G. C., Akber, S., & Roy, A. (2023a). Impact of Outcome-Based Education (OBE) on Learners' Performance in Business Courses. *International Journal of Professional Business Review: Int. J. Prof. Bus. Rev.*, *8*(8), 6.

Saha, G. C., Akber, S., & Roy, A. (2023b). Impact of Outcome-Based Education (OBE) on Learners' Performance in Business Courses. *International Journal of Professional Business Review: Int. J. Prof. Bus. Rev.*, *8*(8), 6.

Saravanan, A., Venkatasubramanian, R., Khare, R., Surakasi, R., Boopathi, S., Ray, S., & Sudhakar, M. (2022). Policy trends of renewable energy and non. *Renewable Energy*.

Sawant, P. (2016). Implementation of outcome based education: A beginning. *Journal of Engineering Education Transformations*, *7*(5), 10–16920. doi:10.16920/jeet/2016/v0i0/85643

Sharma, D. M., Ramana, K. V., Jothilakshmi, R., Verma, R., Maheswari, B. U., & Boopathi, S. (2024). Integrating Generative AI Into K-12 Curriculums and Pedagogies in India: Opportunities and Challenges. *Facilitating Global Collaboration and Knowledge Sharing in Higher Education With Generative AI*, 133–161.

Singh Madan, B., Logeswaran, S., Veerapathran, M., Rai, P., Kumar Singh, S., & B., S. (2024). Engineered Cementitious Composites (ECC) Through Nano-Composite Integration: Enhancing Construction. In *Advances in Chemical and Materials Engineering* (pp. 210–243). IGI Global. doi:10.4018/978-1-6684-8182-0.ch008

Sonia, R., Gupta, N., Manikandan, K., Hemalatha, R., Kumar, M. J., & Boopathi, S. (2024). Strengthening Security, Privacy, and Trust in Artificial Intelligence Drones for Smart Cities. In *Analyzing and Mitigating Security Risks in Cloud Computing* (pp. 214–242). IGI Global. doi:10.4018/979-8-3693-3249-8.ch011

Sreedhar, P. S. S., Sujay, V., Rani, M. R., Melita, L., Reshma, S., & Boopathi, S. (2024). Impacts of 5G Machine Learning Techniques on Telemedicine and Social Media Professional Connection in Healthcare. In Advances in Medical Technologies and Clinical Practice (pp. 209–234). IGI Global. doi:10.4018/979-8-3693-1934-5.ch012

Tirlangi, S., Teotia, S., Padmapriya, G., Senthil Kumar, S., Dhotre, S., & Boopathi, S. (2024). Cloud Computing and Machine Learning in the Green Power Sector: Data Management and Analysis for Sustainable Energy. In Developments Towards Next Generation Intelligent Systems for Sustainable Development (pp. 148–179). IGI Global. doi:10.4018/979-8-3693-5643-2.ch006

Upadhyaya, A. N., Saqib, A., Devi, J. V., Rallapalli, S., Sudha, S., & Boopathi, S. (2024). Implementation of the Internet of Things (IoT) in Remote Healthcare. In Advances in Medical Technologies and Clinical Practice (pp. 104–124). IGI Global. doi:10.4018/979-8-3693-1934-5.ch006

Upadhyaya, G. (2021). Effective Implementation of Outcome-based Education: The Role of Faculty Awareness. *Indonesian Journal Of Educational Research and Review*, 380–391.

Vasudevan, N. (2020). Development of a common framework for outcome based accreditation and rankings. *Procedia Computer Science*, *172*, 270–276. doi:10.1016/j.procs.2020.05.043

Venkatasubramanian, V., Chitra, M., Sudha, R., Singh, V. P., Jefferson, K., & Boopathi, S. (2024). Examining the Impacts of Course Outcome Analysis in Indian Higher Education: Enhancing Educational Quality. In Challenges of Globalization and Inclusivity in Academic Research (pp. 124–145). IGI Global.

Venkatesh, K., & King, C. S. (2021). Challenges and Issues in Implementation of OBE. *Assessment Tools for Mapping Learning Outcomes With Learning Objectives*, 83–96.

Viswanadhan, K., & Rao, N. (2005). Effectiveness of NBA accreditation processes. *National Symposium on Engineering Education (NSEE05)*, 100–108.

Yenugu, S. (2022). The new National Education Policy (NEP) of India: Will it be a paradigm shift in Indian higher education? *Perspectives: Policy and Practice in Higher Education*, *26*(4), 121–129.

Zhen, Y., Luo, J.-D., & Chen, H. (2023). Prediction of Academic Performance of Students in Online Live Classroom Interactions—An Analysis Using Natural Language Processing and Deep Learning Methods. *Journal of Social Computing*, *4*(1), 12–29. doi:10.23919/JSC.2023.0007

KEY TERMS AND DEFINITIONS

Augmented Reality: Augmented Reality is a digital technology that uses visual, auditory, haptic, and olfactory elements to enhance the physical world, commonly used in mobile apps, gaming, and interactive marketing.

Mixed Reality: Mixed Reality (MR) is a technology that merges real and virtual worlds, enabling complex interactions in fields like manufacturing, design, and healthcare, extending beyond VR and AR.

Virtual Reality: Virtual Reality (VR) is a headset-based simulated experience used in gaming, education, training, and virtual tours, providing an immersive environment similar or different from the real world.

Compilation of References

Abad-Segura, E., González-Zamar, M. D., Infante-Moro, J. C., & Ruipérez García, G. (2020). Sustainable management of digital transformation in higher education: Global research trends. *Sustainability (Basel), 12*(5), 21–27. doi:10.3390/su12052107

Adamopoulou, E., & Moussiades, L. (2020). An Overview of Chatbot Technology. *IFIP Advances in Information and Communication Technology, 584 IFIP*. doi:10.1007/978-3-030-49186-4_31

Adeshola, I., & Adepoju, A. P. (2023). The opportunities and challenges of ChatGPT in education. *Interactive Learning Environments*, 1–14. doi:10.1080/10494820.2023.2253858

Adetayo, A. J., & Oyeniyi, W. O. (2023). Revitalizing reference services and fostering information literacy: Google Bard's dynamic role in contemporary libraries. *Library Hi Tech News*. Advance online publication. doi:10.1108/LHTN-08-2023-0137

Adeyinka-Ojo, S., Lee, S., Abdullah, S. K., & Teo, J. (2020). Hospitality and tourism education in an emerging digital economy. *Worldwide Hospitality and Tourism Themes, 12*(2), 113–125. doi:10.1108/WHATT-12-2019-0075

Adıgüzel, T., Kaya, M. H., & Cansu, F. K. (2023). Revolutionizing education with AI: Exploring the transformative potential of ChatGPT. *Contemporary Educational Technology, 15*(3), ep429. Advance online publication. doi:10.30935/cedtech/13152

Ady, J. K. (1999). Computer-mediated communication in a high school global education curriculum: A brochure project. *Social Studies, 90*(4), 159–163. doi:10.1080/00377999909602408

Agrawal, A. V., Pitchai, R., Senthamaraikannan, C., Balaji, N. A., Sajithra, S., & Boopathi, S. (2023). Digital Education System During the COVID-19 Pandemic. In Using Assistive Technology for Inclusive Learning in K-12 Classrooms (pp. 104–126). IGI Global. doi:10.4018/978-1-6684-6424-3.ch005

Ahel, O., & Lingenau, K. (2020). Opportunities and Challenges of Digitalization to Improve Access to Education for Sustainable Development in Higher Education. In *Universities as Living Labs for Sustainable Development. World Sustainability Series*. Springer. doi:10.1007/978-3-030-15604-6_21

Ahmad, C. (2013). *The Effectiveness of Small Group Discussion Method in Teaching Reading.* Perpustakaan.upi.edu.

Ahmad, S., Umirzakova, S., Mujtaba, G., Amin, M. S., & Whangbo, T. (2023). Education 5.0: requirements, enabling technologies, and future directions. *arXiv preprint arXiv:2307.15846.*

Ahmad, S. Z., Bakar, A. R. A., & Ahmad, N. (2018). An evaluation of teaching methods of entrepreneurship in hospitality and tourism programs. *International Journal of Management Education, 16*(1), 14–25. doi:10.1016/j.ijme.2017.11.002

Aithal, P., & Aithal, S. (2020). Implementation strategies of higher education part of national education policy 2020 of India towards achieving its objectives. *International Journal of Management, Technology, and Social Sciences, 5*(2), 283–325. doi:10.47992/IJMTS.2581.6012.0119

Ait-Mlouk, A., & Jiang, L. (2020). KBot: A Knowledge Graph Based ChatBot for Natural Language Understanding over Linked Data. *IEEE Access : Practical Innovations, Open Solutions, 8*, 149220–149230. Advance online publication. doi:10.1109/ACCESS.2020.3016142

Alam, A., & Mohanty, A. (2022). Business models, business strategies, and innovations in EdTech companies: integration of learning analytics and artificial intelligence in higher education. In *2022 IEEE 6th Conference on Information and Communication Technology (CICT)* (pp. 1-6). IEEE. 10.1109/CICT56698.2022.9997887

Alam, A. (2022). Employing adaptive learning and intelligent tutoring robots for virtual classrooms and smart campuses: Reforming education in the age of artificial intelligence. *Advanced Computing and Intelligent Technologies Proceedings of ICACIT, 2022*, 395–406.

Alasadi, E. A., & Baiz, C. R. (2023). Generative AI in education and research: Opportunities, concerns, and solutions. *Journal of Chemical Education, 100*(8), 2965–2971. doi:10.1021/acs.jchemed.3c00323

Aldosari, S. A. M. (2020). The future of higher education in the light of artificial intelligence transformations. *International Journal of Higher Education, 9*(3), 145–151. doi:10.5430/ijhe.v9n3p145

Alenezi, M., & Akour, M. (2023). Digital Transformation blueprint in Higher Education: A case study of PSU. *Sustainability (Basel), 15*(10), 8204. Advance online publication. doi:10.3390/su15108204

Alexander, J. S. (2021). Implementing Outcome Based Education (OBE): Case Studies in a College and School Setting. *Social Action*, 71.

Ali, S. A., Payne, B. H., Williams, R., Park, H. W., & Breazeal, C. (2019). *Constructionism, ethics,and creativity: developing primary and middle school artificial intelligence education.* Paper presented at International Workshop on Education in Artificial Intelligence (EDUAI), Palo Alto, CA, USA.

Ali, F. (2023). Let the devil speak for itself: Should ChatGPT be allowed or banned in hospitality and tourism schools? *Journal of Global Hospitality and Tourism*, *2*(1), 1–6. doi:10.5038/2771-5957.2.1.1016

Almeida, D., Shmarko, K., & Lomas, E. (2021). The ethics of facial recognition technologies, surveillance, and accountability in an age of artificial intelligence: A comparative analysis of US, EU, and UK regulatory frameworks. *AI and Ethics*. Advance online publication. doi:10.1007/s43681-021-00077-w PMID:34790955

Alojail, M., & Khan, S. B. (2023). Impact of digital transformation toward sustainable development. *Sustainability (Basel)*, *15*(20), 14697. Advance online publication. doi:10.3390/su152014697

Alotaibi, N. S., & Alshehri, A. H. (2023). Prospers and obstacles in using artificial intelligence in Saudi Arabia higher education institutions—The potential of AI-based learning outcomes. *Sustainability (Basel)*, *15*(13), 10723. doi:10.3390/su151310723

Alter, S. (2022). Understanding artificial intelligence in the context of usage: Contributions and smartness of algorithmic capabilities in work systems. *International Journal of Information Management*, *67*, 102392. doi:10.1016/j.ijinfomgt.2021.102392

Alters, B. J., & Nelson, C. E. (2002). Perspective: Teaching evolution in higher education. *Evolution; International Journal of Organic Evolution*, *56*(10), 1891–1901. doi:10.1111/j.0014-3820.2002.tb00115.x PMID:12449476

Alvarez, A. J., & Palmero, H. (2022). The inner voices of students in asynchronous online learning approach. *International Journal of Social Sciences and Education Research*, *8*(2), 148–154. doi:10.24289/ijsser.1065915

Alvero, R. (2023). ChatGPT: Rumors of human providers' demise have been greatly exaggerated. *Fertility and Sterility*, *119*(6), 930–931. doi:10.1016/j.fertnstert.2023.03.010 PMID:36921837

Alyasiri, O. M., Selvaraj, K., Younis, H. A., Sahib, T. M., Almasoodi, M. F., & Hayder, I. M. (2024). A Survey on the Potential of Artificial Intelligence Tools in Tourism Information Services. *Babylonian Journal of Artificial Intelligence*, *2024*, 1–8. doi:10.58496/BJAI/2024/001

Al-Zyoud, H. M. M. (2020). The role of artificial intelligence in teacher professional development. *Universal Journal of Educational Research*, *8*(11B), 6263–6272. doi:10.13189/ujer.2020.082265

Anazifa, R. D., & Djukri, D. (2017). Project-Based Learning and Problem-Based Learning: Are They Effective to Improve Student's Thinking Skills? *Jurnal Pendidikan IPA Indonesia*, *6*(2), 346–355. doi:10.15294/jpii.v6i2.11100

Anderson, D. L. (1999). Heuristics for educational use and evaluation of electronic information: A case of searching for shaker history on the World Wide Web. *Journal of the Association for History & Computing*, *2*(2). http://www.mcel.pacificu.edu/JAHC/JAHCII2/INDEX.html

Anderson, T., & Dron, J. (2011). Three generations of distance education pedagogy. *International Review of Research in Open and Distance Learning*, *12*(3), 80–97. doi:10.19173/irrodl.v12i3.890

Aprendemos Juntos 2030. (2020). *V. Completa. Las claves educativas en la era de la inteligencia artificial.* https://www.youtube.com/watch?v=18QBF0LifbY

Araujo, T., Helberger, N., Kruikemeier, S., & De Vreese, C. H. (2020). In AI we trust? Perceptions about automated decision-making by artificial intelligence. *AI & Society, 35*(3), 611–623. doi:10.1007/s00146-019-00931-w

Arcodia, C., Abreu Novais, M., Cavlek, N., & Humpe, A. (2021). Educational tourism and experiential learning: Students' perceptions of field trips. *Tourism Review, 76*(1), 241–254. doi:10.1108/TR-05-2019-0155

Arslan, K. (2020). Eğitimde yapay zekâ ve uygulamaları. *Batı Anadolu Eğitim Bilimleri Dergisi, 11*(1), 71-88. https://dergipark.org.tr/en/download/article-file/1174773

Athota, L., Shukla, V. K., Pandey, N., & Rana, A. (2020). Chatbot for Healthcare System Using Artificial Intelligence. *ICRITO 2020 - IEEE 8th International Conference on Reliability, Infocom Technologies and Optimization (Trends and Future Directions).* 10.1109/ICRITO48877.2020.9197833

Athreya, R. G., Ngonga Ngomo, A. C., & Usbeck, R. (2018). Enhancing Community Interactions with Data-Driven Chatbots - The DBpedia Chatbot. *The Web Conference 2018 - Companion of the World Wide Web Conference, WWW 2018.* 10.1145/3184558.3186964

Audras, D., Zhao, A., Isgar, C., & Tang, Y. (2022). *Virtual teaching assistants: A survey of a novel teaching technology. International Journal of Chinese Education, 11*(2).

Avgeli, V., Dahlan, M. A., Bakir, A., & Wickens, E. (2020). 4IR Impacts on tourism education and industry. *Journal on Tourism & Sustainability, 4*(1), 6–15.

Avnoon, N., Kotliar, D. M., & Rivnai-Bahir, S. (2023). Contextualizing the ethics of algorithms: A socio-professional approach. *New Media & Society.* doi:10.1177/14614448221145728

Ayers, E. L. (1999). *History in hypertext.* Retrieved August 24, 1999 from: http://jefferson.village.virginia.edu/vcdh/Ayers.OAH.html

Babić, S. (2011, May). E-learning environment compared to traditional classroom. In *2011 Proceedings of the 34th International Convention MIPRO* (pp. 1299-1304). IEEE.

Bahroun, Z., Anane, C., Ahmed, V., & Zacca, A. (2023). Transforming education: A comprehensive review of generative artificial intelligence in educational settings through bibliometric and content analysis. *Sustainability (Basel), 15*(17), 12983. doi:10.3390/su151712983

Baidoo-Anu, D., & Ansah, L. O. (2023). Education in the era of generative artificial intelligence (AI): Understanding the potential benefits of ChatGPT in promoting teaching and learning. *Journal of AI, 7*(1), 52–62. doi:10.61969/jai.1337500

Balacheff, N. (1993). Artificial intelligence and real thinking. In C. Keitel & K. Ruthven (Eds.), *Learning from computers: Mathematics education and technology* (pp. 131–158). Springer-Verlag. doi:10.1007/978-3-642-78542-9_6

Balasubramani, R., & Chiplunkar, N. N. (2017). Attainment of programme outcomes through course outcomes in outcome based education: A case study. *Journal of Engineering Education Transformations*, *31*(2), 26–30.

Balula, A., Moreira, G., Moreira, A., Kastenholz, E., Eusébio, C., & Breda, Z. (2019). Digital transformation in tourism education. *Tourism in Southern and Eastern Europe*, *5*, 61–72. doi:10.20867/tosee.05.45

Bamford, M. (2020) *Tracking technology aims to improve online learning for students during COVID-19, ABC News*. https://www.abc.net.au/news/2020-05-08/tracking-technology-aims-to-improve-online-learning/12211996

Bareis, J., & Katzenbach, C. (2022). Talking AI into being: The narratives and imaginaries of national AI strategies and their performative politics. *Science, Technology & Human Values*, *47*(5), 855–881. doi:10.1177/01622439211030007

Basiri, A., Amirian, P., Winstanley, A., & Moore, T. (2018). Making tourist guidance systems more intelligent, adaptive and personalised using crowd sourced movement data. *Journal of Ambient Intelligence and Humanized Computing*, *9*(2), 413–427. doi:10.1007/s12652-017-0550-0

Baskara, R. (2023). Exploring the implications of ChatGPT for language learning in higher education. *Indonesian Journal of English Language Teaching and Applied Linguistics*, *7*(2), 343–358.

Bass, R., & Rosenweig, R. (2000). *Rewriting the history and social studies classroom needs, frameworks, dangers, and proposals*. White Papers on the Future of Technology in Education: U.S. Department of Education. Available: https://www.air.org/forum/Bass.pdf

Bates, A. W. (2019). *Teaching in a Digital Age: Guidelines for designing teaching and learning for a digital age*. Tony Bates Associates Ltd.

Battour, M., Mady, K., Salaheldeen, M., Elsotouhy, M., Elbendary, I., & Boğan, E. (2023). AI-enabled technologies to assist Muslim tourists in Halal-friendly tourism. *Journal of Islamic Marketing*, *14*(5), 1291–1309. doi:10.1108/JIMA-01-2022-0001

Baugh, I. W., & Baugh, J. G. (1997). Global classrooms: E-mail learning communities. *Learning and Leading with Technology*, *25*(3), 38–41.

Baum, S., Ma, J., & Payea, K. (2010). *Education Pays, 2010: The Benefits of Higher Education for Individuals and Society. Trends in Higher Education Series*. College Board Advocacy & Policy Center.

BBC News. (2019) In 360: *Notre-Dame cathedral before the fire - BBC News*. Youtube. https://www.youtube.com/watch?v=mOuvAJRknXk&t=22s

Bearman, M., Ryan, J., & Ajjawi, R. (2023). Discourses of artificial intelligence in higher education: A critical literature review. *Higher Education*, *86*(2), 369–385. doi:10.1007/s10734-022-00937-2

Becker, H. J. (1999). Internet usage by teachers: Conditions of professional use and teacher-directed student use. In *Teaching, Learning, & Computing: 1998 National Survey, Report* (Vol. 1). Center for Research on Information Technology & Organizations, University of California, Irvine.

Belda-Medina, J., & Calvo-Ferrer, J. R. (2022). Using Chatbots as AI Conversational Partners in Language Learning. *Applied Sciences (Basel, Switzerland), 12*(17), 8427. Advance online publication. doi:10.3390/app12178427

Bellan, J. M., & Scheurman, G. (1998). Actual and virtual reality: Making the most of field trips. *Social Education, 62*(1), 35–40.

Benavides, L. M. C., Tamayo Arias, J. A., Arango Serna, M. D., Branch Bedoya, J. W., & Burgos, D. (2020). Digital transformation in higher education institutions: A systematic literature review. *Sensors (Basel), 20*(11), 3291. Advance online publication. doi:10.3390/s20113291 PMID:32526998

Benbya, H., Davenport, T. H., & Pachidi, S. (2020). Artificial intelligence in organizations: Current state and future opportunities. *MIS Quarterly Executive, 19*(4).

Benckendorff, P., & Zehrer, A. (2017). The future of teaching and learning in tourism. In *Handbook of teaching and learning in tourism* (pp. 609–626). Edward Elgar Publishing. doi:10.4337/9781784714802.00055

Bernard, H. R. (2017). *Research methods in anthropology: Qualitative and quantitative approaches*. Rowman & Littlefield.

Berson, M. J. (2002). Reflecting on technology in the social studies: Past, present, and future perspectives. *The International Social Studies Forum, 2*(2), 159–161.

Berson, M. J., Mason, C. L., Heinecke, W. F., & Coutts, C. B. (2001). An examination of beliefs and practices of social studies methods faculty. *The International Social Studies Forum, 1*(2), 89–105.

Berson, I. R., & Berson, M. J. (2003). Digital literacy for cyber safety, digital awareness, and media literacy. *Social Education, 67*(3), 164–168.

Berson, M. J. (1996). Effectiveness of computer technology in the social studies: A literature review. *Journal of Research on Computing in Education, 28*(4), 486–499. doi:10.1080/08886504.1996.10782179

Berson, M. J. (2000a). Rethinking research and pedagogy in the social studies: The creation of caring connections through technology and advocacy. *Theory and Research in Social Education, 28*(1), 121–131. doi:10.1080/00933104.2000.10505900

Berson, M. J. (2000b). The Caribbean online: Exploration through Internet resources. *Social Education, 64*(2), 101–104.

Berson, M. J., & Berson, I. R. (1999). Coming to terms with Mother Nature: Using the Web to educate children about natural disasters. *Social Studies and the Young Learner, 12*(1), 19–21.

Berson, M. J., Berson, I. R., & Ralston, M. E. (1999). Threshing out the myths and facts of Internet safety: A response to "Separating wheat from chaff.". *Social Education*, *63*(3), 60–61.

Berson, M. J., Cruz, B., Duplass, J., & Johnston, H. (2004). *Social studies on the Internet* (2nd ed.). Merrill/Prentice Hall.

Bhat, R., Kamath, C. R., Mathias, K. A., & Mulimani, P. (2022). Practical Implementation of Outcome-Based Education Practices in the Indian Engineering Institutes–Approach An Objective Based Investigation. *Journal of Engineering Education Transformations*, *36*(1). Advance online publication. doi:10.16920/jeet/2022/v36i1/22133

Bhutoria, A. (2022). Personalized education and artificial intelligence in the United States, China, and India: A systematic review using a human-in-the-loop model. *Computers and Education: Artificial Intelligence*, *3*, 100068. Advance online publication. doi:10.1016/j.caeai.2022.100068

Bilotta, E., Bertacchini, F., Gabriele, L., Giglio, S., Pantano, P. S., & Romita, T. (2021). Industry 4.0 technologies in tourism education: Nurturing students to think with technology. *Journal of Hospitality, Leisure, Sport and Tourism Education*, *29*, 100275. Advance online publication. doi:10.1016/j.jhlste.2020.100275

Birhane, A. (2021). The impossibility of automating ambiguity. *Artificial Life*, *27*(1), 44–61. doi:10.1162/artl_a_00336 PMID:34529757

Bogdanovych, A., Rodríguez-Aguilar, J. A., Simoff, S., & Cohen, A. (2010). Authentic interactive reenactment of cultural heritage with 3D virtual worlds and artificial intelligence. *Applied Artificial Intelligence*, *24*(6), 617–647. doi:10.1080/08839514.2010.492172

Bolick, C. M. (2002). Digital history TIP: Preservice social studies teachers' experiences in a technology-rich field initiative. *Journal of Computing in Teacher Education*, *19*(2), 54–60.

Bondarenko, Y. G., & Kozulin, A. V. (1991). The democratization of education: Basic principles. *Higher Education in Europe*, *16*(1), 74–78. doi:10.1080/0379772910160109

Boopathi, S., & Kumar, P. (2024). Advanced bioprinting processes using additive manufacturing technologies: Revolutionizing tissue engineering. *3D Printing Technologies: Digital Manufacturing, Artificial Intelligence, Industry 4.0*, 95.

Bower, M., Kennedy, G. E., Dalgarno, B., Lee, M. J., & Kenney, J. (2015). Design and implementation factors in blended synchronous learning environments: Outcomes from a cross-case analysis. *Computers & Education*, *86*, 1–17. doi:10.1016/j.compedu.2015.03.006

Bozkurt, A., Junhong, X., Lambert, S., Pazurek, A., Crompton, H., Koseoglu, S., ... Romero-Hall, E. (2023). Speculative futures on ChatGPT and generative artificial intelligence (AI): A collective reflection from the educational landscape. *Asian Journal of Distance Education*, *18*(1), 53–130.

Brassler, M., & Dettmers, J. (2017). How to enhance interdisciplinary competence interdisciplinary problem-based learning versus interdisciplinary project-based learning. *The Interdisciplinary Journal of Problem-Based Learning*, *11*(2), 1–12. doi:10.7771/1541-5015.1686

Braun, J. A. (2002). Social studies education and technology: A rock and roll perspective. *The International Social Studies Forum, 2*(2), 167–169.

Braun, J. (1997). Past, possibilities, and potholes on the information superhighway. *Social Education, 61*(3), 49–153.

Braun, V., & Clarke, V. (2006). Using thematic analysis in psychology. *Qualitative Research in Psychology, 3*(2), 77–101. doi:10.1191/1478088706qp063oa

Brennan, J., & Teichler, U. (2008). The future of higher education and of higher education research: Higher education looking forward: An introduction. *Higher Education, 56*(3), 259–264. doi:10.1007/s10734-008-9124-6

Brey, P. (1998). The Politics of Computer Systems and the Ethics of Design. In J. van den Hoven (Ed.), *Computer Ethics: Philosophical Enquiry*. Rotterdam University Press.

Brinkmann, S. (2014). Unstructured and semi-structured interviewing. The Oxford handbook of qualitative research, 2, 277-299.

Brooks, R. M. (2023). Integrity Through Experience: Fostering a Culture of Academic Integrity Through an Experiential Learning Approach. In *Handbook of Academic Integrity* (pp. 287–303). Springer International Publishing. doi:10.1007/978-3-031-54144-5_94

Brown, A. H., & Green, T. D. (2015). *The essentials of instructional design: Connecting fundamental principles with process and practice*. Routledge. doi:10.4324/9781315757438

Bucea-Manea-Ţoniş, R., Kuleto, V., Gudei, S. C. D., Lianu, C., Lianu, C., Ilić, M. P., & Păun, D. (2022). Artificial intelligence potential in higher education institutions enhanced learning environment in Romania and Serbia. *Sustainability (Basel), 14*(10), 5842. doi:10.3390/su14105842

Bulathwela, S., Pérez-Ortiz, M., Holloway, C., & Shawe-Taylor, J. (2021). Could AI democratize education? Socio-technical imaginaries of an edtech revolution. *35th Conference on Neural Information Processing Systems. 1-9.* 10.48550/arxiv.2112.02034

Bulchand-Gidumal, J. (2022). Impact of artificial intelligence in travel, tourism, and hospitality. In *Handbook of e-Tourism* (pp. 1943–1962). Springer International Publishing. doi:10.1007/978-3-030-48652-5_110

Burrell, J., & Fourcade, M. (2021). The society of algorithms. *Annual Review of Sociology, 47*(1), 213–237. doi:10.1146/annurev-soc-090820-020800

Bygstad, B., Øvrelid, E., Ludvigsen, S., & Dæhlen, M. (2022). From dual digitalization to digital learning space: Exploring the digital transformation of higher education. *Computers & Education, 182*, 104463. Advance online publication. doi:10.1016/j.compedu.2022.104463

Cabaleiro-Cerviño, G., & Vera, C. (2020). The Impact of Educational Technologies in Higher Education. *GIST Education and Learning Research Journal, 20*, 155–169. doi:10.26817/16925777.711

Çalışkan, H., & Kaşıkçı, Y. (2010). The application of traditional and alternative assessment and evaluation tools by teachers in social studies. *Procedia: Social and Behavioral Sciences*, *2*(2), 4152–4156. doi:10.1016/j.sbspro.2010.03.656

Calvo, H., & Ruiz, J. (2024). *Sociedad Mexicana de Inteligencia Artificial*. SMIA. https://smia.mx/

Campbell, M., Gibson, W., Hall, A., Richards, D., & Callery, P. (2008). Online vs. face-to-face discussion in a web-based research methods course for postgraduate nursing students: A quasi-experimental study. *International Journal of Nursing Studies*, *45*(5), 750–759. doi:10.1016/j.ijnurstu.2006.12.011 PMID:17306272

Canal del Congreso. (n.d.). *Impulsan regulación de Inteligencia Artificial*. https://www.canaldelcongreso.gob.mx/noticias/17075/ImpulsanregulaciondeInteligenciaArtificial

Cantu, D. A. (1999). An Internet-based multiple intelligences model for teaching high school history. *Journal of the Association for History & Computing*, *2*(3). http://mcel.pacificu.edu/jahc/jahcII3/ index.html

Cantu, D. A. (2000a). Teaching pre-columbian and colonial American history on the Web. *Journal of the Association for History & Computing*, *3*(1). http://mcel.pacificu.edu/JAHC/JAHCIII1/index.html

Cantu, D. A. (2000b). Technology integration in preservice history teacher education. *Journal of the Association for History & Computing*, *3*(2). http://mcel.pacificu.edu/JAHC/JAHCIII2/index.html

Capuano, N., & Caballé, S. (2020). Adaptive learning technologies. *AI Magazine*, *41*(2), 96–98. doi:10.1609/aimag.v41i2.5317

Carbonell, J. R. (1970). AI in CAI: An artificial-intelligence approach to computer-assisted instruction. *IEEE Transactions on Man-Machine Systems*, *11*(4), 190–202. doi:10.1109/TMMS.1970.299942

Carlos, H., Germán, S.-T., & Dixon, S. (2021). Tashi-bot: A intelligent personal assistant for users in an educational institution. In Journal of Management Information and Decision Sciences (Vol. 24, Issue 6).

Carr, F. L. (1999). Using the World Wide Web as a teaching tool in an introduction to American history: Some technical and ethical difficulties. *Journal of the Association for History & Computing*, *2*(3). http://mcel.pacificu.edu/jahc/jahcII3/index.html

Carrillo, C., & Flores, M. A. (2020). COVID-19 and teacher education: A literature review of online teaching and learning practices. *European Journal of Teacher Education*, *43*(4), 466–487. doi:10.1080/02619768.2020.1821184

Chaiprasurt, C., Amornchewin, R., & Kunpitak, P. (2022). Using motivation to improve learning achievement with a chatbot in blended learning. *World Journal on Educational Technology: Current Issues*, *14*(4), 1133–1151. Advance online publication. doi:10.18844/wjet.v14i4.6592

Chan, C. K. Y., & Tsi, L. H. (2023). The AI Revolution in Education: Will AI Replace or Assist Teachers in Higher Education? *arXiv preprint arXiv:2305.01185.*

Chandra, S., Ranjan, A., & Chowdhary, N. (2022). Online hospitality and tourism education-issues and challenges. *Tourism (Zagreb), 70*(2), 298–316. doi:10.37741/t.70.2.10

Chatterjee, S., & Bhattacharjee, K. K. (2020). Adoption of artificial intelligence in higher education: A quantitative analysis using structural equation modelling. *Education and Information Technologies, 25*(5), 3443–3463. doi:10.1007/s10639-020-10159-7

Chaturvedi, R., Verma, S., Ali, F., & Kumar, S. (2023). Reshaping Tourist Experience with AI-Enabled Technologies: A Comprehensive Review and Future Research Agenda. *International Journal of Human-Computer Interaction*, 1–17. doi:10.1080/10447318.2023.2238353

Chaudhry, M. A., & Kazim, E. (2022). Artificial Intelligence in Education (AIEd): A high-level academic and industry note 2021. *AI and Ethics, 2*(1), 1–9. doi:10.1007/s43681-021-00074-z PMID:34790953

Cheng, L., Varshney, K. R., & Liu, H. (2021). Socially responsible AI algorithms: Issues, purposes, and challenges. *Journal of Artificial Intelligence Research, 71*, 1137–1181. doi:10.1613/jair.1.12814

Chen, H. L., Vicki Widarso, G., & Sutrisno, H. (2020). A ChatBot for Learning Chinese: Learning Achievement and Technology Acceptance. *Journal of Educational Computing Research, 58*(6), 1161–1189. Advance online publication. doi:10.1177/0735633120929622

Chen, J., Sun, J., & Wang, G. (2022). From unmanned systems to autonomous intelligent systems. *Engineering (Beijing), 12*, 16–19. doi:10.1016/j.eng.2021.10.007

Chen, L., Chen, P., & Lin, Z. (2020). Artificial intelligence in education: A review. *IEEE Access : Practical Innovations, Open Solutions, 8*, 75264–75278. doi:10.1109/ACCESS.2020.2988510

Chen, Y., Jensen, S., Albert, L. J., Gupta, S., & Lee, T. (2023). Artificial intelligence (AI) student assistants in the classroom: Designing chatbots to support student success. *Information Systems Frontiers, 25*(1), 161–182. doi:10.1007/s10796-022-10291-4

Cheung, S. K., Kwok, L. F., Phusavat, K., & Yang, H. H. (2021). Shaping the future learning environments with smart elements: Challenges and opportunities. *International Journal of Educational Technology in Higher Education, 18*(1), 1–9. doi:10.1186/s41239-021-00254-1 PMID:34778521

Chiu, K. F. C. (2021). A holistic approach to the design of artificial intelligence (AI) education for K-12schools. *TechTrends, 65*(5), 796–807. doi:10.1007/s11528-021-00637-1

Chiu, T. K. (2024). Future research recommendations for transforming higher education with generative AI. *Computers and Education: Artificial Intelligence, 6*, 100197. Advance online publication. doi:10.1016/j.caeai.2023.100197

Chiu, T. K. F., Xia, Q., Zhou, X., Chai, C. S., & Cheng, M. (2023). Systematic literature review on opportunities, challenges, and future research recommendations of artificial intelligence in education. In *Computers and Education* (Vol. 4). Artificial Intelligence., doi:10.1016/j.caeai.2022.100118

Chokur, M. F. S., & Al-Khafaji, S. J. N. (2023). The strategic use of events to revitalize cities: Najaf as a case study. *International Journal of Nonlinear Analysis and Applications*, *14*(8), 265–282.

Chon, K. K. S., & Hao, F. (2024). Technological evolution in tourism: A Horizon 2050 perspective. *Tourism Review*. Advance online publication. doi:10.1108/TR-10-2023-0753

Chui Chui, H. (2022). The QuillBot grammar checker: Friend or foe of ESL student writers. *Journal of Creative Practices in Language Learning and Teaching*, *10*(1).

Chui. (2022). The State of AI in 2022-and a half decade in review. McKinsey. https://www.mckinsey.com/capabilities/quantumblack/our-insights/the-state-of-ai-in-2022-and-a-half-decade-in-review#review

Clayton, K. E., Blumberg, F. C., & Anthony, J. A. (2018). Linkages between course status, perceived course value, and students' preference for traditional versus non-traditional learning environments. *Computers & Education*, *125*, 175–181. doi:10.1016/j.compedu.2018.06.002

Cochrane, T., & Rhodes, D. (2013). iArchi [tech] ture: Developing a mobile social media framework for pedagogical transformation. *Australasian Journal of Educational Technology*, *29*(3). Advance online publication. doi:10.14742/ajet.191

Cohen, L., Manion, L., Morrison, K., & Wyse, D. (2010). *A guide to teaching practice*. Rutledge. doi:10.4324/9780203848623

Colaner, N. (2022). Is explainable artificial intelligence intrinsically valuable? *AI & Society*, 1–8.

Comisi6n Econ6mica para América Latina y el Caribe (CEPAL). (2021). Tecnologías digitales para un nuevo futuro (LC/TS.2021/43). Academic Press.

Cools, H., Van Gorp, B., & Opgenhaffen, M. (2022). Where exactly between utopia and dystopia? A framing analysis of AI and automation in US newspapers. *Journalism*.

Cooper, G. (2023). Examining science education in chatgpt: An exploratory study of generative artificial intelligence. *Journal of Science Education and Technology*, *32*(3), 444–452. doi:10.1007/s10956-023-10039-y

Corbett, J. R. (1995). Cognitive tutors: Lessons learned. *Journal of the Learning Sciences*, *4*(2), 167–207. doi:10.1207/s15327809jls0402_2

Cox, A. C. (1997). Using the stock market game in the social studies classroom. *Social Education*, *61*(6), 347–350.

Cox, A. M., Pinfield, S., & Rutter, S. (2019). The intelligent library: Thought leaders' views on the likely impact of artificial intelligence on academic libraries. *Library Hi Tech*, *37*(3), 418–435. doi:10.1108/LHT-08-2018-0105

Creswell, J. W. (2013). *Qualitative inquiry and research design: Choosing among five approaches*. Sage publications.

Crompton, H., & Burke, D. (2023). Artificial intelligence in higher education: The state of the field. *International Journal of Educational Technology in Higher Education*, *20*(1), 22. doi:10.1186/s41239-023-00392-8

Cuartielles, R., Ramon-Vegas, X., & Pont-Sorribes, C. (2023). Retraining fact-checkers: The emergence of ChatGPT in information verification. *Profesional de La Información/Information Professional, 32*(5), 1-12.

Cuban, L., Kirkpatrick, H., & Peck, C. (2001). High access and low use of technologies in high school classrooms: Explaining an apparent paradox. *American Educational Research Journal*, *38*(4), 813–834. doi:10.3102/00028312038004813

Czarnecki, K. (2018). Less inequality through universal access? Socioeconomic background of tertiary entrants in Australia after the expansion of university participation. *Higher Education*, *76*(3), 501–518. doi:10.1007/s10734-017-0222-1

Dalgic, A., Demir, M., & Ergen, F. D. (2023). Does Perceived Vulnerability Mediate the Effect of Hotel Employees' Resilience on Mental Health Perceptions? *Tourism (Zagreb)*, *71*(1), 77–97. doi:10.37741/t.71.1.5

Dalgıç, A., Yaşar, E., & Demir, M. (2024). ChatGPT and learning outcomes in tourism education: The role of digital literacy and individualized learning. *Journal of Hospitality, Leisure, Sport and Tourism Education*, *34*, 100481. doi:10.1016/j.jhlste.2024.100481

Daniel, G., Cabot, J., Deruelle, L., & Derras, M. (2020). Xatkit: A Multimodal Low-Code Chatbot Development Framework. *IEEE Access : Practical Innovations, Open Solutions*, *8*, 15332–15346. Advance online publication. doi:10.1109/ACCESS.2020.2966919

Danker, A. (2000). Linking technology with social studies learning standards. *Social Studies*, *91*(6), 253–256. doi:10.1080/00377990009602474

Dao, X.-Q. (2023). Which Large Language Model should You Use in Vietnamese Education: ChatGPT, Bing Chat, or Bard? SSRN *Electronic Journal*. doi:10.2139/ssrn.4527476

Das, S., Lekhya, G., Shreya, K., Shekinah, K. L., Babu, K. K., & Boopathi, S. (2024). Fostering Sustainability Education Through Cross-Disciplinary Collaborations and Research Partnerships: Interdisciplinary Synergy. In Facilitating Global Collaboration and Knowledge Sharing in Higher Education With Generative AI (pp. 60–88). IGI Global.

Dauvergne, P. (2021). The globalization of artificial intelligence: Consequences for the politics of environmentalism. *Globalizations*, *18*(2), 285–299. doi:10.1080/14747731.2020.1785670

De Angelis, L., Baglivo, F., Arzilli, G., Privitera, G. P., Ferragina, P., Tozzi, A. E., & Rizzo, C. (2023). ChatGPT and the rise of large language models: The new AI-driven infodemic threat in public health. *Frontiers in Public Health, 11*, 1567. doi:10.3389/fpubh.2023.1166120 PMID:37181697

De Bruijn, H., Warnier, M., & Janssen, M. (2022). The perils and pitfalls of explainable AI: Strategies for explaining algorithmic decision-making. *Government Information Quarterly, 39*(2), 101666. doi:10.1016/j.giq.2021.101666

De Syon, G. (2000). Teaching the space program with the World Wide Web: Challenges and rewards of assigning online readings. *Journal of the Association for History & Computing, 3*(1). http:// mcel.pacificu.edu/JAHC/JAHCIII1/index.html

De Vynck, G., & Tiku, N. (2023). *Google's catch-up game on AI continues with Bard launch.* The Washington Post. https://www.washingtonpost.com/technology/2023/03/21/bard-google-ai/

Dede, C. (2009). Immersive interfaces for engagement and learning. *Science, 323*(5910), 66–69. doi:10.1126/science.1167311 PMID:19119219

Deloitte. (2019). National Transformation in the Middle East a Digital Journey. *Deloitte* https:// www2.deloitte.com/content/dam/Deloitte/xe/Documents/technology-media-telecommunication

Demir, M. (2024). Building Trust and Credibility: Ethical Use of AI in the Service Industry. In M. Demir & A. Dalgic (Eds.), *Revolutionizing the Service Industry With OpenAI Models* (pp. 243–267). IGI Global. doi:10.4018/979-8-3693-1239-1.ch010

Demir, M., & Demir, Ş. Ş. (2023). Is ChatGPT the right technology for service individualization and value co-creation? Evidence from the travel industry. *Journal of Travel & Tourism Marketing, 40*(5), 383–398. doi:10.1080/10548408.2023.2255884

Demir, M., & Demir, Ş. Ş. (2023b). Incorporating artificial intelligence into tourism education at universities: Opportunities and challenges. *Scientific Collection. InterConf*, (181), 106–114.

Demir, M., & Demir, Ş. Ş. (2023c). Reflection of artificial intelligence applications on students' critical and analytical abilities. *Scientific Collection. InterConf*, (184), 459–467.

Demir, M., Demir, Ş. Ş., & Aktürk, O. (2023). The Effects of Distance Education Capabilities and Competencies on Learning Outcomes During COVID-19 in Higher Education Institutions. *Journal of Hospitality & Tourism Education*, 1–12. doi:10.1080/10963758.2023.2191966

Demir, M., Demir, Ş. Ş., & Yaşar, E. (2022). Big data and innovative organizational performance: Evidence from a moderated-mediated model. *Creativity and Innovation Management, 31*(4), 696–709. doi:10.1111/caim.12525

Demir, Ş. Ş., & Demir, M. (2023). Professionals' perspectives on ChatGPT in the tourism industry: Does it inspire awe or concern? *Journal of Tourism Theory and Research, 9*(2), 61–77. doi:10.24288/jttr.1313481

Deng, X., & Yu, Z. (2023). A Meta-Analysis and Systematic Review of the Effect of Chatbot Technology Use in Sustainable Education. In Sustainability (Switzerland) (Vol. 15, Issue 4). doi:10.3390/su15042940

Deng, R., & Benckendorff, P. (2022). Technology-enabled learning. In *Handbook of e-Tourism* (pp. 1687–1713). Springer International Publishing. doi:10.1007/978-3-030-48652-5_129

Dergaa, I., Chamari, K., Zmijewski, P., & Saad, H. B. (2023). From human writing to artificial intelligence generated text: Examining the prospects and potential threats of ChatGPT in academic writing. *Biology of Sport*, *40*(2), 615–622. doi:10.5114/biolsport.2023.125623 PMID:37077800

Deri, M. N., Zaazie, P., & Singh, A. (2023). Digital Future of the Hospitality Industry and Hospitality Education Globally. In *International Handbook of Skill, Education, Learning, and Research Development in Tourism and Hospitality* (pp. 1–23). Springer Nature Singapore.

Dhoundiyal, H., & Mohanty, P. (2022). Artificial intelligence and robotics driving Tourism 4.0: an exploration. In *Handbook of Technology Application in Tourism in Asia* (pp. 1265–1285). Springer Nature Singapore. doi:10.1007/978-981-16-2210-6_57

Díaz-García, V., Montero-Navarro, A., Rodríguez-Sánchez, J. L., & Gallego-Losada, R. (2022). Digitalization and digital transformation in higher education: A bibliometric analysis. *Frontiers in Psychology*, *13*, 1081595. Advance online publication. doi:10.3389/fpsyg.2022.1081595 PMID:36533011

Diem, R. A. (2002). It was twenty years ago today: Prospects for infusing technology in the social studies. *The International Social Studies Forum*, *2*(2), 171–173.

Diem, R. (2000). Can it make a difference? Technology and social studies. *Theory and Research in Social Education*, *28*(4), 493–501. doi:10.1080/00933104.2000.10505920

Dikli, S. (2006). An overview of automated scoring of essays. *The Journal of Technology, Learning, and Assessment*, *5*(1).

Dockterman, D. (2002). *Weaving technology into your teaching*. Tom Snyder Productions, Inc.

Dogru, T., Line, N., Hanks, L., Acikgoz, F., Abbott, J. A., Bakir, S., Berbekova, A., Bilgihan, A., Iskender, A., Kizildag, M., Lee, M., Lee, W., McGinley, S., Mody, M., Onder, I., Ozdemir, O., & Suess, C. (2023). The implications of generative artificial intelligence in academic research and higher education in tourism and hospitality. *Tourism Economics*. Advance online publication. doi:10.1177/13548166231204065

Dokukina, I., & Gumanova, J. (2020). The rise of chatbots-new personal assistants in foreign language learning. *Procedia Computer Science*, *169*, 542–546. Advance online publication. doi:10.1016/j.procs.2020.02.212

Donlan, L. (1999). Come dream with us: Online projects teach more than technology. *Learning and Leading with Technology*, *26*(7), 42–45.

Döring, H. (2019). Public perceptions of the proper role of the state. In *The State in Western Europe Retreat or Redefinition?* (pp. 12–31). Routledge. doi:10.4324/9781315037479-2

Douidi, L., Djoudi, M., & Khentout, C. (2007). Users assistants for e-learning environment over the web. *Journal of Computational Science*, *3*(3), 122–129. doi:10.3844/jcssp.2007.122.129

Drissi, S., Chefrour, A., Boussaha, K., & Zarzour, H. (2024). Exploring the effects of personalized recommendations on student's motivation and learning achievement in gamified mobile learning framework. *Education and Information Technologies*, 1–38. doi:10.1007/s10639-024-12477-6

Druga, S., Otero, N., & Ko, A. J. (2022, July). The landscape of teaching resources for ai education. In *Proceedings of the 27th ACM Conference on on Innovation and Technology in Computer Science Education* Vol. 1 (pp. 96-102). 10.1145/3502718.3524782

du Boulay, B. (2022). Artificial intelligence in education and ethics. In *Handbook of open, distance and digital education* (pp. 1–16). Springer Nature Singapore. doi:10.1007/978-981-19-0351-9_6-2

Dunn, M. A. (2000). Closing the book on social studies: Four classroom teachers go beyond the text. *Social Studies*, *91*(3), 132–136. doi:10.1080/00377990009602456

Duong, C. D., Bui, D. T., Pham, H. T., & Vu, A. T. (2023). How effort expectancy and performance expectancy interact to trigger higher education students' uses of ChatGPT for learning. Interactive Technology and Smart Education. doi:10.1108/ITSE-05-2023-0096

Durairaj, M., Jayakumar, S., Karpagavalli, V., Maheswari, B. U., Boopathi, S., & ... (2023). Utilization of Digital Tools in the Indian Higher Education System During Health Crises. In *Multidisciplinary Approaches to Organizational Governance During Health Crises* (pp. 1–21). IGI Global. doi:10.4018/978-1-7998-9213-7.ch001

Dwivedi, Y. K., Kshetri, N., Hughes, L., Slade, E. L., Jeyaraj, A., Kar, A. K., Baabdullah, A. M., Koohang, A., Raghavan, V., Ahuja, M., Albanna, H., Albashrawi, M. A., Al-Busaidi, A. S., Balakrishnan, J., Barlette, Y., Basu, S., Bose, I., Brooks, L., Buhalis, D., ... Wright, R. (2023). "So what if ChatGPT wrote it?" Multidisciplinary perspectives on opportunities, challenges and implications of generative conversational AI for research, practice and policy. *International Journal of Information Management*, *71*, 102642. doi:10.1016/j.ijinfomgt.2023.102642

Eaton, J. S. (1999). The social studies classroom on the eve of the cyber century. *Social Education*, *63*(3), 139–141.

Egli, A. (2023). ChatGPT, GPT-4, and Other Large Language Models: The Next Revolution for Clinical Microbiology? In Clinical Infectious Diseases (Vol. 77, Issue 9). doi:10.1093/cid/ciad407

Ehman, L. H. (2002). Why haven't secondary social studies teachers adopted information technologies? *The International Social Studies Forum*, *2*(2), 175–178.

Elbanna, S., & Armstrong, L. (2024). Exploring the integration of ChatGPT in education: Adapting for the future. *Management & Sustainability: An Arab Review*, *3*(1), 16–29. doi:10.1108/MSAR-03-2023-0016

Ellaway, R. (2011). E-learning: Is the revolution over? *Medical Teacher*, *33*(4), 297–302. doi:10.3109/0142159X.2011.550968 PMID:21456987

Elliott, A. (2019). *The culture of AI: Everyday life and the digital revolution*. Routledge. doi:10.4324/9781315387185

Emam, R. M. (2023). *The effect of using Chat GPT technology as one of the applications of artificial intelligence in tourism education for students of tourism and hotels institutes by using task Technology fit model*. doi:10.21608/mfth.2023.327915

Ergen, F. D. (2020). Artırılmış ve sanal gerçeklik teknolojilerinin Isparta ilinin kültürel miras alanlarında uygulanabilirliği üzerine bir literatür taraması. *Journal of Tourism Theory and Research*, *6*(1), 62–74. doi:10.24288/jttr.673593

Essel, H. B., Vlachopoulos, D., Essuman, A. B., & Amankwa, J. O. (2024). ChatGPT effects on cognitive skills of undergraduate students: Receiving instant responses from AI-based conversational large language models (LLMs). *Computers and Education: Artificial Intelligence*, *6*, 100198. doi:10.1016/j.caeai.2023.100198

Fabos, B., & Young, M. D. (1999). Telecommunications in the classroom: Rhetoric versus reality. *Review of Educational Research*, *69*(3), 217–259. doi:10.3102/00346543069003217

Farahani, M., & Ghasemi, G. (2024). *Artificial intelligence and inequality: challenges and opportunities*. Qeios., doi:10.32388/7HWUZ2

Farrokhnia, M., Banihashem, S. K., Noroozi, O., & Wals, A. (2023). A SWOT analysis of ChatGPT: Implications for educational practice and research. *Innovations in Education and Teaching International*, *60*, 1–15. doi:10.1080/14703297.2023.2195846

Farrow, E. (2021). Mindset matters: How mindset affects the ability of staff to anticipate and adapt to Artificial Intelligence (AI) future scenarios in organisational settings. *AI & Society*, *36*(3), 895–909. doi:10.1007/s00146-020-01101-z PMID:33223620

Federspiel, F., Mitchell, R., Asokan, A., Umana, C., & McCoy, D. (2023). Threats by artificial intelligence to human health and human existence. *BMJ Global Health*, *8*(5), e010435. doi:10.1136/bmjgh-2022-010435 PMID:37160371

Femenia-Serra, F. (2018). Smart tourism destinations and higher tourism education in Spain. Are we ready for this new management approach? In *Information and Communication Technologies in Tourism 2018: Proceedings of the International Conference in Jönköping, Sweden, January 24-26, 2018* (pp. 437-449). Springer International Publishing.

Fernandez, E. (2024). *Impulsan regulación de la inteligencia artificial*. Canal del Congreso. https://www.canaldelcongreso.gob.mx/noticias/17075/ImpulsanregulaciondeInteligenciaArtificial

Finkel, M., & Krämer, N. C. (2022). Humanoid robots–artificial. Human-like. Credible? Empirical comparisons of source credibility attributions between humans, humanoid robots, and non-human-like devices. *International Journal of Social Robotics*, *14*(6), 1397–1411. doi:10.1007/s12369-022-00879-w

Fitria, T. N. (2021). QuillBot as an online tool: Students' alternative in paraphrasing and rewriting of English writing. *Englisia: Journal of Language, Education, and Humanities*, *9*(1), 183. Advance online publication. doi:10.22373/ej.v9i1.10233

Fitria, T. N. (2022). Avoiding Plagiarism of Students' Scientific Writing by Using the QuillBot Paraphraser. *Elsya : Journal of English Language Studies*, *4*(3). Advance online publication. doi:10.31849/elsya.v4i3.9917

FitzpatrickN.KelleherJ. (2018) On the Exactitude of Big Data: La Bêtise and Artificial Intelligence. *La Deluziana*, doi:10.21427/dfw8-m918

Flores-Vivar, J. M., & García-Peñalvo, F. J. (2023). Reflexiones sobre la ética, potencialidades y retos de la Inteligencia Artificial en el marco de la Educación de Calidad (ODS4). *Comunicar*, *31*(74). Advance online publication. doi:10.3916/C74-2023-03

Floridi, L., & Cowls, J. (2022). A unified framework of five principles for AI in society. *Machine learning and the city: Applications in architecture and urban design*, 535-545

Fontana, L. A. (1997). Online learning opportunities: Implications for the social studies. In P. H. Martorella (Ed.), *Interactive technologies and the social studies: Emerging issues and applications* (pp. 1–25). State University of New York Press.

Fowler, G. A. (2023). *Say what, Bard? What Google's new AI gets right, wrong and weird.* The Washington Post. https://www.washingtonpost.com/technology/2023/03/21/google-bard/

Frye, B., & Frager, A. M. (1996). Civilization, colonization, SimCity: Simulations for the social studies classroom. *Learning and Leading with Technology*, *24*(2), 21–23, 32.

Fullan, M., Azorín, C., Harris, A., & Jones, M. (2023). Artificial intelligence and school leadership: Challenges, opportunities and implications. *School Leadership & Management*, 1–8. doi:10.1080/13632434.2023.2246856

Gaglo, K., Degboe, B. M., Kossingou, G. M., & Ouya, S. (2022). Proposal of conversational chatbots for educational remediation in the context of covid-19. *International Conference on Advanced Communication Technology, ICACT, 2022-February*. 10.23919/ICACT53585.2022.9728860

Ganapini, M. B., Campbell, M., Fabiano, F., Horesh, L., Lenchner, J., Loreggia, A., . . . Venable, K. B. (2023). Thinking fast and slow in AI: The role of metacognition. In *Machine Learning, Optimization, and Data Science: 8th International Conference, LOD 2022, Certosa di Pontignano, Italy, September 18–22, 2022, Revised Selected Papers, Part II* (pp. 502-509). Cham: Springer Nature Switzerland.

Garrison, D. R., & Kanuka, H. (2004). Blended learning: Uncovering its transformative potential in higher education. *The Internet and Higher Education*, *7*(2), 95–105. doi:10.1016/j.iheduc.2004.02.001

Geoffroy, F., Aimeur, E., & Gillet, D. (2002). *A virtual Assistant for Web-Based Training in engineering education. In International Conference on Intelligent Tutoring Systems* (pp. 301-310). Springer Berlin Heidelberg. 10.1007/3-540-47987-2_34

Georgia Tech. (2016). Artificial Intelligence Course Creates AI Teaching Assistant. Available at: https://news.gatech.edu/news/2016/05/09/artificial-intelligence-course-createsai-teaching-assistant

Georgieva, K. (2024, January 14). AI will transform the global economy; let's make sure it benefits humanity. International Monetary Fund. https://www.imf.org/en/Blogs/Articles/2024/01/14/ai-will-transform-the-global-economy-lets-make-sure-it-benefits-humanity

Gerstein, J. (2014). Moving from education 1.0 through education 2.0 towards education 3.0. In L. M. Blaschke, C. Kenyon, & S. Hase (Eds.), Experiences in self-determined learning (pp. 83-97). Amazon.com.

Ghany, S. Y. A., & Latif, M. M. A. (2012). English language preparation of tourism and hospitality undergraduates in Egypt: Does it meet their future workplace requirements? *Journal of Hospitality, Leisure, Sport and Tourism Education*, *11*(2), 93–100. doi:10.1016/j.jhlste.2012.05.001

Gholami, M., Moghadam, P. K., Mohammadipoor, F., Tarahi, M. J., Sak, M., Toulabi, T., & Pour, A. H. H. (2016). Comparing the effects of problem-based learning and the traditional lecture method on critical thinking skills and metacognitive awareness in nursing students in a critical care nursing course. *Nurse Education Today*, *45*, 16–21. doi:10.1016/j.nedt.2016.06.007 PMID:27429398

Gill, S. S., Xu, M., Patros, P., Wu, H., Kaur, R., Kaur, K., & Buyya, R. (2024). Transformative effects of ChatGPT on modern education: Emerging Era of AI Chatbots. *Internet of Things and Cyber-Physical Systems*, *4*, 19–23. doi:10.1016/j.iotcps.2023.06.002

Glenn, A. D. (2002). Thirty years and some of the same issues. *The International Social Studies Forum*, *2*(2), 179–181.

Göktaş, L. S. (2023). ChatGPT Uzaktan Eğitim Sınavlarında Başarılı Olabilir Mi? Turizm Alanında Doğruluk ve Doğrulama Üzerine Bir Araştırma (Can ChatGPT Succeed. *Journal of Tourism & Gastronomy Studies*, *11*(2), 892–905. doi:10.21325/jotags.2023.1224

Gomez, L. I. (2020). *Immersive virtual reality for learning experiences. Radical Solutions and eLearning: Practical Innovations and Online Educational Technology*, 183-198.

Gonda, D. E., & Chu, B. (2019). Chatbot as a learning resource? Creating conversational bots as a supplement for teaching assistant training course. *TALE 2019 - 2019 IEEE International Conference on Engineering, Technology and Education*. 10.1109/TALE48000.2019.9225974

Goralski, M. A., & Tan, T. K. (2020). Artificial intelligence and sustainable development. *International Journal of Management Education*, *18*(1), 100330. doi:10.1016/j.ijme.2019.100330

Gowda, R. S., & Suma, V. (2017, February). A comparative analysis of traditional education system vs. e-Learning. In *2017 International conference on innovative mechanisms for industry applications (ICIMIA)* (pp. 567-571). IEEE. 10.1109/ICIMIA.2017.7975524

Gragert, E. H. (2000, Sept). Expanding international education through the Internet: No longer limited to the global studies and language curriculum. *White Paper from the Secretary's Conference on Educational Technology, U.S. Department of Education*: Washington, DC. Available: https://www.ed.gov/Technology/techconf/2000/ed_gragert.pdf

Grassini, S. (2023). Shaping the future of education: Exploring the potential and consequences of AI and ChatGPT in educational settings. *Education Sciences, 13*(7), 692. doi:10.3390/educsci13070692

Greenman, C. (2017). Exploring the impact of artificial intelligence on the accounting profession. *Journal of Research in Business. Economics and Management, 8*(3), 1451.

Gregorius, R. M. (2017). Performance of underprepared students in traditional versus animation-based flipped-classroom settings. *Chemistry Education Research and Practice, 18*(4), 841–848. doi:10.1039/C7RP00130D

Gubareva, R., & Lopes, R. P. (2020). Virtual Assistants for Learning: A Systematic Literature Review. *CSEDU*, (1), 97–103. doi:10.5220/0009417600970103

Gupta, A., Varun, Y., Das, P., Muttineni, N., Srivastava, P., Zafar, H., Chakraborty, T., & Nath, S. (2021). TruthBot: An Automated Conversational Tool for Intent Learning, Curated Information Presenting, and Fake News Alerting. *ArXiv Preprint ArXiv:2102.00509.*

Gupta, S., Gupta, N., & Chauhan, P. (2022). Controlling the uncontrolled: Over tourism in hill stations of Northern India. *Journal of Positive School Psychology*, 6549–6568.

Gutmann, A. (1987). *Democratic education: With a New Preface and Epilogue*. Princeton University Press.

Habibi, A., Muhaimin, M., Danibao, B. K., Wibowo, Y. G., Wahyuni, S., & Octavia, A. (2023). ChatGPT in higher education learning: Acceptance and use. *Computers and Education: Artificial Intelligence, 5*, 100190. doi:10.1016/j.caeai.2023.100190

Haleem, A., Javaid, M., Qadri, M. A., & Suman, R. (2022). Understanding the role of digital technologies in education: A review. *Sustainable Operations and Computers, 3*, 275–285. doi:10.1016/j.susoc.2022.05.004

Haluza, D., & Jungwirth, D. (2023). Artificial Intelligence and Ten Societal Megatrends: An Exploratory Study Using GPT-3. *Systems, 11*(3), 120. doi:10.3390/systems11030120

Hammady, R., Ma, M., Al-Kalha, Z., & Strathearn, C. (2021). A framework for constructing and evaluating the role of MR as a holographic virtual guide in museums. *Virtual Reality (Waltham Cross), 25*(4), 895–918. doi:10.1007/s10055-020-00497-9

Hardman, P. (2023). *A Brief History of AI in Education: What we have learned in the last 60 years, and where we're going next.* https://drphilippahardman.substack.com/p/a-brief-history-of-ai-in- education?utm_source=substack&utm_medium=email&utm_content=share

Harper, B., Hedberg, J., Corderoy, B., & Wright, R. (2000). Employing cognitive tools within interactive multimedia applications. In S. P. Lajoie (Ed.), *Computers as cognitive tools: No more walls* (pp. 227–245). Erlbaum.

Harper, R. H. (2021). AI: The social future of intelligence. In *Routledge Handbook of Social Futures* (pp. 52–58). Routledge. doi:10.4324/9780429440717-4

Harris, J. (1999). First steps to telecollaboration. *Learning and Leading with Technology, 27*(3), 54-57.

Harry, A. (2023). Role of AI in Education. *Interdisciplinary Journal and Humanity*, *2*(3), 260–268. doi:10.58631/injurity.v2i3.52

Hasanein, A. M., & Sobaih, A. E. E. (2023). Drivers and Consequences of ChatGPT Use in Higher Education: Key Stakeholder Perspectives. *European Journal of Investigation in Health, Psychology and Education*, *13*(11), 2599–2614. doi:10.3390/ejihpe13110181 PMID:37998071

Hattie, J. (2009). *Visible learning: A synthesis of over 800 meta-analyses relating to achievement*. Routledge.

Helm, J. M., Swiergosz, A. M., Haeberle, H. S., Karnuta, J. M., Schaffer, J. L., Krebs, V. E., Spitzer, A. I., & Ramkumar, P. N. (2020). Machine learning and artificial intelligence: Definitions, applications, and future directions. *Current Reviews in Musculoskeletal Medicine*, *13*(1), 69–76. doi:10.1007/s12178-020-09600-8 PMID:31983042

Henin, C., & Le Métayer, D. (2021). Beyond explainability: Justifiability and contestability of algorithmic decision systems. *AI & Society*, 1–14.

He, Q., Zheng, H., Ma, X., Wang, L., Kong, H., & Zhu, Z. (2022). Artificial intelligence application in a renewable energy-driven desalination system: A critical review. *Energy and AI*, *7*, 100123. doi:10.1016/j.egyai.2021.100123

Hickman, E., & Petrin, M. (2021). Trustworthy AI and corporate governance: The EU's ethics guidelines for trustworthy artificial intelligence from a company law perspective. *European Business Organization Law Review*, *22*(4), 593–625. doi:10.1007/s40804-021-00224-0

Hien, H. T., Cuong, P. N., Nam, L. N. H., Nhung, H. L. T. K., & Thang, L. D. (2018). Intelligent assistants in higher-education environments: The FIT-EBOt, a chatbot for administrative and learning support. *ACM International Conference Proceeding Series*. 10.1145/3287921.3287937

Hinton, P. J. (n.d.). *Ivy Tech develops machine learning algorithm to identify at-risk students and provide early intervention.* Google for Education. https://edu.google.com/why-google/customer-stories/ivytech-gcp/

Holmes, W., Bialik, M., & Fadel, C. (2019). *Artificial intelligence in education: Promises and implications for teaching and learning*. Center for Curriculum Redesign.

Holmes, W., Iniesto, F., Anastopoulou, S., & Boticario, J. G. (2023). Stakeholder Perspectives on the Ethics of AI in Distance-Based Higher Education. *International Review of Research in Open and Distance Learning*, *24*(2), 96–117. doi:10.19173/irrodl.v24i2.6089

Holmes, W., Porayska-Pomsta, K., Holstein, K., Sutherland, E., Baker, T., Shum, S. B., ... Koedinger, K. R. (2021). Ethics of AI in education: Towards a community-wide framework. *International Journal of Artificial Intelligence in Education*, 1–23.

Holmes, W., & Tuomi, I. (2022). State of the art and practice in AI in education. *European Journal of Education*, *57*(4), 542–570. doi:10.1111/ejed.12533

HolonIQ. (2023). *2023 Higher Education Digital Transformation Survey*. https://www.holoniq.com/notes/2023-higher-education-digital-transformation-survey

Holstein, K., Aleven, V., & Rummel, N. (2020). A conceptual framework for human–AI hybrid adaptivity in education. *Artificial Intelligence in Education: 21st International Conference, AIED 2020, Ifrane, Morocco, July 6–10, 2020 Proceedings*, *21*(Part I), 240–254.

Holt, M. (2018). Artificial intelligence in modern society. *Integrated Studies*, 138. https://digitalcommons.murraystate.edu/bis437/138

Hong, W. C. H. (2023). The impact of ChatGPT on foreign language teaching and learning: Opportunities in education and research. *Journal of Educational Technology and Innovation*, *5*(1), 1–9. doi:10.61414/jeti.v5i1.103

Hsu, C. H. (2018). Tourism education on and beyond the horizon. *Tourism Management Perspectives*, *25*, 181–183. doi:10.1016/j.tmp.2017.11.022

Huang, Q., & Xia, L. (2016). Inspection of Spatial–Temporal Behavior of Backpackers in Beijing Based on Trajectory. *Wireless Personal Communications*, *87*(4), 1337–1356. doi:10.1007/s11277-015-3056-0

Hudson, D. (1997). *Rewired: A brief and opinionated net history*. Macmillan Technical Publishing.

Hughes, J. (2019). Learning across boundaries: Educator and startup involvement in the educational technology innovation ecosystem. *Contemporary Issues in Technology & Teacher Education*, *19*(1), 62–96.

Humble, K. (2023). Artificial Intelligence, International Law and the Race for Killer Robots in Modern Warfare. In *Artificial Intelligence, Social Harms and Human Rights* (pp. 57–76). Springer International Publishing. doi:10.1007/978-3-031-19149-7_3

Hung, P. K., Liang, R. H., Ma, S. Y., & Kong, B. W. (2024). Exploring the experience of traveling to familiar places in VR: An empirical study using google earth VR. *International Journal of Human-Computer Interaction*, *40*(2), 255–277. doi:10.1080/10447318.2022.2114141

Hussain, Z., Babe, M., Saravanan, S., Srimathy, G., Roopa, H., & Boopathi, S. (2023). Optimizing Biomass-to-Biofuel Conversion: IoT and AI Integration for Enhanced Efficiency and Sustainability. In Circular Economy Implementation for Sustainability in the Built Environment (pp. 191–214). IGI Global.

Hutson, J., Jeevanjee, T., Vander Graaf, V., Lively, J., Weber, J., Weir, G., ... Edele, S. (2022). Artificial Intelligence and the Disruption of Higher Education: Strategies for Integrations across Disciplines. *Creative Education, 13*(12), 3953–3980. Advance online publication. doi:10.4236/ce.2022.1312253

Hwang, G. J., Xie, H., Wah, B. W., & Gašević, D. (2020). Vision, challenges, roles and research issues of Artificial Intelligence in Education. *Computers and Education: Artificial Intelligence, 1*, 100001. Advance online publication. doi:10.1016/j.caeai.2020.100001

Hwang, H., & Park, M. H. (2020). The Threat of AI and Our Response: The AI Charter of Ethics in South Korea. *Asian Journal of Innovation & Policy*, *9*(1).

Ibrahim, M. S., & Hamada, M. (2016). Adaptive learning framework. In *2016 15th International Conference on Information Technology Based Higher Education and Training (ITHET)* (pp. 1-5). IEEE. 10.1109/ITHET.2016.7760738

Igna, I., & Venturini, F. (2023). The determinants of AI innovation across European firms. *Research Policy*, *52*(2), 104661. doi:10.1016/j.respol.2022.104661

Iskender, A. (2023). Holy or unholy? Interview with open AI's ChatGPT. *European Journal of Tourism Research*, *34*, 3414–3414. doi:10.54055/ejtr.v34i.3169

Islam, S. R., Russell, I., Eberle, W., & Dicheva, D. (2022). Instilling conscience about bias and fairness in automated decisions. *Journal of Computing Sciences in Colleges*, *37*(8), 22–31.

Ivanashko, O., Kozak, A., Knysh, T., & Honchar, K. (2024). The Role of Artificial Intelligence in Shaping the Future of Education: Opportunities and Challenges. *Futurity Education*, *4*(1), 126–146. doi:10.57125/FED.2024.03.25.08

Ivanova, M. (2019). Robots, artificial intelligence, and service automation in travel agencies and tourist information centers. In Robots, Artificial Intelligence, And Service Automation In Travel, Tourism And Hospitality (pp. 221-237). Emerald Publishing Limited. doi:10.1108/978-1-78756-687-320191011

Ivanova, V., Toskova, A., Stoyanova-Doycheva, A., Stoyanov, S., & Veselinova, M. (2017, September). Lifelong learning in Virtual education space with intelligent assistants. In *Proceedings of the 8th Balkan Conference in Informatics* (pp. 1-6). 10.1145/3136273.3136287

Ivanov, S., & Soliman, M. (2023). Game of algorithms: ChatGPT implications for the future of tourism education and research. *Journal of Tourism Futures*, *9*(2), 214–221. doi:10.1108/JTF-02-2023-0038

Jadhav, M. R., Kakade, A. B., Jagtap, S. R., & Patil, M. S. (2020). Impact assessment of outcome based approach in engineering education in India. *Procedia Computer Science, 172*, 791–796. doi:10.1016/j.procs.2020.05.113

Jia, S., Chi, O. H., Martinez, S. D., & Lu, L. (2023). When "Old" Meets "New": Unlocking the Future of Innovative Technology Implementation in Heritage Tourism. *Journal of Hospitality & Tourism Research (Washington, D.C.)*. Advance online publication. doi:10.1177/10963480231205767

Jobin, A., Ienca, M., & Vayena, E. (2019). The global landscape of AI ethics guidelines. *Nature Machine Intelligence, 1*(9), 389–399. doi:10.1038/s42256-019-0088-2

Johnson, C., & Rector, J. (1997). The Internet ten: Using the Internet to meet social studies curriculum standards. *Social Education, 61*(3), 167–169.

Kabir, S., Hossain, M. P., Mallik, K., Rahman, M., Islam, M. J., & Khatun, A. (2019). An Extensive Online Examination System With Automatic Assessment Technique. *GUB Journal of Science and Engineering, 6*(01), 54–59. doi:10.3329/gubjse.v6i1.52051

Kalaichelvan, R., & Subramanian, P. (2023). Historical perspective of education 1.0 to education 5.0. In S. Prakash, M. A. Muniammal, M. Maruthavanan, S. Raja Kumar, K. Thangavel, & N. Sundar (Eds.), *Education 5.0: Revolutionizing learning for the future* (pp. 53–56). Thiagarajar College of Preceptors.

Kalbaska, N., & Cantoni, L. (2022). e-Learning in tourism education. In Handbook of e-Tourism (pp. 1667-1686). Cham: Springer International Publishing.

Kalliamvakaou. (2022). Quantifying GitHub Copilot's Impact on Developer Productivity and Happiness. https://github.blog/2022-09-07-research-quantifying-github-copilots-impact-on-developer-productivity-and-happiness

Kallou, S., Kikilia, A., Kalogiannakis, M., & Zacharis, N. Z. (2023). Emotional intelligence development: The implementation of transformative learning through digital technologies in tourism-a study protocol. *International Journal of Technology Enhanced Learning, 15*(2), 180–194. doi:10.1504/IJTEL.2023.130112

Kamalov, F., Santandreu Calonge, D., & Gurrib, I. (2023). New era of artificial intelligence in education: Towards a sustainable multifaceted revolution. *Sustainability (Basel), 15*(16), 12451. doi:10.3390/su151612451

Karam, J. (2023). Reforming Higher Education Through AI. In *Governance in Higher Education: Global Reform and Trends in the MENA Region* (pp. 275–306). Springer Nature Switzerland. doi:10.1007/978-3-031-40586-0_12

Kasneci, E., Seßler, K., Küchemann, S., Bannert, M., Dementieva, D., Fischer, F., Gasser, U., Groh, G., Günnemann, S., Hüllermeier, E., Krusche, S., Kutyniok, G., Michaeli, T., Nerdel, C., Pfeffer, J., Poquet, O., Sailer, M., Schmidt, A., Seidel, T., ... Kasneci, G. (2023). ChatGPT for good? On opportunities and challenges of large language models for education. *Learning and Individual Differences, 103*, 102274. doi:10.1016/j.lindif.2023.102274

Kavitha, K. B., Pradeep Kumar, T.K., Nithiya, S., & Suguna, A. (2023). Implementation of Artificial Intelligence in Education. *International Research Journal of Computer Science, 10*(5), 104-108. . doi:10.26562/irjcs.2023.v1005.01

Keçi, I., & Qosja, E. (2021). Tourism Education During the Pandemic: Is Distance Education a Solution? In Handbook of Research on the Impacts and Implications of COVID-19 on the Tourism Industry (pp. 863-884). IGI Global.

Keiper, T., Harwood, A., & Larson, B. E. (2000, Fall). Preservice teachers' perceptions of infusing computer technology onto social studies instruction. *Theory and Research in Social Education, 28*(4), 566–579. doi:10.1080/00933104.2000.10505924

Kengam, J. (2020). Artificial intelligence in education. *Research Gate*, *18*, 1–4.

Khademi, A. (2023). Can ChatGPT and Bard generate aligned assessment items? A reliability analysis against human performance. *Journal of Applied Learning and Teaching*, *6*(1). Advance online publication. doi:10.37074/jalt.2023.6.1.28

Khogali, H. O., & Mekid, S. (2023). The blended future of automation and AI: Examining some long-term societal and ethical impact features. *Technology in Society*, *73*, 102232. doi:10.1016/j.techsoc.2023.102232

Kim, N.-Y., Cha, Y., & Kim, H.-S. (2019). Future English Learning: Chatbots and Artificial Intelligence. *Multimedia-Assisted Language Learning, 22*(3).

Kim, J., Lee, H., & Cho, Y. H. (2022). Learning design to support student-AI collaboration: Perspectives of leading teachers for AI in education. *Education and Information Technologies, 27*(5), 6069–6104. doi:10.1007/s10639-021-10831-6

Kim, N. (2018). A Study on Chatbots for Developing Korean College Students' English Listening and Reading Skills. *Journal of Digital Convergence*, *16*(8).

Kim, N. J., & Kim, M. K. (2022, March). Teacher's perceptions of using an artificial intelligence-based educational tool for scientific writing. *Frontiers in Education*, *7*, 755914. doi:10.3389/feduc.2022.755914

Kiryakova, G., & Angelova, N. (2023). ChatGPT—A Challenging Tool for the University Professors in Their Teaching Practice. *Education Sciences, 13*(10), 1056. doi:10.3390/educsci13101056

Klutka, J., Ackerly, N., & Magda, A. J. (2018). *Artificial intelligence in higher education: Current uses and future applications*. Learning House.

Kolmos, A., & de Graaff, E. (2014). Problem-based and project-based learning in engineering education. Cambridge Handbook of Engineering Education Research, 141-161.

Kong, S. C., Cheung, W. M. Y., & Zhang, G. (2022). Evaluating an AI literacy programme for empoweringand developing concepts, literacy and ethical awareness in senior secondary students. *Education and Information Technologies*. Advance online publication. doi:10.1007/s10639-022-11408-7

Koo, C., Xiang, Z., Gretzel, U., & Sigala, M. (2021). Artificial intelligence (AI) and robotics in travel, hospitality and leisure. *Electronic Markets*, *31*(3), 473–476. doi:10.1007/s12525-021-00494-z PMID:35603226

Kooli, C. (2023). Chatbots in Education and Research: A Critical Examination of Ethical Implications and Solutions. *Sustainability (Basel)*, *15*(7), 5614. Advance online publication. doi:10.3390/su15075614

Kostka, I., & Toncelli, R. (2023). Exploring applications of ChatGPT to English language teaching: Opportunities, challenges, and recommendations. *TESL-EJ*, *27*(3), 1–19. doi:10.55593/ej.27107int

Kremer, M., & Holla, A. (2009). Improving education in the developing world: What have we learned from randomized evaluations? *Annual Review of Economics*, *1*(1), 513–542. doi:10.1146/annurev.economics.050708.143323 PMID:23946865

Kubiatko, M., & Vaculová, I. (2011). Project-based learning: Characteristic and the experiences with application in the science subjects. *Energy Education Science and Technology, Part B. Social and Educational Studies*, *3*(1), 65–74.

Kucirkova, N., & Leaton Gray, S. (2023). Beyond Personalization: Embracing Democratic Learning Within Artificially Intelligent Systems. *Educational Theory*, *73*(4), 469–489. doi:10.1111/edth.12590

Kuleto, V., Ilić, M., Dumangiu, M., Ranković, M., Martins, O. M., Păun, D., & Mihoreanu, L. (2021). Exploring opportunities and challenges of artificial intelligence and machine learning in higher education institutions. *Sustainability (Basel)*, *13*(18), 10424. doi:10.3390/su131810424

Kumara, V., & Sharma, M. D., Samson Isaac, J., Saravanan, S., Suganthi, D., & Boopathi, S. (2023). An AI-Integrated Green Power Monitoring System: Empowering Small and Medium Enterprises. In Advances in Environmental Engineering and Green Technologies (pp. 218–244). IGI Global. doi:10.4018/979-8-3693-0338-2.ch013

Kurbanov, R. A., Belyalova, A. M., Yarygina, N. A., Schetinina, S. Y., Feshina, S. S., Buslaev, S. I., & Dugarskaya, T. A. (2020). Student attitude to future profession in field of information technology at university training stage. *International Journal of Psychosocial Rehabilitation*, *24*(4), 5019–5026. doi:10.37200/IJPR/V24I4/PR201601

Kurniati, E. Y., & Fithriani, R. (2022). Post-Graduate Students' Perceptions of Quillbot Utilization in English Academic Writing Class. *Journal of English Language Teaching and Linguistics*, *7*(3), 437. Advance online publication. doi:10.21462/jeltl.v7i3.852

Kuziemski, M., & Misuraca, G. (2020). AI governance in the public sector: Three tales from the frontiers of automated decision-making in democratic settings. *Telecommunications Policy*, *44*(6), 101976. doi:10.1016/j.telpol.2020.101976 PMID:32313360

Kwon, S. M., Wardrip, P. S., & Gomez, L. M. (2014). Co-design of interdisciplinary projects as a mechanism for school capacity growth. *Improving Schools*, *17*(1), 54–71. doi:10.1177/1365480213519517

Lagunes, A. (2024) *Hacia un Diagnóstico de la Inteligencia Artificial en México: Implementación Ética y Responsable ANIA-UNESCO*. Senadora Alejandra Lagunes. https://www.alejandralagunes.mx/inteligencia-artificial

Lampoltshammer, T. J., Wallinger, S., & Scholz, J. (2023). Bridging Disciplinary Divides through Computational Social Sciences and Transdisciplinarity in Tourism Education in Higher Educational Institutions: An Austrian Case Study. *Sustainability (Basel)*, *15*(10), 8133. Advance online publication. doi:10.3390/su15108133

Larson, D. B., Harvey, H., Rubin, D. L., Irani, N., Justin, R. T., & Langlotz, C. P. (2021). Regulatory frameworks for development and evaluation of artificial intelligence–based diagnostic imaging algorithms: Summary and recommendations. *Journal of the American College of Radiology*, *18*(3), 413–424. doi:10.1016/j.jacr.2020.09.060 PMID:33096088

Laupichler, M. C., Aster, A., Schirch, J., & Raupach, T. (2022). Artificial intelligence literacy in higher and adult education: A scoping literature review. *Computers and Education: Artificial Intelligence*, *3*, 100101. doi:10.1016/j.caeai.2022.100101

Lee, M. J., & Stuckart, D. W. (2001). Promise and practice of computer technologies in the social studies: A critical analysis. In W. B. Stanley (Ed.), *Critical issues in social studies research for the 21st century* (pp. 209–229). Information Age Publishing.

Lehmann, R., Bosse, H. M., Simon, A., Nikendei, C., & Huwendiek, S. (2013). An innovative blended learning approach using virtual patients as preparation for skills laboratory training: Perceptions of students and tutors. *BMC Medical Education*, *13*(1), 1–9. doi:10.1186/1472-6920-13-23 PMID:23402663

Li, C. H., Yuen, H. Y., Lee, T. T., Tang, W. F., Lee, C. C., Ng, C., & Mak, S. L. (2023). How to Embed AI Applications of Building Management System in Campus Management. In *International conference on WorldS4* (pp. 403-411). Singapore: Springer Nature Singapore.

Li, F., Qi, J., Wang, G., & Wang, X. (2014). Traditional classroom vs e-learning in higher education: Difference between students' behavioral engagement. *International Journal of Emerging Technologies in Learning*, *9*(2), 48. doi:10.3991/ijet.v9i2.3268

Li, H. (2023). AI in Education: Bridging the Divide or Widening the Gap? Exploring Equity, Opportunities, and Challenges in the Digital Age. *Advances in Education. Humanities and Social Science Research*, *8*(1), 355–355. doi:10.56028/aehssr.8.1.355.2023

Lim, M. Y., & Aylett, R. (2009). An emergent emotion model for an affective mobile guide with attitude. *Applied Artificial Intelligence*, *23*(9), 835–854. doi:10.1080/08839510903246518

Limna, P., & Kraiwanit, T. (2023). The role of chatgpt on customer service in the hospitality industry: An exploratory study of hospitality workers' experiences and perceptions. *Tourism and Hospitality Management*, *29*(4), 583–592. doi:10.20867/thm.29.4.9

Lim, W. M., Gunasekara, A., Pallant, J. L., Pallant, J. I., & Pechenkina, E. (2023). Generative AI and the future of education: Ragnarök or reformation? A paradoxical perspective from management educators. *International Journal of Management Education*, *21*(2), 1–12. doi:10.1016/j.ijme.2023.100790

Lin, C. C., Huang, A. Y., & Lu, O. H. (2023). Artificial intelligence in intelligent tutoring systems toward sustainable education: A systematic review. *Smart Learning Environments*, *10*(1), 41–50. doi:10.1186/s40561-023-00260-y

Lin, W. R., Lee, S. S., & Huang, W. S. (2023). A scale for measuring tourists' technological competence. *Journal of Hospitality and Tourism Technology*, *14*(5), 802–814. doi:10.1108/JHTT-09-2021-0276

Liu, B. L., Morales, D., Roser-Chinchilla, J., Sabzalieva, E., Valentini, A., Vieira do Nascimento, D., & Yerovi, C. (2023). Harnessing the era of artificial intelligence in higher education: a primer for higher education stakeholders. https://policycommons.net/artifacts/6942527/harnessing-the-era-of-artificial-intelligence-in-higher-education/7852431/

Liu, L., Subbareddy, R., & Raghavendra, C. G. (2022). AI Intelligence Chatbot to Improve Students Learning in the Higher Education Platform. *Journal of Interconnection Networks*, *22*(Supp02), 2143032. Advance online publication. doi:10.1142/S0219265921430325

Liu, M., Ren, Y., Nyagoga, L. M., Stonier, F., Wu, Z., & Yu, L. (2023). Future of education in the era of generative artificial intelligence: Consensus among Chinese scholars on applications of ChatGPT in schools. *Future in Educational Research*, *1*(1), 72–101. doi:10.1002/fer3.10

Lo, C. K. (2023). What Is the Impact of ChatGPT on Education? A Rapid Review of the Literature. *Education Sciences*, *13*(4), 410. doi:10.3390/educsci13040410

Loos, E., Gröpler, J., & Goudeau, M. L. S. (2023). Using ChatGPT in Education: Human Reflection on ChatGPT's Self-Reflection. *Societies (Basel, Switzerland)*, *13*(8), 196. doi:10.3390/soc13080196

Luan, H., Geczy, P., Lai, H., Gobert, J., Yang, S. J., Ogata, H., Baltes, J., Guerra, R., Li, P., & Tsai, C. C. (2020). Challenges and future directions of big data and artificial intelligence in education. *Frontiers in Psychology*, *11*, 580820. Advance online publication. doi:10.3389/fpsyg.2020.580820 PMID:33192896

Lund, B. D., Wang, T., Mannuru, N. R., Nie, B., Shimray, S., & Wang, Z. (2023). ChatGPT and a new academic reality: Artificial Intelligence-written research papers and the ethics of the large language models in scholarly publishing. *Journal of the Association for Information Science and Technology*, *74*(5), 570–581. doi:10.1002/asi.24750

Madan, B. S., Viraj Dravid, S., Deenadayalan, G., Rathod, P., Arumugam, G., & Boopathi, S. (2024). Innovations and Applications of Engineered Cementitious Composites and Alternative Materials: Reimagining Construction. In Advances in Chemical and Materials Engineering (pp. 53–86). IGI Global. doi:10.4018/978-1-6684-8182-0.ch003

Madhav, A. S., & Tyagi, A. K. (2022). The world with future technologies (Post-COVID-19): open issues, challenges, and the road ahead. *Intelligent Interactive Multimedia Systems for e-Healthcare Applications*, 411-452.

Maguluri, L. P., Arularasan, A., & Boopathi, S. (2023). Assessing Security Concerns for AI-Based Drones in Smart Cities. In Effective AI, Blockchain, and E-Governance Applications for Knowledge Discovery and Management (pp. 27–47). IGI Global. doi:10.4018/978-1-6684-9151-5.ch002

Mahadevan, R., Shivaprakash, N., Khobragade, N., Raju, K., & Rao, V. N. (2013). Implementing a sustainable methodology for assessment of course outcomes and program outcomes in an Indian Engineering institute. *Proceedings of 2013 IEEE International Conference on Teaching, Assessment and Learning for Engineering (TALE)*, 51–54. 10.1109/TALE.2013.6654398

Makridakis, S. (2017). The forthcoming Artificial Intelligence (AI) revolution: Its impact on society and firms. *Futures*, *90*, 46–60. doi:10.1016/j.futures.2017.03.006

Mandalia, S. (2023). Tourism Education in the Digital Era: Navigating Innovation and Transformation. In *International Conference on Social Science and Education (ICoeSSE 2023)* (pp. 509-530). Atlantis Press. 10.2991/978-2-38476-142-5_48

Mane, S. D. (2015). NBA and NAAC Accreditation of UG Engineering Programmes/Colleges in India: A Review. *International Journal of Scientific Engineering and Applied Science*, *1*(6), 2395–3470.

Mantegna, M. (2022). *No soy un robot: construyendo un marco ético accionable para analizar las dimensiones de impacto de la inteligencia artificial*. Academic Press.

Mantello, P., Ho, M. T., Nguyen, M. H., & Vuong, Q. H. (2023). Bosses without a heart: Socio-demographic and cross-cultural determinants of attitude toward Emotional AI in the workplace. *AI & Society*, *38*(1), 97–119. doi:10.1007/s00146-021-01290-1 PMID:34776651

Maqbool, S., Ismail, S. A. M. B. M., Maqbool, S., & Hassan, S. U. (2018). Effects of Traditional Lecture Method and Multi-Sensory Approach on ELT Learners at Graduate Level. International. *Journal of Academic Research in Progressive Education and Development*, *7*(4), 488–505.

Marks, A., Al-Ali, M., Atassi, R., Elkishk, A. A., & Rezgui, Y. (2021). Digital transformation in higher education: maturity and challenges post COVID-19. In Information Technology and Systems: ICITS 2021, Volume 1 (pp. 53-70). Springer International Publishing. doi:10.1007/978-3-030-68285-9_6

Marshall, M. N. (1996). Sampling for qualitative research. *Family Practice*, *13*(6), 522–526. doi:10.1093/fampra/13.6.522 PMID:9023528

Martins, L. L., Gilson, L. L., & Maynard, M. T. (2004). Virtual teams: What do we know and where do we go from here? *Journal of Management*, *30*(6), 805–835. doi:10.1016/j.jm.2004.05.002

Martorella, P. H. (1997). Technology and social studies—or: Which way to the sleeping giant? *Theory and Research in Social Education*, *25*(4), 511–514. doi:10.1080/00933104.1997.10505828

Maslej, N., Fattorini, L., Brynjolfsson, E., Etchemendy, J., Ligett, K., Lyons, T., Manyika, J., Ngo, H., Niebles, J. C., Parli, V., Shoham, Y., Wald, R., Clark, J., & Perrault, R. (2023). The AI Index 2023 Annual Report. AI Index Steering Committee, Institute for Human-Centered AI, Stanford University.

Mason, C. L., & Berson, M. J. (2000). Computer-mediated communication in elementary social studies methods. *Theory and Research in Social Education*, *28*(4), 527–545. doi:10.1080/00933104.2000.10505922

Mason, C., Berson, M., Diem, R., Hicks, D., Lee, J., & Dralle, T. (2000). Guidelines for using technology to prepare social studies teachers. *Contemporary Issues in Technology & Teacher Education*, *1*(1), 107–116.

McCarthy, J. (n.d.). What is artificial intelligence? http://jmc.stanford.edu/artificial-intelligence/what-is-ai/

McGue, S. R., Pelic, C. M., McCadden, A., Pelic, C. G., & Lewis, A. L. (2021). The use of simulation in teaching. *Psychiatria Clinica*, *44*(2), 159–171. PMID:34049640

Mckie, I. A. S., & Narayan, B. (2019). Enhancing the Academic Library Experience with Chatbots: An Exploration of Research and Implications for Practice. *Journal of the Australian Library and Information Association*, *68*(3), 268–277. Advance online publication. doi:10.1080/24750158.2019.1611694

Mele, C., & Russo-Spena, T. (2023). Artificial Intelligence in Services. Elgar Encyclopedia of Services, 356.

Memarian, B., & Doleck, T. (2023). ChatGPT in education: Methods, potentials and limitations. *Computers in Human Behavior: Artificial Humans*, *100022*(2), 100022. Advance online publication. doi:10.1016/j.chbah.2023.100022

Merryfield, M. M. (2000, Fall). Using electronic technologies to promote equity and cultural diversity in social studies education. *Theory and Research in Social Education*, *28*(4), 502–526. doi:10.1080/00933104.2000.10505921

Mhlanga, D. (2023). Open AI in education, the responsible and ethical use of ChatGPT towards lifelong learning. *Education, the Responsible and Ethical Use of ChatGPT Towards Lifelong Learning,* 1-19.

Mhlanga, D., Denhere, V., & Moloi, T. (2022). COVID-19 and the key digital transformation lessons for higher education institutions in South Africa. *Education Sciences*, *12*(7), 464. Advance online publication. doi:10.3390/educsci12070464

Michel-Villarreal, R., Vilalta-Perdomo, E., Salinas-Navarro, D. E., Thierry-Aguilera, R., & Gerardou, F. S. (2023). Challenges and opportunities of generative AI for higher education as explained by ChatGPT. *Education Sciences*, *13*(9), 856. doi:10.3390/educsci13090856

Mikalef, P., Conboy, K., Lundström, J. E., & Popovič, A. (2022). Thinking responsibly about responsible AI and 'the dark side' of AI. *European Journal of Information Systems*, *31*(3), 257–268. doi:10.1080/0960085X.2022.2026621

Miles, M. B., & Huberman, A. M. (1994). Qualitative data analysis: An expanded sourcebook. *Sage (Atlanta, Ga.)*.

Miller, G. J. (2022, March). Artificial Intelligence Project Success Factors—Beyond the Ethical Principles. In *Information Technology for Management: Business and Social Issues: 16th Conference, ISM 2021, and FedCSIS-AIST 2021 Track, Held as Part of FedCSIS 2021, Virtual Event, September 2–5, 2021, Extended and Revised Selected Papers* (pp. 65-96). Cham: Springer International Publishing.

Mills, A., Bali, M., & Eaton, L. (2023). How do we respond to generative AI in education? Open educational practices give us a framework for an ongoing process. *Journal of Applied Learning and Teaching*, *6*(1), 16–30.

Miranda, J., Navarrete, C., Noguez, J., Molina-Espinosa, J. M., Ramírez-Montoya, M. S., Navarro-Tuch, S. A., Bustamante-Bello, M.-R., Rosas-Fernández, J.-B., & Molina, A. (2021). The core components of education 4.0 in higher education: Three case studies in engineering education. *Computers & Electrical Engineering*, *93*, 107278. Advance online publication. doi:10.1016/j.compeleceng.2021.107278

Mirbabaie, M., Brünker, F., Möllmann, N. R., & Stieglitz, S. (2022). The rise of artificial intelligence–understanding the AI identity threat at the workplace. *Electronic Markets*, *32*(1), 1–27. doi:10.1007/s12525-021-00496-x

Mogavi, R. H., Deng, C., Kim, J. J., Zhou, P., Kwon, Y. D., Metwally, A. H. S., ... Hui, P. (2024). ChatGPT in education: A blessing or a curse? A qualitative study exploring early adopters' utilization and perceptions. *Computers in Human Behavior: Artificial Humans*, *2*(1), 100027. doi:10.1016/j.chbah.2023.100027

Moharir, M., Agavekar, R., Bhore, P., Kadam, H., & Bewoor, A. (2022). Effective Implementation of Peer Review as an Active Learning Technique to Attain Course Outcome: A Case Study. *Journal of Engineering Education Transformations, 36*(Special Issue 1).

Molenaar, I. (2022). Towards hybrid human-AI learning technologies. *European Journal of Education*, *57*(4), 632–645. doi:10.1111/ejed.12527

Montenegro-Rueda, M., Fernández-Cerero, J., Fernández-Batanero, J. M., & López-Meneses, E. (2023). Impact of the implementation of ChatGPT in education: A systematic review. *Computers*, *12*(8), 153. doi:10.3390/computers12080153

Moraes, E. B., Kipper, L. M., Hackenhaar Kellermann, A. C., Austria, L., Leivas, P., Moraes, J. A. R., & Witczak, M. (2023). Integration of Industry 4.0 technologies with Education 4.0: Advantages for improvements in learning. *Interactive Technology and Smart Education*, *20*(2), 271–287. doi:10.1108/ITSE-11-2021-0201

Moreira, M. (2000). Aprendizaje significativo. *Recuperado el, 8*, 149-181.

Morellato, M. (2014). Digital competence in tourism education: Cooperative-experiential learning. *Journal of Teaching in Travel & Tourism, 14*(2), 184–209. doi:10.1080/15313220.2014.907959

Mousavinasab, E., Zarifsanaiey, N., & Niakan Kalhori, S., Rakhshan, M., Keikha, L., & Ghazi Saeedi, M. (2021). Intelligent tutoring systems: A systematic review of characteristics, applications, and evaluation methods. *Interactive Learning Environments, 29*(1), 142–163. doi:10.1080/10494820.2018.1558257

Murad, D. F., Iskandar, A. G., Fernando, E., Octavia, T. S., & Maured, D. E. (2019). Towards smart LMS to improve learning outcomes students using LenoBot with natural language processing. *2019 6th International Conference on Information Technology, Computer and Electrical Engineering, ICITACEE 2019*. 10.1109/ICITACEE.2019.8904311

Murati, R. (2015). Conception and Definition of the Democratization of Education. *Journal of Education and Practice, 6*(30), 173–183. https://files.eric.ed.gov/fulltext/EJ1081375.pdf

Murtarelli, G., Gregory, A., & Romenti, S. (2021). A conversation-based perspective for shaping ethical human–machine interactions: The particular challenge of chatbots. *Journal of Business Research, 129*, 927–935. Advance online publication. doi:10.1016/j.jbusres.2020.09.018

Mustafa Kamal, N. N., Mohd Adnan, A. H., Yusof, A. A., Ahmad, M. K., & Mohd Kamal, M. A. (2019). Immersive interactive educational experiences–adopting Education 5.0, Industry 4.0 learning technologies for Malaysian Universities. In *Proceedings of the International Invention, Innovative & Creative (InIIC) Conference, Series* (pp. 190-196). Academic Press.

Nader, K., Toprac, P., Scott, S., & Baker, S. (2022). Public understanding of artificial intelligence through entertainment media. *AI & Society*, 1–14. PMID:35400854

Najbrt, L., & Kapounova, J. (2015). Personalized Guide through Educational Exhibition: Fuzzy Expert System as Museum Exhibition "Virtual Guide". *Journal of Education and Human Development, 4*(1), 159–170. doi:10.15640/jehd.v4n1a15

Nathan, M. J., Koedinger, K. R., & Tabachneck, H. J. M. (2000). Teachers' and researchers' beliefs of early algebra development. *Journal of Mathematics Education Research, 31*(2), 168–190. doi:10.2307/749750

National Council for the Social Studies Curriculum Standards Task Force. (1994). *Expectations of excellence: Curriculum standards for social studies (Bulletin 89)*. National Council for the Social Studies.

Neumann, M., Rauschenberger, M., & Schön, E. M. (2023). "We Need To Talk About ChatGPT": The Future of AI and Higher Education. In *2023 IEEE/ACM 5th International Workshop on Software Engineering Education for the Next Generation (SEENG)* (pp. 29-32). IEEE.

Ng, D. T. K., Leung, J. K. L., Chu, S. K. W., & Qiao, M. S. (2021). Conceptualizing AI literacy: An exploratory review. *Computers and Education: Artificial Intelligence, 2*, 100041. doi:10.1016/j.caeai.2021.100041

Nichols, R. (2022). The cultural evolution of Chinese morality, and the essential value of multidisciplinary research in understanding it. In The Routledge International Handbook of Morality, Cognition, and Emotion in China (pp. 19-37). Routledge. doi:10.4324/9781003281566-3

Nilson, L. (2016). *Teaching at its best: A research-based resource for college instructors*. Jossey Bass.

Nordhaus, W. (2019). Climate change: The ultimate challenge for economics. *The American Economic Review*, *109*(6), 1991–2014. doi:10.1257/aer.109.6.1991

Novelli, C., Taddeo, M., & Floridi, L. (2023). Accountability in artificial intelligence: What it is and how it works. *AI & Society*, 1–12. doi:10.1007/s00146-023-01635-y

Nur Azizah, N., & Tira Erlangga, D. (2023). The effectiveness of quillbot in developing students' literation. *Pustakailmu.Id, 3*(1).

Nurmayanti, N., & Suryadi, S. (2023). The Effectiveness Of Using Quillbot In Improving Writing For Students Of English Education Study Program. *Jurnal Teknologi Pendidikan : Jurnal Penelitian Dan Pengembangan Pembelajaran*, *8*(1), 32. Advance online publication. doi:10.33394/jtp.v8i1.6392

Nuruzzaman, M., & Hussain, O. K. (2020). IntelliBot: A Dialogue-based chatbot for the insurance industry. *Knowledge-Based Systems*, *196*, 105810. Advance online publication. doi:10.1016/j.knosys.2020.105810

O'Brien, C. (2023). 8 Universities Leveraging AI to Drive Student Success. Digital Marketing Institute. https://digitalmarketinginstitute.com/blog/8-universities-leveraging-ai-to-drive-student-success

O'Connor, E. A., & Worman, T. (2019). Designing for interactivity, while scaffolding student entry, within immersive virtual reality environments. *Journal of Educational Technology Systems*, *47*(3), 292–317. doi:10.1177/0047239518817545

Oblinger, D. G., & Oblinger, J. L. (2005). *Educating the Net Generation*. EDUCAUSE.

Oda Abunamous, M., Boudouaia, A., Jebril, M., Diafi, S., & Zreik, M. (2022). The decay of traditional education: A case study under covid-19. *Cogent Education*, *9*(1), 2082116. Advance online publication. doi:10.1080/2331186X.2022.2082116

Odyssey Visual Media. (2019) *Abu Simbel Egypt Virtual Tour | VR 360° Travel Experience* Youtube. https://www.youtube.com/watch?v=_4kBntxPUic&t=2s

OECD. (2016). *Innovating Education and Educating for Innovation: The Power of Digital Technologies and Skills*. OECD Publishing. doi:10.1787/9789264265097-

Open, A. I. (2022, November 30). Introducing ChatGPT. https://openai.com/blog/chatgpt

Ouatu, B. I., & Gifu, D. (2021). Chatbot, the future of learning? *Smart Innovation. Systems and Technologies*, *197*, 263–268. Advance online publication. doi:10.1007/978-981-15-7383-5_23

Ouyang, F., & Jiao, P. (2021). Artificial intelligence in education: The three paradigms. *Computers and Education: Artificial Intelligence*, *2*, 100020. Advance online publication. doi:10.1016/j.caeai.2021.100020

Owe, A., & Baum, S. D. (2021). Moral consideration of nonhumans in the ethics of artificial intelligence. *AI and Ethics*, *1*(4), 517–528. doi:10.1007/s43681-021-00065-0

Owoc, M. L., Sawicka, A., & Weichbroth, P. (2021). Artificial Intelligence Technologies in Education: Benefits, Challenges and Strategies of Implementation. In M. L. Owoc & M. Pondel (Eds.), *Artificial Intelligence for Knowledge Management.* Springer. doi:10.1007/978-3-030-85001-2_4

Page, L., & Gehlbach, H. (2018, January 16). How Georgia State University Used an Algorithm to Help Students Navigate the Road to College. *Harward Business Review*. https://hbr.org/2018/01/how-georgia-state-university-used-an-algorithm-to-help-students-navigate-the-road-to-college

Pahl, R. H. (1996). Digital technology and social studies. In B. G. Massialas & R. F. Allen (Eds.), *Crucial Issues in teaching social studies K– 12* (pp. 341–386). Wadsworth.

Pakdaman, M., Moghadam, M. N., Dehghan, H. R., Dehghani, A., & Namayandeh, M. (2019). Evaluation of the cost-effectiveness of virtual and traditional education models in higher education: A systematic review. *Health Technology Assessment in Action*, 1-14.

Palomares, I., Martínez-Cámara, E., Montes, R., García-Moral, P., Chiachio, M., Chiachio, J., Alonso, S., Melero, F. J., Molina, D., Fernández, B., Moral, C., Marchena, R., de Vargas, J. P., & Herrera, F. (2021). A panoramic view and swot analysis of artificial intelligence for achieving the sustainable development goals by 2030: Progress and prospects. *Applied Intelligence*, *51*(9), 6497–6527. doi:10.1007/s10489-021-02264-y PMID:34764606

Pare, S. K. (2023). Outcome-based Education: Calculating Attainment of Programme Outcome through Course Outcome. *Universities Handbook–34th Edition, 61*, 60.

Park, E. L., & Choi, B. K. (2014). Transformation of classroom spaces: Traditional versus active learning classroom in colleges. *Higher Education*, *68*(5), 749–771. doi:10.1007/s10734-014-9742-0

Paul, A., Thilagham, K., KG, J., Reddy, P. R., Sathyamurthy, R., & Boopathi, S. (2024). Multi-criteria Optimization on Friction Stir Welding of Aluminum Composite (AA5052-H32/B4C) using Titanium Nitride Coated Tool. Engineering Research Express.

Pelletier, K., Robert, J., Muscanell, N., McCormack, M., Reeves, J., Arbino, N., . . . Zimmern, J. (2023). 2023 EDUCAUSE Horizon Report, Teaching and Learning Edition. EDUCAUSE. Erişim adresi: https://library.educause.edu/-/media/files/library/2023/4/2023hrteachinglearning.pdf?#page=18

Pérez, J. Q., Daradoumis, T., & Puig, J. M. M. (2020). Rediscovering the use of chatbots in education: A systematic literature review. In Computer Applications in Engineering Education (Vol. 28, Issue 6). doi:10.1002/cae.22326

Perkin, H. (2007). History of Universities. In J. J. F. Forest & P. G. Altbach (Eds.), *International Handbook of Higher Education. Springer International Handbooks of Education* (Vol. 18). Springer. doi:10.1007/978-1-4020-4012-2_10

Peters, M. A., Jackson, L., Papastephanou, M., Jandrić, P., Lazaroiu, G., Evers, C. W., Cope, B., Kalantzis, M., Araya, D., Tesar, M., Mika, C., Chen, L., Wang, C., Sturm, S., Rider, S., & Fuller, S. (2023). AI and the future of humanity: ChatGPT-4, philosophy and education–Critical responses. *Educational Philosophy and Theory*, 1–35. doi:10.1080/00131857.2023.2213437

Poornima, S. N. (2019). Outcome based education, need for the hour-NBA. *Int. J. Adv. Res. Ideas Innov. Technol*, *5*(2), 1030–1033.

Popenici, S. (2023). The critique of AI as a foundation for judicious use in higher education. *Journal of Applied Learning and Teaching*, *6*(2), 1–12.

Popenici, S. A., & Kerr, S. (2017). Exploring the impact of artificial intelligence on teaching and learning in higher education. *Research and Practice in Technology Enhanced Learning*, *12*(1), 22. doi:10.1186/s41039-017-0062-8 PMID:30595727

Postman, N. (2000). Will our children only inherit the wind? *Theory and Research in Social Education*, *28*(4), 580–586. doi:10.1080/00933104.2000.10505925

Prabhuswamy, M., Tripathi, R., Vijayakumar, M., Thulasimani, T., Sundharesalingam, P., & Sampath, B. (2024). A Study on the Complex Nature of Higher Education Leadership: An Innovative Approach. In *Challenges of Globalization and Inclusivity in Academic Research* (pp. 202–223). IGI Global. doi:10.4018/979-8-3693-1371-8.ch013

Prasad, G., & Bhar, C. (2010). Accreditation system for technical education programmes in India: A critical review. *European Journal of Engineering Education*, *35*(2), 187–213. doi:10.1080/03043790903497294

Prem, E. (2023). From ethical AI frameworks to tools: A review of approaches. *AI and Ethics*, *3*(3), 1–18. doi:10.1007/s43681-023-00258-9

Pretorius, A. (2023). A Pedagogy to Support Learning Analytics: A Case for a Specific Higher Education Institution. In *Handbook of Research on AI and Machine Learning Applications in Customer Support and Analytics* (pp. 56–79). IGI Global. doi:10.4018/978-1-6684-7105-0.ch004

ProFuturo y OEI (2023). *El futuro de la Inteligencia Artificial en educación en América Latina*. Academic Press.

Provenzo, E. F., & Renaud, J. P. (Eds.). (2009). *Encyclopedia of the Social and Cultural Foundations of Education* (Vol. 1-3). Sage. doi:10.4135/9781412963992

Puig, A., Rodríguez, I., Arcos, J. L., Rodríguez-Aguilar, J. A., Cebrián, S., Bogdanovych, A., Morera, N., Palomo, A., & Piqué, R. (2020). Lessons learned from supplementing archaeological museum exhibitions with virtual reality. *Virtual Reality (Waltham Cross)*, *24*(2), 343–358. doi:10.1007/s10055-019-00391-z

Qiao-Franco, G., & Bode, I. (2023). Weaponised artificial intelligence and Chinese practices of human–machine interaction. *The Chinese Journal of International Politics*, *16*(1), 106–128. doi:10.1093/cjip/poac024

Qi, B., Wang, X., & Sutton, P. (2021). Can Nighttime Satellite Imagery Inform Our Understanding of Education Inequality? *Remote Sensing (Basel)*, *13*(5), 843. doi:10.3390/rs13050843

Quiroz-Fabra, J., Valencia-Arias, A., Londoño-Celis, W., & García-Pineda, V. (2022). Technological tools for knowledge apprehension and promotion in the cultural and heritage tourism sector: Systematic literature review. *Human Behavior and Emerging Technologies*, *2022*, 1–12. doi:10.1155/2022/2851044

Rahman, M. M., & Watanobe, Y. (2023). ChatGPT for education and research: Opportunities, threats, and strategies. *Applied Sciences (Basel, Switzerland)*, *13*(9), 5783. doi:10.3390/app13095783

RaneN.ChoudharyS.RaneJ. (2023). Education 4.0 and 5.0: Integrating Artificial Intelligence (AI) for personalized and adaptive learning. *Available at* SSRN 4638365. doi:10.2139/ssrn.4638365

Rangel-de Lázaro, G., & Duart, J. M. (2023). You Can Handle, You Can Teach It: Systematic Review on the Use of Extended Reality and Artificial Intelligence Technologies for Online Higher Education. *Sustainability (Basel)*, *15*(4), 3507. Advance online publication. doi:10.3390/su15043507

Ranoliya, B. R., Raghuwanshi, N., & Singh, S. (2017). Chatbot for university related FAQs. *2017 International Conference on Advances in Computing, Communications and Informatics, ICACCI 2017, 2017-January*. 10.1109/ICACCI.2017.8126057

Rashid, N. A., Lim, L. W., Eng, O. S., Ping, T. H., Zainol, Z., & Majid, O. (2016). A framework of an automatic assessment system for learning programming. *Advanced Computer and Communication Engineering Technology Proceedings of ICOCOE, 2015*, 967–977.

Rashid, S., Fayez, O., Ismail, H., & Khan, R. F. (2021). Digital social support for undergraduate students during COVID-19: Pivotal support for the digital transformation. *Journal of Public Health Research*, *10*(4), jphr.2021.2148. Advance online publication. doi:10.4081/jphr.2021.2148 PMID:34278768

Raza, A., & Sohaib Murad, H. (2008). Knowledge democracy and the implications to information access. *Multicultural Education & Technology Journal*, *2*(1), 37–46. doi:10.1108/17504970810867142

Reddy, M. A., Reddy, B. M., Mukund, C., Venneti, K., Preethi, D., & Boopathi, S. (2023). Social Health Protection During the COVID-Pandemic Using IoT. In *The COVID-19 Pandemic and the Digitalization of Diplomacy* (pp. 204–235). IGI Global. doi:10.4018/978-1-7998-8394-4.ch009

Reinhart, R. J. (2018). *Most Americans already using artificial intelligence products*. https://perma.cc/RVY5-WP9WS

Rejeb, A., Rejeb, K., Appolloni, A., Treiblmaier, H., & Iranmanesh, M. (2024). Exploring the impact of ChatGPT on education: A web mining and machine learning approach. *International Journal of Management Education*, *22*(1), 100932. doi:10.1016/j.ijme.2024.100932

Revathi, S., Babu, M., Rajkumar, N., Meti, V. K. V., Kandavalli, S. R., & Boopathi, S. (2024). Unleashing the Future Potential of 4D Printing: Exploring Applications in Wearable Technology, Robotics, Energy, Transportation, and Fashion. In Human-Centered Approaches in Industry 5.0: Human-Machine Interaction, Virtual Reality Training, and Customer Sentiment Analysis (pp. 131–153). IGI Global.

Rhoades, G. (1991). Graduate Education. In International Higher Education Volume 1: An Encyclopedia (1st ed.). Routledge. doi:10.4324/9780203802748

Riege, A. (2005). Three-dozen knowledge-sharing barriers managers must consider. *Journal of Knowledge Management*, *9*(3), 18–35. doi:10.1108/13673270510602746

Risinger, C. F. (2002). Technology, the social studies, an educational change. *The International Social Studies Forum, 2*(2), 187–190.

Risinger, C. F. (1996). Webbing the social studies: Using Internet and World Wide Web resources in social studies instruction. *Social Education*, *60*(2), 111–112.

Roll, I., & Wylie, R. (2016). Evolution and revolution in artificial intelligence in education. *International Journal of Artificial Intelligence in Education*, *26*(2), 582–599. doi:10.1007/s40593-016-0110-3

Rose, S. A., & Fernlund, P. M. (1997). Using technology for powerful social studies learning. *Social Education*, *61*(3), 160–166.

Rose, S. A., & Winterfeldt, H. F. (1998). Waking the sleeping giant: A learning community in social studies methods and technology. *Social Education*, *62*(3), 151–152.

Rospigliosi, P. (2023). Artificial intelligence in teaching and learning: What questions should we ask of ChatGPT? *Interactive Learning Environments*, *31*(1), 1–3. doi:10.1080/10494820.2023.2180191

Rudak, L. (2013). Spot-The-Difference–Traditional Education Vs. E-Education. Use of E-learning in the Training of Professionals in the Knowledge Society. STUDIO NOA, Cieszyn–Katowice.

Rudolph, J., Tan, S., & Tan, S. (2023). War of the chatbots: Bard, Bing Chat, ChatGPT, Ernie and beyond. The new AI gold rush and its impact on higher education. *Journal of Applied Learning and Teaching*, *6*(1). Advance online publication. doi:10.37074/jalt.2023.6.1.23

Sabzalieva, E., & Valentini, A. (2023). ChatGPT and artificial intelligence in higher education: quick start guide. https://www.ucd.ie/artshumanities/t4media/ChatGPT-and-Artificial-Intelligence-in-higher-education-Quick-Start-guide_EN_FINAL.pdf

Saha, G. C., Akber, S., & Roy, A. (2023a). Impact of Outcome-Based Education (OBE) on Learners' Performance in Business Courses. *International Journal of Professional Business Review: Int. J. Prof. Bus. Rev., 8*(8), 6.

Sah, G. K., Gupta, D. K., & Yadav, A. P. (2024). Analysis of ChatGPT and the future of artificial intelligence: Its effect on teaching and learning. *Journal of AI. Robotics & Workplace Automation, 3*(1), 64–80.

Saif, N., Khan, S. U., Shaheen, I., ALotaibi, F. A., Alnfiai, M. M., & Arif, M. (2024). Chat-GPT; validating Technology Acceptance Model (TAM) in education sector via ubiquitous learning mechanism. *Computers in Human Behavior, 154*, 108097. Advance online publication. doi:10.1016/j.chb.2023.108097

Salas-Pilco, S. Z., & Yang, Y. (2022). Artificial intelligence applications in Latin American higher education: a systematic review. In International Journal of Educational Technology in Higher Education (Vol. 19, Issue 1). doi:10.1186/s41239-022-00326-w

Samuel, J. (2023). *Response to the March 2023'Pause Giant AI Experiments: An Open Letter by Yoshua Bengio, signed by Stuart Russell, Elon Musk, Steve Wozniak, Yuval Noah Harari and others*. Academic Press.

Saravanan, A., Venkatasubramanian, R., Khare, R., Surakasi, R., Boopathi, S., Ray, S., & Sudhakar, M. (2022). Policy trends of renewable energy and non. *Renewable Energy*.

Sarıhan, A., Oray, N. C., Güllüpınar, B., Yanturali, S., Atilla, R., & Musal, B. (2016). The comparison of the efficiency of traditional lectures to video-supported lectures within the training of the Emergency Medicine residents. *Turkish Journal of Emergency Medicine, 16*(3), 107–111. doi:10.1016/j.tjem.2016.07.002 PMID:27857987

Saunders, G. (2000). *Getting Started with On-line Learning*. Winchcombe: Learning Partners.

Saunders, G., & Klemming, F. (2003). Integrating technology into a traditional learning environment: Reasons for and risks of success. *Active Learning in Higher Education, 4*(1), 74–86. doi:10.1177/1469787403004001006

Sawant, P. (2016). Implementation of outcome based education: A beginning. *Journal of Engineering Education Transformations, 7*(5), 10–16920. doi:10.16920/jeet/2016/v0i0/85643

Saye, J. W. (1998). Creating time to develop student thinking: Team teaching with technology. *Social Education, 62*(6), 356–362.

Saye, J. W., & Brush, T. (1999). Student engagement with social issues in a multimedia-supported learning environment. *Theory and Research in Social Education, 27*(4), 472–504. doi:10.1080/00933104.1999.10505891

Schiff, D. (2021). Out of the laboratory and into the classroom: The future of artificial intelligence in education. *AI & Society, 36*(1), 331–348. doi:10.1007/s00146-020-01033-8 PMID:32836908

Schuitema, J., Peetsma, T., & van der Veen, I. (2012). Self-regulated learning and students' perceptions of innovative and traditional learning environments: A longitudinal study in secondary education. *Educational Studies, 38*(4), 397–413. doi:10.1080/03055698.2011.643105

Sembor, E. C. (1997). Citizenship, diversity, and distance learning: Video conferencing in Connecticut. *Social Education, 61*(3), 154–159.

Shah, P. (2023). *Embracing AI in Education.* John Wiley & Sons.

Sharma, D. M., Ramana, K. V., Jothilakshmi, R., Verma, R., Maheswari, B. U., & Boopathi, S. (2024). Integrating Generative AI Into K-12 Curriculums and Pedagogies in India: Opportunities and Challenges. *Facilitating Global Collaboration and Knowledge Sharing in Higher Education With Generative AI*, 133–161.

Shaver, J. P. (1999). Electronic technology and the future of social studies in elementary and secondary schools. *Journal of Education, 181*(3), 13–41. doi:10.1177/002205749918100303

Shaw, C., Yuan, L., Brennan, D., Martin, S., Janson, N., Fox, K., & Bryant, G. (2023). *Generative AI in Higher Education: Fall 2023 Update of Time for Class Study.* Tyton Partners. https://tytonpartners.com/time-for-class-2023/GenAI-Update

Shawar, B. A., & Atwell, E. S. (2005). Using corpora in machine-learning chatbot systems. *International Journal of Corpus Linguistics, 10*(4), 489–516. Advance online publication. doi:10.1075/ijcl.10.4.06sha

Shaw, J., Rudzicz, F., Jamieson, T., & Goldfarb, A. (2019). Artificial intelligence and the implementation challenge. *Journal of Medical Internet Research, 21*(7), e13659. doi:10.2196/13659 PMID:31293245

Shelle, G., Earnesty, D., Pilkenton, A., & Powell, E. (2018). Adaptive learning: An innovative method for online teaching and learning. *Journal of Extension, 56*(5), 17. doi:10.34068/joe.56.05.17

Shi, J., Cai, L. A., & Wolfe, K. (2022). Advancing hospitality and tourism education and research through global crises. *Journal of Teaching in Travel & Tourism, 22*(3), 199–204. doi:10.1080/15313220.2022.2110550

Siemens, G. (2005). Connectivism: A learning theory for the digital age. *International Journal of Instructional Technology and Distance Learning*, 2(1), 3–10.

Siemens, G., & Long, P. (2011). Penetrating the fog: Analytics in learning and education. *EDUCAUSE Review, 46*(5), 30–32.

Singh Madan, B., Logeswaran, S., Veerapathran, M., Rai, P., Kumar Singh, S., & B., S. (2024). Engineered Cementitious Composites (ECC) Through Nano-Composite Integration: Enhancing Construction. In *Advances in Chemical and Materials Engineering* (pp. 210–243). IGI Global. doi:10.4018/978-1-6684-8182-0.ch008

Singh, S., & Thakur, H. K. (2020). Survey of Various AI Chatbots Based on Technology Used. *ICRITO 2020 - IEEE 8th International Conference on Reliability, Infocom Technologies and Optimization (Trends and Future Directions)*. 10.1109/ICRITO48877.2020.9197943

Skavronskaya, L., Hadinejad, A., & Cotterell, D. (2023). Reversing the threat of artificial intelligence to opportunity: A discussion of ChatGPT in tourism education. *Journal of Teaching in Travel & Tourism*, *23*(2), 253–258. doi:10.1080/15313220.2023.2196658

Smith, A., Hachen, S., Schleifer, R., Bhugra, D., Buadze, A., & Liebrenz, M. (2023). Old dog, new tricks? Exploring the potential functionalities of ChatGPT in supporting educational methods in social psychiatry. *The International Journal of Social Psychiatry*, *69*(8), 1882–1889. doi:10.1177/00207640231178451 PMID:37392000

Smith, H. (2021). Clinical AI: Opacity, accountability, responsibility and liability. *AI & Society*, *36*(2), 535–545. doi:10.1007/s00146-020-01019-6

Snipes, S. (2023). Transforming Education With AI: Guide to Understanding and Using ChatGPT in the Classroom. Ai4 Press.

Soliman, M. (2022). Pedagogical Intelligence in Virtual Reality Environments. In *Learning with Technologies and Technologies in Learning: Experience, Trends and Challenges in Higher Education* (pp. 285–302). Springer International Publishing. doi:10.1007/978-3-031-04286-7_14

Songkram, N., Chootongchai, S., Khlaisang, J., & Koraneekij, P. (2021). Education 3.0 system to enhance twenty-first century skills for higher education learners in Thailand. *Interactive Learning Environments*, *29*(4), 566–582. doi:10.1080/10494820.2019.1592197

Sonia, R., Gupta, N., Manikandan, K., Hemalatha, R., Kumar, M. J., & Boopathi, S. (2024). Strengthening Security, Privacy, and Trust in Artificial Intelligence Drones for Smart Cities. In *Analyzing and Mitigating Security Risks in Cloud Computing* (pp. 214–242). IGI Global. doi:10.4018/979-8-3693-3249-8.ch011

Southworth, J., Migliaccio, K., Glover, J., Glover, J. N., Reed, D., McCarty, C., Brendemuhl, J., & Thomas, A. (2023). Developing a model for AI Across the curriculum: Transforming the higher education landscape via innovation in AI literacy. *Computers and Education: Artificial Intelligence*, *4*, 100127. doi:10.1016/j.caeai.2023.100127

Sreedhar, P. S. S., Sujay, V., Rani, M. R., Melita, L., Reshma, S., & Boopathi, S. (2024). Impacts of 5G Machine Learning Techniques on Telemedicine and Social Media Professional Connection in Healthcare. In Advances in Medical Technologies and Clinical Practice (pp. 209–234). IGI Global. doi:10.4018/979-8-3693-1934-5.ch012

Steinbauer, G., Kandlhofer, M., Chklovski, T., Heintz, F., & Koenig, S. (2021). A differentiated discussion about AI education K-12. *Kunstliche Intelligenz*, *35*(2), 131–137. doi:10.1007/s13218-021-00724-8 PMID:34007103

Stewart, J., & Gorman, C. (2024). Authentic Assessment and Embedding Sustainable Literacy and Technology Skills in Tourism Education. *Irish Journal of Academic Practice*, *11*(2). https://arrow.tudublin.ie/ijap/vol11/iss2/10

Stoll, C. (1999). *High-tech heretic*. Doubleday.

Strielkowski, W., Korneeva, E., & Gorina, L. (2022). Sustainable development and the digital transformation of educational systems. *Intelektinė ekonomika, 16*(1), 134-150. doi:10.1016/S0883-0355(99)00012-9

Su, J., Zhong, Y., & Ng, D. T. K. (2022). A meta-review of literature on educational approaches for teaching at the K -12 levels in the Asia-Pacific region. *Computer and Education: Artificial Intelligence*, *3*, 100065. doi:10.1016/j.caeai.2022.100065

Suthers, D., Connelly, J., Lesgold, A., Paolucci, M., Erdosne, E., Toth, J., & Weiner, A. (2001). Representational and advisory guidance for students learning scientific inquiry. In K. D. Forbus & P. J. Feltovich (Eds.), *Smart machines in education* (pp. 7–35). American Association for Artificial Intelligence.

Sweeney, P. (2022). Trusting social robots. *AI and Ethics*, 1–8. PMID:35634257

Tangonyire, R., & Mayaki, B. (2024). Social Media and its Democratizing Impact on Africa's Education: A Critique. *Chiedza. Journal of Arrupe Jesuit University*, *25*(1), 22–34.

Tian, X., Risha, Z., Ahmed, I., Lekshmi Narayanan, A. B., & Biehl, J. (2021). Let's Talk It Out. *Proceedings of the ACM on Human-Computer Interaction, 5*(CSCW1). 10.1145/3449171

Tirlangi, S., Teotia, S., Padmapriya, G., Senthil Kumar, S., Dhotre, S., & Boopathi, S. (2024). Cloud Computing and Machine Learning in the Green Power Sector: Data Management and Analysis for Sustainable Energy. In Developments Towards Next Generation Intelligent Systems for Sustainable Development (pp. 148–179). IGI Global. doi:10.4018/979-8-3693-5643-2.ch006

Tiwari, C. K., Bhat, M. A., Khan, S. T., Subramaniam, R., & Khan, M. A. I. (2023). What drives students toward ChatGPT? An investigation of the factors influencing adoption and usage of ChatGPT. Interactive Technology and Smart Education. doi:10.1108/ITSE-04-2023-0061

Tlili, A., Shehata, B., Adarkwah, M. A., Bozkurt, A., Hickey, D. T., Huang, R., & Agyemang, B. (2023). What if the devil is my guardian angel: ChatGPT as a case study of using chatbots in education. *Smart Learning Environments*, *10*(1), 15. doi:10.1186/s40561-023-00237-x

Todorov, J., Valkanov, V., Stoyanov, S., Daskalov, B., Popchev, I., & Orozova, D. (2018). Personal assistants in a virtual education space. *Practical issues of intelligent innovations*, 131-153.

Togola, A., Ahmed, S., & Jadaan, T. (2019). Barriers of knowledge transfer between globally distributed teams in ICT product development. *Proceedings of the 52nd Hawaii International Conference on System Sciences.* 5568-5577. 10.24251/HICSS.2019.670

Tolkach, D., & Pratt, S. (2021). Travel Professors: A YouTube channel about tourism education & research. *Journal of Hospitality, Leisure, Sport and Tourism Education, 28*, 100307. Advance online publication. doi:10.1016/j.jhlste.2021.100307 PMID:36569348

Tong, M. S., Zheng, H. Q., & Wan, G. C. (2019). Improvement of Education Method by Using Artificial Intelligence Technology. In *2019 IEEE International Conference on Engineering, Technology and Education (TALE)* (pp. 1-5). IEEE. 10.1109/TALE48000.2019.9225891

Tóth, Z., Caruana, R., Gruber, T., & Loebbecke, C. (2022). The dawn of the AI robots: Towards a new framework of AI robot accountability. *Journal of Business Ethics, 178*(4), 895–916. doi:10.1007/s10551-022-05050-z

Tran, T. N., & Tran, H. P. (2023, November). Exploring the role of ChatGPT in developing critical digital literacies in language learning: a qualitative study. *Proceedings of the AsiaCALL International Conference, 4*, 1-17. 10.54855/paic.2341

Tuo, Y., Ning, L., & Zhu, A. (2021). How artificial intelligence will change the future of tourism industry: The practice in China. In *Information and Communication Technologies in Tourism 2021: Proceedings of the ENTER 2021 eTourism Conference, January 19–22, 2021* (pp. 83-94). Springer International Publishing.

Tuomi, I. (2020). The Impact of Artificial Intelligence on Learning, Teaching, and Education. Policies for the future. *European Union.*

Ülkü, A. (2023). Artificial intelligence-based large language models and integrity of exams and assignments in higher education: The case of tourism courses. *Tourism & Management Studies, 19*(4), 21–34. doi:10.18089/tms.2023.190402

UNESCO. (2020). *La ciudadanía digital como política pública en educación en América Latina.* Oficina Regional de Ciencias para América Latina y el Caribe.

UNESCO. (2023). *Global Education Monitoring Report 2023: Technology in education – A tool on whose terms?* UNESCO. doi:10.54676/UZQV8501

Upadhyaya, A. N., Saqib, A., Devi, J. V., Rallapalli, S., Sudha, S., & Boopathi, S. (2024). Implementation of the Internet of Things (IoT) in Remote Healthcare. In Advances in Medical Technologies and Clinical Practice (pp. 104–124). IGI Global. doi:10.4018/979-8-3693-1934-5.ch006

Upadhyaya, G. (2021). Effective Implementation of Outcome-based Education: The Role of Faculty Awareness. *Indonesian Journal Of Educational Research and Review*, 380–391.

Van Doren, C. (2022). *Breve Historia del Saber.* Booket Paidós.

Van, N. T., Irum, S., Abbas, A. F., Sikandar, H., & Khan, N. (2022). Online Learning—Two Side Arguments Related to Mental Health. *International Journal of Online & Biomedical Engineering, 18*(9), 131–143. Advance online publication. doi:10.3991/ijoe.v18i09.32317

Vasconcelos, M. A. R., & dos Santos, R. P. (2023). Enhancing STEM learning with ChatGPT and Bing Chat as objects to think with: A case study. *Eurasia Journal of Mathematics, Science and Technology Education, 19*(7), em2296. Advance online publication. doi:10.29333/ejmste/13313

Vasudevan, N. (2020). Development of a common framework for outcome based accreditation and rankings. *Procedia Computer Science, 172*, 270–276. doi:10.1016/j.procs.2020.05.043

Vázquez-Cano, E., Mengual-Andrés, S., & López-Meneses, E. (2021). Chatbot to improve learning punctuation in Spanish and to enhance open and flexible learning environments. *International Journal of Educational Technology in Higher Education, 18*(1), 33. Advance online publication. doi:10.1186/s41239-021-00269-8

Venkatasubramanian, V., Chitra, M., Sudha, R., Singh, V. P., Jefferson, K., & Boopathi, S. (2024). Examining the Impacts of Course Outcome Analysis in Indian Higher Education: Enhancing Educational Quality. In Challenges of Globalization and Inclusivity in Academic Research (pp. 124–145). IGI Global.

Venkatesh, K., & King, C. S. (2021). Challenges and Issues in Implementation of OBE. *Assessment Tools for Mapping Learning Outcomes With Learning Objectives*, 83–96.

Vincent-Lancrin, S., & Van der Vlies, R. (2020). *Trustworthy artificial intelligence (AI) in education: Promises and challenges.* Academic Press.

Visvizi, A. (2021). Artificial intelligence (AI): Explaining, querying, demystifying. *Artificial Intelligence and Its Contexts: Security, Business and Governance*, 13-26.

Viswanadhan, K., & Rao, N. (2005). Effectiveness of NBA accreditation processes. *National Symposium on Engineering Education (NSEE05)*, 100–108.

Vivar, J. M. F., & Peñalvo, F. J. G. (2023). Reflexiones sobre la ética, potencialidades y retos de la Inteligencia Artificial en el marco de la Educación de Calidad (ODS4). *Comunicar: Revista científica iberoamericana de comunicación y educación*, (74), 37-47.

Wachtel, G., Schmöcker, J. D., Hadas, Y., Gao, Y., Nahum, O. E., & Ben-Moshe, B. (2021). Planning for tourist urban evacuation routes: A framework for improving the data collection and evacuation processes. *Environment and Planning. B, Urban Analytics and City Science, 48*(5), 1108–1125. doi:10.1177/2399808321994575

Wagman, M. (1997). *Cognitive science and the symbolic operations of human and artificial intelligence: theory and research into the intellective processes.* Praeger Publishers.

Walczak, K., & Cellary, W. (2023). Challenges for higher education in the era of widespread access to Generative AI. *Economics and Business Review, 9*(2), 71–100. doi:10.18559/ebr.2023.2.743

Wang, T., Lund, B. D., Marengo, A., Pagano, A., Mannuru, N. R., Teel, Z. A., & Pange, J. (2023). Exploring the potential impact of artificial intelligence (AI) on international students in higher education: Generative AI, chatbots, analytics, and international student success. *Applied Sciences (Basel, Switzerland), 13*(11), 6716. Advance online publication. doi:10.3390/app13116716

Welty, W. M. (1989). Discussion Method Teaching. *Change, 21*(July/August), 40–49. doi:10.1080/00091383.1989.9939866

Weng, Z., Tang, J., & Liu, K. (2021, October). The Impact of Free Preschool Education on Educational Inequality in China. In *2021 6th International Conference on Modern Management and Education Technology (MMET 2021)* (pp. 462-472). Atlantis Press. 10.2991/assehr.k.211011.085

White, C. S. (1997a). Information technology in U.S. social studies classrooms: Potentials and realities. Washington DC: Office of Educational Research and Improvement. (ERIC Document Reproduction Service No. ED 421 415)

White, C. S. (1997b). Technology and social studies: An introduction. *Social Education, 61*(3), 147–148.

Whitworth, S. A., & Berson, M. J. (2003). Computer technology in the social studies: An examination of the effectiveness literature (1996– 2001). *Contemporary Issues in Technology & Teacher Education, 2*(4). http://www.citejournal.org/vol2/iss4/socialstudies/ article1.cfm

Whitworth, S. A., Owings Swan, K., & Berson, M. J. (2002). Handheld computing in the social studies. *Social Education, 66*(3), 174–179.

Wieser, M., Schöffmann, K., Stefanics, D., Bollin, A., & Pasterk, S. (2023, October). Investigating the Role of ChatGPT in Supporting Text-Based Programming Education for Students and Teachers. In *International Conference on Informatics in Schools: Situation, Evolution, and Perspectives* (pp. 40-53). Cham: Springer Nature Switzerland. 10.1007/978-3-031-44900-0_4

Wikipedia. (2024). ChatGPT. Available at: https://en.wikipedia.org/wiki/ChatGPT

Wiley, D. (2017). What is open pedagogy? In E. Mays (Ed.), *A Guide to Making Open Textbooks with Students* (pp. 9–16). Rebus Community.

Woltering, V., Herrler, A., Spitzer, K., & Spreckelsen, C. (2009). Blended learning positively affects students' satisfaction and the role of the tutor in the problem-based learning process: Results of a mixed-method evaluation. *Advances in Health Sciences Education : Theory and Practice, 14*(5), 725–738. doi:10.1007/s10459-009-9154-6 PMID:19184497

World Bank. (2023, October 11). Education overview. https://www.worldbank.org/en/topic/education/overview

Wu, R., & Yu, Z. (2023). Do AI chatbots improve students learning outcomes? Evidence from a meta-analysis. *British Journal of Educational Technology*, 1–24. doi:10.1111/bjet.13334

Xu, W., & Ouyang, F. (2022). The application of AI technologies in STEM education: a systematic review from 2011 to 2021. In International Journal of STEM Education (Vol. 9, Issue 1). doi:10.1186/s40594-022-00377-5

Xu, J., Tavitiyaman, P., Kim, H. J., & Lo, S. K. J. (2022). Hospitality and tourism higher education in the post-COVID era: Is it time to change? *Journal of Hospitality & Tourism Education, 34*(4), 278–290. doi:10.1080/10963758.2022.2056044

Xu, X., Su, Y., Zhang, Y., Wu, Y., & Xu, X. (2024). Understanding learners' perceptions of ChatGPT: A thematic analysis of peer interviews among undergraduates and postgraduates in China. *Heliyon*, *10*(4), 1–13. doi:10.1016/j.heliyon.2024.e26239 PMID:38420484

Yallop, A. C., Gică, O. A., Moisescu, O. I., Coroş, M. M., & Séraphin, H. (2023). The digital traveller: Implications for data ethics and data governance in tourism and hospitality. *Journal of Consumer Marketing*, *40*(2), 155–170. doi:10.1108/JCM-12-2020-4278

Yamin, M. M., Ullah, M., Ullah, H., & Katt, B. (2021). Weaponized AI for cyber attacks. *Journal of Information Security and Applications*, *57*, 102722. doi:10.1016/j.jisa.2020.102722

Yang, H., Kim, H., Lee, J. H., & Shin, D. (2022). Implementation of an AI chatbot as an English conversation partner in EFL speaking classes. *ReCALL*, *34*(3), 327–343. Advance online publication. doi:10.1017/S0958344022000039

Yang, Y., Shang, H., Jamal, N., & Ullah, F. (2023). Video resources recommendation for online tourism teaching in interactive network. *Mobile Networks and Applications*, *28*(3), 1–12. doi:10.1007/s11036-023-02193-9

Yao, W. (2020). Educational Equity in the age of artificial intelligence—taking the construction of rural teachers as an example. *The US-China Education Review: A, 10*(4), 9-18.

Yaşar, E., & Gafar, B. Ü. (2024). Metaphorical perceptions of undergraduate tourism students towards the concepts of English and Professional English: The case of Türkiye-Spain. *Journal of Tourism Theory and Research*, *10*(1), 1–11. doi:10.24288/jttr.1269672

Yenugu, S. (2022). The new National Education Policy (NEP) of India: Will it be a paradigm shift in Indian higher education? *Perspectives: Policy and Practice in Higher Education*, *26*(4), 121–129.

Yiğit, S. (2023). Yapay Zekâ Gastronomi Eğitimine Katkı Sunabilir Mi? ChatGPT Örneği. *Journal of Tourism & Gastronomy Studies.*, *11*(3), 1970–1982.

Yildirim, Y., Arslan, E. A., Yildirim, K., & Bisen, I. (2021). Reimagining education with artificial intelligence. *Eurasian Journal of Higher Education*, *2*(4), 32–46. doi:10.31039/ejohe.2021.4.52

Young, A. T., Amara, D., Bhattacharya, A., & Wei, M. L. (2021). Patient and general public attitudes towards clinical artificial intelligence: A mixed methods systematic review. *The Lancet. Digital Health*, *3*(9), e599–e611. doi:10.1016/S2589-7500(21)00132-1 PMID:34446266

Yousuf, M., & Wahid, A. (2021, November). The role of artificial intelligence in education: Current trends and future prospects. In *2021 International conference on information science and communications technologies (ICISCT)* (pp. 1-7). IEEE. 10.1109/ICISCT52966.2021.9670009

Yu, D., Rosenfeld, H., & Gupta, A. (2023) 'The "AI divide" between the Global North and the Global South', *World Economic Forum*. Available at: https://www.weforum.org/agenda/2023/01/davos23-ai-divideglobal-north-global-south/

Yuan, H., Qian, Y., Yang, R., & Ren, M. (2014). Human mobility discovering and movement intention detection with GPS trajectories. *Decision Support Systems*, *63*, 39–51. doi:10.1016/j.dss.2013.09.010

Zafrullah, Z., Hakim, M. L., & Angga, M. (2023). ChatGPT open AI: Analysis of mathematics education students learning interest. *Journal of Technology Global*, *1*(01), 1–10.

Zajda, J., & Vissing, Y. (Eds.). (2022). *Discourses of globalisation, ideology, and human rights* (Vol. 14). Springer. doi:10.1007/978-3-030-90590-3

Zawacki-Richter, O., Marín, V. I., Bond, M., & Gouverneur, F. (2019). Systematic review of research on artificial intelligence applications in higher education–where are the educators? *International Journal of Educational Technology in Higher Education*, *16*(1), 1–27. doi:10.1186/s41239-019-0171-0

Zeng, J. (2020). Artificial intelligence and China's authoritarian governance. *International Affairs*, *96*(6), 1441–1459. doi:10.1093/ia/iiaa172

ZhaiX. (2022). ChatGPT user experience: Implications for education. *Available at* SSRN 4312418.

Zhai, X., Chu, X., Chai, C. S., Jong, Y. S. M., Istenic, A., Spector, M., Liu, J. B., Yuan, J., & Li, Y. (2021). A Review of Artificial Intelligence (AI) in Education from 2010 to 2020. *Complexity*, *2021*, 1–18. Advance online publication. doi:10.1155/2021/8812542

Zhang, B., Zhu, J., & Su, H. (2023). Toward the third generation artificial intelligence. *Science China. Information Sciences*, *66*(2), 1–19. doi:10.1007/s11432-021-3449-x

Zhang, Y., Wu, M., Tian, G. Y., Zhang, G., & Lu, J. (2021). Ethics and privacy of artificial intelligence: Understandings from bibliometrics. *Knowledge-Based Systems*, *222*, 106994. doi:10.1016/j.knosys.2021.106994

Zhao, H. (2011). Introducing ICT in a Traditional Higher Education Environment. In S. Lin & X. Huang (Eds.), *Advances in Computer Science, Environment, Ecoinformatics, and Education. CSEE 2011. Communications in Computer and Information Science* (Vol. 216). Springer. doi:10.1007/978-3-642-23345-6_25

Zhen, Y., Luo, J.-D., & Chen, H. (2023). Prediction of Academic Performance of Students in Online Live Classroom Interactions—An Analysis Using Natural Language Processing and Deep Learning Methods. *Journal of Social Computing*, *4*(1), 12–29. doi:10.23919/JSC.2023.0007

Zhu, C., Sun, M., Luo, J., Li, T., & Wang, M. (2023). How to harness the potential of ChatGPT in education? *Knowledge Management & E-Learning*, *15*(2), 133.

Zhu, M., Sari, A., & Lee, M. H. (2018). The impact of flipped classroom design on student performance and perceptions in the learning of mathematics in higher education: A meta-analysis. *Educational Technology Research and Development*, *66*(2), 427–453.

Zmyzgova, T. R., Polyakova, E. N., & Karpov, E. K. (2020). Digital transformation of education and artificial intelligence. In *2nd International Scientific and Practical Conference "Modern Management Trends and the Digital Economy: from Regional Development to Global Economic Growth" (MTDE 2020)* (pp. 824-829). Atlantis Press. 10.2991/aebmr.k.200502.134

Zuiderwijk, A., Chen, Y. C., & Salem, F. (2021). Implications of the use of artificial intelligence in public governance: A systematic literature review and a research agenda. *Government Information Quarterly*, *38*(3), 101577. doi:10.1016/j.giq.2021.101577

About the Contributors

Mahmut Demir graduated from Cukurova University Mersin School of Tourism and Hotel Management in1993. He earned his master's degree (2002) and Ph.D. degree (2009) from Dokuz Eylül University, Department of Tourism Management. He started to work as an academic at Mugla University in 1997. He has been working at the Isparta University of Applied Sciences, Tourism Faculty as a professor since 2012. In 2011 he was invited by The Sheffield Hallam University in the UK, where he worked as a visiting scholar for three months. He is the president, board member, and founder member of the International Center of Social Sciences and Education Research (ICSER). Along with ICSER, Prof. Dr. Mahmut DEMIR organized fifteen international conferences between 2015-2020. He is editor in chief of both "Journal of Tourism Theory and Research" and "International Journal of Social Sciences and Education Research". His research interest includes tourism, travel and Hospitality management, organizational behavior, human research management, digitalization and innovation in tourism.

* * *

Munir Ahmad is a seasoned professional in the realm of Spatial Data Infrastructure (SDI), Geo-Information Productions, Information Systems, and Information Governance, boasting over 25 years of dedicated experience in the field. With a PhD in Computer Science, Dr. Ahmad's expertise spans Spatial Data Production, Management, Processing, Analysis, Visualization, and Quality Control. Throughout his career, Dr. Ahmad has been deeply involved in the development and deployment of SDI systems specially in the context of Pakistan, leveraging his proficiency in Spatial Database Design, Web, Mobile & Desktop GIS, and Geo Web Services Architecture. His contributions to Volunteered Geographic Information (VGI) and Open Source Geoportal & Metadata Portal have significantly enriched the geospatial community. As a trainer and researcher, Dr. Ahmad has authored over 50 publications, advancing the industry's knowledge base and fostering innovation in Geo-Tech, Data Governance, and Information Infrastructure, and Emerging Technologies. His commitment to Research and Development (R&D) is evident in his role as a dedicated educator and mentor in the field.

Mariam Ali is Business entrepreneur Co- founder of ertglob. She has served as Business instructor, Curriculum innovation director and Vice Principal in International Technical Colleges in Saudi Arabia. Her area of research includes Education models in digital age, Business models in digital era, Digital enterprenureship and role of Vocational education for labor upskilling and job Market employability gaps.

Luis Antonio Bernal Marín is a full-time Research Professor in the Animation and Visual Effects Engineering program at the Universidad Politécnica de Baja California. Additionally, he serves as the head of the Audio workshop, focusing on audiovisual production and teaching courses in 3D animation and visual effects. He graduated from the Bachelor's program in Communication Sciences at the Universidad Autónoma de Baja California, specializing in audiovisual production and media communication. He holds a Master's degree in Multimedia Design from the Universidad Xochicalco. With a decade-long career in audiovisual production in digital media in Mexicali, Baja California, Mexico, and seven years of experience in higher education teaching.

Sampath Boopathi is an accomplished individual with a strong academic background and extensive research experience. He completed his undergraduate studies in Mechanical Engineering and pursued his postgraduate studies in the field of Computer-Aided Design. Dr. Boopathi obtained his Ph.D. from Anna University, focusing his research on Manufacturing and optimization. Throughout his career, Dr. Boopathi has made significant contributions to the field of engineering. He has authored and published over 210 research articles in internationally peer-reviewed journals, highlighting his expertise and dedication to advancing knowledge in his area of specialization. His research output demonstrates his commitment to conducting rigorous and impactful research. In addition to his research publications, Dr. Boopathi has also been granted one patent and has three published patents to his name. This indicates his innovative thinking and ability to develop practical solutions to real-world engineering challenges. With 17 years of academic and research experience, Dr. Boopathi has enriched the engineering community through his teaching and mentorship roles.

E. Ivette Cota-Rivera received a M.Eng. from the Autonomous University of Baja California (UABC, Universidad Autonoma de Baja California). In 2016, she received her Ph.D. in Energy Engineering and is currently working as a pro fessor in the Energy Engineering program at the Polytechnic University of Baja California (UPBC, Universidad Politecnica de Baja California). Her research interests include energy efficiency and sustainability, artificial intelligence, energy science and technology, as well as programming.

Sanny F. Fernandez is an academician who has been teaching for 27 years now since 1997.Three years with the grade school and high school department at Assumption-Iloilo, General Luna St., Iloilo City. Fourteen years at Colegio de San Jose in Jaro, Iloilo City, and 10 years up to the present at Iloilo State University of Fisheries Science and Technology (ISUFST), main campus in Tiwi, Barotac Nuevo, Iloilo, Philippines. He finished his Bachelor in Secondary Education (BSED) major in Mathematics in 1995 at Central Philippine University (CPU), Jaro, Iloilo City. He graduated with his Master of Arts in Education (MAED) with a specialization in Mathematics in 2012 and a Doctor of Philosophy in Education (PhD in Ed) major in Educational Management in 2019, both degrees were obtained at West Visayas State University (WVSU) in La Paz, Iloilo City. He handles general, professional, and major subjects in mathematics in the College of Education. He is a professor in educational management, research, and statistics subjects in the School of Graduate Studies at ISUFST. He held various designations as publication adviser, director of student affairs, director for advancement and linkages, dean of the College of Education, and program chair in Educational Management in the master's and doctorate programs. He has published and presented various papers to research conferences locally and abroad and won the Best Presenter Award. He also serves as editor and peer-reviewer to several internationally indexed online journals. His passion for teaching and love for learning propelled him to write as a co-author of a chapter in this book.

Martha González graduated with a Bachelor's degree in Fine Arts from the Autonomous University of Baja California, and holds a Master's degree in Arts from the same university, graduating with honors. Recipient of the Santander Meta program scholarship to attend the Augmented Reality bootcamp at CENTRO, Mexico City in 2023. Full-time professor since 20022, affiliated with the Animation and Visual Effects Engineering department at the Polytechnic University of Baja California. With 18 years of teaching experience at the undergraduate level in academic programs related to art, architecture, design, and animation. Interested in researching new technologies, innovation, sustainability, and teaching related to the artistic field.

Catherine Hayes is Professor of Health Professions Pedagogy and Scholarship at the University of Sunderland, UK. She is a UK National Teaching Fellow and Principal Fellow of the UK Higher Education Academy. As a graduate of Podiatric Medicine in 1992, Catherine was a Founding Fellow of the Faculty of Podiatric Medicine at the Royal College of Physicians and Surgeons (Glasgow) in 2012 and was awarded Fellowship of the Royal College of Podiatry (London) in 2010. She is currently Programme Leader of the University of Sunderland's Professional Doctorate pathways for the DBA, EdD, DPM and DProf.

Maria Kainat has completed her studies at the Department of Computer Science, University of Agriculture Faisalabad, Pakistan.

Snehalatha M. is working as an Associate Professor in the Department of Career Development in SRM Institute of Science and Technology has about 27 years of teaching experience. Her areas of research include Mathematical Modeling and Stochastic Processes.

Maida Maqsood did MS in English from Government College Women University, Sialkot. Throughout her academic journey, she has achieved notable successes that have strengthened her foundation in literature, education and linguistics. Her Master's research reflects her dedication to exploring critical themes in literature with the use of linguistics style. Additionally, her active participation in different conferences and seminars, such as The International Conference on Modern Trends in Applied Linguistics, and 7th ASNeT International Multidisciplinary Academic Conference 2024 (AIMAC 2024) highlight her commitment to staying updated with current trends in her field.

Abelardo Mercado Herrera is Doctor of Science and Master of Science from the National Institute of Astrophysics, Optics and Electronics, specializing in Astrophysics, Postdoctorate in Astrophysics from the Institute of Astronomy of the National Autonomous University of Mexico, Electronics Engineer from the Autonomous University of Baja California . He is a specialist in the mathematical-statistical description of stochastic and/or deterministic processes, nonlinear systems, complex systems, chaos theory, among others, as well as their application to physical phenomena such as astronomy, economics, finance, telecommunications, science social etc., in order to determine the underlying dynamics in such processes, and if necessary, their connection with real physical variables and possible prediction. He has worked on the development of various electronic circuits, interfaces and programs to carry out electrical tests in the industry, as well as in scientific instrumentation, applied to telemetry, infrared polarimetry, optics and spectroscopy. He has also specialized in image analysis, measurement techniques and noise reduction.

Krishna Kumari R. is working as an Assistant Professor in the Department of Career Development Centre in SRM Institute of Science and Technology has about 8 years of teaching experience. Her areas of research include Formal Languages and Automata Theory, Theory of Computation. She holds a diverse array of qualifications including M.Sc., M.Phil., M.Ed., TNSET, and a Ph.D. She has authored a total of 25 publications, all indexed in SCOPUS, with 17 being published post-Ph.D. Additionally, she has authored 3 books/book chapters and holds 1 patent published and 1 granted. She serves as a reviewer in 4 SCOPUS indexed journals and 2 SCOPUS and ESCI indexed journals. Dr. Krishna Kumari has been a resource person for 3 Faculty Development Programs (FDPs), presented at 2 conferences/symposiums, and chaired 2 conferences. She has also attended 3 workshops and participated in 10 FDPs. Furthermore, Dr. Krishna Kumari is an active member of 10 professional memberships, showcasing her commitment to professional development and academic excellence.

Jonai Wabwire is a seasoned communication expert, trainer of journalists and author with a passion for exploring the intricacies of human interaction. With a background in Mass Communication, Wabwire has dedicated his career to unraveling the dynamics of communication in various contexts. Holding a doctorate degree in Communication and Media from Kisii University, Wabwire has combined academic knowledge with real-world experience to provide valuable insights into effective communication strategies. Throughout his professional journey, Wabwire has conducted extensive research on topics in communication. His work has been published in various academic journals, books and presented at international conferences, earning him recognition as a thought leader in the field. Jonai Wabwire has also collaborated with diverse organizations, guiding them through the challenges of communication in modern work environments.

Index

A

B

C

D

E

G

H

I

L

M

N

O

P

Q

R

S

T

V

W

www.ingramcontent.com/pod-product-compliance
Lightning Source LLC
LaVergne TN
LVHW081335300926
849161LV00008B/1979

9798369316665